TROUBLED
BUT NOT
DESTROYED

TROUBLED BUT NOT DESTROYED

AUTOBIOGRAPHY OF
DR. DAVID M. GITARI
RETIRED ARCHBISHOP OF THE
ANGLICAN CHURCH OF KENYA

ISAAC PUBLISHING

*Troubled But Not Destroyed: Autobiography of Dr. David M. Gitari,
Retired Archbishop of the Anglican Church of Kenya*

Isaac Publishing, 6729 Curran Street, McLean VA 22101

Financial assistance towards this publication has been received from The Drummond Trust, 3 Pitt Terrace, Stirling, and is gratefully acknowledged. Warm gratitude is also expressed to the Barnabas Fund for its very significant support for this publication.

Library of Congress Control Number: 2014950950

ISBN: 978-0-9916145-4-7

Book design by Lee Lewis Walsh, Words Plus Design

Printed in Kenya by Majestic Printing Works Ltd, Nairobi

Archbishop David Gitari of Kenya
– global African Anglican leader

David Mukuba Gitari (1937–2013), first Bishop of the Diocese of Mount Kenya East (1975–1997) and Archbishop of Kenya (1997–2002), was one of the first post-colonial global African Christian leaders.

He came to prominence in Kenya in 1975 when he gave a series of six bible expositions on the Voice of Kenya radio. J.M. Kariuki M.P. had been found murdered in the Ngong Hills. Gitari expounded Cain's murder of Abel. He was 'carpeted' by VoK and told his sermons had been disturbing. Gitari replied that the gospel of Jesus Christ is very disturbing, especially to sinners.

Biblical exposition set the pattern for his preaching, proclaiming orthodox Christian faith to the whole of society and the powers that be.

He was elected first bishop of the new Diocese of Mount Kenya East in 1975 at the age of 38, only four years after ordination as a deacon. He drew round him gifted people from all parts of the world and inspired love and loyalty in those who worked with him. He took as a motto Jesus' growth in favour with God and man (Luke 2:52) and promoted culturally appropriate evangelism, appointing camel borne evangelists for nomads in the north of his diocese, and social action through establishing Christian Community Services (CCS) and a team of 'barefoot' health workers.

He demonstrated a new style of leadership by identifying younger gifted leaders and releasing them into ministry. He saw no incompatibility between mainstream Anglicanism and being an evangelical church leader. He moved evangelicalism on from being a movement in the Church for evangelicalism to being an expression of the church's faith itself.

He challenged President Moi especially over his abolition of the secret ballot in 1987. In 1989 he was the object of an assassination attempt in his own home, which was widely believed to have been instigated by the state authorities.

At the 1988 Lambeth Conference, he piloted through a change in the church's discipline for people in polygamous marriages before their baptism. In 1998, he provided leadership for Lambeth 1.10 on human sexuality, thereby consolidating Anglican orthodoxy as a global movement with significant leadership from Africans.

He served as a member of the Anglican-Roman Catholic International Commission, vice-moderator of the Commission for World Mission and Evangelism of the World Council of Churches, chairman of the Theological Commission of the World Evangelical Fellowship, the founder chairman of the African Theological Fraternity and the founder chairman of the Oxford Centre for Mission Studies and of its journal *Transformation*. He chaired the Conference of African Churches with the World Bank in 2000.

When installed as Archbishop in 1997, he announced the date of his retirement for 2002 aged 65 and established the Philadelphia Centre on his farm in Embu. In 1998 he was awarded an honorary doctorate by the University of Kent.

He kept a daily diary from his early years. His autobiography is an unparallelled resource for African Church history in the twentieth century.

Contents

Acknowledgements

During the ten years I have been writing this autobiography, a number of people spent many hours typing from my hand-written manuscripts. Peris Njeri, my daughter in-law and Nancy Njura typed most of the chapters. I am also grateful to Ruth Waceke Njiru, who typed the appendices.

Eva Macharia, who was my able secretary when I was the Archbishop of Kenya between 1997 and 2002, helped in searching for important documents in the archives of the Province during the formative stages of this autobiography.

I found it very difficult to write the chapter on the third president of Kenya, Mwai Kibaki. I am however grateful to the one time Comptroller of State House, John Matere Keriri, for reading my first draft of the chapter and for making useful suggestions and corrections. I am also very pleased that the Revd Dr John Karanja, a Professor of Church History and African studies at the Trinity Lutheran Seminary at the Ohio State University, USA, visited and stayed with me at my Philadelphia home in Kirinyaga county, during which time he read the whole manuscript and made useful suggestions to improve the book. My long-term friend since our university days at Royal College (later University of Nairobi), Archbald Githinji, also read the manuscript and reminded me of important events that he felt should have been included in the book. I also appreciate the encouragement that I was given by Eunice

Njeri Sahle, a Kenyan scholar from Kirinyaga who is currently an Associate Professor at the University of North Carolina at Chapel Hill, USA.

The Anglican Bishops in Kenya and members of the Provincial Synod have constantly urged me to complete the book, which they knew that I have been writing since my retirement. They have been waiting for the publication of the autobiography and I thank them for their encouragement and patience.

I am also grateful to my son John Mwendwa, a communicator by profession, for reading the whole manuscript and editing it.

Finally I wish to express my gratitude to Chris Sugden for preparing the manuscript for publication and ensuring that it receives the widest circulation in various parts of the world.

Dedication

This book is dedicated to my parents, Samuel Mukuba and Jessie Njuku, who taught me about Jesus Christ from my childhood and instructed me in the Christian faith. Their commitment to the church created in me an irresistible desire to offer my life to the full-time service of Christ and his Church. The book is also dedicated to my sons, Samuel, Jonathan and John, and their wives, who gave me every encouragement to write the book. I also dedicate the book to my grandchildren, who have given me much joy in my retirement.

Introduction

A good number of scholars have approached me with the intention of writing my biography and I have given them every encouragement and a good number have interviewed me. However no complete biography has so far been published even though chapters about my ministry as a bishop of the church have appeared in a number of publications. The Ven. Patrick Benson used my case study for his thesis for his master of philosophy degree. The thesis, entitled "Church Confrontation with State During Kenya's Nyayo Era: Causes and Effects", was submitted to the Open University, England in November 1993. Bishop Gideon Githiga published his doctoral thesis for the Open University entitled "The Church as the Bulwark against Extremism" (Oxford, Regnum, 2001), which summarises the "Development of Church-State Relationship in Kenya, with particular reference to the years after Independence from 1963-1992". The book refers to my prophetic ministry and is also dedicated to me.

John Karanja, the leading Anglican Church historian, authored *Founding an African Faith – Kikuyu Anglican Christianity, 1900-1945*, published by Uzima Press in 1999, which he dedicated to me for my "commitment to upgrading the academic standards of clergy and dedication to church". He wrote a scholarly article on the biblical, prophetic ministries of Henry Okullu and me. The article was published by the *Anglican and Episcopal History* Volume LXXV in December 2006. Karanja describes

Okullu's hermeneutical methodology as extrapolation and my methodology as a good example of evangelical biblical hermeneutic and more pragmatic. John Casson also wrote a thesis on my holistic ministry for his diploma studies. I am also aware that Eunice Njeri Sahle, an associate professor at the University of North Carolina at Chapel Hill, USA, is also doing research on my prophetic ministry.

In 2009 Palgrave Macmillan in the United States of America also published a book entitled *Religion and Politics in Kenya: Essays in Honour of a Meddlesome Priest.* "Meddlesome priest" refers to me, and Ben Knighton, formerly the principal of St Andrews College of Theology and Development, Kabare, which I founded in 1977, edited nine essays in the book. The book was launched in Nairobi in January 2010. The contributors of the essays include: Ben Knighton, John Lonsdale, Galia Sabar, Julias Gathogo, John Chesworth, Jacqueline Klopp and Paul Gifford. All these are reputable scholars with first hand knowledge of Kenya. Hilary Ng'weno, a great communicator, has produced a documentary about my life in his series "The Making of a Nation". I thank him for leading the way in telling the world about me through the electronic media. So various attempts have been made to tell my story but it was still my wish to write my own autobiography before researchers publish my biographies. No one writing my story can get all the facts correct except me. I wanted to write my own story so that future biographers can use it as an important resource in their research about my life.

My father was the first literate person in Ngiriambu village. From 1920 to 1960 he kept a daily written record of what was happening to him. For instance, he recorded all the names and dates of all the children born in the area he served as a lay reader for 40 years. I have the custody of the records he kept and many people who do not know when they were born come to see me and I give them the actual dates of their birth to their great delight. Since 1988 when I moved my residence from Embu in Eastern Province to Philadelphia Place in Kirinyaga County, I have kept what I call a "Daily Occurrence Book", following in the footsteps of my father. At the end of each day I write all that has happened to me. Each occurrence book is 576 pages and in hard cover. I am currently writing the 25th volume. These books have been of great help in writing this autobiography.

I started writing my story soon after my retirement in 2002. I was however not in a hurry to complete it and have it published, for I very much wanted to include my observations on the way Kenya would evolve after the removal of KANU after 40 years in power. I retired from my position as

Archbishop of Kenya almost at the same time as President Daniel arap Moi, who had ruled the country for 24 years, retired from his own. His hand-picked successor, Uhuru Kenyatta, was defeated by Mwai Kibaki, who became the third president of Kenya. It is now more than a decade since KANU was removed from power.

The delay in publishing this autobiography has enabled me to include a chapter on the regime of President Kibaki. The autobiography, in addition to chapters on my family background, education, ministry to students and the Bible Society of Kenya and service to the Church of Christ as a Bishop and Archbishop of the Anglican Church of Kenya, includes chapters on my relationship with the first President, Mzee Jomo Kenyatta (1963-1978) and the second President, Moi (1978-2002). It has been my joy to witness the way Kenya has been ruled by a coalition government led by the third President for a decade. Though the second president ruined the country economically, the change of guard proves the words of Studdert Kennedy true that "when a country changes its government, it only pushes one set of sinners out and puts another set in. The most passionate idealists are never completely free from egocentricity and partisan bias". The worst ethnic clashes in Kenya took place after KANU was removed from power.

The main purpose of writing this autobiography is that future biographers will have access to credible resource material. But it is also my desire that the present generation and posterity will have the story as told by the actor. I also wish to share with readers the things I hold dearly in life: commitment to the Lord Jesus Christ, serving him and his church with absolute dedication and rendering sincere service to God's people and to Kenya. It has been my passionate conviction that even if I am *troubled,* I must never give up hope in life and with St Paul, I say, "I am troubled but not destroyed" (2 Corinthians 6:9). My prayer and hope for Kenya is that it may have leaders who are "capable, God fearing, trustworthy and incorruptible" (Exodus 18).

May God bless you as you read my story.

David M Gitari
March 2012

List of Abbreviations

AACC	All African Council of Churches
ACC	Anglican Consultative Council
ACK	Anglican Church of Kenya
AFCK	Agricultural Finance Corporation
AIC	African Inland Church
APP	African People's Party
ARCIC	Anglican Roman Catholic International Commission
ASWOM	Association of Women in the Ministry
BCMS	Bible Churchmen's Missionary Society (now Crosslinks)
BD	Bachelor of Divinity
CAPA	Council of Anglican Provinces of Africa
CCS	Christian Community Services
CMS	Church Missionary Society (Now Church Mission Society)
CPK	Church of the Province of Kenya
CWME	Commission on World Mission and Evangelism
DC	District Commissioner
DEB	District Education Board
DRC	Democratic Republic of Congo
ECK	Electoral Commission of Kenya
ECUSA	Episcopal Church in the United States of America (now The Episcopal Church)
EER	External Partners of Rwanda
EZE	Evangelische Zentralstelle für Entwicklungshilfe eV (Protestant Association for Cooperation in Development)
FOCUS	Fellowship of Christian Unions
GSU	General Service Unit
HIPC	Highly Indebted Poor Countries
HIV/AIDS	Human Immunodeficiency Virus/Acquired Immune Deficiency Syndrome
IALC	International Anglican Liturgical Commission
ICC	International Criminal Court
ICDC	Industrial and Commercial Development Corporation
IDP	Internally Displaced Persons
IFES	International Fellowship of Evangelical Students
IMF	International Monetary Fund
INFEMIT	International Fellowship of Evangelical Mission Theologians
IVF	Inter-Varsity Fellowship

KADU	Kenya African Democratic Union
KAMA	Kenya Anglican Men's Association
KANU	Kenya African National Union
KAPE	Kenya African Primary Examination
KBC	Kenya Broadcasting Corporation
KCPE	Kenya Certificate of Primary Education
KCSE	Kenya Certificate of Secondary Education
KFA	Kenya Farmers Association
KNTC	Kenya National Trading Corporation
KPCU	Kenya Planters Co-operative Union
KPU	Kenya People's Union
KSCF	Kenya Student Christian Fellowship
KTDC	Kenya Tourism Development Corporation
LCWE	Lausanne Committee for World Evangelisation
MP	Member of Parliament
MRI	Mutual Responsibility and Interdependence
MU	Mothers Union
NCCK	National Council of Churches of Kenya
NCCU	National Coffee Co-operative Union.
NET	Nairobi Evangelistic Enterprise
NGO	Non Governmental Organisation
NICA	National Independent Church of Africa
OCPD	Officer Commanding Police Division
ODM	Orange Democratic Party.
PAFES	Pan African Fellowship of Evangelical Students
PAG	Pentecostal Assemblies of God
PBTE	Provincial Board of Theological Education
PC	Provincial Commissioner
PCEA	Presbyterian Church of East Africa
PIMC	Partners in Mission Consultation
RC	Roman Catholic
RPF	Rwandese Patriotic Front
SCM	Student Christian Movement
SDA	Seventh Day Adventist
TEE	Theological Education by Extension
UK	United Kingdom
UMCA	Universities Mission to Central Africa
USA	United States of America
VOK	Voice of Kenya
WB	World Bank
WCC	World Council of Churches
WEF	World Evangelical Fellowship

Chapter 1

Family Background

Kirinyaga County is the granary of Central Kenya. Even during times of famine in the central and other parts of Kenya, you can still find home-grown maize and beans being sold at Kutus, the commercial and geographical centre of the County. The most prominent feature of the district is Mount Kenya, the roof of Kenya and second highest mountain in Africa. Mount Kenya literally means *the dwelling place of God*.

The beauty of Mount Kenya is best seen from various points in Kirinyaga County, especially at Ngiriambu, the village where I was born. The austere opulence of this mountain is best captured when the golden rays of the sun first strike it in the morning; beholding this is breathtaking and a most memorable experience. You not only see the majestic crown of snow that caps the mountain, but you can also see the panoramic valleys sculptured by thousands of years of melting snow as they cascade to the forest that covers the base of the mountain. These waters, alongside those that flow from the Aberdare Ranges, give rise to the tributaries of Kenya's longest and most voluminous river, the Tana, which pours into the Indian Ocean.

These southern slopes of Mount Kenya are among the most productive parts of Kenya. In the past, traditional foods such as arrowroots, sweet potatoes, yam, millet, sorghum, and bananas, among many others, were grown here in plenty. Some of the best-quality tea and coffee is grown in the higher regions while Kenya's largest rice fields are found in the plains of Mwea, fed by the Rivers Thiba and Nyamindi.

But an interesting feature about this area is that the numerous families that reside in Ndia and Gichugu can trace their roots to sections of the central-lower Eastern Province occupied by the Kamba people, particularly Kitui District. This is because whenever there was severe famine, the Kamba travelled westwards to seek famine relief on the southern slopes of Mount Kenya.

And it so happened that there was very severe famine in Kitui district in the year 1899. Mutaa, the wife of Ngila Nzuki, took little Mukuba, her only son, on a long journey in search of food. They joined a convoy of other travellers from Mutonguni in Kitui with a hope of reaching Kirinyaga, where food was plenty. This was not a journey for nine-year old Mukuba. The scorching heat, exhaustion from the trek, and the scarce offerings of food and water would have more than adequately conspired against the will to survive. But whenever the journey became too much for the boy, Mutaa would urge him on:

"Mukuba, my son!" she would say. "Keep going. We shall soon get to the place where there are plenty of arrow roots, sweet potatoes, millet and sorghum, and not to mention maize, beans and milk." This would encourage the boy to keep pace and the convoy never left them behind.

The main obstacle to this journey was the mighty Tana river. One of the shallowest points of the river was at Riakanau in Mwea. Here hungry travellers would find representatives from various families from Ndia and Gichugu waiting to welcome them into their own homes further north towards the Mount Kenya forest.

Gituku, a resident of Ngiriambu village, had sent his son Muruakieu Njagi to go to welcome a family willing to be hosted at Ngiriambu. Mutaa and her son Mukuba accepted the gesture and Muruakieu carried the boy shoulder-high most of the way on a journey of about fifty kilometres. On arrival, Gituku welcomed Mutaa and her son and gave them plenty of food. Mutaa enjoyed the warm hospitality of Gituku and decided to settle for some time in the new environment.

At the dawn of the new century, Mutaa received the sad news of the death of her husband, Ngila Nzuki. After mourning his death for some time, she agreed to be the third wife of Gituku, who also adopted her son, Mukuba. Mutaa had five children with Gituku but they all died in infancy. The only child who grew to become an adult was Mukuba.

When Mukuba Gituku came of age in about 1910, he underwent the circumcision rite of passage in a ceremony with his young contemporaries. At initiation, different age-groups were given different names and theirs was branded *wakanene*. In 1914, just as the First World War was beginning, a good number of young people from the *wakanene* age group went to Mombasa in search of "greener pastures". It took them three days to walk from Ngiriambu to Nairobi. They then boarded the train to Mombasa. This first ride on the train fascinated the young men as it snaked through the savannahs of the Tsavo. They also saw numerous animals such as zebras, giraffes, elephants, buffaloes, and many more. But the sight of these animals did not excite them (unlike tourists), as they were a familiar feature back home at the time and they even co-existed with humans.

Once they got to Mombasa, an Indian known at Cieti employed Mukuba as a servant of the house. Soon after, Mukuba made his first contact with missionaries from the Church Missionary Society (CMS). He decided to register as a student at the mission centre after he was informed that they offered evening classes. He persuaded his two mates from Ngiriambu village, Gukemba and Ndwiga, to join him for the evening classes and they all learnt how to read and write. It was at the Mission Centre that these young people were introduced to the Gospel. They soon accepted the Good News of Jesus Christ. They developed a desire to share the message with the people at Ngiriambu, 640 kilometres away back home.

One day as they were praying, the Holy Spirit said to them, "Set Mukuba Gituku apart for me to do the work for which I have called him." After further prayer and fasting, they laid hands on Mukuba in prayer and blessing and sent him off. He travelled by train back to Nairobi, where he was met by Daniel Ngure, an employee of the East African Standard, which was the first newspaper in Kenya. Zakayo Karanja, who also hailed from Ngiriambu village, was also present. They trekked back home and arrived at Ngiriambu in late 1919.

CMS missionaries had by 1910 set up the first mission station in Kirinyaga at Kabare, 14 kilometres west of Ngiriambu. However, the missionaries were yet to reach Ngiriambu. Mukuba Gituku became the first Christian to preach the Gospel of Jesus Christ at Ngiriambu. He started by trying to preach the gospel when there were large social gatherings, especially during circumcision ceremonies. At first, the community rejected his message.

He studied the Gospels again and found that Jesus did not start by addressing huge crusades but that his approach was to start with the twelve disciples. Mukuba changed tack. He selected twelve young people and each morning held prayers with them and taught them how to read and write. In the afternoon he sent them two-by-two to go and teach other young people what they had learnt in the morning. This was repeated day after day and a large number of people simultaneously learnt how to read and write.

At the beginning he encountered many problems. Parents would interrupt his lessons and call their sons to go and tend to the cows, goats and sheep. Mukuba had to resort to giving gifts such as salt and sugar and even a cup or two of the local brew, *muratina*, to persuade parents to let their sons join and and to continue with the classes. Those who went the full course were given the Gospel of Mark (which was the only Scripture then available in Kikuyu) to learn God's word by themselves. In 1920, Revd Mr Rampley, the CMS missionary at Kabare, heard that someone had established a church at Ngiriambu. Rampley sought Mukuba out and they teamed up and worked together.

In those days the Kikuyus were not burying their dead but left them in the wild to be eaten by hyenas. One day Rampley and Mukuba went on a hunting trip and shot dead a few buffaloes, slaughtered them and laced parts of the carcasses with poison. They then put the poisoned meat in strategic places around the forest. The following day 98 hyenas were found dead. The hyena menace came to an abrupt end and people were taught to bury the dead. It was interesting that my father was carrying out the ministry of Christ even before he was either ordained, confirmed or even baptised.

The missionary baptised Mukuba on 25 April 1920 and he was given the name Samuel. On 23 June 1921, he was confirmed by the then Bishop of Mombasa, the Rt Revd Richard Stanley Heywood. Rampley and Mukuba teamed up in planting churches in Ngiriambu, Thumaita and Ngariama near Mount Kenya forest. Harun Njege and Jeremiah Kabui became the founding elders of the churches in Thumaita and Ngariama respectively. Between 1933 and 1934 my father was enrolled as a student at St Paul's Bible College, Limuru. The school had been established at Mombasa in 1903 and was moved to Limuru in 1930. He however could not be ordained on completing his studies as a forerunner, Musa Mumai, had already been ordained in 1929 and was in charge of Kabare parish. This parish covered the whole of the present-day Gichugu District and parts of Mwea. The missionaries were convinced that the parish could not afford to pay the salaries of two priests.

Rampley conducted the first service of holy matrimony at St Andrew's Church, Kabare on 24 October 1924. This wedding was between Samuel Mukuba and Jessie Njuku, an orphan who was among the first community of believers. The wedding reception was held at Ngiriambu and attended by 33 people, who contributed a then very impressive 38 shillings.

One of the most impressive characteristics of Mukuba was that he kept a daily written record of the events relating to him in excellent handwriting. Just as an indicator of the detail of his records: I have the names of all the guests who attended the wedding reception and the amount of money each guest contributed. He also kept a record of all children born in the area by name, the date of birth and the names of the parents. He was effectively the official registrar of births of his time.

God blessed Mukuba and Jessie Njuku with a total of 11 children. Unfortunately three of them died in infancy. Those who lived to be adults were Hannah Mutaa (Micere, 1925), Harun Njagi (1930), Peninah Muthoni (1933), Stanley Nzuki (1935), David Mukuba Gitari (1937), Mary Wanjiru (1940), Eliud Njiru (1943), and Fridah Wangeci (1948).

I am therefore the fifth child of Samuel and Jessie Mukuba. I was brought up in a first-generation Christian home. We lived a simple life. In the early years we stayed in a two-bedroom house: one for all the children, both my brothers and sisters, and a second one for my parents. A fireplace separated the two rooms. Later my parents put up a separate room for the boys. Our sisters took great care over us and dearly loved us. I could say that they spoilt us in a way because when they found any one of us washing clothes they would say, "That is not your work," and they would take it on.

My parents were so committed to the mission of the church that in our home compound there was a chapel and every day my father would ring the bell at 6.00am for morning prayers and again at 6.00pm for evening prayers. He would start the service whether or not there was a congregation in attendance. But the bell served another communal purpose. Watches were virtually unheard of at this time so the community relied on Mukuba's bell to inform them on when the time had reached either 6.00am or 6.00pm.

Near our home was the source of a spring known as Karumba. Villagers had to descend through a canopy of vegetation and undergrowth to get their supply of crystal clear and clean water at the bottom the valley. The story that follows may sound stranger than fiction to some, but has been corroborated by a consistent thread of witnesses. Before the advent of Christianity, the local community believed that there were many demons in the Karumba valley. This was because people who went to draw water early in the morning could hear eerie voices in the underbrush, but they never saw anyone. One day a woman went to fetch water a little too early and was beaten with sticks by invisible forces.

"Why have you come to disturb us too early?" she heard as she scurried up the hill in panic. When Mukuba's bell started ringing, the same witnesses testified that the demons vacated Karumba Valley one night and went chanting that Mukuba's bell has disturbed them so much that they had gone to take up new residence in Mount Kenya forest.

My mother Jessie was taught how to read and write by my father and she in turn passed the skills to her children long before they joined school. She taught me how to read and write in 1943. My parents were highly respected for enlightening and liberating the people from superstition, retrogressive culture and fear. For instance, according to Kikuyu custom if a woman gave birth to twins, the two children were abandoned to die as they were considered a bad omen. An infant who developed the upper teeth first suffered the same fate.

On 8 April 1923, Mukuba was informed that there were plans to throw a child to the hyenas at the valley of palm trees known as Kariru. He instructed his wife, Jessie, and Naomi, another Christian woman, to prepare to go and save the baby. It was not until 6.00pm that a number of people left the village to go and throw the child away. Mukuba, Jessie and Naomi followed them at a distance until they found the point where the child was abandoned. The child was still alive but had leaves stuck in his mouth and nostrils. My mother took the boy home and took care of him. He was called Alfred Karanja.

When his parents became Christians two years later, they were given their child back on condition that they would not harm him. My parents continued to support Alfred Karanja. He went on to upper primary school at Kaaga in Meru from 1932 to 1934. My parents paid his school and college fees and even his dowry before he got married. He was later trained as a pharmacist and worked in various government hospitals for many years. He was ever grateful to Samuel and Jessie. We considered him to be the first born son of the Mukuba family. As the Lausanne Covenant states, "Because man is God's creature, some of his culture is rich in beauty and in goodness. Because he has fallen, all of it is tainted with sin and some of it is demonic."[1]

---

1 J. D. Douglas (ed.), *Let the Earth Hear His Voice*. Minneapolis: World Wide Publications, 1975, Clause 10. (Report of the 1974 International Congress on World Evangelization held at Lausanne.)

My father was known to be very generous. He used the money he saved during his time in Mombasa to start the church and school at Ngiriambu. During the initial years he paid from his own pocket the teachers whom he had recruited. I have a record of names of many people to whom he loaned money but it would appear that he never asked them to pay him back. My parents were also very hospitable. Many visitors who called in at our home did not go away without drinking a cup of tea.

Mukuba was a very good farmer and won top prizes at agricultural shows. He was also very committed to the ministry of the church. He considered Monday to Saturday as the period to prepare the sermon for Sunday. This he did in the evenings after discussion and story-telling with elders in the village who used to visit our *thome* (fire-place) outside the homestead. I used to enjoy listening to the stories as the elders shared their life experiences. My father was a great storyteller.

My father, Mukuba, was man of extraordinary courage. To the best of my knowledge he was the first person in Gichugu division to refuse to allow his daughter to undergo female genital mutilation (FGM). My second sister Peninah Muthoni suffered greatly for being the first girl not to undergo this retrogressive rite of passage. At the height of the rebellion against British colonial rule, Mau Mau freedom fighters went looking for her so as to circumcise her forcibly but she was well protected. Many people said that she would never get a husband just for this reason. But in about 1954, she was married to Elphas Kanyua Mutema and together they had eight children.

Samuel was also full of mercy. During the emergency, when the colonial government launched an all-out offensive against pro-freedom forces, he had been appointed as a member of the committee screening Mau Mau suspects. This committee held its sittings at Kiamutugu, the headquarters of Ngariama Location. During one hearing, the local colonial District Officer pierced a suspect with a knife, and pushed it at least four inches into one of his thighs in a bid to coerce him into admitting that he was a member of the Mau Mau. My father stood up in protest, saying that it was illegal to torture suspects into making confessions. He then declared that he had resigned from the committee.

The freedom fighters heard about his stance and resolved to do him no harm. Before this, it was usual for the Mau Mau to visit homes at night and force occupants to take an oath of allegiance. One night they visited our home to administer the oath to my father and his household. But before they could do this, a hippopotamus emerged from the dark, forcing them to flee and take refuge in my father's granary. In the morning they met my father and assured him that their experience the previous night had convinced them never to administer the oath to this man of God.

My father was a man of prayer. Before we went to bed, he conducted prayers for the whole family. There is no doubt that God heard his prayers though he was neither rich nor poor. God blessed him and his family for many years. He went to be with the Lord on 3 October 1970. My mother lived on until 2 January 2000. Born in 1898, she saw a bit of the 19th century, lived through the entire 20th century and saw the dawn of the 21st century. She was 102 years old when she passed away. Even in her advanced age she could still read her Bible without the aid of spectacles. She was beloved, admired and respected as a woman of great faith.

I must admit that my inspiration to join the full-time ministry of the Church came from my parents, who were always praying that one of their children would follow their footsteps and join the ministry of the Church.

Chapter 2

Early Education

Humble Beginnings

My father, Samuel Mukuba, had founded Ngiriambu Primary School in the 1920s. It was built on flat land that overlooked Karumba valley. The valley was covered by a thick forest with many indigenous trees such as *Miringa* and *Mikoigo*. There was one *Mururi* that had become the tallest and thickest of all the trees. When it fell down in the 1990s, the tremor was felt through the village.

The school building was one block with walls made of mud and thatched with grass. It was partitioned into three classrooms by movable structures because it served as both a school and a church. On Sundays the partitioning was removed to create space for worshippers. Every Friday the pupils had to patch the floor with a mixture of cow dung and ash to make it presentable for worship on Sunday.

I first went to school in 1943 but I was told I that I was too small, so I joined Standard A in 1944. I then proceeded to Standard B in 1945 then qualified to join Standard 1 in 1946. The Primary School offered studies up to Standard 5. The fee was 50 cents per term, but some of the pupils could not afford that amount. Most of the boys wore only a shirt or sheet with no underwear or shorts.

Discipline was an important part of our primary education. Every time a teacher entered a classroom, the pupils stood up.

"Good morning pupils!" he would say.

"Good morning teacher!" we would respond.

We were not supposed to speak to a teacher with our hands in our pockets. Pupils who were caught misbehaving were punished by caning.

We accepted this discipline and even had a song for it: *Mwalimu uhure na uthomithie wega* which meant, "Teacher, beat me, but teach me well." A good number of pupils from non-Christian families wore amulets provided by traditional medicine men as protection from sickness or bad luck.

When I started going to school, I had the unmistakable experience of hearing the voice of Jesus, who spoke to me in a wonderful, sweet voice. I had this experience three times as I was walking to school and have never forgotten it. The voice gave me encouragement and provided clear assurance and confirmation that the living Lord Jesus Christ is risen.

I sat for the Standard 5 National Examination in 1950. There were very few schools with upper primary school (they were known as intermediate schools spanning classes 6 to 8) in those days. Those from the region who passed their examinations could either join Kagumo school in Nyeri or Kangaru school in Embu. Though I had worked very hard, I failed in the examination. Only five of my fellow classmates went to Kangaru School but I was very surprised that I was not among the five as I used to perform better academically than the five who qualified.

By this time the people of Ngariama had put up a Standard 6 class at Ngiriambu under the headship of Marclus Njiru. I was persuaded to join this class in January 1951. An intermediate school had been started at Kabare in 1949. I joined Kabare Intermediate School in 1952 for Standard 7 and proceeded to Standard 8 in 1953. I sat for my Standard 8 (KAPE) in 1953 with the hope of joining Kangaru Secondary School. Again, I failed the examination to my great surprise and shock. I was, however, invited to join St Mark's Teachers' Training College at Kigari, Embu. I joined the college in 1954 and I was deeply grateful that at last I was in an institution with very good facilities.

After three days, however, the Principal, Catherine Paul, and her deputy, Bedan Ireri, called for me and I could never have been prepared for what they told me.

"We have decided to send you back home because you are too short and cannot reach the blackboard." Even before I could mentally process what they had told me, they added, "Go back home, ask your mother to feed you for one year, following which you will automatically be accepted into the college." It took me a long time to overcome the shock of that decision. The following day the Revd Neville Langford-Smith (who later became the first Bishop of Nakuru) gave me a ride in his car, from Kigari to Kabare. I was admitted to repeat Standard 8 in 1954. It seemed to me that my tenure at Kabare was interminable.

I re-sat my (KAPE) examination at the end of the year. This time I was the only student from Kabare Upper Primary School (Intermediate) who was selected to join Kangaru Secondary School, in 1955. During the first two years at Kabare I was staying at the house of the Revd Musa Njiru, who was the Vicar-in-Charge of the parish and a great friend of my father. He lived together with his two youngest sons, who were also in primary school. My father was convinced that it would be better for me to live in the house of the pastor than anywhere else. But this proved to be the most difficult time in my life. Though my parents sent me to Kabare with enough food, the boys would cook my food and refuse to let me eat. I was hungry most of the time and I often had to buy ripe Kikuyu bananas for lunch.

In 1953, the Kabare Mission became a centre where many people came to seek refuge from the Mau Mau. A home guard garrison was established there with about 50 fighters. They used to prepare stiff porridge or *ugali* in huge sufurias. But each person was expected to provide the stew or milk accompaniment for himself. I would join the home guards at supper time, take my share of *ugali* and eat it in the darkness, without any stew or milk. One weekend I went home and left two shillings in my box. When I came back, the two brothers had broken into the box and taken the money. When I reported the matter to their father, he became very furious with me for making "false allegations" against his children. This forced me to seek alternative accommodation, very much against the wish of my father.

I will close on this episode with one incident that had a long term impact on my life. One day, the vicar sent his youngest son and me to Ithareini Market to do some shopping. After crossing Kiringa River, we jumped onto a bus and hung on to its ladder through the journey. We thought it would stop at Ithareini two kilometres away; unfortunately it did not. I jumped out in panic, fell down and broke my left hand. Njiru's son also jumped to the ground but fortunately he was not injured. I was put on a donkey cart and was in great pain for the two hours that I was being ferried to Kerugoya Hospital. I was treated by a Dr Ang'awa but my hand never healed completely. But the Lord seemed to say, "My grace is sufficient for you, for my power is made perfect in weakness" (2 Corinthians 12:9). As a

Bishop, I have used the hand to confirm thousands of people who might not even notice its weakness. This is one of those weaknesses that has humbled me and made me empathise fully with all those who suffer from serious disabilities.

I therefore fully appreciate the words of St Paul when he says, "That is why, for Christ's sake, I delight in weaknesses, in insults, in hardships, in persecutions, in difficulties. For when I am weak, then I am strong" (2 Corinthians 12:10). The Revd Musa Njiru, who was later made a Canon of St James and All Martyrs Cathedral, Murang'a by Bishop Obadiah Kariuki, deeply appreciated my election as the first Bishop of Mt Kenya East in 1975 and gave me full support.

I joined Kangaru School, Embu, in January 1955. During my time at Kangaru, I became closely associated with Peterson Muchangi, who was the school bursar. He was a keen member of the East African Revival Movement. He invited students who had accepted Jesus Christ as their personal Saviour to go to his house for weekly fellowship meetings. I attended these meetings regularly though I found it difficult to confess sins, as I did not always know what sins to confess!

I also attended fellowship meetings in Embu town but I was concerned with the legalistic attitude of some of the brethren. At the end of each meeting we would go outside and stand in a circle and embrace one another while singing the revival song *Tukutendereza*. Then one day they refused to embrace me because I had parted my hair as was common during that time. The brethren also condemned girls who wore necklaces or earrings.

However, I attended the fellowship meetings throughout my Kangaru days. The revival movement that began at Gahini in Rwanda in the 1930s and spread to Uganda, Kenya and Tanzania was and remains a spiritual movement that challenged Christians to greater commitment to Jesus Christ. The Brethren declared that being baptised was not enough, and that each individual needed to receive Jesus Christ as a personal saviour and make a public confession of his or her sins. The brethren courageously refused to take the Mau Mau oath, which involved drinking animal blood and rejecting Christianity. They boldly said they could not exchange the blood of Jesus Christ their Saviour for that of animals. For this, many of those in Central Kenya died as martyrs. But over the years, the revival movement has been weakened by introverted ministry, legalism and leadership conflicts.

I was the founder of the Christian Union at Kangaru school and was its chairman during the four years I studied there. I encouraged members of the

Christian Union to teach Sunday School in the neighbouring villages. We had groups teaching at Kangaru and Gatunduri villages as well as within Embu town. I was nicknamed "the Man of the Bible" as I was always carrying my Bible and reading it in the dormitory. I was assigned to Mbeere House and I led prayers each night before we slept. One night I went to Embu House to pray for the students in the dormitory when a cheeky student switched off the lights. The House Master, Mr Muhoya, came and switched them back on only to find me standing right in the middle of the dormitory.

"What are you doing in this dorm at this hour?" he asked in fury. I replied that I was praying for the students. To everyone's amazement, he quickly retreated and shut the door behind him.

Though I hated games, I was responsible for the tennis court, which was regularly used by Mr Muhoya and a few other teachers. I also disliked athletics. There was a cross-country race organized once every year and it was compulsory for every student to run the marathon. I once participated in that race and despite making every effort I managed to take the second-last position. One day I was forced to play football for Mbeere House and I scored a goal only to be told that I was offside. I have never tried to play football since that day.

I may not have won accolades in athletics or school games but utilized my talents and abilities in other ways and achieved some milestones of my own. I wrote a play that was cast by the members of the Christian Union and staged before all the students and teachers at school. Mr Cobb, our headmaster and a great educationist and disciplinarian, also watched the play.

The school used to do very well in the final Cambridge "O"-Level Examinations. Among the teachers then was Mr Jeremiah Nyagah, the first headmaster of the school, who later became one of the few Kenyan representatives to the Legislative Council before independence and one of the longest-serving members of parliament in independent Kenya. When Mr Cobb left the school to go to the Ministry of Education Headquarters in Nairobi, the Revd William Owen became our headmaster. He was nicknamed Kagori (a small animal skin) because he always wore a skin jacket.

I sat the Cambridge "O"-Level Examination in November 1958. The Sunday before the examinations began, I left the school to worship at the church in Embu town and to attend fellowship meetings as usual. My classmates were by then doing some last-minute reading commonly referred to as "cramming" and they wondered where I was going at such a critical time. When the results were released I had scored a First Division with credits in every subject. I was offered a place at Royal Technical College, Nairobi (later the University of Nairobi), which I joined in September 1959.

The Royal Technical College, Nairobi

From January to July 1959, the Revd Michael Lapage, the supervisor of Anglican schools in Embu District, employed me as an untrained teacher at Kiburu Intermediate school in Ndia Division. I was earning Ksh 149 per month but when the "O"-level examination results were released, my salary was increased to Ksh 449. At the end of March, I was paid a total of Ksh 1,347. This was the first time I had received such a large amount of money. I continued teaching at Kiburu until September 1959, when I joined Royal Technical College, Nairobi.

The Royal Technical College, Nairobi (incorporating the Gandhi Memorial Academy) was originally a project of the Indian community in Kenya, who wanted to build a technical college for their children. The colonial government persuaded the community to make the college multi-racial. The college opened its doors to students in 1956. I joined the college in September 1959. When I joined the college, there were 200 Indian students and only 100 Africans from Kenya, Uganda and Tanzania.

I joined the Faculty of Arts to study Geography, English Literature and Mathematics. I was forced to do mathematics very much against my will. I had a strong credit in the subject in my "O"-level results, but despite having done well, I knew that the subject was not to my liking. I spent one whole day doing one calculus exercise and got only 4%. I became very depressed and appealed to the authorities to allow me to take history instead of maths. This request was eventually accepted. In those days, one could take "A"-level studies at either Makerere or the Royal Technical College. After two years I passed the "A"-levels and in September 196, I started undertaking my Bachelor of Arts degree from the University of London as an external student.

I graduated in May 1964, six months after Kenya became independent. By that time, the college had changed its name twice. It became Royal College, Nairobi and later became the Constituent College of the University of East Africa, with President Nyerere as its first Chancellor. President Nyerere himself conferred us with degrees in April 1964 in the presence of Mzee Jomo Kenyatta, the first President of Kenya.

My closest friends at the Royal College, Nairobi were Archibald Githinji and Evanson Mwaniki, who had come from Alliance High School. Githinji had a very good sense of humor and kept us laughing all the time. Mwaniki was also an accomplished musician and often played the organ during the Christian Union meetings. Githinji climbed the ranks of the civil service to become the Permanent Secretary in the Office of the President responsible for Defence. Mwaniki worked with Shell Company and eventually became the Managing Director there and later the Chairman of the national carrier, Kenya Airways.

One day, shortly after joining the college, I was going for lunch at the halls of residence when I overheard two engineering students, Athumani and Mimano, say that there is no God. I stopped and challenged them over this and they told me to prove that indeed God existed. They were third-year engineering students and had very persuasive arguments for their claim. I found it very difficult arguing with them and I eventually told them the only thing I could do was to pray for them. Athumani told me that I "would suffer the consequences if they found me accusing them to God"!

Years later, I was surprised to find Mimano (who at the time was the Manager of Kenya Railways) sitting at the front pew of St Andrew's PCEA Church, Nairobi, as one of the elders of the church. At the end of the service I asked him what had drawn him to the church after he had once told me that he did not believe in the existence of the Supreme Being. He told me that as a result of my prayers he had come to believe in God and had accepted Jesus Christ as his personal saviour. It was a great joy to know that my prayers for an ardent, self-confessed atheist had borne fruit and had at last been answered.

The first semester at the Royal Technical College was very difficult for me. I was so depressed that I could not concentrate on my studies and had to be admitted to the university sanatorium. I even started wondering whether I had made the right decision in joining the college. While at Kangaru School, Embu, I had felt a strong call to join the sacred ministry. I even went to St Paul's United Theological College, Limuru and met the Revd Allan Page, who told me that I could not join the college because I was "too educated". The college took only Standard 8 graduates and there was no college that offered advanced theological studies in Kenya at that time. I asked Revd Mr Page whether I could go to England to study theology but he advised me against this, arguing that "no African could understand Greek and Hebrew"!

I then sought the advice of Leonard Beecher, then the Bishop of Mombasa, over my wish to join the ministry. He sent his chaplain to visit me at the university sanatorium. The Bishop's advice was that I should continue with my secular studies at the Royal Technical College, as these would shape my future ministry in the Church. I accepted this advice and continued with my studies. With the benefit of hindsight, I can now confidently say that advice of Bishop Beecher set me in the right direction.

The University Christian Union was the most active organization in the University. The Chairman was Joseph Musembi and I succeeded him in 1960. Stephen Talitwala was the Treasurer of the Christian Union. He later became the Vice-Chancellor of Daystar University. It was during my time as the chairman that we invited the Revd John Stott to conduct the first mission to the university. Stott travelled from Ghana with a swollen eye as he had been bitten by a mosquito. His presentations were well attended but only one, my friend Archibald Githinji, responded to the invitation to accept Jesus Christ as his personal saviour. I know this might have discouraged Stott but those of us who were already committed Christians were greatly encouraged by his ministry. We were encouraged to know that the Gospel of Christ can be defended intellectually.

After graduating from the Royal College Nairobi in May 1964, I became a teacher at Thika High School. I was the first African university graduate to teach at the School. Mr Lomas, the Headmaster gave me one of the houses given to Africans, which did not have servant quarters as the houses designated for Europeans had. Among those I taught in Thika High School was Paul Muite, who later became one of the key players in the reform movement that led to the restoration of multi-partyism in Kenya. He was also a member of parliament and a very gifted lawyer. There was also Immanuel O'kubasu, who later became a Court of Appeal Judge.

During our days at the Royal College, the students held only one demonstration against the authorities and the college was never closed. In about 1963, the students decided to demonstrate along what is now called Uhuru Highway. The purpose of the demonstration was to demand the construction of an underground footpath across the highway. We had to cross the road dangerously at least four times a day, walking between our halls of residence and lecture rooms, many times ducking past speeding vehicles. In protest we wore red gowns and walked in single file and blocked the cars at the roundabout (between the University and St Paul's Chapel). We were not very many students then, so after crossing the road, we would return to the starting point and repeat this several times.

The traffic jam extended to the Westlands area, two and half kilometres away. No police officers turned up and we retreated to our classes at about 9.00am. The students tried to repeat the demonstration at lunchtime to get some attention but the police were there in full force. Some students were arrested and taken to the Central Police Station. Another group of students went to demand the release of their colleagues. More students were arrested and charged with behaving in a manner likely to cause a breach of the peace. The government finally agreed to construct the underground tunnel, which I understand is not regularly used these days as it has become a security risk.

During our days at the Royal College Nairobi, we took plenty of interest in the politics of the day. I joined university when the state of emergency was still in force. This was at the height of the clamour for independence and for the release of Mzee Jomo Kenyatta, who later became the first president of Kenya. The students often invited the African nationalist leaders of the day to come and address us. Tom Mboya was the most popular politician among the students. He was admired for his eloquence, courage and efficiency as the Secretary General of KANU. Other popular speakers were James Gichuru, Julius Kiano and Paul Ngei. We also invited freedom fighters from other African countries. Among them were Mwalimu Julius Nyerere, Kenneth Kaunda of Zambia and Joshua Nkomo of Zimbabwe.

I was present during the first Madaraka Day celebrations on what is now Harambee Avenue on 1 June 1963, when Kenya was granted internal self-government. I was also present at Uhuru Gardens when Kenya was granted full independence on 12 December 1963. These were very exciting days for the African students on campus. We welcomed the pledge that our political leaders would fight against poverty, ignorance and disease.

In 1963, the University of East Africa was established with three constituent colleges, one in each country: Makerere College for Uganda, Nairobi University College for Kenya and University of Dar es Salaam for Tanzania, with the President of Tanzania, Mwalimu Julius Nyerere as the first chancellor. I was one of the graduates during the first graduation ceremony held in the great court of Nairobi College and Mwalimu Nyerere conferred us with degrees. We graduated six months after independence and we were in great demand to serve the civil service of the new nation. Nairobi University College became the University of Nairobi in 1970, when it became autonomous. I surprised many college mates and friends when I decided to serve as a minister of the Gospel instead of going to undertake better paying jobs in the civil service or in the private sector. I felt strongly that my calling was in the service of Christ and His Church.

Tyndale Hall, Bristol

While at Thika High School, I met the Revd David Adeney, who encouraged me to become a Travelling Secretary of the Pan African Fellowship of Evangelical Students (PAFES) now called FOCUS. Arrangements were made by Dr Oliver Barclay, the General Secretary of the Inter-Varsity Fellowship in Britain for me to undertake one year of theological studies at Tyndale Hall, a theological college in Bristol in the United Kingdom. I joined the college in September 1965 and did part of the diploma course. I remember attending a philosophy class taught by the Revd Anthony Thiselton. At the end of the class one student approached me and said he was deeply concerned that I had not understood what the lecturer was saying. He offered to come to my room to explain the content of the lecture. I declined his offer and informed him that we should wait for the results of the essay we were asked to write on the same subject. When the results were returned, I was the leading student with 19/20 marks and my friend had only 5/20 marks.

It was not my wish to study theology for only one year. My wish was to undertake a Bachelor of Divinity at the University of London for three consecutive years. The Inter-Varsity Fellowship that had sponsored me felt all I needed was some advanced Bible knowledge so that I could return home and minister among university students in Eastern Africa.

A researcher recently found a letter in the archives of Trinity College, Clifton in Bristol written by the Principal, the Revd Stafford Wright, in February 1966 to Dr Oliver Barclay, which says in part:

> The reason why I am writing to you is because of the position of David Gitari, we all agree that he has outstanding abilities. It would be a very great pity if he has to leave with only half of the Diploma completed. We feel that every effort should be made for him to remain for at least one more year, and if he completes his diploma we should then consider very seriously whether he should take the London B.D.... we can guarantee that he is a first class man, and money should be spent on his training rather than on training others whom we have little knowledge and who probably will not get much out of their time in England.

Despite this appeal, the Inter-Varsity Fellowship was unwilling to finance my diploma studies for a second year. I returned home after one year of studies and worked as a lay chaplain at the University of Nairobi as well as General Secretary of the Pan African Fellowship of Evangelical Students. During this time I co-coordinated the work of PAFES from Cairo to Zimbabwe. My colleague Gottfried Osei-Mensah co-coordinated the work in West Africa. I made several visits to Egypt, Sudan, Ethiopia, Uganda, Tanzania, Malawi, Zambia and Zimbabwe. I encouraged the formation and strengthening of Christian Unions in the Universities in those countries. I however felt deeply that I needed more theological training. Dr Oliver Barclay, the General Secretary of the Inter-Varsity Fellowship, agreed to grant me a scholarship to return to Bristol for three years to complete my studies.

In 31 December 1966 I was married to Grace Elizabeth Wanjiru Gatembo. She had undertaken her "O"-levels at Alliance Girls High School, and had trained as a Nurse at Kenyatta Hospital, where she emerged the second-best student. The wedding was conducted by Bishop Obadiah Kariuki at St James and All Martyrs Cathedral, Murang'a. Our first born son, Samuel Mukuba, was born in October 1967. So I returned to Tyndale Hall, Bristol with my wife Grace and our eleven-month old son, Sammy.

I enjoyed the New Testament lectures by the Revd Denis Tongue enormously. The Revd Stafford Wright was our Principal, who was later succeeded by the Revd Dr Jim Packer. Among our lecturers were the Revd John Wenham, the Revd Dr Colin Brown, the Revd Anthony Thiselton and the Revd John Tiller. We occasionally went across the Downs (beautiful, open and very well-tended green grounds) to Clifton College to attend some of the lectures, and the students at Clifton also came to Tyndale Hall for lectures. At Tyndale Hall we held annual competitions in the art of reading the Bible. I enrolled for the contest. A student of English extraction came to discourage me from taking part in the competition since English was my second language. I, however, insisted that I would not remove my name. When the competition came, I was declared the best Bible reader and was given a gift of a new Bible. I also won the prize the following year. The adjudicators told my fellow competitors that I won the first prize because I had read 2 Corinthians 12: 1-10 "as if I was the writer".

In the summer of 1970, Dr Oliver Barclay gave me an air ticket to return to Kenya to look for a new job and also to conduct a mission to the University of Salisbury in Rhodesia, now Zimbabwe. The main speaker at the mission was Bishop Muzorewa, who impressed me greatly. Though the university was multi-racial, the white and black students could not interact beyond their own races, to the point that even students in the same class did not know each other by name.

Before returning to Britain I went to see Dr Wilfred Stott, the Principal of St Paul's United Theological College, Limuru, to ask him whether I could teach at Limuru on completion of my studies. To my surprise, he told me that "no African can teach at St Paul's as there is no money to pay the salary of African tutors". I then went to see the newly enthroned first Archbishop of the Anglican Church of Kenya, the Most Revd Festo Olang', to request him to offer me a job in the Diocese of Nairobi. He advised me to write to him about a month before completion of my studies. I wrote him a letter in May 1971 and he replied and indicated that there were no vacancies in the Diocese of Nairobi. On receiving his letter I was very disturbed that I might return home only to find myself jobless.

After a week, I received another letter from the Revd John T. Mpayeei requesting me to succeed him as General Secretary of the Bible Society of Kenya so that he could concentrate on translation of the Bible into the Maasai language. I accepted his offer reluctantly because I felt that I was not as well trained to sell Bibles as to expound the message of the Bible.

So in July 1971 I took a flight from Heathrow Airport with my wife and my son Sammy, who was now four years old. We stopped at Libya's second largest city, Benghazi, now synonymous with the uprising against the long-time leader of the country, Muammar Gaddafi (since deceased). As we were flying over Uganda our plane was intercepted by the soldiers of Idi Amin. They demanded to be shown the passport of each passenger. We did not land at the Jomo Kenyatta International Airport until about 3 am.[2] To my great surprise my mother was there to welcome us, though many others who had come to meet us at 11.00 pm could not wait any longer.

---

2 David Gitari's son John Mwendwa explains what happened:

"The Ugandan military had taken over government institutions including the civil aviation authority and the control tower. My understanding is that Uganda by then had no airforce capable of intercepting planes mid air and therefore could only communicate with pilots using the normal channels. The pilot was ordered to land (presumably in Entebbe) after which soldiers boarded the plane to check all the passports. My understanding is that Idi Amin was paranoid against any potential threat and his neighbours. At some point and I am not certain if it was by this time, Amin became pro-Palestine and was on the hunt for Israeli nationals to gain favour with the Arab world."

Chapter 3

The Road to Ordination

Ministry to the Students

The Kenya Students Christian Fellowship (KSCF) was founded in August 1959 at Alliance High School, Kikuyu. The inaugural meeting was attended by bishops, moderators, several other Church leaders, and evangelical schoolteachers from Britain associated with the Inter-Varsity Fellowship (IVF). Secondary school students who were attending a Christian Union conference at the same time were invited to attend the inaugural meeting. The KSCF draft constitution was adopted and the first National Council was elected. Students had two seats in the council of ten. I was elected as one of the two student representatives on the grounds that I was going to join the Royal Technical College Nairobi in September of the same year. In 1960, Gordon Mungeam, a history lecturer and one of the advisors of the college Christian Union wrote a letter to the Chairman of KSCF suggesting that I should not be a member of the council so that I could concentrate on my academics. I was therefore replaced by Joseph Musembi, the chairman of the Christian Union.

I remember that when I attended the first meeting of the council, I had to travel to Nairobi from Kiburu Intermediate School where I was teaching. Michael Lapage had agreed that I could ride in his car with him so long as I waited for him at Kagio market. He was travelling from the Kigari Mission Centre to Nairobi to attend the same meeting. James S. Mathenge, who was a student at Makerere University, gave me a lift on his bicycle from Kiburu to Kagio about five kilometres away. We arrived in good time only to see Lapage speed past us in his car. He had apparently forgotten that he had offered to give me a lift. I had to take a bus to Nairobi via Sagana and Fort Hall (now Murang'a) but I arrived at Church Army College, (now Carlile College) just before the meeting started at 2.00pm. Mathenge, who later became a seasoned civil servant, recalls with great amusement that he once gave the future Archbishop of the Anglican Church of Kenya a lift on his bicycle.

Before I joined the Royal Technical College, Nairobi, I visited a number of institutions around the Mount Kenya region, including Chogoria Boys High School, Kaaga Teachers College, Meru, and Tumutumu Teachers College and Njiiri's High School, encouraging Christian Unions. In 1961, I was again elected to represent the students on the KSCF Council and I remained a member until I went to Bristol in September 1965. When Harry Cotter was appointed Secretary of the Scripture Union in Kenya, KSCF appointed him as the first full-time Travelling Secretary. I worked closely with him when I was General Secretary of the Pan African Fellowship of Evangelical Students (1966 to 1968). We organized annual conferences and I was often one of the speakers.

After graduating with a Bachelor of Divinity Degree from the University of London in 1971, I attended the KSCF conference held at Machakos Boys High School as one of the speakers. I was greatly concerned that all the other speakers were insisting that the proof that one was Spirit-filled was to speak in tongues. The Pentecostal/Charismatic movement was now spreading like bush fire in secondary schools. On Saturday evening I decided to read to the conference 1 Corinthians chapters 12, 13 and 14. I made very few comments but I emphasised that speaking in tongues was one of the gifts of the Spirit and it was wrong to insist that every Spirit-filled person must speak in tongues. After all St Paul considered one who prophesies as greater than one who speaks in tongues, unless he interprets, so that the Church may be edified (1 Corinthians 14:5). Again he says, "I thank God that I speak in tongues more than all of you. But in the church I would rather speak five intelligible words to instruct others than ten thousand words in a tongue."

When I finished reading the three chapters, one of the speakers stood up and said, "This evening the Holy Spirit has been quenched." He then invited students to stay for all night prayers that the Holy Spirit might return to the conference.

The following Sunday morning there was another prayer meeting and one person prayed, "God deliver us from the demon of theology!" The response was a big Amen! At the end of the meeting I stood to correct the misconception. I said it is very wrong to call theology demonic for the word "theology" means the knowledge of God. The election for the new KSCF Council was held in the afternoon of that Sunday and I was elected as the new Chairman of the Fellowship. I remained the Chairman until 1975, when I was consecrated the Bishop of Mt Kenya East. One of my joys during that time was to note that some of the members of the council who had opposed my position about speaking in tongues at Machakos had accepted my position on gifts of the Holy Spirit. Among them was the Revd Dr MacMillan Kiiru, who has remained a faithful friend since then.

During my time as the Chairman, most of the meetings of the Council were held at the boardroom of the Bible Society of Kenya in Nairobi. I gave Bible studies in nearly all KSCF annual conferences and visited and spoke in many secondary schools. We formed the Nairobi Evangelistic Team (NET) in the capital city, which conducted weekend missions to many secondary schools throughout Kenya. The team included Edward Kizza, a Ugandan who was a lecturer in mathematics at the University of Nairobi, Joseph Musembi, my former classmate at the university, who later became a Pastor of the African Inland Church, and Rahab Kamau and Helen Chege, who both trained as teachers and were later appointed to head secondary schools. We used our own resources to visit the various schools and there are people I still meet who tell me that they accepted Jesus Christ when NET conducted missions in their institutions.

I preferred expository preaching in my ministry to the students, and indeed in all my addresses. I was first inspired to this by the Revd Tom Houston, who founded the Nairobi Baptist Church in the early sixties. My friend Joseph Musembi and I used to attend evening services at the Baptist Church at the Nairobi Arboretum, which was a walking distance from the halls of residence. Houston's sermons at the Baptist Church were based on a specific passage of the Bible. After introducing the passage, he would analyse the passage verse by verse and then apply the message of the text to challenge the congregation. He was definitely the best Bible teacher I had met. Later I was greatly moved by the Revd John Stott, who conducted the first mission to the University of Nairobi when I was the Chairman of the Christian Union. His books were also helpful to me in preparing my sermons. I also bought a complete set of William Barclay's New Testament *Daily Study Bible* published by the St Andrew's Press, Glasgow. I bought the set at KSh 2 per copy at the Methodist Church of Kenya office in Nairobi when I was a university student. I find these commentaries most helpful to date. When my family vacated the house rented by the Bible Society of Kenya at David Osieli Road at Westlands, I advised KSCF to purchase the house. This property has been a great blessing to KSCF.

The Student Movements

The Pan African Fellowship of Evangelical Students (PAFES), now the Fellowship of Christian University Students (FOCUS), was founded in 1958. The Christian Union of Kumasi College of Arts, Science and Technology became the first member of PAFES and was followed by the Christian Union of the Royal Technical College, Nairobi and that of the University of Ghana (LEGON). The first Travelling Secretary was Dr Alonzo Fairbanks, an African-American who was appointed in 1960. After completing my one-year theological studies at Tyndale Hall, Bristol, I was appointed Travelling Secretary for Eastern and Central Africa. Gottfried Osei-Mensah became Travelling Secretary in West Africa.

Before I started my studies in Bristol, I attended a one-month training course for student travelling secretaries from Latin America, Europe, Asia and Africa held at Casa Moscia in Switzerland. Moscia is a conference centre on the shores of Lake Locarno. The facility had been bought by the Evangelical Christian Students Movement of German Switzerland in 1957. Dr Hans Burki, the then General Secretary of the Switzerland Fellowship of Evangelical Students, organized the course in Moscia. It was here that I first met Samuel Escobar and Rene Padilla of Latin America, Chua Wee Hian of Singapore and Dr Isabelo Magalit of the Philippines. They all played important parts in ministering to university students in their respective regions and countries. This was the first time I had ever attended a Christian leadership conference overseas and I found the experience most useful. The venue of the conference on the shores of Lake Locarno is one of the most beautiful places that I have ever visited. Dr Burki took us for a walk in the foothills of the Alps. I remember that we visited a remote village where children were amazed to see a black person for the first time. They approached me with great trepidation and wondered what had happened to my skin.

PAFES was affiliated to the International Fellowship of Evangelical Students (IFES), which was founded in Boston in 1947 with Dr Stacey Woods, the General Secretary of the Inter-Varsity Christian Fellowship of North America, as its first General Secretary. Hence the aims and functions of PAFES were the same as those of IFES. The founders of IFES were concerned that the Student Christian Movement (SCM) had become too liberal. Hence the fellowship aimed at upholding the fundamental truths of Biblical Christianity, seeking to awaken and deepen personal faith in the Lord Jesus Christ and to further evangelistic work among students throughout the world.

I earlier indicated that I had visited various universities and colleges through Sudan, Ethiopia, Uganda, Kenya, Tanzania, Zambia, Malawi and what is now Zimbabwe as the Secretary General of PAFES. But the differences in the schools of thought were manifested overtly during my first visit to the newly established University of Malawi and Zomba Teachers Training College, where I found myself in the midst of a very hostile group of students. I had just delivered what I thought was a good lecture about Christian faith, but nothing had prepared me for the shock during the question and answer session that followed.

The first question: "Who has sent you here to Malawi?" The second question: "Why waste your time coming to evangelize people who are already Christians instead of going to preach to the nomads of Northern Kenya?"

The atmosphere was so hostile that I felt like David in Psalms 55: 6-8, who said:

Oh, that I had the wings of a dove!
I would flee far away
And stay in the desert
I would hurry to my place of shelter [Nairobi]
Far from tempest and storm.

I later learnt later that the students had been encouraged to be hostile to me by those who thought that I had gone to criticise the Student Christian Movement (SCM), to which they belonged. When, however, I visited the University the following year, I was warmly received, and the students were full of apologies for what had happened the previous year.

I visited the University of Dar-es-Salaam a number of times during the two years. The contact person was Professor Denis Osborne, who was the advisor of the university Christian Union. Bishop Alfred Stanway conducted two missions to the university and I assisted him on both occasions. I also assisted Revd John Stott when he conducted a mission there when I was General Secretary of the Bible Society of Kenya.

I also regularly visited Christian Unions at the University of Addis Ababa, Gondar and Alemeya College of Agriculture. In Addis Ababa, the Christian Union meetings were normally held at Makene Yesus Christian Centre.

During this period, Christian students were greatly inspired by the visits of A.T. de B. Wilmot, who was a businessman based in West Africa, and also by David Bentley-Taylor, formerly a missionary to China and Indonesia. When I was in Bristol with my family, we were often invited by David to spend Christmas at his spacious home in Hereford. David was such a hilarious and interesting speaker that students attended his meetings in large numbers. David Adeney, the Associate General Secretary of IFES for Asia, also visited us. He is the one who encouraged me to join the students' ministry.

During the two years that I was the General Secretary of PAFES, we lived in a bungalow bought by the University of Nairobi Chaplaincy Committee. I had been appointed as a lay chaplain to the University of Nairobi in addition to my work with PAFES. The bungalow was an ecumenical centre. Through the leadership of David Barrett, funds were raised to construct a Students Christian Centre, now known as Ufungamano House. The Protestants contributed two-thirds of the funds and Catholics contributed one-third. During our stay, various meetings were held by Catholic and other Christian students but at different times. Ufungamano House has now become a household name, as it was here that religious leaders from the Anglican, Catholic, Presbyterian, Muslim, Hindu and other faiths met regularly to strategise and advance the cause of democratic governance, a process that put Kenya well on course to achieving a new constitution.

When I was an undergraduate at the University of Nairobi (1959–1964), I noticed that the Christian student world was divided between the evangelicals and the liberals. The church in Kenya was founded by evangelical missionary organisations from Europe and America, but I was not aware of these divisions until I went to the university. Christian Union advisors from Britain had come from the background of the Inter-Varsity Fellowship and they discouraged us from inviting speakers who were not of that background. This polarisation disturbed me, especially because I did not fully understand issues that divided evangelicals and liberals. I initiated a forum to debate the matter, which was held at St Julian's Centre at Limuru and attended by students from Makerere and Nairobi universities.

Tom Houston represented the evangelicals' view and Stanley Booth-Clibborn presented the other view. We were deeply impressed by both speakers. But we also felt that these divisions from Britain were being imposed on us and that we needed fully to understand the issues within our context and take an independent stand without external pressure.

The debate that I chaired left me convinced that the evangelical position was more plausible. But the tendency of evangelicals to concentrate more on spiritual matters and to ignore the socio-political issues that also affect the whole individual left much to be desired.

The International Congress on World Evangelization held at Lausanne in July 1974 was a great landmark in my ministry. The congress was convened by the Billy Graham Association and was attended by about 4,000 Christians representing 151 countries. The theme of the Congress was "Let the Earth Hear His Voice". At the end of the Congress the evangelicals adopted "The Lausanne Covenant," an historic 15-clause document. Clause 5, entitled "Christian Social Responsibility", states in part:

> We affirm that God is both the creator and the judge of all men. We, therefore, should share his concern for justice and reconciliation throughout human society and for liberation of men from every kind of oppression. Because mankind is made in the image of God, every person regardless of race, religion, colour, culture, class, sex or age, has an intrinsic dignity because of which he should be respected and served, not exploited. Here too we express penitence both for our neglect and for having sometimes regarded evangelism and social concern as mutually exclusive... We affirm that evangelism and social political involvement are both part of our Christian duty. For both are necessary expressions of our doctrine of God and man, our love for our neighbour and our obedience to Jesus Christ. The message of salvation implies also a message of judgment upon every form of alienation, oppression and discrimination, and we should not be afraid to denounce evil and injustice wherever they exist...[3]

3 J. D. Douglas, *ibid.*, p. 4.

So evangelicals from all parts of the world repented for having put a wedge between evangelism and social political involvement. Twelve months after Lausanne, I was consecrated and enthroned as the first (and last) Bishop of the Diocese of Mt Kenya East. I was thrust into this position as an evangelical deeply committed to evangelism and an evangelical ready to be deeply involved in social-political activities and prepared courageously to denounce evil and injustice wherever they might be found in the Diocese of Mt Kenya East and my country, Kenya.

The Bible Society of Kenya

I became the third General Secretary of the Bible Society of Kenya in September 1971. I learnt from my predecessor, the Revd John Mpayeei, that the ministry of the Bible Society was threefold; translation, publication, and distribution of Bibles. During the four and a half years I was the General Secretary we completed translation of the Bible in KiMeru and, along with Dr Stevenson, supervised the translation of Kisii and Luhya Bibles. The proposal to include the extra-canonical books or apocrypha in the Luhya Bible caused some tension, as the translators were opposed to the move. We had to hold a special meeting at the Cathedral of the Good Shepherd, Nakuru, to resolve the dispute.

The Gospel of Mark was also translated into the Turkana language and I had the joy of taking the first ever scriptures to the people and Christians of Turkana. Revd Mr Mpayeei gave us his personal Land Rover to deliver the books. After passing Kapenguria and Amudant, we crossed into the borders of Uganda and were stopped by Idi Amin's soldiers but they did not harass us. When we entered Turkana at about 10.00pm, we were stopped by young people who were asking for water to drink. They were travelling to Lodwar for interviews for training as policemen. We gave them all the water we had. Our vehicle broke down four kilometres from Lodwar Town and we had to spend the night in the vehicle. We sent Pastor Karume (later Chief Chaplain of Prisons) to go and seek help in Lodwar town. We were able to attend the inaugural service to dedicate the first Gospel translated into the Turkana language.

Most of the men in the service did not wear anything below their waist lines while the women did not wear anything above their waistlines. I remember wondering whether they were real Christians. But when they started singing "Stand up, stand up for Jesus", my doubts were cast away.

The measure of success of a Bible Society is determined by the number of Scriptures it sells. During my tenure, Kenya sold more Scripture in proportion to its population than any other society in Africa. Being the Secretary of the Bible Society gave me the unique opportunity of having access to all Christian denominations in Kenya. I came to know the various Christian leaders across virtually all the churches and I travelled the vast reaches of the country to promote the sales of Bibles.

Soon after my appointment, we advertised for the post of Promotions Officer. We interviewed two people and the then provost of the Cathedral of Good Shepherd, Nakuru, got the job but for some reason he tried to get me removed from my position. He had tried to forge my signature in a letter he had written to apply for a job as the General Manager of Uplands Bacon Factory. The letter he had written was returned to us. The board found him guilty of forgery and we had no option other than to sack him. I was deeply shocked that a priest could commit such a crime.

I resigned as the General Secretary of the Bible Society of Kenya on 31 December 1975, as I had already been elected and enthroned as the first Bishop of the Diocese of Mt Kenya East. The election was held in April 1975 and I was enthroned at Emmanuel Church, Kigari, on Sunday 20 July 1975 in the presence of about 20,000 people.

Chapter 4

The Ordained Ministry
of the Church

I had prepared myself for the full ministry of the Church for about twelve years (1959 to 1971). My calling was mainly to young intellectuals. I very much wanted to commend the Gospel of Jesus to students in secondary schools and the University of Nairobi. The Archbishop, the Most Revd Festo Habakkuk Olang', did not accept my offer, most likely on the advice of his Archdeacon, the Ven. Ken Stovold. At that time, I was only the fourth Anglican Kenyan to obtain a University degree in Theology after Dr John Mbiti, the Revd Thomas Kalume (who became a Member of Parliament) and the Revd Henry Okullu (who at that time was the Editor of Target Newspaper).

When, however, I was employed by the Bible Society, the Archbishop agreed to make me a deacon in November 1971. I was attached to St Mark's Church, Westlands. I preached the first sermon there in January 1972 and was surprised the following day when I received a letter from the Archbishop informing me that I was no longer allowed to preach anywhere in the Anglican Diocese of Nairobi. The complaint against my teachings had apparently originated from the congregants of English descent, who were more than 50% of the total population in the church. I found it strange that the Archbishop did not call me to defend myself and that he took the decision without hearing my side of the story. The "irritating" sermon was based on the book of Revelation 3:15-16: "I know your deeds, that you are neither cold nor hot. I wish you were either one or the other! So because you were lukewarm – neither hot nor cold – I am about to spit you out of my mouth."

When I became the Bishop of Nairobi and the Archbishop of the Anglican Church of Kenya, I visited St Mark's Church, Westlands in 1997 and I reminded the congregation that I had once been barred from preaching anywhere in the Diocese. There was a remnant of the 1972 congregation who recalled my experiences 25 years earlier. Though I had been barred from preaching in the Diocese of Nairobi, I was now the Bishop of the Diocese with Episcopal authority to preach in every Anglican Church in Nairobi and throughout Kenya. This confirms that God works in mysterious ways His wonders to fulfil. As the General Secretary of the Bible Society I had travelled all over the country and made contact with various Christian leaders of all denominations. For regular Sunday worship, I joined St Andrew's Presbyterian Church, Nairobi, and virtually became the assistant to the Revd George Wanjau. He made me responsible for the University of Nairobi students' service which was held at the church between 9.00am and 10.30am. This was very satisfying for me as I was able to minister to the university students.

In December 1972, I was ordained a priest by the Bishop of Mt Kenya, the Rt Revd Obadiah Kariuki, in a colourful service held at St James and All Martyrs Cathedral, Murang'a. In June 1974, the position of the Provost of All Saints Cathedral, Nairobi fell vacant as the Very Revd Henry Okullu had been elected the second Bishop of the diocese of Maseno South. My name was suggested as his possible successor by Joel Buku but Archdeacon Stovold told the panel that I had no parish experience. This was true but he was the one who advised Archbishop Olang' not to give me the opportunity to have parish experience.

In April 1975, I was elected the first (and last) Bishop of the new Diocese of Mt Kenya East, which was carved out of the diocese of Mt Kenya. The diocese comprised the Administrative Districts of Kirinyaga, Embu, Meru, Isiolo, Marsabit, Mandera and Wajir. It constituted one third of the total surface area of Kenya. Soon after the elections, Archbishop Festo telephoned me while I was at the offices of the Bible Society and asked me to go and see him immediately.

"Yesterday," the Archbishop declared, "you were elected the Bishop of Mt Kenya East!"

I was not sure how to react to the news but realized that I needed answers.

I asked him, "How is it that only last year I could not be appointed provost for the All Saints Cathedral for not having parish experience and now I am being called to serve at a position of even higher responsibility?"

The Archbishop looked rather embarrassed and could not answer that question. I asked him to give me time to pray and consult with my family and friends before I considered taking up the position.

Meanwhile the flamboyant and charismatic Member of Parliament for Nyandarua North, Josiah Mathenge Kariuki, had been assassinated and his body had been found in a thicket at Ngong' Hills on 3 March 1975. He had risen to national prominence and his death had caused a major political crisis. The National Council of Churches of Kenya requested me to give six live talks on what was then the only broadcasting station, the state-owned Voice of Kenya (VOK) (later renamed Kenya Broadcasting Corporation). The programme was called "Lift up your hearts", each of a five-minute duration leading up to the prime seven o'clock morning news bulletin. I based the six talks on the first stanza of the National Anthem:

O God of all Creation
Bless this our Land and Nation
Justice be our Shield and Defender
May we dwell in Unity
Peace and Liberty
Plenty be found within our Borders

After giving the fourth talk, I was summoned to the VOK Headquarters to explain my devotional talks. I got there at about three o'clock and was kept waiting for an hour. I was eventually called into an office and found seven gentlemen ready to grill me. When I said "Good afternoon!" no one responded except Revd Mr Gichuhi, who was in charge of Religious Broadcasting. They had already obtained my manuscripts of the sermons and the chairman of the broadcaster, James Kangwana, finally explained why I had been summoned.

"Your sermons this week are very disturbing," he said. "Your reference to Cain killing his brother Abel (Genesis 4) may make listeners assume that you were referring to the assassination of J. M. Kariuki."

I told him that if my sermons were disturbing, then they had served their purpose, as the gospel of Jesus Christ is very disturbing, especially to sinners.

"Every human being is created in the image of God and has sanctity for which they should be served and not be exploited or eliminated," I replied. I pointed to each member of the panel, reminding every one of them that they were created by God in his image and no one has the right to take their lives.

Kagwana, told me that, if that was the point I was making, then I should continue with the talks I had prepared for Friday and Saturday.

On Sunday, I delivered a summary of the talks at the Nairobi Baptist Church and it was broadcast live on state radio. On Monday I received a call from VOK to say that the text of my sermon had to be delivered to State House, Mombasa, where Mzee Jomo Kenyatta was on a working holiday. The handwritten manuscript was typed out by my secretary at the Bible Society and sent to Mombasa. As I did not know what might happen to me, I decided to take a holiday and went to my village at Ngiriambu, in Kirinyaga District. I was advised by my friends to keep away from Ngong Hills during the holidays.

After a month I returned to my office and was visited by Jeremiah Nyagah, the then Minister for Agriculture. He came to advise me to accept my election as the first Bishop of Mt Kenya East. He was a member of the ten-man Electoral College that had unanimously elected me. He told me that they had never expected that I would decline the offer. Indeed, they wanted the Diocese to be divided because they felt they had a well qualified candidate to be the first Bishop. He had just arrived from Commonwealth meetings in Jamaica and informed me that the Archbishop wanted the Electoral College to meet urgently and elect another person because I was not keen.

After the minister left, I received a telephone call from the then Head of Civil Service and Secretary to the Cabinet, Geoffrey Karekia Kariithi, who requested me to go and see him. I was certain that the government had finally taken a position on my radio talks on the sanctity of human life and armed myself with scripts of the sermons just in case. I then went to the third floor of Harambee House ready for a second round of grilling from state agents. But on entering his office, I found only Kariithi. He moved from his desk and offered me a seat on the nearby sofa set, which made me feel a little more at ease.

To my surprise, he asked me why I had not accepted the offer to be the Bishop of Mt Kenya East. I was so surprised by the question that I decided to accept the offer immediately. Kariithi then picked up the phone and telephoned Archbishop Olang' and together they fixed the date of my consecration and enthronement for Sunday 20 July 1975. Then Kariithi told me that my radio talks on the National Anthem were the talking point of top civil servants. He however told me to keep on challenging all injustices in society.

I was consecrated and enthroned as the Bishop of Mt Kenya East at Emmanuel Church, Kigari, on Sunday 20 July 1975. I however, continued serving as the General Secretary of the Bible Society of Kenya until 31 December 1975.

Chapter 5

Bishop of the Diocese
of Mt Kenya East

My family moved from Westlands, Nairobi, to Embu town on 31 December 1975. The young family occupied one of the wooden houses inherited from the diocese of Mt Kenya and adjacent to the present St Paul's Cathedral, Embu. Even before I was consecrated and enthroned as Bishop, the leading laymen had constituted the Diocesan Development Committee. The committee was chaired by G. K. Kariithi, at that time the Head of Civil Service, Secretary to the Cabinet and also the Permanent Secretary in the office of the President. The other members of the committee were Jeremiah Nyagah, the then Minister for Agriculture, Joel Gatungo, Treasurer of the Kirinyaga County Council, Johnson Ndegwa of the Teachers Service Commission, John Nyagah, the Embu Town Clerk, Nelson Kivuti, M.A.N. Karanga, Benson Wamai, James Njogu, Simeon Kanai, Grace Ikahu and Beatrice Kanini.

The committee was keen to ensure that the new diocese had the necessary facilities to enable the Bishop to perform his duties. They had bought a large house belonging to Dr Kanyama, which was converted into a diocesan office. The committee went ahead and made the necessary plans to have the diocese financially inaugurated before the end of 1975. The inauguration ceremony was held at Embu Stadium in December 1975. The Archbishop of Canterbury, the Most Revd and Rt Hon. Donald Coggan, was the guest preacher and the guest of honour was Daniel arap Moi, the Vice President of

Kenya. In his sermon, based on Acts 2:42, Archbishop Coggan expounded the four pillars on which the diocese should be founded. They were teaching, fellowship, prayers and Eucharist.

The Vice President conducted the fundraising, which realised a total of Ksh 370,000. Then President Jomo Kenyatta sent a gift of Ksh 2,000. Most of the money was used to purchase property in Nairobi to generate income. Among those present during the inauguration ceremony were the Most Revd Festo Olang', the Archbishop of Kenya, and the Most Revd Janani Luwum, the Archbishop of the Church of the Province of Uganda, who in 1977 died as a martyr during the reign of terror of Idi Amin. The World Council of Churches was holding its fifth Assembly in Nairobi at that time (23 November to 10 December 1975) and fifteen international delegates were able to participate in the inaugural service. The Archbishop of Canterbury was most amused to see a cow being auctioned to raise funds for the new diocese. Also present was Charles Njonjo, the Attorney General, who had accompanied the Archbishop of Canterbury.

I started the diocesan office at Embu assisted by five other full time employees, who included Archdeacon Bedan Ireri, the Revd Epaphras Nthiga the Youth Secretary, a typist and a gardener/watchman. The Bishop combined the duties of Administrative Secretary, Accountant, Development Secretary, Education Secretary and Office Messenger. In April 1976, Grace, my wife, completed her training as a secretary at Kyanda College and succeeded the typist as my secretary. She had already resigned from her nursing job at Kenyatta Hospital to take care of our first-born son Sammy. A dedicated mother, she served the Diocese as a secretary for two years before she retired to concentrate more on caring for our three boys. She proved to be one of the best secretaries I have ever had, as she was always punctual, efficient, humble, duty-conscious and dedicated to her work. She remained the chair lady of the Mothers Union from 1976 to 1986, where she excelled in her work and is remembered for the prayers for the families that she introduced. She returned to nursing, her profession of training, and worked at the Chogoria Mission Hospital. She studied Midwifery at Pumwani Hospital in Nairobi and went on to undertake a Higher Diploma in Education at the Kenya Medical Training College, where she was a top student, and has had a distinguished career training nurses at senior levels, including at St Joseph's Mission Hospital in Transmara and the School of Nursing at the Consolata Mission Hospital, Mathari, Nyeri, which has topped national examinations.

We had three children: Samuel Mukuba Gitari, Jonathan Mwangi Gitari and John Mwendwa Gitari. Samuel studied accounts at Kimathi Institute and started off as a banker. He was known for his speed and efficiency at his station at Barclays Bank and received merit awards for fastest cashier and a merit award for the fastest data entry clerk. He later felt the call to enter full-time ministry in the church and proceeded to pursue a higher diploma in theology at Church Army and a postgraduate diploma in theology. He is the Chaplain at St John's Community Centre in Pumwani and is making an impact as the Coordinator of the HIV/AIDS Programme for the Diocese of Nairobi. Jonathan Mwangi Gitari studied electrical and electronics engineering at the Kenya Polytechnic before undertaking a degree in information systems and technology at the United States International University, Nairobi. He has been a Consultant and Information Technology Project Coordinator for the United Nations Nairobi offices (UNON). He has held management positions in various organisations and now implements security projects, including design, build, installing and configuring of integrated access control systems in ORAD. John Mwendwa Gitari, a journalist by profession, studied communications at Daystar University and later undertook postgraduate fellowships in journalism, democracy and broadcast management in the United States. He rose through the ranks from reporter to the news editor at Kenya's first private television station, Kenya Television Network, before he moved to K24 Television. He has won several local and international awards, such as the CNN Africa Journalist of the Year in Television, won top prize for the Peter Jenkins East African Award for Environment and Conservation, the UNESCO HIV/AIDS Red Ribbon Awards for Eastern and Southern Africa among others.

By 1990, the number of full-time employees at the diocesan office had increased from six to 141. This number included 37 employees of the Christian Community Services, 49 priests and evangelists employed by Diocesan Missionary Association and employees of St Andrew's College of Theology and Development. During the fifteen years, the number of parishes increased from 19 to 93, an increase of 390% or an average annual growth of 4.7%. In 1976 we had 150 congregations and by 1990 the number had increased to 420. The number of clergy serving in the Diocese increased from 30 in 1976 to 119 in 1990 and 16 candidates for ministry were undergoing training at St Andrew's, Kabare, and St Paul's, Limuru. In addition there were 15 Church Army sisters and captains and 15 women who had undertaken three years of theological training and had been commissioned as deaconesses, as the province had not as yet agreed to the ordination of women. The province gave consent to the ordination of women in June 1990, just before the diocese of Mt Kenya East was divided into two.

We started off with fewer than 100 licensed lay readers in 1976 and by 1990 there were 431 lay readers and many catechists or evangelists. As a result of hard pastoral work through the combined effort of clergy and laity, about 150,000 people had been baptized during the fifteen years and I had confirmed about 90,000 people. An average of 40 new members were being received into the fellowship of the Anglican Church every Sunday. The fame of the Diocese of Mt Kenya East spread far and wide and many visitors from other Anglican dioceses in Kenya and overseas came to visit the diocese to find out why there was such rapid growth and enthusiasm. In 1980, I was appointed by the Council of Anglican Provinces of Africa (CAPA) to be the director of the annual one-month courses for newly consecrated bishops in Africa. Most of those courses were held at St Julian's Centre at Limuru. I continued directing those courses, assisted by the Ven. John Kago, until about 1994.

Reasons for the Phenomenal Growth of the Diocese of Mt Kenya East

Holistic Application of the Mission of Jesus and His Church

The initial challenge by the Archbishop of Canterbury during the December 1975 inaugural service of the diocese that the four pillars of the church should be TEACHING, FELLOWSHIP, REGULAR EUCHARIST AND PRAYER (Acts 2:42) was taken seriously. My participation at the Lausanne Congress on World Evangelization in July 1974 opened my eyes to understanding the holistic mission of the church. I understood the manifesto of Jesus as contained in Luke 4:18-19 in a new way. Jesus entered the Nazareth synagogue on the Sabbath day and read a passage from Isaiah where it was written:

> The spirit of the Lord is upon me,
> because he has anointed me
> to preach good news to the poor
> He has sent me to proclaim freedom

For the Prisoners
And recovery of the blind,
To release the oppressed
To proclaim the year of the Lord's favour.
(Isaiah 61:1-2)

To announce that the time has come when the Lord will save his people is to proclaim "jubilee". According to Leviticus 25 the jubilee in the 50th year was celebrated by proclamation of freedom to all the inhabitants of the land. "During this jubilee year, all property that had been sold shall be restored to the original owners or their descendants, and anyone who had been sold as a slave shall return to the family" (Leviticus 25:10). Hence Jesus saw his task as that of announcing Jubilee, which had now become a metaphor for the release of those who were oppressed by injustice. The poor to whom Jesus was called to preach the good news were not only those who were spiritually poor but also those who were economically and socially oppressed by the structures of society. In November 1983, I based my charge to the fifth synod of the Diocese on Luke 2:52: "And Jesus increased in wisdom, and in stature, and in favour with God and man." I told the synod, "Just as Jesus grew in four dimensions, so every child born in this world should be given a chance to grow in the same way." The development of each individual should be in those four areas:

MENTAL DEVELOPMENT
PHYSICAL DEVELOPMENT
SPIRITUAL DEVELOPMENT
SOCIAL DEVELOPMENT

During the fifteen years, we understood our mission as the continuation of the mission of Jesus, who told his disciples "As the Father has sent me, I am sending you" (John 20:21).

In his ministry Jesus went through all the towns and villages, preaching the good news of the kingdom, and healing every disease and sickness (Matthew 9:35). This holistic understanding of the Gospel meant that we were not only going to evangelise and to respond to the spiritual needs of the people, but we were also going to respond to the physical needs of God's people, for a human being is a psychosomatic (spirit/body) unit and the two cannot be separated.

Partners in Mission Consultations (PIMC)

One of the most important decisions made by the 1968 Lambeth Conference was the establishment of the Anglican Consultative Council (ACC), which was scheduled to meet once every two years. Later it was found more appropriate to hold meetings once every three years. All the Anglican provinces were to be represented by either two or three people. There was to be a fair representation of bishops, clergy and laity. The first meeting of the ACC was held at Limuru, Kenya, in 1972. The meeting worked out the guidelines for Partners in Missions Consultations, a new concept that was to replace the concept of mutual responsibility and interdependence in the body of Christ (MRI) adopted during the Anglican Congress held in Toronto, Canada, in 1963.

The first PIMC in Kenya was held in Nairobi in 1976 and each diocese was requested to submit its priorities, which were discussed by delegates from other dioceses and partners from various parts of the Anglican Communion. I knew so little about this concept that the only priority I submitted on behalf of the Diocese of Mt Kenya East was the need for a camel and mule for the Revd Andrew Adano, to carry out his ministry among the pastoralist communities in Northern Kenya. One partner from the Episcopal Church of America (ECUSA) asked me with a light touch whether "a second-hand camel would be okay".

In 1977 I was appointed to represent Kenya during the Partners in Mission Consultation of ECUSA. The consultation was held at Louisville, Kentucky. The external partners spent the first week getting some orientation on the USA and ECUSA. We were divided into groups and sent to the eight provinces of ECUSA. I went to Province Seven and held meetings at Sacramento in California. During the last week, we gathered at Louisville once again and worked out the priorities of each province and the whole church. This was my first visit to the USA and it was quite an eye-opener. I returned to Kenya re-energized to ensure that we made proper arrangements for the second Partners in Mission Consultation, which we held in the coastal town of Mombasa in 1981.

The Provincial Synod appointed me to be the Provincial Co-coordinator of the PIMC. I encouraged every parish, deanery, archdeaconry and diocese to work out its ten priorities for the next five years and in doing so to invite partners from other parishes, deaneries, archdeaconries and dioceses related to the constituency under review. The external partners who came from

Australia, America, Canada, England, Ireland, South Africa, Uganda, Tanzania, Sudan and West Africa were first sent to various dioceses before gathering in Mombasa to discuss and adopt the priorities of the Province. I also co-coordinated the third PIMC held at St Andrews, Kabare, in early 1988.

When guidelines for drawing up the priorities were properly followed, then each parish, deanery and archdeaconry ended up with an effective five-year development plan. The external partners in each case were to scrutinize the priorities by questioning the validity or necessity of each priority. This exercise proved to be very useful, as the church was no longer going to do its work without well-conceptualized five-year development plans. In the Diocese of Mt Kenya East, I chaired meetings of the PIMC at deanery level. Out of the priorities of each parish, the diocese was able to draw up its priorities for the next five years. The agreed ten priorities of the Diocese for the period 1986 to 1990 were as follows;

- Evangelism
- Pastoral Care
- Teaching Ministry
- Agriculture and Rural Development
- Social Welfare
- Health
- Education
- Construction
- Appointments
- Communications

The priorities at every level were reviewed from time to time. Every time I paid an Episcopal visit to a parish, I checked whether the parish was implementing its laid-down priorities. I told the eighth and the last synod of the Diocese of Mt Kenya East, "There is no doubt that the concept of Partners in Mission Consultation has helped us to understand the extent of our mission and has made us get used to the process of a five year development plan."

Equipping God's People for Every Good Work

St Andrew's College of Theology and Development

St Paul wrote to Timothy, "All scripture is God-breathed and is useful for teaching, rebuking, correcting and training in righteousness, so that the man of God may be thoroughly equipped for every good work" (2 Timothy 3:16-17). The growth of the diocese can also be attributed to the emphasis we placed on training. The last synod of the diocese of Mt Kenya East held at Kahuhia in 1975 had recommended that the new dioceses of Mt Kenya and South should continue training their clergy at Macgregor Bible School at Weithaga, as starting a new Bible college would be prohibitive. I met Bishop Sospeter Magua so that we could discuss how the two dioceses were going to make use of the Bible School. I found out that our philosophies on training differed so greatly that I decided that it was imperative to establish a theological college for the diocese of Mt Kenya East. Bishop Magua wanted to select mature people from the East African Revival Movement and give them six months' training at Weithaga and then ordain them. I wanted well-qualified young people who were committed Christians and who had scored at least a 3rd division in their form four examinations. They would then undergo a three-year theological education before ordination.

The theological college had humble beginnings, starting in the diocesan office in Embu in May 1977, and was moved to St Andrew's, Kabare, in 1978. By the time of the division of the diocese of Mt Kenya East in 1990, St Andrews had trained 125 men and eight women. Twenty of these men were from other ACK dioceses and eight were from Sudan, Ethiopia and Tanzania. It did not take long for the province to recognize St Andrew's as the leading Anglican theological college in Kenya, a status it still enjoys to date.

The diocese refused to follow the short cut of ordaining people without proper theological training. We also encouraged clergy to advance their theological studies at St Paul's, Limuru or overseas. I was the first principal of St Andrew's and was succeeded by the Revd Canon Steven Houghton, who was very reluctant to leave his station and ministry in Northern Kenya. He returned to Marsabit after one year to continue with his work of translating the Bible into the Borana/Oromo language. Stephen was succeeded by Gideon Ireri, who later became Bishop of Mbeere after working as principal for eight years. Patrick Benson served as the acting principal before Gideon returned from St John's, Nottingham, where he attained his Bachelor of Divinity Degree. Other principals who served after the diocese was divided were Graham Kings, Wellington Chege, Ben Knighton and the current Principal, Canon Moses Njoroge. The partners who made generous contributions for the construction of the theological college and its ministry were World Vision, EZE of Germany, ECUSA, Bread for the World, CMS and BCMS (now Crosslinks), and the Diocese of Chelmsford, which financed the construction of the library and chapel.

It is important to note that a number of St Andrew's alumni went on to pursue further studies and several now have Doctor of Philosophy degrees in theology from various distinguished universities. These include the Revd Canon Dr Moses Njoroge, who has been the principal of the college, the Revd Canon Prof Joseph Galgalo, the Vice-Chancellor of St Paul's University, his colleagues the Revd Dr Zablon Bundi, the Revd Dr Kabiru Gatumu and Ph.D. candidate the Revd Lydia Mwaniki, and Kenyatta University lecturer the Revd Dr Julius Gathogo. St Andrew's is also proud that a number of its alumni are now bishops of the church, including the Rt Revd Daniel Munene, Bishop of Kirinyaga, the Rt Revd Moses Masamba Nthuka, Bishop of Mbeere, the Rt Revd Charles Mwendwa, Bishop of Meru, the Rt Revd Joseph Kagunda, Bishop of Mt Kenya West, the late Bishop Andrew Adano and the late Bishop William Waqo, who was the Provincial Secretary of the Anglican Church in Kenya

St Andrew's, Kabare, started training office secretaries under the able leadership of the Revd Pamela Wilding. There were also courses available to train community health workers and accountants. To equip the laity for God's work, I invited the Revd Canon Keith Anderson to come and initiate the Theological Education by Extension (TEE) program. He co-coordinated advanced-level TEE from his base in Kerugoya town. Newton Gatimu started TEE at parish level for lay readers, catechists and other interested lay people. Others who served in the TEE department included Joyce Karuri, Jane Karira, Dr Peter Williams and the Revd Titus Ngotho. Some of the lay people who undertook certificate level TEE felt called to full-time ministry and underwent further training at St Andrew's, Kabare, before ordination.

Christian Community Services (CCS)

The aims and functions of the original Diocesan Development Committee was to ensure that the bishop and his team had adequate facilities to enable them to perform their duties efficiently. In addition to the diocesan office, the committee started building the bishop's house even before my family and I had moved to Embu. The committee had also made plans to build a cathedral and a theological college. The committee was at first very reluctant to involve the diocese in such activities as agriculture, health and water development, because some felt that they were the responsibility of the government.

By this time, Bethuel Kiplagat, the then Deputy General Secretary of the National Council of Churches of Kenya (NCCK), had visited me and promised to support human development activities in the diocese. A special meeting of the Diocesan Development Committee was held at the Ruiru home of the Chairman, G. K. Kariithi. John Kamau, the General Secretary of NCCK, and Kiplagat addressed the meeting. This meeting was the crucial turning point in convincing members to see development in terms not only of construction, but also of human development.

Following the advice of Bethuel Kiplagat, the committee invited CORAT Africa to undertake a feasibility study in the diocese in early 1977. CORAT Africa sent four teams to study health, agriculture, education and administration. The health team, led by Professor Colin Forbes of the School of Medicine of the University of Nairobi, advised us against starting a hospital, saying a health team should concentrate on primary health care. The education team, composed of the Revd Donald Dain and Richard Odeng', visited all our church-sponsored secondary schools in the diocese and recommended that we employ a diocesan Education Secretary and two religious education advisors. They recommended that we hold an annual Education Sunday and invite schools and institutions of learning for prayers and fundraising to support the diocese. The founder of CORAT (Africa), Bishop Stuart Snell, evaluated the administration of the diocese and suggested ways in which we could make it more efficient and effective in its mandate.

The Department of Education was set up in January 1978 with Godfrey Muriithi as the first Education Secretary. The Revd Ephantus Mwaniki was appointed Religious Education Advisor for Embu district and Bernard Koigi took the same position in Kirinyaga district. The funds raised during annual Education Sundays were enough to support the education programme of the diocese. By 1980, the full-time members of staff in the department had increased to seven. These included a financial advisor to *harambee* (self-help) schools and a film operator.

Those who graced the Annual Education Sundays as chief guests were almost always the cabinet minister or assistant minister for education, or permanent secretaries. The first fundraising, held at Kangaru School, Embu, in January 1978 realized Ksh 205,000. By the time of the division of the diocese, a total of Ksh 4,500,000 had been raised locally to support the department. Most of the money was donated through sponsored schools and parishes. In 1976 the diocese sponsored 101 Primary schools with 45,500 pupils and 1,323 teachers. There were also 28 sponsored secondary schools with 8,000 students. By 1990 the number of sponsored primary schools had increased to 145 while the number of sponsored secondary schools had increased to 52. We also had eight sponsored polytechnics and five special schools.

The Board of Education under the chairmanship of Johnson Ndegwa regularly visited secondary schools to preach and to celebrate holy communion, attended meetings the boards of governors of various schools, organized seminars for accounts clerks in *harambee* secondary schools, conducted a film ministry, organised educational tours for secondary school heads, granted bursaries to needy students and participated in preparing syllabuses and teaching materials for religious education at all levels. Schools posting the best CPE, "O"-Level, "A"-Level and later KCPE and KCSE results were given trophies during Education Sundays. The education team also represented the sponsor during the appointment of new members to the boards governing various schools while assisting schools in resolving problems and disputes such as strikes.

By the time of its division in 1990, the diocese of Mt Kenya East had the most elaborate and effective education program in the Anglican church of Kenya and one of the best among other religious sponsors. The greatest challenge that we faced during the fifteen years was the abuse of authority by government officials in the Ministry of Education who failed to respect the rights of the sponsor as enshrined in the 1969 Education Act. The Act clearly stated that the Minister shall appoint the heads of schools and the chairman of Board of Governors in consultation with the sponsor. This was often ignored and many times we had to protest to the ministry when such decisions were made without consultation. However there was no doubt that our effort to become an effective sponsor not only raised morale, but also promoted spiritual and academic well-being within our schools.

Primary Health Care

We knew that we had to hire a full time director of Community Services if the diocese was to provide services effectively in primary health care and play its role in rural development. The Episcopal Church of the United States of America offered the services of Kerk Burbank, a committed Christian layman with ten years' experience in marketing, public relations, advertising and organisational development. Burbank arrived in May 1979. His first task was to write a proposal for a primary health care programme. The Central Protestant Development Agency of Germany (EZE) accepted the proposal and gave us the initial grant of Ksh 3,500,000 for three years. Because of our transparency and demonstrated accountability in the use of the funds, EZE continued renewing and increasing the grants throughout the 15 years of the diocese and beyond. Funds were also received from USAID for family planning and child survival programs. By 1990 we had received grants totaling Ksh 28,555,424. The department was well co-coordinated by Anne Njeri Murage, a highly qualified nurse.

The Primary Health Care Programme had five components: setting up village (local church) health committees, training of community health workers (CHW), mobile clinics, family planning and child survival. The local church health committee had to identify a person (usually the evangelist or catechist) who would undergo six weeks of training at St Andrew's, Kabare, and upon graduation, would return to his or her village and teach the community on the causes of the commonest diseases in the area and how to prevent them. Being a trained evangelist, he or she would cater for the spiritual as well as the physical needs of the community. The syllabus at St Andrew's was developed according to the guidelines of the World Health Organization (WHO). During the first graduation ceremony, the Eastern Province Director of Health Services acknowledged that we were the first organisation in Kenya to train CHWs in accordance with the recommendations of the WHO. Hundreds of thousands of people die of preventable diseases each year and the WHO had observed that if developing countries borrowed from the Western model, which was highly dependent on graduate medical doctors, then it would take a long time for medical services to percolate through to rural and grassroots communities. After all, most medical doctors tend to concentrate their clinics and operations in urban areas. It also takes up to seven years or more after secondary school education to train a medical doctor, a long and expensive venture by any standard.

The CHW training is a practical approach that focuses on only nine of the commonest diseases namely malaria, pneumonia, diarrhoea, intestinal worms, measles, anaemia, upper respiratory tract infection (URTA), and meningitis. HIV/AIDS was factored in during the 1990s. The CHWs return to their villages to teach the community how to prevent these diseases. By the time we divided the diocese in 1990, there were about 400 CHWs scattered all over the diocese with the life-saving message that "prevention is better than cure". We had also established about 16 centres, which were visited by our Community Health Mobile Unit for immunisation of infants and for ante-natal and post-natal care, among many other services. The centres were supposed to be at least five kilometres from the nearest government dispensary or health post. This programme was a great blessing to many in the vast remote areas who may never have enjoyed medical care. There were many more clients seeking assistance with family planning than those who went to government hospitals. Kerk Burbank returned to America in 1982 and was succeeded by the Revd Josphat Mugweru, who consolidated the work until 1989, after which Anne Murage became the acting director. In the meantime, the name Christian Community Services, which was coined by the Diocese of Mt Kenya East, was adopted by all other dioceses of the Anglican Church of Kenya.

Meanwhile the spread of the HIV infection and deaths associated with AIDS had reached alarming levels and the pandemic was declared a national disaster in 1999. In 1994, the diocese of Kirinyaga approached Trinity Church, New York, who agreed to give us a three-year grant to set up the AIDS Awareness Creation Programme. We were able to employ a team of four people: a nurse, a social worker, a lady who was living positively with HIV and a driver. We equipped the team with a television set and a video cassette player to enable maximum exposure of real-life stories of people affected and infected by HIV/AIDS. The team visited schools, churches, open-air markets, and numerous public places creating awareness of HIV and AIDS. This was the first ever HIV/AIDS awareness programme in Kirinyaga district. Its success encouraged Trinity Church in New York to commit more funds for co-ordination of HIV/AIDS programs at the provincial level.

In early 1985 my wife and I visited Stuttgart, Germany, at the invitation of Dr Walter Arnold and the Revd Albrecht Hauser of the Evangelical Lutheran Church of Wurttemberg. The church had partnered with the diocese of Mt Kenya East for more than a decade on a number of ventures and had annually given us funds for evangelism in northern Kenya and for theological education. In the previous year, there was severe famine throughout Kenya and we had received generous funds for famine relief. I could just have continued making appeals for famine relief but while in the hotel where we were staying, I had a vision of starting a programme to increase food production in various districts of the diocese to increase their productivity and capacity to feed themselves sustainably instead of depending on handouts year after year. I wrote a simple proposal and shared the vision with Bread for the World, based in Stuttgart. The proposal was improved and expanded by Stephen Githendu, an agriculturist who had been seconded to the diocese by the Ministry of Agriculture. Bread for the World then sent Peter Rottach to Kenya to discuss the proposal further. The organisation agreed to fund an integrated programme to be based in six stations in various parts of the diocese.

The first station was established at the Isiolo District Centre and when it became successful other stations were established at Wanguru in Kirinyaga district, Mitunguu in Meru district, Sololo in Moyale district, Macumo in Embu district and Mayori in Mbeere district. In the dry areas of Sololo in Marsabit district and in Isiolo district, demonstration farms were established for crops suitable for semi-arid areas and veterinary services were made available for those with domestic animals, especially camels, cows and goats. Through the vision, the directors of CCS were able to model those centres into sustainable models for development. These centres virtually replaced government farmers' training centres and agricultural extension services programmes, which seem to have died a natural death during the Moi regime. The once robust centres that had by then collapsed included Kamweti in Kirinyaga and Kanguru in Meru districts. Before starting the six centres, the diocese made use of these dormant government centres to train farmers.

When the diocese was divided in 1990, Monica Hoffman of EZE recommended that the department of Christian Community Services remain as a single unit serving the various sees. The CCS office at Kerugoya continues to co-ordinate the human development services of the four dioceses carved out from the former Diocese of Mt Kenya East: Kirinyaga, Embu, Mbeere and Meru. J. S. Mathenge has served as chairman and Bishop Henry Kathii as vice-chairman for nearly two decades.

Quality Departmental Heads

The growth of the Diocese of Mt Kenya East was by and large due to the quality and calibre of the men and women appointed to head various departments. I could not have succeeded if it were not for the very able team of senior staff who took up various appointments. From the humble beginnings we set up a Diocesan Appointment Committee that advertised, short-listed and interviewed all employees. I refused to employ or fire any member of staff on my own. It also became our policy to offer people employment on the basis of their ability, irrespective of where they came from. We therefore managed to have a highly qualified team of senior staff. The Revd Jephthah Gathaka was the first and very able Administrative Secretary. He was succeeded by James Njogu, a layperson with plenty of experience in local government administration.

Robert Martin, a Crosslinks missionary, was seconded to us to serve as the diocesan accountant and he was very efficient in his work. He was succeeded by Jane Mbario, a highly qualified lady from Embu. These two accountants created a sense of confidence among Christians in the diocese that their finances were well managed. Our overseas partners were so deeply impressed by our accountability, transparency and efficiency that they increased their grants from time to time. The directors of CCS, Kerk Burbank, the Revd Josphat Mugweru and later the Revd Ben Kanina were among the ablest directors of development in the province. Stephen Githendu did a superb job as the Coordinator of Rural Development and so did Anne Murage in the Community Health Department. The Revd Joyce Karuri Kirigia did a commendable job in the Communications Department.

Through her initiative, the diocese of Kirinyaga was able to produce a hymn book in Kikuyu called *Nyimbo cia Gucanjamura Ngoro*, which can be simply translated to mean "hymns to warm up our hearts". This hymn book has made worship more vibrant and jubilant. Joyce was later to co-ordinate a project that published *Our Modern Services*, a Kenyan prayer book, which has been hailed all over the world. She also co-coordinated the production of a new hymn book for the Anglican Church of Kenya with tunes gathered from various parts of Kenya. She was later invited to represent Africa on the executive of the International Anglican Liturgical Committee. We had an efficient and effective education team referred to earlier. Able archdeacons such as the Ven Marclus Itumu, the Ven Ephantus Muriuki, the Ven Titus Ngotho, the Ven Jeremiah Njogu and the Ven Major Phinehas Nyagah also served the diocese. The Mothers Union was served well by Virginia Karani and Janet Ruita, while the Revd Epaphras Nthiga was very gifted in his ministry among the youth.

The departmental heads admired my leadership in that I did not unnecessarily interfere with their work. I delegated my responsibilities to these people and I gave the space to each person to perform his or her duties without interference. I occasionally held meetings with them so as to receive reports from the various departments. The working environment was very good and the morale was very high. I consider this as one of the key reasons for the rapid growth of the Diocese.

Mobilisation of the Laity

The other major reason for rapid growth of the diocese was mobilization of the laity. It was the laity in Embu and Kirinyaga who requested that the Diocese of Mt Kenya East be created and on becoming the first Bishop, I found the laity to be highly committed to supporting the work of the diocese. I only encouraged this already existing enthusiasm. There were individuals who held high office or key positions in the land who took it as a great privilege to use their gifts to support the ministry of the bishop and the diocese. They included Jeremiah Nyagah, one of the longest serving members of parliament and cabinet ministers, who supported the diocese wholeheartedly, G. K. Kariithi, J. S. Mathenge, and Luka Galgallo, M. A. N. Karanga, John Nyagah, Johnson Ndegwa, Joel Gatungo (our treasurer for many years), Nelson Kivuti, Grace Ikahu, Beatrice Kanini and many others. We encouraged every congregation and parish to mobilise lay people and involve them in the ministry of the church.

The Mothers Union of the Mt Kenya East diocese was the most dynamic movement in the Diocese. We took regular statistics and found that two-thirds of regular worshippers were women. Women made church gatherings very lively. Everywhere I went I was welcomed by dancing women. They cleaned and beautified the churches and cooked for visitors. They supported parishes by doing various projects such as building vicarages and multi-purpose halls, and providing furniture and utensils, among numerous other positive contributions they made. They met regularly for fellowship and capacity building. Though the number of Christian women active in the church was far greater than that of men, they were outnumbered by men at the various levels of decision-making. I encouraged the various departments and bodies of the church, albeit without much success, to implement the recommendation of the World Council Churches that the decision-making bodies of churches should have not less than 40% women.

Ordination of Women

The other factor that contributed to the growth of the diocese was the decision to train suitably qualified women and to prepare them for the full-time ministry of the church. Women had always enrolled as students from the time St Andrew's College was moved to Kabare. Naturally some of the women did better academically than their male classmates but on completion of their training, women could only be commissioned as deaconesses. This was very frustrating to women as they were not getting a chance to make full use of their talents. The 1978 Lambeth Conference had recommended that each Province discuss the possibility of the ordination of women and take a decision. The Synod of Mt Kenya East diocese debated that motion in 1978, 1981, and 1983 but the motion was lost every time mainly because the clergymen voted against it. The motion was finally passed in 1986. But it was not until the eve of the division of the diocese in June 1990 that the Province accepted the ordination of women. By that time there were 16 women who had successfully undergone ministerial training.

The first women to be made deacons were the Revd Pamela Wilding, the Revd Edith Njoki Njiri and the Revd Joyce Mutitu Cendi. The ceremony to make them deacons was held at Kutus in July 1992. My proposal to make women deacons was vehemently opposed by two archdeacons on grounds that the decision to ordain women was made by the diocese of Mt Kenya East and not by the new diocese of Kirinyaga. I therefore had to convene a special session of the synod of Kirinyaga to adopt over 100 resolutions made by the synods of the Mt Kenya East diocese from 1975 to 1990. The special synod adopted all 100 resolutions including the one on ordination of women. The two archdeacons were conspicuously absent during the synod and the vote.

By the end of 1997, I had ordained a good number of women to serve in the diocese of Kirinyaga. By that time, the women trained at St Andrew's since its inception in 1977 were about 30. The ordained women brought unique talents to the ministry of the church. In their pastoral work, they could sometimes venture into areas where male priests found difficulty. Some of them excelled in the administration of parishes. I posted one of the women priests to a parish that had lagged behind in payment of diocesan quotas, and within a very short time she had cleared the arrears.

Financial Support

The parishes continued to give financial support for the ministry of the diocese though some parishes were struggling to clear their quota. During the fifteen years of the existence of the diocese, the parishes contributed a total of Ksh 30,186,122 plus grants of Ksh 25,781,115 towards evangelism, theological education, St Andrew's Institute, Theological Education by Extension and the ministry of the Mothers Union. The grants came from the Anglican Church of Canada, ECUSA, EZE, the Evangelical Lutheran Church of Wurttemberg, Germany, WCC, Tearfund, Diocese of Chelmsford, the international office of the MU, World Vision, CMS and BCMS. In addition a total of Ksh 78,500,800 was received for human development, most of which came from EZE of Germany. When we wanted to embark on major projects such as the construction of the cathedral and the theological college we refused to be discouraged by the doubting Thomases who would say, "There is no money."

I often said, "By faith we shall do great things." I strongly believed that resources were abundant among the Christians and our task was to find ways and means of making them give generously and sacrificially for God's work. By faith we were able to build the largest Anglican Cathedral in the ACK outside Nairobi, which was consecrated in 1987 in the presence of five primates and 45 bishops from Africa who had come to attend a pre-Lambeth Consultation in Nairobi. When the diocese was divided, Kirinyaga diocese appointed the Revd John Kangangi to be the Director of Stewardship and he moved Christians to give generously and joyfully for God's work. At the beginning of each year we held a stewardship seminar that was attended by six officials from each parish. The diocese gave an account of how the income of each preceding year was spent and presented the budget for the new year. The delegates participated in the allocation of quotas and returned home satisfied at being part of the exercise.

Chapter 6

Bishop of the Diocese of Kirinyaga

During the seventh synod of the diocese of Mt Kenya East, held at St Andrew's Church Kabare in April 1988, it was proposed that the see be divided into two and a commission was appointed to look into the matter, under the chairmanship of Johnson Ndegwa. The secretaries to the commission were Henry Kathii and the Revd Jephthah Gathaka. A special synod of Mt Kenya East was called in April 1989 to receive the report of the commission. The commission had done such a thorough job that the motion to subdivide the diocese was supported by 245 delegates with only one objection and two abstentions. The synod resolved that the new Diocese of Kirinyaga comprise Kirinyaga District in Central Province, and Meru, Isiolo and Marsabit Districts in Eastern Province. It was also resolved that the Diocese of Embu comprise Embu District in Eastern Province, and Wajir and Mandera Districts in North Eastern Province. All the assets and liabilities of the Diocese of Mt Kenya East were divided with such transparency that there were no complaints from any quarters. It was resolved that the diocese be formally divided on 1 July 1990. The Electoral College for the diocese of Embu was elected by the synod of Mt Kenya East, which subsequently elected the then Vicar-General, the Revd Moses Njue, to become the first Bishop of Embu. Moses had been one of the first Education Secretaries in the diocese and had also served for five years as a missionary of the diocese to the Evangelical Lutheran Church of Wurttemberg in Germany.

The farewell service at St Paul's Cathedral, Embu, was held on Sunday 1 July 1990, and was attended by thousands of people. I based my sermon on Joshua 1:1-10. I reminded the congregation that when Moses died, his successor Joshua was commanded by God to be "strong and very courageous. Be careful to obey all the law my servant Moses gave you; do not turn from it to the right or to the left, that you may be successful wherever you go" (Joshua 1:7). Moses Njue, who was holding my pastoral staff during the sermon, was subsequently elected the first Bishop of Embu and was consecrated and enthroned in September of the same year.

From the Cathedral, the Christians of Embu and Kirinyaga dioceses travelled to the boundary of the two districts and said goodbye to one other at the Rupingazi bridge. Tears flowed freely, especially among the women of the new Embu diocese as they witnessed the bishop who had served them for 15 years go, not to return again in that position. A convoy of 19 vehicles escorted me to Kerugoya and under a tree at St Thomas' Church we said prayers for the new diocese. St Thomas' Church, Kerugoya, became the cathedral of the new diocese and it was there that I was enthroned as the first bishop of the diocese of Kirinyaga.

The Diocese of Kirinyaga started with 59 parishes served by 62 clergymen, eight deaconesses, nine Church Army officers and 311 lay readers. By the end of 1996, there were 99 parishes served by 115 clergy, of whom 14 were women. At that time the Diocese of Kirinyaga had more parishes and clergy than any other diocese in the ACK. It was therefore resolved that the diocese be divided into two in January 1997. The new Diocese of Meru was to serve the people of Meru South, Meru Central, Meru North and Tharaka Districts in Eastern Province. The new Kirinyaga diocese was to serve the people of Kirinyaga District in Central Province, and Isiolo, Marsabit and Moyale Districts in Eastern Province. Henry Partridge, a CMS Missionary from New Zealand and a tutor at Bishop Hannington College, Mombasa, became the first bishop of the Diocese of Meru in January 1997.

I appointed Andrew Adano to be my assistant bishop in 1991. He succeeded Robert Beak, who had been my assistant in the Diocese of Mt Kenya East for five years. The assistant bishop was stationed in Marsabit and had special responsibilities of oversight among the people of northern Kenya and the nomadic communities there, but he came down south to assist me whenever the need arose. It was a great blow to the diocese and to the entire church when Andrew died in a helicopter accident in Marsabit on Sunday 28 July 1996, together with a number of civil servants. Andrew had taken a lift to join me at Kutus for a ceremony to make deacons when the fatal crash happened in Marsabit. In honour of his unique ministry among the pastoralists, NCCK commissioned my son, John Mwendwa, to research his life and to write his biography. The book, entitled "The Gospel on Camel's Back", was published by NCCK in 1998. In his preface to the book, the author says, "Adano was only 48 years old at the time of his death, and had served for 22 years. Yet in this short time he was blessed, with much patience, selfless commitment and determination, he was able to share his blessings with many of those around him. He revealed a faith and devotion to Christ that shone through his love of God and for his people. His ultimate desire was to see his flock changed and transformed by the word and spirit of God."[4] And Mutava Musyimi, the General Secretary of NCCK, in introducing the book says, "As his story reveals, Bishop Adano stood firmly for truth, honesty, peace, reconciliation and as a Christian servant leader model worth emulating."[5]

In 1990 we started building temporary offices for the new diocese at Kutus, which is the geographical and commercial centre of Kirinyaga District. The offices were not ready at the time of division and we were accommodated for the first few months at the CCS offices at Kerugoya, ten kilometres away from Kutus. Towards the end of the year, rumours were spreading that our wooden offices still under construction were going to be burnt by members of the youth wing of the Kenya African National Union (then the ruling and only political party in Kenya, as the country was constitutionally a single-party state).

I went to see the General Manager of the Kenya Power and Lighting Company (KPLC) to plead with him to authorise the supply of power to our offices. In my presence, he telephoned the regional office in Nyeri telling them to give the connection top priority. By the time I returned from Nairobi at 5pm, it was a relief to be able to switch on the lights and members of staff occupied the new offices the following day. I was planning to build a complex of permanent buildings to host a spacious chapel, a large meeting hall and offices. I was not able to fulfil this vision, however, as I was relocated to Nairobi. The Diocese of Kirinyaga was however able to build spacious permanent offices in Meru in preparation for the split of the diocese

---

4 John Mwendwa, *The Gospel on a Camel's Back: The Story of Andrew Adano Tuye.* Nairobi, Kenya: National Council of Churches of Kenya, 1998, p. ix.

5 *Ibid.*, p. vi.

in 1997. It also completed construction of St Stephen's Evangelist Training Centre, Marsabit, with assistance from the Evangelical Lutheran Church of Wurttenberg. The new diocese also assisted in the construction of St Thomas' Church, Kerugoya, which became the cathedral of the new diocese.

I had served as the bishop of Kirinyaga for seven years and by the end of 1997 had ministered to the people of Kirinyaga for 22 years running. At the time of my departure, the Kirinyaga diocese was vibrant, viable and served by a large number of well-trained clergy, both men and women. The lay people had given enthusiastic support to the bishop and the church. Many observers pointed to the diocese as a good model of what an Anglican diocese should be.

Archbishop Gitari Academy

In 1980, the leaders of Ngariama location met at Kiamutugu Secondary School and resolved to build a technical secondary school within the location. Nahashon Njuno, who was the Member of Parliament for Gichugu constituency, was charged with responsibility of searching for suitable land to put up this public utility. A steering committee was picked under the chairmanship of the Member of Parliament and with Justus Githei as secretary. The meeting also resolved unanimously to request the Bishop of the Diocese of Mt Kenya East to sponsor the institution. I was present during the meeting, accepted the request and also became the vice-chairman of the committee.

Within a very short time Njuno approached the District Forester, who agreed to set aside 33 acres on the southern side of Njukiini forest for the institution. The ministry cleared the land and promised the committee that after utilizing the 33 acres fully, seven more acres would be made available. I approached Henry Kathii (now bishop of Embu), who was the chairman of Kamuthatha Boarding Primary School, which we also sponsored, to look for good architectural drawings for the institution. Henry gave us drawings for the construction of dormitories for boys and girls and classrooms.

We tried in vain to get the school registered for a whole ten years (1980-1990). Government officials advanced all kinds of reasons against the formation of the institution. We were told it was no longer the policy of the government to approve technical secondary schools. We then decided to build a boarding primary school for children between Standard 4 and Standard 8. The Ministry of Education shockingly refused to register the school. It must be understood that this was a time of immense political expediency and intrigue, and that any development activity was viewed with great suspicion if it was not part of the strand of patronage that served the interests of KANU and its officials through the various grassroots branch offices at district and regional level all the way to the party National Executive Council. This patronage also pervaded every level of the civil service and was perpetuated by the provincial administration through chiefs, district officers, provincial commissioners, and security and intelligence agents, and found expression in the executive arm of government, the cabinet and the party NEC. Loyalty to this machinery mainly determined the career path for civil servants and politicians and became the litmus test for the development agenda upon which communities, constituencies and entire regions could benefit from or be deprived of the crumbs that fell from the table of the masters. Under this myopic approach, entire communities failed to benefit from numerous projects that would have catalysed positive change.

Following the unnecessary resistance that we were getting over the registration of the school, it was clear that KANU operatives in the district had told then President Daniel arap Moi that the purpose of the project was for Njuno and myself to build our political profiles. The situation became so bad that Njuno resigned as chairman of the school and I took over the position. To improve his relationship with the President, Njuno was reconciled to his arch-rival in KANU District branch politics, James Njiru, a move that in a way redefined Kirinyaga politics in parliament. Njiru subsequently helped Njuno to recapture the strategic chairmanship of the Gichugu KANU Branch by rigging the election to oust G. K. Kariithi in about September 1988.

In 1990, the committee built three classrooms but one night 23 iron sheets were vandalised. I requested the District Commissioner to give me a permit to hold a meeting at the site of the school and the permit was granted. Two days before the meeting, however, the Chief of the Location came to my house very early in the morning to inform me that my licence had been cancelled. I told the Chief to go and tell the DC that the meeting would continue as planned "whether he liked it or not"! Through the church network, I invited the people of Ngariama to come for the meeting at ACK St Magdalene Church, Kanjuu, that Sunday afternoon. They came in their hundreds. The DC sent the District Officer for Kianyaga and a contingent of policemen to stop the meeting. But they found it difficult to evict me from the church. I even invited the DO to come forward and greet the congregation. The point here is that numerous vital and well-intended projects in many parts of the country, whether in roads, health care or agriculture, and many other grand social and economic projects could not take off or were sabotaged merely out of political rivalry, worldly ego and personality conflicts, and ill-conceived perceptions that certain projects would threaten the status quo. All these factors were perpetuated by lack of visionary leadership. The situation was however greatly improved when the country reverted to multi-party democracy.

The Diocese of Mt Kenya East was subdivided into the Dioceses of Kirinyaga and Embu on 1 July 1990. The diocese of Kirinyaga advanced a loan of Ksh 2,000,000, which enabled the school to construct dormitories for 400 children. It was opened to the first Standard 4 and 5 pupils in 1991 and Irene Murage became the first headmistress of the school, which was originally called St Augustine Academy. It was named after St Augustine Kiaumbui, the Anglican parish that the school was in. I continued to hold the position of chairman of the school until 1997, when I was consecrated and enthroned as the third Archbishop of the Anglican Church of Kenya. The Revd Amos Kinyua, the Vicar-in-Charge of Kiaumbui church who had until then been the vice-chairman succeeded me as chairman when I relocated to Nairobi. It was Kinyua who proposed that the name of the school be changed to Archbishop Gitari Academy in my honour for the services I had rendered to the school and the diocese. The proposal was approved by the school committee, the Diocesan Education Committee and the Synod of the Diocese of Kirinyaga. The Revd Amos Kinyua was later succeeded by Bernard Makanga as the chairman.

When I retired as the Archbishop of Kenya and took up permanent residence at my Philadelphia Place home, I was approached in 2003 by the District Education Board to be one of the two representatives of the Board on the school committee. I found that the school had a new head teacher, Lydia Mutegi. During the first meeting I was unanimously elected chairman of the committee. I had a deep desire to expand the school and create a secondary school in it. The school had 33 acres and only three acres had been fully utilised. There was also great demand for boarding secondary schools in the district and indeed in the country as a whole, as the number of schools nationally could not absorb the tens of thousands of primary school graduates. It was my vision to have a centre where quality education could be provided. At first the parents unanimously approved my plans but the idea was sabotaged and to the present day the 30 acres of land remain idle and numerous children have lost the opportunity of a quality preparation for the future.

My philosophy of education drastically differed from that of the head of the school. I strongly believed that the purpose of education is not merely to pass examinations but to prepare young people for life. Most of my lectures on education were based on Luke 2:52, where Luke says, "And Jesus grew in wisdom, stature and in favour with God and man." In other words Jesus grew intellectually, physically, spiritually and socially. I strongly believe that education without those four dimensions of growth is not complete. Students at the school were made to spend hours studying so that the school gained only the reputation of good academic performance. There was very little time given to games or other extra-curricula activities such as music and drama. There was also neither transparency nor accountability in the way the school was being run.

After three years as school chairman, I received one day a letter signed by both the head teacher and the acting assistant chief of Kanjuu sub-location revoking my appointment as a member of the school committee. That was on 10 February 2006. This came as a great surprise to me. as I knew that the head of a school had no power to revoke membership of any committee member. I consulted the highest authority in the Ministry of Education, Science and Technology, who confirmed to me that the procedure of appointing and revoking members of committees running primary boarding schools was similar to the procedure that applied to secondary schools. The members are appointed by the Minister for Education at the recommendation of the District Education Board. I also wrote a letter to the then Minister for Justice and Constitutional Affairs and MP of the constituency in which the school is situated and delivered it personally to find out whether a head of a school could legally revoke the appointment of any member to the school committee. It is now seven years since I wrote that letter and I have not yet received a reply.

Though I received a letter from the then District Education Officer on 6 June regretting the manner in which the head teacher communicated the matter to me, I was not satisfied by the failure of the ministry to deal with issues that were of great concern to the founders of the school. I also did not like the way I was unceremoniously removed from the committee. I appreciate that the school has continued to perform well academically and is one of the leading public schools in the district. But it was even doing much better when we started the school and from the point when pioneer pupils started sitting national exams, the Kenya Certificate of Primary Education, in 1994. At one time it was rated twelfth nationally and at another time it was seventh in the whole country. Yet at that time the school was involved in many extra-curricula activities. Children who are made to memorise content like parrots may pass very well in primary school, but may find studies at secondary and post-secondary school level to be very difficult.

The school has great potential and I hope that the leaders of Kirinyaga County can reclaim it and convert it into a centre for excellence in education. Though I have no bitterness, I find it strange that the school that I founded and that is named in my honour had no space for me. My vision has been forgotten. We are now under a new constitutional dispensation and I hope that the devolved county of Kirinyaga will make the education of our children meaningful by equipping our children for life in all four dimensions: intellectual, physical, spiritual and social. The county has 30 acres available to establish a centre of excellence in education. It was good news to learn that the head teacher has at last been removed from heading the school with effect from January 2012. Now I can freely visit the school named after me and renew my vision to build a secondary school and make it into a centre of excellence.

Chapter 7

The Province

Secretary of the House of Bishops

The House of Bishops is composed of all the bishops in the Anglican Province of Kenya. I first attended the meeting of House of Bishops on 13 October 1975, three months after being consecrated and enthroned as the Bishop of Mt Kenya East. The meeting was chaired by Archbishop Festo Olang' and was also attended by Bishops Peter Mwang'ombe of Mombasa, Neville Langford-Smith of Nakuru, James Mundia of Maseno North and Assistant Bishops Manasses Kuria of Nakuru, Ezbon Ngaruiya of Mt Kenya South, and Crispus Nzano of Nairobi. Bishop Henry Okullu sent an apology as he was on an official trip to Australia, while Bishop Obadiah Kariuki was hospitalised. During the meeting I was unanimously elected the Secretary of the House by virtue of being the youngest bishop by consecration and enthronement. In the same tradition, Sospeter Magua, who had succeeded Obadiah Kariuki as bishop of Mt Kenya South, was elected Secretary in November 1976. He continued in that position until his resignation in October 1980. The House abandoned the tradition of electing the youngest bishop and elected me to succeed Sospeter Magua. I remained the secretary of the house for fourteen years until 1994, when I was succeeded by Bishop Samson Mwaluda of the diocese of Taita-Taveta.

I recall three major issues that were discussed during the first meeting I attended. The Bishop of Mombasa, Peter Mwang'ombe, wanted to be allowed to appoint two elderly senior priests (the Ven. Kiteto and the Ven. Nathaniel Mweri) to be his Assistant Bishops. He had already informed them of his intention and they were already using the title "Assistant Bishop designate." The archbishop informed the bishop that it was wrong to promise the two archdeacons that he would appoint them before he had received the consent of the archbishop and of the House of Bishops. The House did not consider it necessary to have two assistants in the diocese of Mombasa and preferred that only one assistant be appointed, if absolutely necessary. The archbishop did not accept this request and the matter was deferred until "such a time the Holy Spirit gives a very clear guidance concerning this matter." Bishop Peter Mwang'ombe humbly apologized and accepted the guidance of the House.

The House also discussed fund-raising events, commonly referred to as *harambees*. While appreciating the spirit of fund-raising, the House discouraged the holding of *harambees* on the day of the consecration of a church. The House also felt that as far as possible we should avoid the use of church fund-raising ceremonies as political platforms by politicians. It was also recommended that leaders who came to worship where a bishop or archbishop was present should not get undue prominence. The centre of attention should be the leader of the Church and especially in the proclamation of the Gospel of Jesus Christ.

The third issue concerned church weddings where the bride is pregnant. The chairman of the meeting, Archbishop Olang', who raised the issue, gave the example of how he was approached by a prominent personality who wanted him to conduct the wedding of his daughter at the All Saints Cathedral, Nairobi, which he consented to do. But when the couple came for counselling he saw that bride was at an advanced stage of her pregnancy. He told the couple that the wedding would be conducted in the vestry and not in the sanctuary and that the congregation would not be allowed to witness the ceremony. The bride burst into tears and went to see her father. A compromise was reached, however, when it was agreed that the congregation would be allowed into the sanctuary. The procession of the bride and her maids would pass through the sanctuary on its way to the vestry where the wedding would be conducted. After the wedding, the married couple would have the recessional procession through the sanctuary. There was to be no singing at all. Though this was the first meeting of the House of Bishops that I was attending I felt constrained to disagree with the chairman. I said it was wrong to deny the congregation the opportunity to witness the couple takes marriage vows and say:

I N take you N
to be my wedded wife /husband
to have and hold from this day forward,
for better for worse,
for richer for poorer, in sickness and in health,
to love, cherish and worship
till death do us part,
and this is my solemn vow.

I was convinced that what makes a wedding a holy matrimony is not the condition of the bride. It is God who made the state of marriage holy when he said at the time of the creation of Adam and Eve that "For this reason, a man will leave his father and mother and be united to his wife, and they will become one flesh" (Genesis 2:24). We call a church building "holy" because it has been dedicated and set apart for worship. But those who enter the holy place of worship are both saints and sinners. Similarly both saints and sinners can enter into a holy matrimony. Bishop Neville Langford–Smith took an even more surprising position that "it is not a sin for a girl who intends to be married to become pregnant, it is a mistake!" After further discussion it was agreed "that the attitude of the minister towards those who have anticipated their marriage should be to help them pastorally, and bring them to a point of repentance. The wedding, if the bride is pregnant, should be performed publicly in the church and not in the vestry. In this way the couple will be given the opportunity of making solemn vows before God and the congregation".

On 14 March 1977, Archbishop Festo Olang' convened an urgent meeting of the House of Bishops to discuss the worsening situation in Uganda under the leadership of the tyrant Idi Amin. Amin had ordered the assassination of the Archbishop of Uganda, Rwanda, Burundi and Boga-Zaire, the Most Revd Janani Luwum, and two government ministers, who were all murdered on 16 February 1977. The bishops met with heavy hearts and decided to issue a press statement in protest that afternoon. The statement was signed by the Archbishop, Henry Okullu, James Mundia, Manasses Kuria, Ezbon Ngaruiya, Sospeter Magua, Crispus Nzano and me. After the death of Luwum, many Ugandans fled into exile. The wife of Luwum and her children were given refuge in Kisumu by Bishop Henry Okullu. Bishop Melkizedek Otim and his family were given a place to stay at Kigari, Embu district, in my Mt Kenya East jurisdiction. The House of Bishops discour-

aged Archbishop Olang' from travelling to Uganda to take part in the consecration ceremony of the bishop of the new diocese of Mityani for security
reasons. The centennial celebrations of the Anglican Church of Uganda
could not be held in the country and the House of Bishops decided to hold
a special service of celebration at All Saints Cathedral, Nairobi, in July 1977,
which was attended by many Ugandan refugees who were staying in Kenya.

The first Archbishop of ACK, the Most Revd Festo Olang', gave good
leadership to the church in Kenya and he laid a solid foundation for the
Province. He was humble, firm and hard-working. Over time, my relationship with the Archbishop became very cordial and he began to appreciate the
gifts that God had given me. The Archbishop retired on 11 November 1979.
He was highly respected not only in the Anglican Church, but also by our
ecumenical partners and society at large. He knew how to relate to the government of the day. As I have often said, "The relationship of church leaders
to those in authority should be like our relationship with fire – if you get too
close then you will get burnt, and if you get too far, then you will freeze."
Hence it is necessary to keep a safe strategic and critical distance so that you
can support and praise the leadership when they do what is right and criticise them fearlessly when they go wrong. Festo kept a strategic distance from
the powers of the day. In 1985, I invited the retired Archbishop to the celebration of the tenth anniversary of the diocese of Mt Kenya East. He came
and spent a week in the diocese and he was welcomed enthusiastically everywhere we went and he was given numerous gifts in all the places we visited.

When the Archbishop retired, he left office in a disturbing manner. The
bishops of Mt Kenya South, Nakuru and I were blamed for the unceremoni-
al way that he left office. The blame has been greatly exaggerated, especially
by the Kenyan Media. I will put the record straight. One year before the
Archbishop was due to retire, the chancellor of the diocese of Mt Kenya
South, John Gacuhi, raised the issue during the meeting of the Standing
Committee held in about January 1979. Gacuhi wanted the issue to be discussed so that proper arrangements could be made for the retirement of the
Archbishop. The Archbishop, who was in the chair, told Gacuhi that he was
out of order. No one raised the issue for the rest of the year and by the time
it came up, it was already too late. In October 1979, the Archbishop sent
notice calling for a meeting of the Provincial Synod to be held on 13
November 1979 at the All Saints Cathedral, Nairobi. Gacuhi wrote a letter
to the Archbishop to inform him that he could not chair that meeting as he
would have reached his retirement age on Saturday 11 November. When the

Archbishop received this letter, he convened a special meeting of the Standing Committee of the Provincial Synod on Saturday 11 November in the hope that the committee would discuss the matter of his retirement and consider extending his tenure in office. The letter convening the meeting did not give adequate notice and the meeting was boycotted by the three bishops who were eventually blamed by the media. The meeting was nevertheless held at Imani House, Nairobi, and it had the requisite quorum. Since the meeting was to discuss the retirement of the Archbishop, the Dean of the Province, Bishop Peter Mwang'ombe, took the chair and the agenda was discussed in the absence of the Archbishop. I did not attend the meeting but I was informed that the members present felt that to take a decision to extend the tenure of the Archbishop when bishops from three out of seven dioceses were not present would be unwise. Hence the Standing Committee resolved that the Archbishop should retire at midnight on Saturday 11 November 1979 on reaching the retirement age of 65 years.

This decision was conveyed to the Archbishop, who was deeply affected. But it should be noted that had the Archbishop allowed discussion of his retirement to take place earlier in the year, then there would not have been any last-minute crisis. The bishops who did not attend the special meeting of the Standing Committee were blamed for what had happened. But the meeting, which had a quorum, could have legally extended the tenure of the office of the Archbishop even if it was for a period of six months. Those who did not attend the meeting therefore should not be blamed for the unceremonious retirement of the first Archbishop. The Archbishop was however so much affected that he declined the invitation to participate in the consecration of his successor, Manasses Kuria, in August 1980. The House of Bishops sent me as an emissary to visit the retired Archbishop at his Maseno Home and try to convince him to change his mind. I travelled together with my entire family and arrived at the official residence of Bishop James Mundia in Kakamega late at night. The following day Mundia took us to see the Archbishop, who received me and my family well. He however remained adamant and declined to participate in the enthronement ceremony.

About four years after the enthronement of the Most Revd Manasses Kuria as the second Archbishop, the House of Bishops decided to visit his predecessor and his wife at his Maseno home. After holding a meeting of the House of Bishops at St Philip's Maseno, we were led to his home by Archbishop Kuria. We were also joined by representatives of the House of Clergy and the House of Laity. The Bishops presents were James Mundia,

Henry Okullu, Laadan Kamau, Daniel Omollo and me. A cheque was presented to the Archbishop from the Province. He hosted us at a very elaborate luncheon and after we had eaten, the retired Archbishop said, "I deeply appreciate the visit and assure all of you of my deep love for the Anglican church and my willingness to continue being of service to the church during the days of my retirement."

After those words there was much rejoicing and the retired Archbishop said the closing prayers and pronounced the benediction.

Election of the Second Archbishop

The Rt Revd Manasses Kuria was elected Archbishop of the Anglican Church of Kenya unopposed in June 1980, and the service of his enthronement was held at All Saints Cathedral, Nairobi, in August the same year. The occasion was graced by the second President of Kenya, Daniel arap Moi. All the Bishops were present except Bishop Henry Okullu, who was on official duty overseas. From the moment Archbishop Kuria was enthroned, the media in Kenya repeatedly gave the impression that the then Attorney General, Charles Njonjo, manipulated the election process, leading to the defeat of Okullu. A missionary from Australia who was a tutor at St Philip's Maseno Bible School and a great admirer of the bishop had confidentially written a 19-page thesis to prove that Okullu was the right person to have been elected the second Archbishop, if it were not for the interference of the Attorney General. The writer argued that there was a long struggle for leadership in Kenya between Luos and Kikuyus. In the past this struggle was between Oginga Odinga and Jomo Kenyatta. But after the passing away of Jomo Kenyatta in 1978, the same struggle continued. This time however, the struggle of the two tribes was manifested through Bishop Okullu and the then Attorney General Charles Njonjo. The writer was of the opinion that Henry Okullu could take leadership of the Luos by either being the Archbishop of the Anglican Church or as the Vice-President of Kenya. The writer went as far as to suggest that the Luo community wanted to revive the initial partnership of Luos and Kikuyus in the leadership of Kenya. Paul Mbuya, the chairman of the Luo Union, had gone to see then President Jomo Kenyatta, so that the political partnership of the two communities could be revived. He persuaded the President to appoint a Luo to replace Daniel arap Moi as the Vice-President. Asked to suggest a Luo who could be appointed as Vice-President, Paul Mbuya proposed Bishop Okullu. This plan could not work, according to the writer, as the Attorney General was allegedly planning to have the Bishop assassinated so that he could not take political or religious leadership. This confidential document had been sent to all primates of the Anglican Church in the world for prayers for the bishop, who was allegedly in danger of being eliminated.

Soon this confidential document fell into the hands of the Attorney General, who asked the House of Bishops to address the issues raised in the document and take appropriate action. The House of Bishops met under the chairmanship of Archbishop Kuria and Bishop Okullu appeared before the meeting. He convinced the bishops that he was not aware of the alleged document and had not even read it. My proposal that a letter should be sent to all primates to correct the impression was rejected and it was agreed that the matter should not be pursued any further. I was deeply impressed by Bishop Okullu who, though rather disturbed, remained very calm when this document was being discussed and he remained very willing to accept the wisdom of the House of Bishops concerning the matter.

To shed some light on the events surrounding the election, the 1979 constitution of the ACK stated that "any three members of the Standing Committee of the Provincial Synod together may nominate any Bishop or Priest of any Diocese of the Anglican Communion in good standing as a candidate for election to the vacant Archbishopric". Each diocese was represented in the Standing Committee of the provincial synod by the diocesan bishop, a priest and a layman. Since a person could not nominate himself as a candidate, one more nomination was required from one other member of the standing committee from another diocese for one to be properly nominated as a candidate. Bishop Okullu was able to get two individuals from his diocese to nominate him but he was not able to get the required third person from another diocese to sign his forms. He was therefore not a candidate for the election. The Attorney General therefore did not stop Bishop Okullu from being elected to be the second Archbishop because Okullu was unable to get three members of the executive committee of the Provincial Synod to nominate him.

But the Attorney General occupied a powerful position and he did interfere with the election, albeit in a different manner. The bishop of Mombasa, the Rt Revd Crispus Nzano, had been legally nominated by three members of the Standing Committee and so had the bishop of Nakuru, Manasses Kuria. Just before the date of the election, the Attorney General telephoned Bishop Nzano and prevailed upon him to withdraw his candidacy, to which the Bishop obliged. So when we met at the All Saints Cathedral, Nairobi, in June 1980, the Chancellor, James Hamilton, informed us that two candidates were legally nominated but Bishop Nzano had withdrawn. He therefore declared Manasses Kuria elected unopposed as the second Archbishop of the ACK. I stood up to request that Bishop Nzano tell the Electoral College the reasons for his withdrawal. Bishop Nzano however declined to give any reason. Years later, Bishop Nzano informed me that it was a telephone call from the then Attorney General that made him withdraw his candidature.

In his autobiography, entitled *Quest for Justice* and published in 1977 by Shalom Publishers and Training Centre, Bishop Okullu devotes chapter 11 to discussing the Archbishop's election in 1980 (see pp. 97-107). He says that his candidature was blocked by Kikuyu tribalism. To prove that he says, "On one occasion while we were staying at the CPK Guest House in Nairobi with Bishop David Gitari of Mt Kenya East, I opened the subject. Bishop Gitari is one of the better educated Kenyan Bishops, and I was hoping for a very objective conversation. Gitari surprised me by saying that since Olang' (from Western Kenya) had been the Archbishop, this time you from Western Kenya are to be prepared to work with an Archbishop from Central Province." Deeply hurt, the bishop continues, I asked Gitari if the deciding factor in the election of the new Archbishop must be geographically considered. When Gitari saw my manuscript, he denied that he had made such remarks" (see p. 103).

Now that I have an opportunity of writing my autobiography, I feel constrained to put the record straight. Bishop Okullu had asked me to meet him in Nairobi to discuss the forthcoming election of the Archbishop and I accepted his invitation. We met in his room at the ACK Guest House and he told me that since we were both university graduates he did not know why I was not supporting him. In response I told the bishop very frankly that Bishop James Mundia and the Luhyas could not support his candidature because of the ongoing boundary row at Maseno between the Dioceses of Maseno North and Maseno South. Then I told him that predominantly Kikuyu dioceses could also not support him as they believed he had a deep prejudice against Kikuyus. The reason for this is that when he was the editor of Target Newspaper, the paper was highly anti-Kikuyu. The Bishop was not expecting this reply from me. He confessed that he had not known Kikuyus very well, as he had spent most of his working days in Uganda. He told me that in Kampala, he had befriended only one Kikuy,u who was a librarian at Makerere University. He was also quick to tell me that when the Kikuyus killed Tom Mboya, he was incensed by them but when they also killed J. M. Kariuki, a fellow Kikuyu, he changed his attitude.

I also reminded him of an incident in 1970 when I had just returned from Rhodesia and wanted to see him as an editor to discuss the situation in the country. When I entered his office, he did not even greet me but told me, "I give you one minute." I just left his office deeply shocked and went to Nation House, where I delivered newspaper cuttings carrying reports of the then president of Rhodesia urging more Europeans to migrate to Rhodesia and have as many babies as possible to increase the white population there. The *Nation* published the story the following day. I never told Bishop Okullu that 1980 was the turn for a Kikuyu to be elected Archbishop. I have never been a tribalist in my service to the church and the nation. I remember in those days being invited to a luncheon by the Attorney General, Charles Njonjo, and a number of Anglicans from the Kikuyu community. Njonjo was very worried that Okullu might be elected the second Archbishop. During the luncheon, Njonjo accused me of being a friend to Okullu. My reply was that all my brother bishops including Okullu are my friends.

Bishop Okullu was able to recover from the missed opportunity to serve as the second Archbishop. He moved on to play his part as a member of House of Bishops responsibly and supported Archbishop Kuria to the best of his ability. I recall one occasion when a priest from Nyanza who was serving in the diocese of Nairobi started taking issue with the archbishop in public. Bishop Henry Okullu issued a press statement rebuking him for attacking the head of the Anglican Church. This press statement from the Bishop of his home diocese silenced the priest once and for all. As time went on, and we interacted many times, Bishop Okullu became a good friend of mine and many times he was the first person to nominate my name to undertake tasks in which he believed I was gifted. I always found his contribution in the House of Bishops very sensible and useful and many times he helped us in sorting out some of the problems and dilemmas we encountered. Outsiders who knew Okullu through the media might have concluded that he was an arrogant bishop. To the contrary, I found him a humble man of God with a zeal for the Gospel and a vision for a just society.

It is also likely that Bishop Okullu was ultimately reconciled to Charles Njonjo. When the bishop died in 1999, Njonjo attended nearly all the meetings for the preparation of the funeral and made the most generous financial contribution to meet funeral expenses. He was also present at the funeral service at the All Saints Cathedral, Nairobi, and at his burial place in Bondo.

As we continued serving together in the church as bishops, Henry, who at first might have thought that I was too evangelical or too heavenly-minded to be of any earthly use came to realise that we had a lot more in common and that our theological convictions were very similar. We both preached and practised a holistic gospel and we both courageously challenged those in authority against injustice. In his autobiography, he makes several favourable references to me. In early 1983, Henry was invited to London to appear before the interviewing panel for the vacant post of General Secretary of the Anglican Consultative Council. Before going for the interviews he sought the counsel of the House of Bishops. Archbishop Kuria informed him that he had strongly recommended his name to the primates. Henry then recalls my response: "I would not recommend that Bishop Okullu should go out of Kenya at this time when his services are most needed."

The interviewing committee appointed Sam Van Culin of ECUSA to succeed Bishop John Howe of Scotland. Bishop Okullu was informed of the reason why he was not given the job: "The committee discovered in you, a person totally committed to the service of his church and nation and his people, to take you from your diocese and from Kenya would mean an extremely painful separation." Bishop Okullu adds in his autobiography, "The opinion of Bishop Gitari that I should not leave Kenya at this time was confirmed" (see pp. 104-106). Bishop Okullu writes of his admiration of my courageous prophetic ministry, which led to my house being raided by thugs in 1989. He also appreciates the part I played in organising and chairing National Pastors Conferences in 1980 and 1986.

Chapter 8

The House of Bishops 1980–1994

When the Church of the Province of Kenya (now ACK) was created in 1970, there were only six dioceses: Mombasa, Nairobi, Nakuru, Mt Kenya, Maseno North and Maseno South. During the first decade, only one new diocese was added to the original six, the diocese of Mt Kenya East. During the next decade (1980 to 1990), five more sees were created. These were Eldoret (1983), Mt Kenya Central (1984), Machakos (1985), Nambale (1987), and Embu (1990). The new bishops consecrated and enthroned during these ten years were Alexander Kipsang Muge, George Njuguna, Benjamin Nzimbi, Isaack Namango and Moses Njue. When Manasses Kuria became Archbishop and moved to Nairobi, Laadan Kamau succeeded him as Bishop of Nakuru. Laadan retired on 31 December 1989 and was succeeded by Stephen Njihia.

The other persons who had joined the House of Bishops during the second decade were the the Rt Revd Daniel Jonathan Omollo, Assistant Bishop of Maseno South, who was consecrated in January 1982, the Rt Revd Robert Beak, Assistant Bishop of Mt Kenya East, consecrated at St Andrew's, Kabare, in July 1984, the Rt Revd Isaak Namango, Assistant Bishop of Maseno North, consecrated in 1984, and the Rt Revd Haggai Nyang', the assistant Bishop of Maseno South, who was consecrated in January 1990. Omollo, Namango and Nyang' were later to become Bishops of the new Dioceses of Maseno West, Nambale and Southern Nyanza. The number of the members of the House had increased from six in 1970 to twelve in 1990, a 100% increment.

The Right Revd Peter Mwang'ombe: Bishop of Mombasa

The first major problem that the second Archbishop confronted concerned some serious allegations made against the bishop of Mombasa, the Rt Revd Peter Mwang'ombe, by a Church Army sister working in the diocese. In August 1980, there was an East African Revival Brethrens Convention held in Wundanyi, Taita and attended by thousands of people from all over the country. During the convention, the lady publicly confessed to having committed a sin with the bishop ten years earlier (1970), which led to her pregnancy and birth of a son. Bishop Sospeter Magua advised the Archbishop in my presence at ACK Guest House, Mombasa to write to Bishop Mwang'ombe and advise him to resign with immediate effect. When Bishop Mwang'ombe received the letter, he refused to resign and continued with his Episcopal duties in the diocese. He consulted his lawyers, who filed a case in the civil courts against the Province, the Diocese of Mombasa and the Archbishop. Attempts to persuade the bishop to withdraw the civil case were futile. The court proceedings continued in camera and a ruling was delivered in October 1980 in which the bishop lost the case. He was invited to attend the meeting of the House of Bishops on 11 November 1980. Bishop Mwang'ombe attended the meeting briefly but refused to discuss the allegations made against him, as he had already lodged an appeal in a higher court and he needed the advice of his lawyers before he could discuss the matter with the bishops.

The Archbishop informed the forum that he would rather that the matter was settled in accordance with church procedures for disciplining a bishop rather than have the dispute settled via civil court. He further said that the matter could also be settled pastorally rather than legally. In response Bishop Mwang'ombe stood up, shook hands with the Archbishop and the six bishops present and then left to go and look for his lawyers. After he left, the House decided to appoint a Commission of Enquiry made up of two bishops to probe the allegation that the bishop had behaved in a manner unbecoming of a bishop. The two bishops visited Mombasa and interviewed the person who had made the allegations. She said that she went public because the sin that she had committed ten years earlier had troubled her so much and for too long that she decided to accept Jesus Christ as her saviour and confess the sin publicly. Bishop Mwang'ombe also appeared before the probe team but refused to discuss the matter. He submitted a letter to the secretary of the House in which he stated, "What I want is the case against me to be heard in the Court of Appeal during which the person who has made the allegations and any other witness will give evidence and be cross examined by my lawyers."

The House of Bishops having received the report of the Commission concluded that there was enough evidence that the subject had behaved in a manner unbecoming of a bishop and had been given sufficient opportunity to defend himself but had refused to co-operate.

The House advised the Archbishop to demand the immediate resignation of Bishop Mwang'ombe and that he vacate the diocesan house with effect from 1 December 1980. Bishop Mwang'ombe refused to either resign or vacate the diocesan house. The case against the church was heard by the Court of Appeal in March 1981 but was adjourned until August 1981. Bishop Mwang'ombe did not vacate the diocesan house until July 1981 and the appeal case was not even heard in August as was expected. In July he wrote a rather vague letter of resignation. After vacating the diocesan house he moved to his home near Kanamai. Meanwhile the Rt Revd Crispus Nzano, the Assistant Bishop, was enthroned as Bishop of Mombasa on 22 March 1981.

This rather unfortunate event cannot be concluded without reporting that some years after the retirement of Bishop Mwang'ombe, the House of Bishops and the Provincial Synod decided to send a team composed of bishops, clergy and laity to pay a pastoral visit to the bishop and his wife. At this time they had moved to their home in Voi. The team led by His Grace Archbishop Manasses Kuria left Nairobi early in the morning, was joined by Thomas Malinda at Athi River and got to Voi in the early afternoon. We were met by Bishop Crispus Nzano about a kilometre away from the home of Bishop Mwang'ombe. When we arrived, we found a good number of family members and women who had come to join the bishop and his wife Mariamu in welcoming us. When we entered the bishop's house, he knelt down and wept with joy and then he embraced and shook hands with us. We were served with a delicious meal. We then sang songs of praise and had a good fellowship with the bishop, his wife and all present. We then gave him a cash gift of contributions from all the dioceses. Bishop Mwang'ombe and his wife received the gift warmly. After the prayers for the bishop and his family, we left for Nairobi. We were left with no doubt that Mwang'ombe loved the church that he had served for fourteen years as a diocesan bishop and as the Dean of the Province. We were deeply moved by the tears he shed.

These events raise questions on the issue of public confession, which the East African Revival has insisted on ever since its beginning in the early 1930s. John Stott, the renowned evangelical theologian and preacher, wrote a book entitled *Confess Your Sins: The Way of Reconciliation*. Stott recommends that if one has committed a sin against God, he/she should repent of the sin before God only. If one has sinned against a neighbour, for instance the wife or the husband, then he or she should go to the person whom he or she has sinned against and humbly repent of the sins. However if a sin becomes a scandal to the whole church, then the sinner should publicly confess his or her sins to the church. There are some sins which if confessed publicly can cause more problems than blessings to the church. When I was the Bishop of Mt Kenya East, I had to visit a congregation where public confession of sin by one of the elders had caused a huge crisis among the young people in the church. The elder had named the young girl he had committed the sin with and this came as a great shock to the youth in the church. The elder insisted that this public confession of the sin brought great peace to his troubled heart. On their part, the young people felt greatly offended that the church elder that they had trusted so much could commit such a sin with a fellow young member of their group. The person named became so troubled that she deserted the church. The lady who confessed her sins in the Wundanyi Revival Convention should have been advised on how best to handle the situation. This is probably why some churches prefer auricular confession or confessing before a priest rather than going public.

Another issue that arises is whether it was right or not for Bishop Mwang'ombe to go to court and sue the Province and the diocese over the allegations made against him. Most unfortunately, a precedent had already been set in the Anglican Church of Kenya when a priest in the Diocese of Nairobi filed a suit in a civil court against Archbishop Festo Olang' over his having been transferred from one parish to another. With the intervention of the then Attorney General, the court ruled in favour of the priest to the great embarrassment of the whole Church. Since that time a good number of Anglican priests have preferred to go to civil court against their superiors. It is my considered opinion that those who feel that they have been offended should in the first instance follow church procedures in seeking justice. Civil suits should be filed in court only when all avenues of appeal in the constitution of the church are exhausted. Our Lord Jesus Christ told his disciples:

> "If your brother sins against you, go and tell him his fault, between you and him alone. If he listens to you, you have gained your brother. But if he does not listen, take one or two others along with you, that every charge may be established by the evidence of two or three witnesses. If he refuses to listen to them, tell it to the whole church and if he refuses to listen to the whole church, let him be to you as a gentile and a tax collector" (Matthew 18:15-17; see also Corinthians 6:1-8).

Conflict Resolution in the Diocese of Mt Kenya South

Bishop Sospeter Magua and his wife Peninah died in a tragic road accident at Kabati near Thika on 25 September 1982. Nelson and Diana Kivuti came to my house in Embu at about lunchtime that fateful Saturday afternoon. Kivuti was in tears when he asked me whether I had heard the news.

"What news?" I asked him.

"Bishop Sospeter Magua is dead!"

I got into my car and drove to the scene of the accident about 80 kilometres away, where I found Heshbon Mwangi and the bishop's daughter-in-law. The body of the late bishop was still trapped in the car. The wife of the bishop died on arrival at the Thika District Hospital. The police did not get to the scene until about 5pm. By this time the Ven. John Kago and his wife had arrived from Karatina and were shocked to see the body of the bishop. During the 7.00pm KBC news bulletin, the President Daniel arap Moi informed Kenyans about the death of the bishop and his wife.

The death of Bishop Magua caused a crisis in the diocese of Mt Kenya South. The process to elect a new bishop was set in motion but five members of the Electoral College from Murang'a district refused to participate in the election. At that time, the diocesan Electoral College was composed of six priests and six laymen who were also the elected members of the diocesan Standing Committee. The Christians of Murang'a had figured that if the election of the bishop was held, then a candidate from Kiambu would succeed the late Magua, who also hailed from Kiambu, because seven out of the twelve electors were from Kiambu. Greatly concerned about this crisis, I collected five nomination forms from the Provincial Chancellor and took them to Murang'a, where I met the five members of the Electoral College and tried to convince them to nominate their preferred candidate, but they would not budge. The Revd Heshbon Mwangi, the undisputed leader of the Revival Movement in central Kenya, was the rallying point of the people of Murang'a in their refusal to participate in the election unless the diocese was split into two.

The Archbishop had set the timeline for the election of the successor of Bishop Magua in accordance with the Provincial constitution. The nomination papers were sent to the diocesan Electoral College and the closing date for the nomination was 15 March 1983. The election was scheduled for 15 April 1983. Thirty-nine congregants from Murang'a sent a memorandum to the Archbishop, which was copied to all the bishops, demanding that the diocese be divided before the elections. Copies of the memorandum were also sent to the media. I went to see Archbishop Manasses Kuria concerning this crisis and I offered to address the members of the synod from Murang'a to find out why they were unwilling to have their delegates participate in the elections. The Archbishop consented to my proposal and I went to St James and All Martyrs Cathedral to address the Christians of Murang'a. I was accompanied by John Kibuchi, the Chancellor of the diocese of Mt Kenya East. The Cathedral was filled to capacity not only by members of the synod, but also by representatives of every parish in Murang'a and Nyeri. My attempt to persuade the congregation to allow their members of the Electoral College to participate in the election of a new bishop fell on deaf ears.

Instead, and very much against my will, they unanimously passed a resolution that I should act as the bishop of the Mt Kenya South Diocese, until the crisis was resolved. Kibuchi returned to Nairobi and reported what had transpired. When the Archbishop heard that the meeting resolved that I should act as their bishop, he ordered me to keep away from Mt Kenya South and have nothing to do with the diocese. The Archbishop thought that I had gone to Murang'a to undermine his authority. Yet I had gone there only to assist him to solve the problem and as a result of the events, he gravely misunderstood my zeal to intervene on his behalf. A special meeting of the provincial synod was convened on 18 November 1983 to discuss this issue. The motion to divide the diocese was moved by Kibuchi and was seconded by the Provincial Chancellor, Paul Kihara Kariuki. The meeting unanimously resolved that the diocese be divided into two. The two new sees would be called Mt Kenya South and Mt Kenya Central. Meanwhile a member of the Provincial Synod from Kiambu issued a press statement that was published in the *Daily Nation*, claiming that I wanted the diocese of Mt Kenya South to be divided so that I could gain more votes for the next election of an Archbishop. The bishops stood in solidarity with me in denouncing the statement as baseless.

The constitutional crisis emanated from the demand by the people of Kiambu that the constitutional article on the election of a Bishop be followed to the letter, whereas those from Murang'a were demanding that the diocese be divided first before the election was held. The house of the Bishops held an emergency meeting at St Philip's Bible School, Maseno, on 6 May 1983 before going to pay the courtesy call on retired Archbishop Festo Olang' that I described earlier. Bishop Henry Okullu told the meeting that "we have confused the public by giving the impression that those who want the diocese to be divided are making unconstitutional demands and that those who want the bishop to be elected first are the ones who are following the constitution". There is nothing in the constitution that could have stopped the Archbishop from calling the Synod to discuss the sub-division of the Diocese soon after the death of Bishop Magua. Bishop Laadan Kamau said:

> …the most frightening thing is to have a few people who happen to have votes electing a bishop they want, while thousands of people might not agree with such a choice. A person elected should be such that the whole Christian Community is virtually in agreement with electors. To do otherwise is a disservice not only to the person elected, who might not get the support he ought to get, but also to the diocese and the whole church. This is a situation which must be avoided so that it does not appear as if we are imposing a bishop on reluctant section of the diocese. If subdivision of the diocese will bring peace to the troubled diocese, then we better go ahead, call the Synod and subdivide the diocese.

The House of Bishops unanimously passed a resolution that "the Archbishop, as the bishop of the diocese of Mt Kenya South is strongly advised to convene a special session of the diocesan Synod to decide on the creation of two dioceses from the existing diocese". The special Synod was held at St James and All Martyrs Cathedral, Murang'a, on 24 June 1983 and unanimously resolved that the diocese be divided into two. The two new dioceses were called Mt Kenya South and Mt Kenya Central. Subsequently a special Provincial Synod was convened on 18 November 1983 to discuss the issues. The provincial chancellor, Paul Kariuki, eloquently defended the motion to divide the Diocese. The motion was passed unanimously. This constitutional crisis reminds us of the words of St Paul that "the law kills but the Spirit gives life". (2 Corinthians 3:6), and Jesus said, "The Sabbath was made for man not man for Sabbath" (Mark 2:27). A constitution offers useful guidance to any institution or country. However, there are times when we can become slaves to the written law. As there is no constitution that is perfect, it is important to review constitutions from time to time especially when they become a problem instead of a blessing.

For instance, when Archbishop Manasses Kuria retired in September 1994, we were unable to elect a successor for two years. The constitution stated that the election of an archbishop could not take place until all the vacant sees were filled first. At that time we had problems in electing bishops for the dioceses of Kajiado and Maseno North. The problem was resolved in 1996 when I was the Dean of the Province (see chapter 10). The diocese of Mt Kenya South was divided on 1 January 1984, and the process of election of bishops of the two dioceses commenced. Bishop John Mahiani was the only candidate nominated for the new see of Mt Kenya Central. He was consecrated on 18 March 1984 at St James and All Martyrs Cathedral, Murang'a.

Election and Consecration of the Bishop of the New Diocese of Mt Kenya South

No sooner had the crisis surrounding the division of Mt Kenya South Diocese been resolved than another challenge emerged, this time concerning election of the bishop of the residual diocese of Mt Kenya South. The Ven. Dedan Kamau and The Ven. John Kago were nominated as candidates for the bishopric of the new see. A letter signed by 200 Christians of Mt Kenya South was sent to the Archbishop and all bishops alleging that Dedan Kamau was not a priest of good standing. A special meeting of the House of Bishops was convened at Nambale during the occasion of the consecration of the Assistant Bishop of Maseno North on 5 January 1984. A special commission of five people was appointed to look into this matter and subsequently the two candidates were requested to withdraw their names and not to accept their nominations in the election that was to follow.

It was resolved that the Provincial Election Panel would take over the role of nominating candidates from the diocesan Electoral College. Subsequently the Provincial Panel nominated the Revd George Njuguna, a tutor at St

Paul's United Theological College, Limuru. Then the Archbishop added the name of the Revd Samuel Muturi, the Principal of McGregor Bible School, Weithaga. The name was rejected by the Provincial Panel by more than 50% of its members. However the Archbishop insisted that he had power to add a name to the list of candidates. At this juncture, Bishop Alexander Muge sued the Archbishop in a court of law. The case received wide publicity in both print and the electronic media. The court ruled that the Provincial constitution did not give the Archbishop the powers that he claimed to have. The Electoral College of Mt Kenya South subsequently elected the Revd George Njuguna as the Bishop of Mt Kenya South. He was consecrated and enthroned at St Andrews Pro-Cathedral, Kiambu on Sunday 16 September 1984. He was succeeded by the Rt Revd Peter Njenga in June 1996.

Chapter 9

Bishop Alexander Kipsang' Muge

The diocese of Nakuru was divided on 1 January 1983 thus creating the new Diocese of Eldoret. Alexander Kipsang' Muge, an ex-policeman who fought during the *shifta* war in North Eastern Province in 1964-65, was elected the first Bishop of Eldoret. He was consecrated and enthroned on 11 June 1983 at the age of 35 years. In 1970 he had accepted Jesus Christ as his personal saviour and was baptised by the Revd John Kago on 5 October 1970. He resigned from his job as an elite General Service Unit (GSU) policeman in 1973 and joined St Philip's Bible College, Maseno, to study theology and to prepare himself for the ministry of the church. He was ordained a deacon by Archbishop Festo Olang' in 1976 and became a curate of St Stephen's Church, Jogoo Road. He also served as a curate of St Mark's Church, Westlands. He very much wanted to go to Britain to advance his studies in theology but the Diocese of Nairobi was not willing to sponsor him or even to allow him to raise funds for his studies. He resigned and joined the Diocese of Mt Kenya South and organized successful fundraising ceremonies that realized sufficient funds to enable him to study at London Bible College from 1979 to 1982. On his return he became the assistant Provost of All Saints Cathedral, Nairobi, and a year later he was elected and enthroned as the first Bishop of the Diocese of Eldoret.

Within a short time, Bishop Muge became one of the most outspoken bishops in the Anglican Church of Kenya. Both he and Bishop Henry

Okullu were often quoted in the media. They both knew the secret of having their Sunday sermons covered by the media. They would ensure that their written Sunday sermons were delivered to the various newsrooms by Friday with the rider that they were embargoed until after they had preached the sermons on Sunday. The press did not discover me until June 1986 when the influential *Weekly Review* put my portrait on the front cover of the magazine. By that time the portraits of Muge and Okullu had appeared many times on front cover of the *Weekly Review.*

Bishop Alexander Muge was seen by Kenyans as a very courageous bishop as he fearlessly took the administration of the then President Daniel arap Moi to task over various injustices and lack of proper governance. He was from the Kalenjin community, just like Moi, and this show of independence greatly impressed Kenyans. But it should be noted that Bishop Muge did not also hesitate to criticise the leadership of his own church. As stated earlier in this book (chapter 8), within a year of his becoming Bishop, he challenged Archbishop Manasses Kuria for assuming powers that the church constitution did not give him. Besides Muge, a number of other bishops were also dissatisfied with the leadership of the Archbishop.

One of the complaints was that Archbishop Kuria was offering clergy from other dioceses employment in the Diocese of Nairobi without in any way consulting bishops of the affected dioceses. Then there was his ordaining of candidates indiscriminately without adequate theological education, making unilateral decisions affecting various boards and committees without any reference to those boards and committees, and making a clergyman of doubtful character a canon of All Saints Cathedral, Nairobi. The said clergyman had, during a visit to California, USA, claimed that he was the bishop-elect of the new diocese of Mt Kenya South even before the elections were held. He had even been presented with an Episcopal staff while in America. Though aware of these facts, the Archbishop went ahead to try to make him a canon of the Cathedral. The House of Bishops protested and he was never installed as a canon. Bishop Henry Okullu and I were requested to draft a statement on how to improve the working relationship with the Archbishop. The Archbishop very graciously apologised to the House of Bishops and accepted the Memorandum of Understanding dated 18 June 1984.

On 11 March 1984, Bishop Muge informed the House of Bishops that a rumour was being spread in Eldoret that he was involved in a plot to assassinate Stanley Metto, then MP for the Mosop constituency. The bishop indicated that he had already reported the matter to the police. The bishops were unanimous in assuring Bishop Muge that they would stand in solidarity with him but did not wish to issue a press statement as this would only help to drive the rumour mills. The Archbishop however visited the Commissioner of Police and discussed the allegation. The now defunct but once dreaded Special Branch unit investigated the matter and concluded that the story was a fabrication by Metto.

There was a separate incident on 10 June 1989 when Bishop Muge wrote a letter to the Archbishop and sent copies to all bishops to say that he would not attend a meeting of the House of Bishops to be held on 19 June 1989. He boycotted the meeting to protest against Bishop Daniel Jonathan Omollo who had employed Lukas Wadenya as Director of Community Services in his diocese without the consent of the Diocese of Eldoret. At that time Lukas was one of the most qualified and able persons for that position in the Province and was highly respected by our overseas partners. During the meeting of 19 June 1989, the House of Bishops passed the following resolution:

> This House of Bishops deplores the behaviour of Bishop Muge boycotting the meeting of the House for no good reason and for making an allegation concerning the employment of Lucas Wadenya by the Diocese of Maseno West without checking the facts (Min 13/89).

Bishop Muge also boycotted another meeting in January 1990 and the House expressed concern about his absence and requested Bishop Henry Okullu, Crispus Nzano, John Mahiaini and George Njuguna to have fellowship with Muge over the matter (see Min of 22 Jan 1990). Muge however went ahead to attend the Standing Committee of the Provincial Synod in June 1989 and also in January 1990. The main concern at this time was a fresh crisis that had arisen following the division of the Diocese of Nambale. The Diocese of Maseno North was subdivided on 1 January 1987, creating the Diocese of Nambale, but the election of a bishop to serve the diocese was delayed as the Christians of Katakwa archdeaconry started demanding to have a diocese of their own. They also refused to co-operate in the election of the bishop of the new diocese. Most of the people in Katakwa were Teso and the others who proposed the new diocese were Luhyas. The Teso people felt that if the election went ahead, another Luhya would be elected as their bishop and they were opposed to this because they wanted one of their own to be the Bishop of Katakwa. Isaac Namango was subsequently elected the Bishop of Nambale and was consecrated and enthroned on 30 August 1987.

The Christians of Katakwa refused to be part of Nambale diocese and on 25 November 1987, 40 people from Katakwa stormed into Chapter House at the All Saints Cathedral, Nairobi, where the House of Bishops was meeting and demanded to be allowed to have their own diocese. They had a fall-back position that if this was not possible, they would ask to be attached to the diocese of Eldoret.

The Provincial Standing Committee of the Synod meeting on 27 November 1987 referred the matter to the synod of Nambale for action. The Synod of Nambale met in April 1988, and rejected the request of the Katakwa archdeaconry, as no formal request had been made by the archdeaconry to split the diocese. The Diocesan Synod also advised Bishop Namango to withdraw the licenses of all clergy who were behind the split in the diocese. During the meeting of the Provincial Standing Committee of the Synod held on 23 June 1989, a commission was appointed under the chairmanship of Bishop Benjamin Nzimbi to look into the problem of the troubled Diocese. The other members of the commission were Bishop Jonathan Omollo, the Ven. Elijah Ramtu, the Very Revd Peter Njenga, Charlotte Kea and Symon Kariuki. On hearing about the appointment of this commission, the majority of the people of Katakwa rejected the commission. More than 50 people from Katakwa camped outside Bishopsbourne, the official residence of the Archbishop next to State House in Nairobi and the Archbishop refused to address them. The Archbishop called for a special meeting of the Provincial Standing Committee of the Synod to discuss the Katakwa issue, which had now attracted the attention of the media, especially the *Daily Nation*, whose chairman at the time was a prominent Anglican layman from Katakwa. In one banner headline in the *Nation*, I was accused by the "sons of Katakwa" for "not advising the Archbishop to agree to divide the diocese".

The Standing Committee met in this delicate environment and decided to appoint a new commission under the chairmanship of Bishop George Njuguna of Mt Kenya South. The other members of the commission were Bishop Crispus Nzano, Provost Gideon Ireri, the Ven. David Kariuki, Jacob Obara and Ambassador John Mbugua. Meanwhile another bus load of Christians from Nambale had come to show their opposition to the Christians of Katakwa who were camping at Bishopsbourne. The people of Katakwa, led by Moses Ote, accepted the resolution of the committee and a service of thanksgiving was held at the cathedral, attended by all parties concerned. There was repentance, forgiveness and rejoicing.

The Diocese of Katakwa virtually came into *de facto* existence on 28 June 1989 with the Archbishop holding an oversight role. The Njuguna Commission reported its findings to the Standing Committee of the Provincial Synod. On 26 January 1990, the commission recommended that the Standing Committee of Provincial Synod should accept the creation of the Diocese of Katakwa during its next meeting in June 1990. To ensure that the provincial constitution was followed, the Diocese of Nambale was requested to meet before June 1990 to endorse the division. The Diocese of Maseno South was requested to exercise Episcopal oversight over Katakwa as it had two bishops (Okullu and Omollo). Two senior Teso priests who held divergent views and led the opposing groups were removed from Katakwa. The Ven. Eliud Okiring and the Ven. Stephen Emuria were posted to other dioceses. The diocese of Katakwa became a *de jure* diocese on 1 January 1991, and Eliud Okiring was elected the first bishop of the diocese on 2 March 1991. He was consecrated and enthroned on 19 May 1991.

In June 1989, Bishop Muge wrote a letter to the House of Bishops to state that his diocese had allowed him to go on sabbatical leave from September 1989 to June 1990 and that retired Archbishop Harold Lee Nutter of the Diocese of Fredericton, Brunswick, Canada, would take care of the spiritual welfare of the diocese in his absence. Bishop Muge was not present to give reasons for these arrangements and the Archbishop and Dean of the Province were requested to raise the matter with him. Bishop Muge turned up at the meeting at of the House of Bishops at Chapter House looking very unsettled. He took his seat for less than five minutes then suddenly left for an unknown destination. For the remainder of 1989 and 1990, he looked most uncomfortable in the meetings of the NCCK. He would attend the meetings for only a few minutes, disappear for a while and then return for a few more minutes until delegates started getting very suspicious of him. But the people who knew Muge very well knew that he was very fond of making telephone calls, and one could guess that every time he left the meeting, he was going to call his friends and other contacts he had established.

Visit to Canada 1988

It will be appropriate at this point to give an account about my visit to Canada with Bishop Muge in November 1988. Muge had until this point been a very close friend of mine. He used to telephone me almost twice a week and would even wake me up at midnight to ask me why I was sleeping when Kenya was burning. I was invited to give a series of theological lectures at Wycliffe Theological College, Toronto, in Canada in November 1988. When I arrived at the airport, Bishop Muge was there to meet me, as he was already in Toronto. We spent the night in the same hotel, and on the following day he left for the Diocese of Fredericton in East Canada, which was a partner diocese of Eldoret. He was later scheduled to return to Toronto to attend meetings of the synod of the Anglican Church of Canada as an observer.

A day before I left Toronto for Ottawa, two young Kenyans who were working in Toronto visited me. One informed me that he was a grandson to one of the first Anglican priests in Murang'a, and that he had worked with the Kenya Air Force until the time of the attempted coup d'état against the administration of President Moi that took place on 1 August 1982. The student went on to tell me that when the coup failed, he went or fled into exile to Tanzania and eventually found his way to Canada. The second gentleman told me that he had worked as a caterer at the National Assembly but resigned and worked in one of the Hotels in Diani beach, on Kenya's south coast. He said that he soon discovered that the Special Branch personnel were on his trail and he also fled to Tanzania and eventually took refuge in Canada. I asked the two young men whether they belonged to *Mwakenya* (an underground organization of young political activists that had been proscribed by the government) but they said no. They however told me that they regularly received *Mwakenya* publications and that they favourably quoted sermons of Muge and myself. I told them that I was interested in reading the publications and they promised to deliver them to me that evening. They also expressed their strong desire to meet Bishop Muge, whose courage they admired greatly. I told them that he would be back in Toronto before the end of the month and they gave me their telephone contacts to give to Muge. The two young men delivered the *Mwakenya* publications, which I read and left at the hotel for them to pick up. I then left for Ottawa, where I met the Kenyan Ambassador to Canada and also the former editor-in-chief of the *Daily Nation*, George Gethii, who had also taken refuge in Canada and who was at this time a born-again Christian. He gave me a vivid testimony of his spiritual pilgrimage.

From Ottawa I telephoned Bishop Muge to inform him that there were two young men who were waiting to see him when he returned to Toronto. I later learnt that the Bishop met both young men three times and recorded all that they said in a small tape recorder that he had concealed in his pocket. They seem to have explicitly declared to him that they were indeed members of the *Mwakenya* movement and gave him names of *Mwakenya* followers in Europe and America. Accounts indicate that Muge informed State House about his contact with the group and that he was even given the go-ahead to hold a meeting in London with representatives of the proscribed group drawn from all over Europe. It turned out that Muge was given money by government operatives to organise that meeting and the person in charge of Special Branch at that time travelled to London to facilitate the meeting. Muge returned to Kenya in mid-December 1988 loaded with plenty of secrets and literature on *Mwakenya* and with the full knowledge of the government. Being caught with such material at this time in Kenya's history could lead to arrest, torture, detention without trial or at worst, death.

Bishop Henry Okullu confided in me how Bishop Muge tried to persuade him to accompany him to State House, Nairobi, to meet the President and brief him on his contacts with *Mwakenya*. One morning, the two bishops went to the house of Hezekiah Oyugi, the then powerful Head of the Civil Service who was to take them to see the President. Bishop Okullu told me that he was very surprised to see his colleague in possession of *Mwakenya* literature but Bishop Muge told him he had the necessary authorisation from the government. Bishop Okullu soon became very uncomfortable about the prospect of the meeting with the President, a meeting that eventually did not happen. Around Christmas 1988, the President said there were some bishops who were traveling overseas to meet with *Mwakenya* and who were not disclosing their mission to the government. I started getting concerned and one day I telephoned Muge to ask him what he had told the President about our visit to Canada. Muge told me not to worry.

At this time I was on the board of governors of Kagumo Teachers Training College. We met some time in March 1989, and agreed that all the members of the board should attend the graduation ceremony in April 1989, which was to be graced by the President. I got a telephone call from the Principal of the college, the Revd Michael Kagume, early on the day of the graduation. He told me that the Provincial Commissioner of Central Province had advised that I should not attend the ceremony as "the President does not want to see you".

I told the Principal that we had agreed that all members of the board should attend the graduation ceremony and welcome the President. I told the Principal that I was going to stand by the decision of the board rather than adhere to the wishes of the PC and the powers that be. However, when I saw the headlines in a publication of the KANU-owned *Kenya Times* newspaper, I changed my mind and decided not to attend the graduation ceremony. On the previous Sunday as I was preaching at St Thomas' Church, Kerugoya, two KANU Youth Wingers called Wakuthira and Kibaki tried to grab the microphone from me but were overpowered by the churchwardens and their attempts to heckle me were drowned by the singing of the congregation. (KANU had an organised youth wing countrywide that was sometimes used to effect its overt and covert political agenda.)

During the graduation ceremony, President Moi said, "If someone does not like the sermon of a preacher, he should not grab the microphone but should walk away. However Bishop Gitari must tell the nation what he had gone to do in Canada in November 1988 and whom he met while in Canada." This statement was given wide publicity by the media. I tried to telephone Bishop Muge in Eldoret to enquire from him once again what he had told the President that I had gone to do in Canada. I was informed that Bishop Muge was admitted to the Nairobi Hospital. I drove to the hospital early in the morning and found the bishop just after he had been discharged.

I showed Muge the newspaper report of what the president had said at Kagumo College about my visit to Canada, which also said that I must give names of all the Kenyans that I had met in Canada. Muge responded that I should not worry as he was going to call a press conference to answer President Moi's request to me to make a public statement on the matter. On the same day Muge called a press conference where he said, "Bishop Gitari should not be asked whom he met in Canada." In his statement, which was published by the daily newspapers, Bishop Muge said that he was the one who met *Mwakenya* in Canada and had informed the President about it. He exonerated me from any wrong. However his statement immediately started ripples in Christian leadership circles. The question that many were asking was whether Bishop Muge had gone to Canada on behalf of the government or of the church. An urgent meeting of NCCK was called at this time, as member churches were getting concerned about my own life, because politicians were launching salvos at me for not having disclosed that I had met members of *Mwakenya* in Canada. On the same day that NCCK was meeting to discuss the issue, Bishop Muge had requested the Dean of Province, Bishop James Mundia, to convene the meeting of the House of Bishops as the Archbishop was out of the country.

In the morning I delivered a letter to State House giving names of all the Kenyans that I had met in Canada in November 1988. At about 3.00am, I got a strange telephone call from a person from the Telephone Exchange Headquarters in Nairobi who, speaking in Kikuyu, informed me that he had intercepted a telephone call between Bishop Muge and the then Head of Civil Service, Hezekiah Oyugi. This is what the caller said: "I heard Mr Oyugi telling Muge to ensure that Bishop Gitari apologises to the President for having met *Mwakenya* in Canada and for not having declared that he had such a meeting."

The House of Bishops met at Chapter House in the afternoon and Muge was there to tell the bishops to persuade me to apologise to the president. Bishop Henry Okullu was very disturbed by Muge's request. He told the House that "this matter depends on where one was trained". He said that in the college where he went to study theology he was made to understand that "if a man came to his house early in the morning and confessed to the Bishop that he had killed his wife, the first thing is not to take a telephone and report the matter to the police but to give him counseling". He said that having been trained as a policeman the first thing that Muge would do was to "report the matter to the police". Bishop Okullu went on to say that "a Bishop has a duty to meet sinners and saints anywhere on earth and no one including the President should question a religious leader in his pastoral ministry". Bishop Okullu's intervention silenced Bishop Muge. I was however called out of the meeting to see a person who had been sent by Oyugi to see me. That person was none other than my friend Nelson Kivuti, a personal secretary to Oyugi. Kivuti came with a draft of a letter that I was supposed to issue to the press on the same day. The press statement indicated that I should say that "I love President Moi... my diocese and I pray for him regularly... I uphold the rule of law..." among other things.

I returned to the meeting of the House of Bishops with the draft letter but Bishop Okullu was against my issuing such a statement. I then received a telephone call from the Provincial Chancellor, Paul Kihara Kariuki, requesting that I meet him in the office of lawyer Paul Muite at 6.00pm later that day. When I met the two lawyers, they advised me not to issue any statement of apology, as I had committed no crime. I recall them telling me that my greatest advantage was that Kenyans respected me greatly for my courageous stand on issues of injustice in Kenya. "That overwhelming public support is your greatest protection," they told me. They went on to say that if I started showing signs of cowardice, then the general public would be greatly upset and would abandon me. But if I stood firm, even those in authority would hesitate to do any harm to me. I accepted the advice from the lawyers.

I later learnt that State House had telephoned all the daily newspapers to check whether they had received my written apology.

At that time I was preparing to go to San Antonio, Texas, to attend a meeting of the World Council of Churches. I went to the Central Bank of Kenya for tax clearance, as that was the requirement at that time. I met the deputy Governor of the Bank, who was once my geography teacher at Kangaru School, Embu. He told me that he could not clear me because I had become controversial, and he had to consult the ministry of Finance and the Office of the President before I could buy foreign currency. I had to wait for some hours but was eventually cleared. I travelled to America and was away for ten days. By the time I returned the matter had cooled down.

Much as I admired Bishop Muge for his courage, I must also add that he seemed to have been compromised after our visit to Canada. He had been 100% with the church in fighting for justice and truth. But soon after the trip he seemed to have shifted 100% to the side of State House. This made him very uncomfortable, as Christian leaders seemed to have lost some degree of confidence in him. His depression, which led him to be admitted to the Nairobi Hospital, could have arisen from a feeling that he had betrayed his brother bishop. But in August 1990, the bishop took a courageous step to become again the Muge we knew. The President had appointed a commission chaired by the Vice-President, George Saitoti, to gather information from all over Kenya on the "KANU WE WANT." The commission went to Eldoret on Friday 3 August 1990 and Muge presented a most scathing attack on Moi's government. The *Weekly Review* of 10th August 1990 wrote a full length article entitled "Muge reverts to type", which is hereby reproduced.

Muge Reverts to Type

Bishop Alexander Kipsang Muge of the Church of Province of Kenya's Diocese of Eldoret is once again on the warpath. After appearing to have made peace with his political critics and softened his critical stance, he returned with a bang on Friday last week with a hard-hitting memorandum to the Kanu Review Committee. His detractors, predictably, rose up in arms. As if that was what he expected, Muge took position for battle and by Tuesday this week, he was back in his element as one of the government's foremost critics and as a leading player in Nandi District Politics. For the best part of this year, Muge appeared to have softened considerably to the extent of winning praise from some of his foes in the political arena. Notable among them was the minister for energy, Nicholas Biwott, who praised Muge in parliament early last month for not jumping on the multi-party bandwagon.

Biwott's praise was justified in the sense that, unlike on many other issues over which Muge has been known to take a stand contrary to that of the government, he was steadfast in his support of the one-party system. In his memorandum to the committee he maintained the same stand, which was in sharp contrast to that of the entire CPK hierarchy, which, through Archbishop Manasses Kuria, had clearly been in favour of pluralism. Indeed, Muge had retreated to the background as his fellow clerics rose to the forefront in advocating change and this appeared to place him firmly in the one-party camp. Most of the views Muge presented to the committee were not new but an item touching on the presidency, wittingly or otherwise, set him against the very political personalities with whom he appeared to have made peace. Muge charged that there was a "clique of cabinet ministers" who had formed a ring around the President and were "by and large engaged in activities which are driving a wedge between the president and the people". Muge went on to state that the isolation campaign began during the campaign for the 1988 elections, when one senior minister for education and Kanu's national chairman, Peter Oloo Aringo, "raised a hue and cry that the election was to be a clear battle between Nyayo followers and anti-Nyayo forces". Aringo's utterances, according to Muge, divided Kenyans into two opposing camps.

The next day, the President, without mentioning Muge's name, accused the bishop of misjudging the general feelings of the public when it came to his relationship with the people. President Moi told a goodwill delegation from Nyanza Province that, contrary to what Muge claimed, it was a few rich people who were, in fact, out to drive a wedge between him and his faithful supporters. The president said, "I was surprised to hear a bishop say that I was being isolated from the people by a clique. He does not understand members of the public. If anybody understands Kenyan society, it is me and it was wrong for him to say that." Muge had, in his recommendations to the committee, explained how several African presidents had fallen as a result of misinformation and mis-advice from a clique of selfish leaders. He singled out the founder president of Ghana, the late Dr Kwame Nkurumah, and former Ugandan president Dr Milton Obote as some of the leaders who fell as a result of deliberate alienation from the general public. Nkurumah, Muge told the committee, was loved dearly by his people but he fell after he was "misinformed that a free and fair election was set to usher in his political opponents who could completely surround and weaken him". Nkurumah's response, said Muge, was to rig the elections in favour of his political clique and, in the process, he "betrayed the trust people had bestowed on him".

If Muge's analogy was disquieting to President Moi, a number of politicians found it unpalatable. After the president's rebuff, Muge issued a press release in which he expressed his displeasure that the President might have reacted after receiving complaints from the same clique of ministers bent on protecting their own positions. He directly attacked three cabinet ministers, among them Peter Oloo Aringo and the Minister of Co-operative Development, John Cheruiyot, with the latter being singled out because of a different battle of Nandi politics in which Muge has openly played a partisan role. In a press release, Muge returned to some of the issues raised in the memorandum and claimed that those attacking him were the same people who had used the privileged positions and their closeness to the President to frustrate the public. Muge then went on to allege that some corrupt senior government officials continued to enjoy privileges even after the press highlighted shoddy deals in which they were involved. He urged the President to set up an independent commission of inquiry to probe, "some cabinet ministers and civil servants". The inquiry, Muge suggested, should be composed of church leaders and lawyers. Members of the public, he said were eager to know who the cabinet minister was, for instance, who was involved in an irregular Ksh 81 million deal with the Kenya Planters' Co-operative Union (KPCU) and the allocation of a plot formerly owned by former vice-president Joseph Murumbi. Muge also cited grabbing of land in Uasin Gishu by a cabinet minister and a senior civil servant who, he claimed, kicked out poor people after using money borrowed from the government to purchase the land. "It is deplorable for cabinet ministers who claim to serve *wananchi* to use their positions to oppress the very people they claimed to serve," asserted Muge.

Scathing remarks have been Muge's trade mark over the years but last week's outburst was intriguing in that they came at a time when Muge was assumed to have reformed enough to win praise from Biwott, who told parliament last month that Muge was "misled into believing there was something genuine (in multi-party advocacy) until he discovered that he was being misled." Rare appreciation, indeed, from a man who has had no time for Muge in the past; it was probably the best description of Muge's changed image. Early last year, the two had a showdown when Biwott angered church leaders by stating that they had closed ranks with the government after realizing the futility of their militancy against the political establishment. "Who is Biwott, anyway?" questioned Muge in response to Biwott's remarks. He asserted that Biwott was a nobody in the republic of Kenya in his personal capacity. Muge was at the time firmly in the camp of outspoken clergymen, who included his counterparts in the CPK Dr. Henry Okullu of Maseno South and Dr David Gitari of Mt. Kenya East as well as the Revd Timothy Njoya of the Presbyterian Church of East Africa.

Muge's attack raised a hullabaloo among politicians, who felt that the attack was unfair. The strongest objection came from leaders in Nandi, Uasin Gishu and Biwott's home district, Elgeyo Marakwet. The Uasin Gishu Kanu Chairman, Jackson Kibor, went as far as telling Muge exactly who Biwott was. The MP for Kerio Central, Paul Chepkok, who saw Muge's onslaught on Biwott as an affront to the entire Elgeyo Marakwet leadership, went so far as to announce a demonstration in the district to condemn Muge. But the demonstration never took place. In Nandi, a nominated MP, Ezekiel Bargetuny, was the only politician who went for Muge, but his statement was cautiously worded, saying only that Biwott had merely expressed the desire to see good relations between the Church and the state.

Mysterious Death of Bishop Alexander Muge

Muge died in a tragic road accident eleven days after he appeared before the Saitoti Commission. Three days before his death, on 14 August 1990, Peter Okondo, then Minister for Labour, had issued a threat to both Bishop Okullu and Bishop Muge. He had warned that, should Okullu and Muge step in his Busia constituency, they would "see fire and may not come out alive". Muge responded by issuing a press statement defying Okondo's threats, telling the nation that he would be at St Stephen's Church, Busia, on Tuesday 14 August 1990. Muge and his team, in a convoy of several diocesan vehicles, arrived at Busia on time and received a warm welcome from hundreds of worshippers at the church. The team left Busia at 12.30pm, had lunch at Kakamega Golf Hotel, and travelled back via Webuye. Muge's car led the convoy and at Kipkerion, 30 kilometres from Eldoret, his car was hit by an oncoming lorry and Muge died instantly. The death of Muge shocked the nation and there were demands from all quarters that Peter Okondo resign his cabinet post. Okondo yielded to pressure and resigned. The Very Revd Peter Njenga organised a memorial service at All Saints Cathedral in Nairobi, which was attended by thousands of people, including a good number of cabinet ministers and politicians. Bishop Okullu preached a sermon in which he made reference to the story of a child who pointed out "the king was naked" though he was supposed to be wearing his new expensive robes.

Concerning my statement during the service, the *Weekly Review* reported, "Gitari, too, received wild applause with this sermon dwelling on numerous occasions that Muge had stood out in the fight for justice. Gitari recalled the murders of JM Kariuki and Robert Ouko, and pointed out that the government's inability to solve the cases left the public wondering whether some stones were too heavy to turn. 'There can be no peace if we do not discover the mastermind behind the plot to kill Bishop Muge'" (*Weekly Review*, 12 August 1990).

The body of Bishop Muge was interred at the compound of St Stephen's Cathedral in Eldoret after a service attended by about a million people at Eldoret Stadium. I also attended the ceremony but I was not given a chance to address the congregation despite demands by mourners. Soon after Muge's death, the then Attorney General, Justice Matthew Guy Muli, pledged to set up a public inquest to determine the circumstances leading to Bishop Muge's death. The commission, however, was never appointed, though the driver of the lorry was charged with careless driving and was imprisoned for seven years. The real course of Muge's death remains unresolved, just like those of J. M. Kariuki and Robert Ouko. Hence the culture of impunity has continued unabated.

It is my considered opinion that the greatest mistake that Muge made was to be inconsistent. From 1983 to November 1988, Muge, together with other courageous church leaders, challenged injustices in Kenya fearlessly. From December 1988 to July 1990 he rubbed shoulders with the powers that be and State House in particular. Then all of a sudden, in early August 1990, he reverted back to the Muge we knew, as the Kenya *Weekly Review* article stated. "Within a few days Muge was dead. His inconsistency was his undoing."

But Muge died a great hero, resulting from the fact that he returned to his fearless position of challenging injustices. His death was mourned throughout the country. Thousands of people attended his funeral service at All Saints Cathedral, Nairobi. The clergy in their hundreds carried his coffin from the Lee Funeral Home in a procession through Valley Road to the Cathedral. The funeral service at Eldoret Stadium was attended by an estimated one million people. When the history of the Church in Kenya is written, the late Bishop Muge will appear as one of the greatest Anglican bishops in modern times.

Chapter 10

The Dean of the Province

The Most Revd Manasses Kuria retired as Archbishop of the Anglican Church of Kenya on reaching the retirement age of 65 years in July 1994. I was elected unopposed to be the Dean of the Province to succeed Bishop Henry Okullu, who had also retired. In the absence of the Archbishop, I also served as the acting Archbishop until the election of the successor to Archbishop Kuria. Elections of the third Archbishop of the ACK could not be held owing to a constitutional problem. All the vacant sees were supposed to be filled before the election could proceed. The purpose of this tradition was to ensure that all dioceses (except Nairobi) were to be represented by their own bishop at the Electoral College, which was composed of all diocesan bishops as well as the elected members of the Provincial Standing Committee (one priest and one layperson from each diocese). When the Archbishop retired, the sees of Kajiado and Maseno North were vacant. The Revd Bernard Njoroge had been elected Bishop of the new diocese of Kajiado but was rejected by the majority of Christians from the Masaai community there. Simon Oketch had also been elected the Bishop of Maseno North but his opponent went to court to contend that at the time of his election, he had not as yet reached the mandatory age of 40 years. The two controversies went on for two years and with time became increasingly difficult to solve. Meanwhile leaders and congregations were becoming impatient about the church not having an Archbishop.

The constitution was finally amended so that even if there were vacant sees, the election of the Archbishop could proceed. The vacant sees would be represented by a senior priest appointed by the House of Bishops in consultation with the Standing Committee of the diocese whose Episcopal see was vacant. After the amendment of this clause, the election of the third Archbishop was held in November 1996. Five candidates were validly nominated: Benjamin Nzimbi, Joseph Wasonga, Stephen Kewasis, Horace Etemesi and myself. Horace withdrew his candidature on the day of election. The process of election began at about 10.00am and ended at 10.00pm. During the first balloting, there were 201 voters. I received 101 votes and the other three candidates together got 100 votes. But I could not be declared Archbishop-elect owing to the requirement that one had to have a two-thirds majority vote. In further balloting, Stephen Kewasis and Benjamin Nzimbi were eliminated and Wasonga and myself were left for subsequent balloting. It was not until ballots were cast for a sixth time that it was declared that I had acquired the requisite majority of 133 votes against 66 for Wasonga. On the day that I was elected Archbishop, I received a message from the Chaplain of the Kenyatta National Hospital that my sister Hannah Micere, the first born of our family, had passed away that morning. It was declared that I had the majority vote and Bishop Joseph Wasonga broke the news to the Electoral College and he led prayers for me, for my family and for the loss. My sister had been admitted in the hospital four months earlier following an accident in Nairobi. That day was a day of joy and sorrow for the family.

During the two years as the Dean of the Province I presided over the celebrations of the 150 years of the existence of the Anglican Church of Kenya. The first CMS Missionary, Dr Johannes Krapf, a German from Tubingen, had arrived at Mombasa in 1844 and started missionary work at the coast and within a short time he had learnt sufficient Swahili to enable him to write an English/Swahili Dictionary and to translate parts of the Bible into Swahili. He also travelled into the hinterland and while in Kitui, he became the first white man to see Mt Kenya. He gave the mountain the name, which became the name of our country, Kenya. The 150 years were celebrated with one group walking from Mombasa, retracing the footsteps of Dr Krapf, and the other walking from Mumias, where Bishop James Hannington was at first buried. The missionary was killed alongside his companions on 29 October 1885 as he was going to Uganda and the last words found in his journal stated, "Go tell your master that I have purchased the road to Uganda with my blood." The climax of the two walks was a gathering at All Saints

Cathedral, Nairobi, to celebrate the 150 years. The trek from Mumias was led by Bishop Stephen Kewasis of Eldoret and those who walked from Mombasa were led by Bishop Alfred Chipman of Mt Kenya West. The Mombasa and Nairobi walkers included young people from CMS England.

The 150 years were also marked by publication of a book entitled *Rabai to Mumias: a short history of CPK 1844-1994*, prepared by the Provincial Unit of Research. The book was compiled by a committee chaired by Samuel arap Ngeny, the lay secretary of the Provincial Synod and manager of Uzima Press, which published the book. The climax of celebrations was a visit by the Archbishop of Canterbury, the Most Revd and Rt Hon George Carey, from 9 to 15 December 1994. During his stay, the Archbishop also visited Kisumu and Mumias and also addressed clergy at All Saints Cathedral, Nairobi. On Jamhuri Day (Kenya's independence day), he was the only religious leader who said prayers at the celebration. Retired Archbishop Manasses Kuria and I accompanied the Archbishop of Canterbury to pay a courtesy call on President Moi at State House, Nairobi. The Archbishop of Canterbury raised a number of issues of justice and peace with the President.

When Archbishop Kuria handed over to me as the Dean of the Province and Acting Archbishop, he did not inform me of a problem that was about to erupt into the public domain concerning the bishop of Mt Kenya South. The Archbishop had left for the USA and had been away for several months. Some members of the Standing Committee of the diocese of Mt Kenya South had written a letter to the Archbishop accusing their bishop of conduct unbecoming his office. I very reluctantly had to chair several meetings of the House of Bishops to try my brother bishop. This was a very agonising time, as the press kept the story in the headlines. Bishop Horace Etemesi of the Diocese of Butere was of very great help to me. He offered to accompany me to the Synod of the Diocese of Mt Kenya South, where the Bishop and Synod came to an amicable agreement. Bishop George Njuguna agreed to resign and the diocese agreed to give him all his retirement benefits. After his retirement I took over as the Bishop of Mt Kenya South until the election and enthronement of Peter Njenga as his successor in June 1996.

The Diocese of Kajiado was also in turmoil and I had to visit Kajiado four times when I was the Dean of the Province to discuss with the Synod the crisis over the election of the Bishop. Though Bernard Njoroge had been legally elected by a small majority, it became virtually impossible to consecrate and enthrone him. At one time the Provincial Synod was held at St Mark's Westlands and three buses of Christians from the Maasai community arrived at the venue and almost caused chaos. Bernard arrived at about the same time, was chased away and had to take refuge at the vicarage. At about this time, I accepted an invitation to induct Simon Oriedo as the Vicar of St Faith Church, Ongata Rongai in the Diocese of Kajiado. Bernard Njoroge organized young people to stop me from performing the ceremony. When I entered the church leading a long precession of clergy from Kajiado, Kirinyaga and Nairobi, there was a scuffle in the church and one priest was hit with a chair and bled profusely. Bernard lay prostrate on the holy table and I watched in shock as he asked me to beat him up. The police came in time to restore peace. I inducted Revd Simon Oriedo as the new parish priest, preached and administered holy communion. Meanwhile Bernard was taken to Mater Hospital, where he told the dailies that I hit him with the Holy Staff, a claim that was totally false. This incident was reported to the Provincial Synod and the Synod decided to disqualify Njoroge from taking the office of bishop. Elections for the first Bishop of Kajiado started afresh and Jeremiah Taama was elected unopposed. He was consecrated and enthroned on 3 August 1997. Hence Bernard himself solved the problem of Kajiado by attacking the acting Archbishop while performing his duties. The problem of Maseno West was also solved. Those opposed to election of Simon Oketch went to court, but judgment was made in favour of Simon and we consecrated him in Kakamega on 17 December 1995.

Chapter 11

Third Archbishop of ACK
1997–2002

I was enthroned as the third Archbishop of ACK at All Saints Cathedral, Nairobi on Sunday 12 January 1997. The occasion was attended by thousands of people and was graced by His Excellency President Daniel arap Moi and the Primate of the Anglican Church of Canada, who preached the sermon. The ceremony was held a day before the WCC Sokoni (Market Place) conference started at Karen. Most of the 500 international delegates attended the enthronement ceremony and Dr Konrad Raiser, the General Secretary of WCC, spoke during the ceremony.

Also present was Canon John Peterson, the General Secretary of the Anglican Consultative Council, and the Revd Christopher Carey of CMS, who travelled all the way from London to attend the ceremony. The Primates of Cape Town, Tanzania, and Uganda were also represented. All the ACK Bishops and Christians from all over the country attended. The *Kenya Times* of 19 January 1997 carried a banner story of the occasion with a photograph of me shaking hands with President Moi. The *Sunday Times* report is reproduced here:

Ecstatic Day for Kenyan Anglicans

The Anglican Church in Kenya enthroned Revd Dr David Mukuba Gitari as its third Archbishop in a colourful ceremony witnessed by thousands of Christians and church leaders from all over the world including State President Daniel arap Moi. (APS staff writers Osman Njuguna and Joseph Owiti, who participated in the historic occasion, filed this report).

On January 12, 1997 the Church of the Province of Kenya (CPK) enthroned Rev Dr David Mukuba Gitari as its third archbishop and Bishop of Nairobi Diocese. It was a well attended ecstatic and colourful ceremony witnessed by a cross section of Christians from Kenya, Anglican Primates from Africa and Canada, representatives of ecclesiastical organizations, members of the diplomatic corps in this East African Country, Government and opposition leaders.

Guests started arriving at Nairobi's All Saints Cathedral grounds as early as 7.30 am and many had taken their seats inside the church and under the tents pitched outside by 8.00 am. President Moi was ushered into the cathedral at 9.45 am. The organizers, anticipating a big turn-out had positioned monitors at strategic points for those who could not secure places inside.

The more than six-hour ceremony kicked off with a procession from the nearby Uhuru Park, accompanied by a church band playing trumpets and drums to the tune of Christian Hymns. The Kirinyaga Diocese Mothers' Union ululated as they sang praises to their past immediate bishop now taking the lead of the CPK.

The ceremony proper began at about 10.30 am when the Provincial Chancellor Paul Kariuki Kihara read the mandate followed by the archbishop-elect knocking thrice at the Cathedral's main entrance and saying aloud: "Open for me the gates of righteousness, I will enter them and give thanks to the Lord!"

The elaborate ceremony was conducted by the acting CPK Dean Bishop Benjamin Nzimbi, assisted by Bishops Samson Mwaluda and Joseph Wasonga and the Provost of the Cathedral the Very Revd Peter Njoka.

As Rt Revd Gitari was led through the Declaration of Assent and Oath by the CPK Provincial Chancellor, he elicited laughter from the congregation as he swore to leave office "not later than midnight" upon attaining the retirement age of 65 years.

Born on September 16, 1937, Archbishop David Gitari should retire mid-September 2002. He was elected the third archbishop of the CPK on November 20 1996. His Predecessor Manasses Kuria headed the church from 1980 to 1994 having taken over from the first Archbishop Festo Olang' who led the province from 1970 to 1979.

The day's sermon was delivered by the Most Rev Michael Peers, the Primate of the Anglican Church of Canada who was also representing the Archbishop of Canterbury George Carey. He described Dr Gitari as one "known to many of us in many places around the world in the Anglican Communion and beyond, respected and one who brings respect" to the church in Kenya and the wider church of Christ. Archbishop Peers, basing his preaching on the oneness in Jesus Christ and community, told the congregation that at the present time, people are looking for security in what is locally known and familiar and that attitude "sometimes bears with it terrible consequences". He noted that as people try to express who they are, they are at times compelled to defend themselves against anybody and sometimes everybody. Africa, he added, has not been spared such consequences.

Dignitaries who delivered greetings included President Moi, who congratulated Archbishop Gitari upon his enthronement as the third Primate of the CPK. In his brief "sermon" received with thunderous clapping by the congregation, the President reminded the new archbishop that as a leader he had a very difficult task ahead of him. The head of State also challenged Christians to manifest Christ in their lives and to preach the gospel while there was still time. He reminded them that it is indeed difficult today in "a world of confusion" to be a Christian. Moi who extensively quoted from the Epistles of St Paul also pledged his support to the work of the church regardless of denominational affiliation.

The World Council of Churches (WCC) Secretary General Dr Konrad Raiser congratulating Archbishop Gitari upon his enthronement, also promised the CPK support, solidarity and friendship from the ecumenical council. Dr Raiser reiterated President Moi's message to the new archbishop and reminded his fellow church leader that being a bishop "today is not an easy job. We are surrounded by witnesses of bishops who had to go all the way to offer their very lives."

The All Africa Conference of Churches (AACC) Secretary-General Revd Jose Chipenda prayed that God completes the work he began in Gitari at a very early age. He was referring to the fact that David Gitari started teaching Sunday School at the age of 12 years and preached his first sermon at the age of 15.

The Secretary-General of the National Council of Churches of Kenya (NCCK) Revd Mutava Musyimi, in his congratulatory message stressed on the unity of the church in Kenya, saying the council looked forward to working more closely as Protestant churches, with other churches and the Government.

Referring to the message by the State President, Father Michael Ruwa, representing the 22 Catholic Bishops in Kenya, stressed the importance of enhancing oneness and prayed that working relations between Catholics and Anglicans would be strengthened not only in Kenya but in the region and worldwide.

Bishop Renz of the Evangelical Lutheran Church of Wuerttemberg Stuttgart, Germany told the congregation of the long-term relations between the CPK particularly the Diocese of Mt Kenya East and the Evangelical Lutheran Church of Wuerttemberg. The Evangelical Church awarded Archbishop Gitari the Martin Luther Silver Medal as a symbol "of the joy we have in the union with Christ". The new archbishop also wore what Bishop Renz described as a "huge pair of shoes," a gift from the same church, a symbol that the CPK Primate will be required to cover a longer distance as an archbishop.

The message from the Archbishop of Canterbury George Carey was read by his representative, the Anglican Primate of Canada. The head of the world wide Anglican Communion described Gitari as "no stranger to the Anglican Communion" and offered prayers for the growing and vibrant Province of Kenya. Welcoming Dr Gitari, the newest primate to the Anglican Consultative Council (ACC) which comprises 36 provinces, Archbishop Carey assured the CPK and their new leader of support and love, saying ACC looked forward to working with them.

Other congratulatory messages were received from the conference of the Anglican Communion in Africa and the project for Christian Muslim-Relations in Africa (PROCMURA).

Kenya's 20 CPK bishops representing the 22 dioceses in the country and clergy of the Nairobi Diocese professed and promised true canonical obedience to the new archbishop and bishop respectively.

Delivering his Charge, the newly enthroned archbishop thanked the 201 members of the Provincial Electoral College for electing him as the third archbishop of CPK last November. He said he felt deeply overwhelmed by the trust and confidence the entire church had shown by charging him with the responsibility of leading CPK during these last four years of the 20th century and the end of the Second Millennium of the Christian era, as well as ushering the CPK into the 21st century and the Third Millennium.

Referring to the AACC Seventh Assembly to be held in Addis Ababa, Ethiopia, next October, Archbishop Gitari challenged African Churches to meditate on the assembly theme "Troubled but not Destroyed" saying it is right and proper for churches in Africa to be reminded that indeed "we are troubled but not destroyed". He highlighted incidences that portray the persecution of the Church in former communist countries in Eastern Europe, China and Africa over the past decades and in recent years emphasizing that although troubled, the confessing church was not destroyed but upheld its witness at very difficult times.

On matters that touch on the Anglican Church in Kenya specifically, Archbishop Gitari noted the CPK has experienced various internal problems, some of which appear during the election of bishops and the division of dioceses. He expressed hope that the provincial constitution would be reviewed with a hope of amending the clauses which have been more of a problem than a blessing to the church. He also noted that as the "salt of the earth and light of the world" the church should choose its leaders without being influenced by tribalism or ethnicity and conduct its affairs with transparency and accountability. He also said that the Church needs to have well equipped and trained pastors of the flock. To this end, he added, "adequate and intensive theological training will be needed of all those aspiring to be ordained into priesthood." He noted that in the past, due to the fast growth of the Church, the leadership has been tempted to ordain people with little general and theological education.

The archbishop also assured the congregation and Kenyans in general of the CPK's commitment in the struggle against poverty, ignorance and disease, However, he noted that there is a need to go beyond the fight against the above mentioned and seek their root causes.

The new archbishop caused laughter when he said that when the church asks what the root causes of various ills are, some politicians tell "us to keep away from politics and confine ourselves to purely spiritual matters… if asking why there are so many road accidents in

Kenya is a political question, then we as church leaders will ask that question many a time and will persistently sensitize our Government to repair the roads... urge the traffic police to stop receiving bribes from drivers of unroadworthy vehicles, for these are some of the causes of carnage and loss of lives on the roads."

Archbishop Gitari reminded the Church of its duty to constantly preach the doctrine of sanctity of human life.

My Charge During My Enthronment

I was elected the third Archbishop of the Anglican Church of Kenya and Bishop of Nairobi in November 1996. As stated in the *Kenya Times* article, the President, Daniel arap Moi, was gracious enough to attend my enthronement. Also present were a number of government ministers, Members of Parliament and delegates attending a meeting of the World Council of Churches, led by the General Secretary, Konrad Raiser. The Primates of various provinces of Africa (CAPA) attended the service, and the representative of the Archbishop of Canterbury and Primate of Anglican Church of Canada, the Most Revd Michael Peers, preached the sermon.

In my charge read from the throne entitled "Troubled but not Destroyed" I dealt with the issues of constitutional reform, the battle against poverty, ignorance and disease, transformation of society, the struggle for justice and sanctity of human life, and the good stewardship of the gifts God has given us, such as land, environment and other resources. I also dealt with the issue of human rights, including regular, free and fair elections, the right to free expression and association with others in political parties, labour organisations and other social movements.

I called for the strengthening of the executive, legislature and judiciary in ways that enable them to enforce the checks and balances necessary for good governance. I called for the enforcement of the rule of law so that predictability, fairness and accountability can be assured for all citizens and investors alike. I underlined the fact that corruption had virtually become a way of life in Kenya and quoted the then German Ambassador, who had said a few days before my enthronement that "what makes corruption so bad is that it slows down economic development, distorts the allocation of resources and creates economic structures which benefit only a few". I called upon all people to join hands to arrest this cancer of corruption.

I reminded the congregation that in a world where access to global markets comes via the information superhighway, an open communication system with access to information is essential. I emphasized that there was need to free the media and the airwaves to enable the free expression of views, the cornerstone of democracy. I noted that there is no doubt that liberalised electronic media accommodating many radio and television stations encourages a business and investment climate to flourish when ideas and information flow freely.

In conclusion of my charge I reminded the congregation that the President in his New Year speech had called 1997 the year of reconciliation. I said in this year of reconciliation we want to feel that we have quick access to decision-makers, government ministers, top civil servants, etc. This, I said, will promote meaningful dialogue and understanding. I informed the congregation that the State House and the house of the Anglican Bishop of Mombasa were built so close to one another so that the Governor and the Bishop could have quick access to one another for fellowship, consultation and prayers. I said, "I am now moving to that house called Bishopsbourne as the Archbishop of Kenya. Being so close to State House, I hope we shall have many opportunities of consultation over a cup of tea with our beloved President either at State House or at Bishopsbourne." (Note: the full text of my charge will be found in the publication entitled *Eight Great Years 1994 – 2002,* edited by J. K. Kirigia, Nairobi, Anglican Church of Kenya, 2002).

During the six years I was the Archbishop of ACK my main task was to fulfill the promises I made in my charge during the enthronement service. I revisited this charge just before my retirement on 16 September 2002. Most of the promises that I made were fulfilled, but some achievements were not even mentioned in my charge. I consider the following to be some of the major achievements during my short period as the Primate of the ACK.

Information Technology

Soon after my enthronement, I was visited by Judith Gillespie of Trinity Church on Wall Street, New York. She was very keen to support us in entering the millennium of information technology in style. Trinity Church gave us funds to enable us to install email and internet services in every diocesan office in Kenya where there was electricity. We quickly started the processes to make this possible and were able to buy computers for every diocesan office and every ACK institution in the entire province. Robert Kilonzo was identified as the man to implement the project. He travelled throughout the country installing modern computers fitted with the latest software into 41 offices. This was very new to many officers and Kilonzo organized courses for secretaries and other staff to train in computer skills, how to access and send email and use the internet.

Networked to each other and to the rest of the world via email and the internet, the Anglican Church of Kenya had effectively joined the information superhighway. This technology made a world of difference and brought a new dynamism to the various churches in the far reaches of the country. They could now create content and store data more efficiently and communicate and obtain information faster, which made them more effective in decision-making and in the execution of their mandate. By the time of my retirement, communicating with my fellow bishops had become very efficient and fast. I could send important information to the bishops at the touch of a button.

Formation of Kenya Anglican Men's Association

Soon after my retirement, Thomas Malinda, an outstanding Anglican layman from the diocese of Machakos, wrote to inform me that the greatest achievement of my leadership was the formation of the Kenya Anglican Men's Association (KAMA). He predicted that KAMA was going to be a great movement in the Anglican Church of Kenya. Branches of KAMA have now been established in all the dioceses of ACK. Some dioceses have appointed full time coordinators of KAMA and men are being mobilised for active membership of the association. Before the advent of KAMA, there had already existed (from 1985) the Fathers Union or Fathers Associations in a number of dioceses. Each association had its own constitution but there was no coordination at the provincial level. I had strongly felt that there was need to establish a National Anglican Men's Association. I called a number of meetings in 2000 and 2001 to harmonise the constitutions. The Provincial KAMA received the blessings of the Provincial Synod in July 2001.

The ten aims and objectives of KAMA are:

1. To promote God's Kingdom and to set forth His glory.
2. To help its members to grow in spirit, mind and body and to be nurtured in faith for every good work.
3. To encourage its members to play an active part in the mission of the church.

4. To promote Christian principles in national, civic and community life.

5. To encourage its members to undertake acts of Christian service for the distressed, disadvantaged, or disabled.

6. To encourage its members to use the gifts God has given them as good stewards of God's varied grace.

7. To encourage its members to use their resources in supporting the work of the Church at all levels.

8. To encourage Anglican lay men and women to play a positive role as Christians in the political, social and economic life of the nation.

9. To honour the institution of marriage as ordained by God and to promote Christian family values.

10. To promote Christian fellowship, love and unity in the Church and the society and to promote spiritual enthusiasm among its members.

The motto of KAMA is taken from Joshua 24:23, "As for me and my house, we will serve the Lord." The provincial uniform is a navy blue suit with ties to match, or a clerical collar for clergy. The members also wear a badge. After retirement I wrote a handbook for KAMA entitled *We will serve the Lord*, which is an exposition of the aims and objectives of KAMA. The handbook was launched on 30 November 2004 during the first National Conference of KAMA held at Kiambu Boys High School and attended by 250 delegates from all over Kenya.

Liturgical Renewal

Our Modern Services

When I was enthroned as the third Archbishop of the ACK in January 1997, I considered liturgical renewal as a major priority in my ministry. It was therefore a great joy for me to launch the prayer book *Our Modern Services* during my farewell service held at All Saints Cathedral, Nairobi on 15 September 2002. In the preface of the book, I wrote:

This book is a gift to the Anglican Church of Kenya in the 3rd millennium of the Christian era, and the 21st century. It was a great desire to see the church develop a new alternate prayer book that would be both relevant and contemporary because the 1662 Book of

Common Prayer, great and useful as it has been, has nevertheless been culturally outlived.

The compilation of *Our Modern Services* was the work of a Provincial Liturgical Committee chaired by the Ven. Sam Mawiyoo and Bishop Gideon Githiga. The committee was co-coordinated by the Revd Joyce Karuri Kirigia, who marshaled all her talents to ensure that the book became a reality. The *Our Modern Services* book, which has so many interesting liturgies, has been acclaimed as a great work of liturgical renewal not only in Africa but also throughout the Anglican Communion. Some of the liturgies, especially the service of the Holy Communion, are being used in institutions and churches in other parts of the communion. The impact of this book has not as yet been felt in Kenya except in theological colleges and churches where English is used as the language of worship. As a matter of urgency, the book should be translated into other Kenyan languages.

Tumsifu Mungu – A Kenyan Hymn Book

The Provincial Liturgical Committee commissioned a number of leading musicians in Kenya to compose a Kenyan hymn book. By the time of my retirement, the committee had compiled 543 songs and choruses, blending rhythms and genres from across the country and beyond. The songs are all arranged and harmonised in sola and staff. The musicians who compiled this book were Blasto Ooko, William Kimanyasyo, Noah Omolo, Aggrey Lugalya, Victor Mutinda, Gilbert Oricho, Timothy Mwangi, Patrick Mulayo, Chric Sikuku, Zebedi Muga, Grace Kiseu and David Thyaka. The group was co-coordinated by the Revd Joyce Karuri Kirigia. My challenge to the Province is to have this great work of art published so that many Christians throughout Kenya, Eastern Africa and beyond can have access to the book. Currently only one master copy is in existence. The impact of this hymn book in liturgical renewal will never be felt until it is published.

Revision of the Constitution

In my charge during my enthronement as Archbishop, I had said, "It is my hope that the Provincial Constitution will be reviewed with a hope of amending those constitutional clauses which have been more of a problem to the church than a blessing." The fourth constitution was based on the drafts prepared by Bishop Okullu's Commission, established in November 1992, which submitted its draft in 1998. It was also based on Bishop Wabukala's Commission, which submitted its report in July 2000. The refining of the draft was the work of a number of diocesan chancellors led by the then Provincial Chancellor, Tom Onyango, the Chancellors of Mt Kenya South (Mugure Thande) and Mt Kenya Central (Kimani Kairu) and myself. We spent many hours in the last three months of 2001 and the first two months of 2002 refining the constitution. Despite its shortcomings, the constitution is a great improvement on the preceding three constitutions of 1970, 1982 and 1992. The fourth constitution is not supposed to be a permanent document, as the church has to keep on reviewing the clauses of the constitution and amend those that may prove to be a hindrance to the mission of the church.

In my charge, I also made reference to the review of the National Constitution. I said, "For the same reasons, we should fully support the review of our National Constitution before the next election in order to reflect the changes which have taken place in the political arena. The change from a single party to a multi-party system means the constitution should be reviewed to take account of new realities, the aim being making the country more democratic." The details of my involvement in National Constitutional Reforms are also to be found in the book *Eight Great Years (October 1994 to September 2002)*.

Chapter 12

Reforming the Anglican Church of Kenya

My consecration as a bishop in July 1975 enhanced my desire to see the church reformed. At the diocesan level, I was determined to reform the concept of the mission of the church. There were many Christians who thought that the mission of the church was only to evangelise or win souls for Christ. But, convinced that the Gospel of Christ was concerned about the whole human being – his and her body, mind and spirit – I embarked on proclaiming a holistic Gospel. It was in the diocese of Mt Kenya East that the term Christian Community Services (CCS) was coined, and this was now adopted in the whole province. We took evangelism and pastoral work seriously but we also embarked on community health, water provision, agricultural projects to improve food production and family incomes, social work, and many other projects.

I was appointed the chairman of the Provincial Board of Theological Education (PBTE) in 1980 and I remained chairman until I became the Dean of the Province in 1994. This position provided me with numerous opportunities to play a role in catalysing reforms in the church. I encouraged the clergy interested in further theological studies to take sabbatical leave and join recognised theological seminaries both locally and overseas. I recommended a good number of them for academic scholarships, which they took up mostly in Britain and in the USA. I strongly believed (and I still do) that well trained and educated clergy are a great asset to the church of Christ.

Though St Paul was not one of the twelve disciples, once converted, he became a great asset to the church of Christ not only to the early church, but also to this present day. Being highly educated, he was able to articulate the message of Jesus intellectually and set out to evangelise the Gentiles. He wrote more epistles than any of the 12 disciples.

As chairman of the PBTE, I was greatly concerned that some Bishops were ordaining clergy after only a short period of theological study or after "crash programmes". In view of this, the PBTE made it policy that no one would be ordained without being recommended by the congregation in which he/she regularly worships, and only after being interviewed by bishops' examining chaplains and having successfully undertaken a minimum of three years theological education in a recognised institution. This recommendation was adopted by the Provincial Synod but some bishops ignored it.

As the Chairman of PBTE, I called three Theological Conferences to discuss pertinent issues in the life of the church. The first conference was held at the ACK Guest House, Likoni, Mombasa, in May 1981. The conference was attended by 37 delegates; 27 of them were University graduates. We discussed the theme "The Mission of the Church in Changing Society." The report of the conference was published and discussed by the House of Bishops, the Provincial Standing Committee of the Synod and the Provincial Synod. The second PBTE conference was once again held at the ACK Guest House, Mombasa, and was attended by 60 theologians from all nine dioceses in the Province. The Archbishop and five bishops attended the conference and observers from CMS, Tanzania, ECUSA, PCEA, Methodist Church of Kenya. Evangelical Fellowship of Kenya and Daystar College also participated in the deliberations. The theme of the conference was "Let the Church be the Church." One of the facilitators was Andrew Kirk, a theologian from England.

The third conference, the theme of which was "Liberating the Church for Mission", was held at St Andrew's College of Theology and Development, Kabare, in October 1986. It was attended by 80 participants from all the twelve dioceses of the Province, seven of whom were Bishops. I convened and chaired all three of these conferences and tabled their recommendations to the House of Bishops and the Provincial Synod and its Standing Committee. As a result of these conferences, the Provincial Synod adopted most of the recommendations. The following are some of the most important recommendations adopted by the Synod:

Church and Polygamy

During the first PBTE conference (1981), I presented a paper on the Church and polygamy. The paper generated plenty of discussion. The conference made the following recommendations:

Church and Polygamy
Minutes of the Provincial Synod of November 1982 – Min. 22/82

The Church of the Province of Kenya is convinced that monogamy is God's plan for marriage and that it is the ideal relationship for the expression of love between a husband and a wife. Nevertheless this teaching is not easily understood in many Kenyan cultures in which polygamy is widely practiced and is socially acceptable. While it teaches monogamy, the church must be pastorally sensitive to the widespread existence of polygamy.

People who were Polygamists before becoming Christians

That a person who becomes a polygamist before becoming a Christian shall on accepting the gospel be baptized with his believing wives and children on condition that he shall not take any other wives. The Bishop may confirm such a polygamist, his wives and children after further instructions in the Christian faith.

Motion carried by 46 votes, 3 against, 1 abstention.

People who become Polygamists while already Christians

A Christian who becomes a polygamist deprives himself the privileges of participation in holy communion, standing as a sponsor in baptism and in holding office as a member of church committee or parish council. Also that in keeping with the teaching of St Paul, no polygamist should hold office as a Bishop, Priest, Deacon or Lay Reader. The Bishop shall have the discretion to re-admit a polygamist to full privileges of Lay Church membership after due consideration of the following circumstances with regard to each individual case:

1. The lapse of a notable period of time
2. The polygamist's repentance for his faults in breaking the vows which he made at his marriage
3. The acceptability of such re-admission in the eyes of the local church

4. Special factors operating in an individual case which made it hard for the polygamist to resist taking a second wife.

Motion carried by 43 votes for, 3 against and 1 abstention.

Distribution of Bread by Lay Readers During the Eucharist

During my first four years as a bishop I had got increasingly concerned about the role of lay readers in the church. The practice at that time was that the bishop licensed lay readers who had been recommended by their respective local church committees and parish councils. They were examined by archdeacons before their names were recommended to the diocesan bishop for licensing. There were two licences. One was a general licence to enable the lay reader to assist the parish priest in his various pastoral responsibilities, such as visiting the sick, burial services, etc. There also was a second special licence issued to some lay readers to assist the priest in the distribution of wine only during Eucharist. The licence had to be renewed each year by the bishop. I was not theologically convinced that lay readers should distribute only wine and not bread. This appeared to make bread a superior element to wine. I was convinced that the work of the priest was to consecrate bread and wine and to let the lay readers assist him in distributing both elements. I also did not see the need for yearly renewal of all licensed lay readers. It was tedious work spending hours signing Lay Readers' licenses.

I expressed my concerns during the meeting of the House of Bishops held at Imani House on 26 March 1979 and chaired by Archbishop Festo Olang'. The Bishops supported my sentiments and agreed that "If a Diocesan Bishop gives authority, Lay Readers can assist in distribution of bread". (See Min 2/79.) Where this decision was put into practice, it was a great relief to both clergy and the communicant. It was a tedious task for one priest to distribute bread alone to as many as 600 communicants while several lay leaders were mere observers. The distribution of bread could in some cases last for hours. It appears as if some dioceses are not aware of this recommendation and I would urge all the bishops and the Provincial Synod to adopt it.

During the same sitting, the bishops, after careful consideration, agreed that there was no reason why a diocesan bishop could not authorise a deacon to preside at Holy Communion, but they also agreed to leave the matter to the discretion of the Bishop (see Min 2/79). The ACK has been criticized for allowing deacons to preside over the Eucharist. We have been advised that if we have a shortage of clergy, then we should shorten the period a person must serve as a deacon so that he can assume the duties of a priest once he has taken the necessary vows. But many congregations feel that it is better to have regular Holy Communion where there is a deacon than wait for several weeks before the parish priest comes to celebrate the Eucharist.

The International Anglican Liturgical Committee and the ACC have been revisiting the ideas of Roland Allen, who had proposed that where there is shortage of priests, then a respected lay reader in the local church can be ordained to priesthood and serve his church as priest mainly for the purposes of celebrating Eucharist. Such a local priest does not require theological training and should remain permanently in his local church but under a trained parish priest.

Guidelines for Funerals of Christians

When I was the Archbishop of the ACK, I went to Maseno to attend the funeral of the retired bishop of Maseno North, the Rt Revd James Mundia. The funeral began at 10.00am and ended after 6.00pm. I went home greatly concerned that we can spend the whole day burying one person. The funeral took such a long time because all the 26 Members of Parliament who were present were invited to speak. The wife of the bishop, who was not feeling well on that day, spoke for three hours non-stop while supported by two women, each holding one of her arms. Most of her speech was repetitive. After the service ended and as we were taking the casket for burial, the Mothers Union from various archdioceses took over the programme. They carried beautifully coloured sheets while singing and placed them on the coffin. At about 5.00pm I told the diocesan Bishop that I could not bear it any longer as I had to return to Kisumu airport to catch my plane for Nairobi before 6.00pm.

If this trend continued, our priests, who are burying an average of three people per week, would be spending about 40% of their time burying the dead. I felt it was imperative that we put in place new guidelines in the Anglican Church for funerals. I drafted the guidelines and distributed copies to all diocesan bishops. The following guidelines were tabled by the secretary of PBTE at the 14th Ordinary Session of Synod held at All Saints Cathedral, Nairobi in May 1999.

Funerals

Realizing that Kenya is a multi-cultural society it is difficult for this Synod to have a policy on funerals which can be made compulsory to every culture in Kenya. However as believers in the gospel of Christ, we can agree on those aspects of our culture which are contrary to scriptures and common sense, which we can reject. We can also agree on aspects of our culture on which the scriptures are silent which therefore can be left to the local decision. Yet there are other aspects of our cultures which are not contrary to the scriptures and can therefore be upheld. In view of the above this Synod wishes to give the following guidelines to be further considered by the dioceses.

3.1 That as far as possible, bodies of the dead should not be kept for a period exceeding seven days.

3.2 That preliminaries which are not part of the service be done before the service begins. That as far as possible the service should not be more than two hours.

3.3 To save time we recommend that we reduce the number of speakers. Some speeches can be made before the person presiding over the funeral arrives.

3.4 That there is only one main service either at home or in the church where all messages of condolences shall be given and only committal of the body shall be done at the graveside.

3.5 That for those who die far from their ancestral home and family members feel strongly the need to bury their beloved one at the ancestral home, there is a strong case to have a service in church at the place where the person who has died was a regular worshipper so that those who knew him and who cannot travel to far distances have a chance to participate in the farewell service. In such a case it may be necessary to hold another service at the place of burial.

3.6 We recommend that the viewing of the body be done by the family and friends who go to the mortuary to collect the body and that the viewing of the body is discouraged for the others. However where there is a strong local feeling of the necessity of viewing the body, the matter be left to the discretion of the family and the local church and be done before or after the service.

3.7 We urge the local church and relatives of the deceased to give full support and guidance to the widow/widower and their children and that they respect their feelings and encourage them to live Christian lives.

3.8 We condemn the habit of the in-laws taking away any of the property of the dead person from his or her immediate family members, i.e. the wife and the children, unless the will of the dead person spells out that some of his property be given to the extended members of the family.

3.9 The African culture has not yet accommodated itself the practice of cremation. But if a Christian in his or her will, wishes his body to be cremated the church will accept that wish.

3.10 We are convinced that the funeral service is a wonderful opportunity for extending pastoral care to those who have lost their loved ones as well as an opportunity for the proclamation of the gospel. Hence the clergy and the lay readers should not refuse to conduct a Christian burial service to any member of the church who has not been excommunicated even if he/she might have backslidden. Even where there are serious doubts about the faith of the dead person, and the church might not want to use the liturgy of the church or wear church robes, the presence of the church leaders should be there to minister to the living.

3.11 We discourage the use of a lot of money on the funeral which often leaves the family poorer than before. We recommend that funeral expenses be reduced by not;

- Buying an expensive coffin.
- Cementing the grave.
- Buying expensive new clothes for the dead.
- Feasting before, during and after the funeral.
- Transporting the body to the ancestral home where there are meager funds to hire vehicles.
- And such other activities that are money consuming.

3.12 The Synod considers the position or direction of burying the body as immaterial (note: Some cultures put the body in a sitting position before burial).

3.13 The Synod believes in the doctrine of communion with saints and encourages the remembrance of the dead during worship in our churches.

3.14 During the funeral service either at the church or at home, we consider the master-of-ceremonies to be the highest ranking church leader (Bishop, Priest or Lay-Reader) present. He/she is the one licensed to bury the dead. He/she should be at liberty to ask assistance in non-liturgical matters from a lay person.

Tabled by the Chairman of the Provincial Board of Theological Education (PBTE).

These resolutions were approved by the 14th Provincial Synod held at All Saints Cathedral, Nairobi, on 5-6 May 1999. The Synod recommended that the guidelines be discussed further by the Diocesan Synods to enable the Provincial Synod to come up with the final guidelines (see Minute 13.3/ps/99). The Provincial Synod adopted the guidelines for funerals in the Anglican Church during the Special Synod held at the main hall of the All Saints Cathedral in July 2000. See Min SPS/07/2000.

Baptism of Children of Unmarried Mothers

The 1981 PBTE conference discussed the issue of infant baptism of unmarried mothers' children or single mothers. The practice of the church was not to baptise such children until they reach the age of discretion and are taught the catechism. The conference was of the view that "As far as infant baptism is concerned, the important issue is whether the child will be brought up in the Christian faith or not... The infant can be baptized if there is assurance that his/her mother or custodian will bring up that child in Christian faith and teach the child the vows which were made by his/her parents and god-parents during the baptism." The conference outlined conditions under which the child of a single mother could be baptised. The Provincial Synod of November 1982 adopted the conditions drawn up by the first PBTE conference, which were as follows;

a)   That if the infant is being brought up by his unwed mother, she will be expected to show signs of repentance over a reasonable period of time after which the Bishop will give written authority for the child to be baptized.

b)   That if the child is being brought up by a Christian guardian, for instance a grandmother, and there is an assurance that the child will be brought up in the Christian faith, the child may be baptized, with written authority from the Bishop after a period of six months since the request to baptize the child was made.

c)   If the mother was raped, the child should be baptized once the fact of the rape is established, with the Bishop's written consent.

d) That an unwed mother whose child is baptized as per clause (a) and (c) above shall promise to lead a virtuous life thereafter.

e) However, care shall be taken to treat each case upon its own merit.

Recognition of Marriage Under Customary Law

The first PBTE Conference was concerned that a Christian man and woman who live as husband and wife under customary law are considered as if they are living in sin until their marriage is blessed in church. Under the prevailing practice, they could not participate in Holy Communion nor have their infants baptised until they had their marriage blessed in church. During the November 1982 Provincial Synod, the following motion, which I proposed and was seconded by the Revd Canon Dedan Kamau, was carried unanimously:

> The Church of the Province of Kenya is convinced that a non-polygamous person who is married in accordance to the traditions of his ethnic group or tribe and has fulfilled all the requirements of the traditions such as consent of parents, dowry, etc., and it is recognized by the community that he is married, such a person is truly married. CPK shall not in future make re-marriage in church a condition for baptism or admittance to the Holy Communion. The Local Pastor in exerting this decision may however exercise his pastoral care and encourage such a couple to have their marriage blessed in church. Each case will be looked into on its own merit (see Minute 21/82).

The Synod passed another resolution proposed by Bishop Henry Okullu and seconded by M.W. Ombaka, which stated that:

> whereas we recognize a civil or customary marriage with its own context, we nevertheless note that a Christian marriage has the added blessings of being solemnized and vows taken before God and the assembled congregation of his people (Minute 20/82).

Ordination of Women

The 1978 Lambeth Conference debated the ordination of women at great length. The debate nearly split the Communion but a compromise motion was agreed upon. It was resolved that every Province should debate the ordination of women and those who resolve to ordain them should go ahead and do so. Whatever decision is taken, the Provinces which ordain women and those which do not should remain friendly to one another. In 1980, Bishop Henry Okullu ordained the first Kenyan woman to the diaconate and priesthood. The Bishop was impatient, because he believed the Province was moving too slowly in taking a decision on this matter. During the Provincial Standing Committee of the Synod held in October 1980, the following resolution was made: "Although the ordination of women was accepted in principle by the Province, many Christians do not fully understand its implications and it is recommended that all diocesan Synods should debate the matter and communicate the results of the votes for and against, to the Archbishop."

The first PBTE Conference discussed this issue and gave guidelines on the kind of motion which should be debated at all levels. The conference recommended that the motion to be debated should read as follows:

That this committee/council/synod resolves that women who are called to the sacred ministry and are carefully examined by their respective church committees, Parish Councils, Diocesan selection committees and PBTE and are found to have a genuine calling and necessary qualities and who successfully complete their training for the ordained ministry may be ordained to the Diaconate and to the Priesthood.

The motion was discussed by the sixth Synod of November 1982, but the Synod said that while "the issue of ordination of women is a very fundamental issue and while accepting in principle that the ordination of women is commendable, nevertheless it recommends the dioceses to discuss the issue fully and report their recommendation to the seventh session of the Synod when a final decision on the matter shall be made."

It was further resolved that "Notwithstanding anything hereinbefore contained or implied, there shall be no ordination of women in any diocese within the Province in any circumstances until the Synod makes a final decision at its next meeting" (Minute 23/82).

The majority of the dioceses did not seem to have considered debating the ordination of women as a priority. Hence the matter could not be discussed during the next three ordinary sessions of the Provincial Synod. It was not until the 10th Synod held in June 1990 that the Province was able to take a position on the issue.

Five dioceses – Maseno North, Maseno South, Nambale, Mt Kenya East and Maseno West – had approved the motion to ordain women. Six dioceses reported that they were considering the matter: Nairobi, Nakuru, Mt Kenya Central, Machakos and Mombasa. The diocese of Mt Kenya South had discussed the matter and had resolved that it was not a priority. The Provincial Synod made the following resolution:

> This Provincial Synod of CPK meeting at All Saints Cathedral Church Hall from 26-27 June 1990 allows those Dioceses of this Province which have approved ordination of women to the Diaconate and to Priesthood to go ahead and ordain them.

The motion was carried by 48 votes for, 8 against and 5 abstentions.

Soon after I returned from the 1978 Lambeth conference I had set in motion efforts to enable Christians in the Diocese of Mt Kenya East to understand the issue of ordination of women in the Anglican Communion and I informed them of the deliberations of the just-ended Lambeth Conference. I visited every deanery in the diocese and chaired special meetings to discuss the matter. Christians were at liberty to give their own views on whether women should be ordained or not. Then I called the Third Ordinary Session of the Diocesan Synod, which was held in 1979. The motion was debated but was lost.

I tabled the motion again during the fourth ordinary session of the Synod held at St Mark's College, Kigari, in December 1981 and the motion was lost by 95 votes against and 46 in favour. The motion was debated during the fifth ordinary session of the Synod held at St Mark's College, Kigari, in December 1983, and the motion was once again lost; 79 delegates voted in favour while 110 voted against the motion. In all three instances, it was the House of Clergy who consistently and vehemently protested and remained against the ordination of women. In each case, a majority of the laity voted in favour of the motion, but attitudes were changing over time. The sixth ordinary session of the Synod was held at St Andrew's Church, Kabare, in April 1986. During the Synod the following motion was debated:

> This Synod resolves that women who are called to the sacred Ministry and are carefully examined by their respective church com-

mittees, Parish Councils, the Diocesan Selection Committee and where necessary by PBTE and are found to have a genuine calling and necessary qualities for the Lord's Service and who successfully complete their training for ordained Ministry, may be ordained to the Diaconate subject to approval of such a move by the Provincial Synod.

I moved the motion from the chair and I was seconded by Walter Mathagu; 175 delegates voted in favour of the motion, 44 voted against it and 28 abstained. Of those who voted in favour of the motion, 146 were the laity and 29 were clergy. 32 of those who voted against the motion were clergy and 12 were laity. So eight years of debate, deliberation, discussion and persuasion helped Christians to surmount prejudices and inform themselves on the issues pertaining to ordination of women; finally the motion was at last carried by an overwhelming vote.

The diocese had started preparing women for ministry in 1977. The first two women to join St Andrew's, Kabare, were Nancy Kirera and Jessie Githinji. On completion of their training, I commissioned them as deaconesses while I made their fellow classmates deacons of the church. By the time the diocese accepted ordination of women in 1986, there were quite a number of women who were suitably qualified but whom we could not ordain yet, as the Province had not as yet approved the ordination of women. It was not until June 1990, the eve of the sub-division of the Diocese of Mt Kenya East, that the Provincial Synod gave its nod to the dioceses that had approved the ordination of women to go ahead. The diocese was split into two (Kirinyaga and Embu). On 1 July 1990, I chose to move to Kirinyaga to start the new diocese.

The Standing Committee of the Synod of the Diocese of Kirinyaga met at Kutus in December 1991 and expressed concern that I had not yet ordained women to the diaconate. I authorised the bishops' examining chaplains to interview those women who had successfully competed their training at St Andrew's but the chairman of the committee declined to interview them, and the qualified women said that they were not psychologically ready for ordination, which was due in a week's time. Their ordination was postponed until July 1992.

In June 1992 two senior clergymen threatened to go to civil court if I ordained women. Their argument was that the resolutions of Mt Kenya East Synod were not applicable to the new Diocese of Kirinyaga. Consequently I called a special Synod of the Diocese of Kirinyaga at St Paul's, Kutus, on 6 June 1992. I tabled 100 resolutions that had been passed by the Diocese of Mt Kenya East from 1975 to 1990, and all resolutions were passed unanimously in the record time of less than one hour. The two senior clergy were conspicuously absent and did not even send an apology. This paved the way for the ordination of the first three women to the diaconate. They were Edith Njiri, Joyce Cendi and Pamela Wilding. By the time I was enthroned as the third Archbishop of the ACK, there were more trained ordained women in the Mt Kenya region than in all other dioceses combined. Some of the women trained at St Andrew's were also serving as priests in other dioceses, such as Nairobi, Kitui and Maseno South.

In my capacity as chairman of PBTE, I called all women who were serving the church as deacons, priests and Church Army sisters for a one-day conference at my Philadelphia Place rural home. More than 30 women turned up and by the end of the day, they had formed ASWOM, the Association of Women in the Ministry, for the purposes of having regular fellowship and strengthening one another. The role women are playing in the ministry has transformed the Anglican church of Kenya and I thank God for the part I played in sensitising the church to accept the ministry of women.

Chapter 13

International Activities and Travels

During my 33 years of service and ministry, I have travelled regularly to many parts of the world. I can only summarise the activities that constituted these international travels.

Lausanne Congress on World Evangelization

As stated in chapter 3 of this book, the Lausanne Congress on World Evangelization was held in Switzerland in the summer of 1974. The congress was convened by Billy Graham and his team to discuss the evangelization of the world under the theme "Let the Earth Hear His Voice". After the conference, I was invited to join the strategy working group, which held meetings in Monrovia in Los Angeles, California, USA. The group was chaired by the Revd Tom Houston, the founder of the Nairobi Baptist Church, whom I had known since my student days. The group presented its report during a conference held at Pattaya, Thailand, in June 1980. A number of theologians representing nationalities from the developing world – Africa, Asia and Latin America – (who considered themselves as representing two-thirds of the world) were dissatisfied with the way the conference was going, saying it was avoiding critical issues that they felt concerned them and that were relevant to their situations back home. I called for a special meeting of theologians from developing countries and we drafted a letter of protest, which was circulated to all attendants by Chris Sugden, whom I had met for the first time in

Bangalore in 1978. One-third of the delegates came to the meeting that I called and chaired. This gathering led to the formation of what later became the International Fellowship of Evangelical Mission Theologians (INFEMIT). I outline the issues that led to this development in more detail on page 134.

I also attended a consultation on the relationship between evangelism and social responsibility held at the Reformed Bible College in Grand Rapids, Michigan, USA, from 16-23 June 1982. The consultation was jointly sponsored by the Lausanne Committee for World Evangelization and the World Evangelical Fellowship (WEF). Fifty evangelical leaders from 27 countries attended the consultation. The participants represented a broad spectrum of theological perspectives. The final statement of the consultation appeared as *The Grand Rapids Report on Evangelism and Social Responsibility: An Evangelical Commitment*, which was edited by John Stott and published in 1983. A valuable summary of the consultation appears in the preface to the official report written by Dr Bong Rin Ro and the Revd Gottfried Osei-Mensah, which states:

> Our conclusion was that there are at least three relationships between evangelism and social responsibility which are equally valid; namely, that Christian social concern can be a *consequence* of evangelism, can be a *bridge* to evangelism, and should be a *partner* of evangelism. It was especially pointed out concerning the latter that in our Lord's ministry, proclamation and service went hand in hand. His words explained His works and His works dramatized His words. Both His words and works were expressions of His compassion for people (Bruce Nicholls [ed.], *In Word and Deed*. Exeter: The Paternoster Press, 1985, p. 8).

The consultation made a distinction between social service and social action: "Social service covers activities related to relieving human need, philanthropy, seeking to minister to individuals and families and works of mercy. Social action has to do with removing the causes of human need, political and economic activity, seeking to transform the structures of society, and the quest for justice."

World Evangelical Fellowship

The World Evangelical Fellowship (WEF) was set up in 1951 at Woudschoten in the Netherlands by members of the formerly British-based

World Evangelical Alliance, founded in 1846. Membership to WEF is open to the national fellowship of evangelical believers in any country and represents an adequate cross-section of evangelical life and interests. There are also associate members and individual members. Membership is open to all who accept without mental reservation the statement of faith, which includes belief in the Holy Scriptures as originally given by God, divinely inspired, infallible and entirely trustworthy, and their supreme authority in all matters of faith and conduct. The statement of faith also includes belief in one God, eternally existent in the three persons of the Trinity, the incarnate Lord Jesus Christ, the salvation of the lost, the Holy Spirit, and the resurrection of both the saved and the lost.

The purposes of WEF are threefold:

a) Furtherance of the Gospel (Philippians 1:11)

b) The defense and confirmation of the Gospel (Philippians 1:7)

c) Fellowship in the Gospel (Philippians 1:5)

The World Evangelical Fellowship convened a consultation on "The Nature and Mission of the Church" held at the Billy Graham Centre, Wheaton College, Wheaton, Illinois, USA, in June 1983. The consultation, commonly referred to as WHEATON 83, brought together 370 men and women from 60 countries. I was invited to attend this consultation and to assist Patrick Sookhdeo in chairing the second of the three tracks on "The Church in New Frontiers in Missions".

I contributed a paper entitled "The Unity and Diversity of the World Wide Church", which was published in the official report of track two, edited by Patrick Sookhdeo under the title *New Frontiers in Mission*, by the Paternoster Press, Exeter, UK in 1987 (see pages 88-100). My first contact with WEF, however, was in September 1976, when I was invited to attend a gathering of the WEF Theological Commission held at St Chrischona, near Basel, Switzerland. The theme of the conference was "Church and Nationhood." I prepared a paper entitled "Church and Nationhood in a Changing World", which I presented at the conference. My paper and eight other papers were edited by Lionel Holmes, and published by the WEF Theological Commission in 1978. (See *Church and Nationhood*. New Delhi: Statesman Press, 1978, pp. 21-28.) The conference also produced THE BASEL LETTER, which was sent to member churches of WEF. During the consultation at Basel, I was requested to become the chairman of the WEF

Theological Commission. I remained the chairman until 1986, when I retired during a consultation held in Singapore.

Kenneth L. Dawning of the Africa Inland Mission came to Nairobi in 1962 to set up an Africa Evangelical office. This became the Association of Evangelicals of Africa and Madagascar in 1966. Dr Byang Kato of Nigeria became the first African General Secretary of AEAM. This evangelical association did not want any churches that were affiliated with the National Council of Churches of Kenya (NCCK) to become members unless they pulled out of NCCK. The Association behaved as if it was the only true representative of evangelicals in Africa. We reminded the Association that most of the mainstream churches in Kenya that founded the NCCK (such as ACK, PCEA, MCK, AIC, etc.) were evangelical and could not pull out of NCCK just to join AEAM.

Our views were supported by A. Morgan Derham, the General Secretary of the British Evangelical Alliance, who visited Kenya in 1967. Dawning held that "the evangelical fellowship had purposes of spiritual renewal that were distinct from some of the projects of the NCCK, such as representation of Christian interests before the government, and that there were leaders of NCCK who were also affiliated with the World Council of Churches causing confusion in the minds of evangelicals". (See David M. Howard, *The Dream that Would Not Die*" [WEF]. Exeter: Paternoster Press, 1986, p. 75.) Owing to this attitude, the main evangelical churches in Kenya (except AIC) have kept away from AEAM and have continued their membership and support for NCCK, AACC and WCC.

World Council of Churches

I have had the privilege of attending four of the General Assemblies of the WCC, beginning with the Nairobi Assembly in 1975. The venues and themes of the Assemblies were as follows;

1975 Nairobi – Jesus Christ Frees and Unites
1983 Vancouver – Jesus Christ, the Life of the World
1991 Canberra – Come Holy Spirit, Renew the Whole Creation
1998 Harare – Turn to God, Rejoice in Hope

I helped to plan the assembly held in Nairobi, especially the opening worship. Attending these assemblies gave me great inspiration as I interacted with Christians of different traditions from various parts of the world, particularly during group discussions. I was also deeply impressed by the thoroughness with which the WCC organises its assemblies. Major decisions were made after thorough discussion and debate, which usually took three weeks.

After the Vancouver Assembly, I was appointed Vice-Chairman of the Commission of World Mission and Evangelism (CWME). In that capacity I attended meetings of the Commission at Limuru in Kenya, Porto Allegro in Brazil (May 1988), Singapore, Romania, Potsdam in East Germany and San Antonio in Texas, USA. I considered myself a bridge builder between evangelicals and ecumenists and was at one time the chairman of the WEF Theological Commission as well as the Vice Chairman of the WCC Commission on World Mission and Evangelism. During the CWME meetings in Romania and prior to the Canberra assembly, I presented a paper on mission and evangelism, which was well received.

The CWME conference in Potsdam, East Germany, was held in July 1986, three years before the collapse of the Berlin Wall. I had to go by air to an airport in West Germany from where I was picked up and driven to the border wall that divided West and East Germany in Berlin. Crossing from the well-developed infrastructure of West Berlin, one could note the virtual decay of the city of Potsdam outside East Berlin. I asked one East German student who was at the conference what she hated most about her country. "It is the fact that I cannot go to West Germany to visit my relatives just because of a wall. That is what I hate most," she replied.

The delegates also visited the Mayor of Potsdam. He spoke at length, praising Russia for having delivered East Germany from the horrors of Nazism. I therefore count it as a great miracle of our time that the Berlin Wall came tumbling down in November 1989, signaling the end of scientific Marxism in Eastern Europe.

During the meetings at Potsdam, the delegates travelled by bus for an hour to Wittenberg, the city of the reformer Martin Luther. We were taken around the place where Luther once lived with his family, which became the centre of reformation. We also visited the parish church where Luther regularly preached, and the Castle Church, where Luther compiled 95 theses against Catholicism. This was where Luther was buried. We were informed that during the time of Luther, one in every two inhabitants of Wittenberg was a university student.

During the meetings at Potsdam, Dr Cecilia Sweemer gave a primary lecture on HIV/AIDS. I was so impressed by her presentation that I invited her to come to Kenya and address the NCCK National Pastors Conference, which was due to be held at the Kenyatta University from 18 to 22 August 1986. She accepted the invitation and gave the lecture to the 1,200 pastors on Tuesday 19 August 1986. At that time there were only 26 known cases of HIV/AIDS in Kenya. To the best of my knowledge, this was the first ever public lecture on HIV/AIDS in Kenya, and that it was presented to such a huge gathering of leaders who had significant influence in their communities was a huge milestone.

International Fellowship of Evangelical Mission Theologians (INFEMIT)

As indicated at the beginning of this chapter, a good number of evangelicals from the developing world and a few like-minded people from the USA and the UK felt dissatisfied with the way the Lausanne Consultation on World Evangelization (COWE) held in Pattaya, Thailand, in June 1980 was avoiding discussions on social, political and economic issues that were of concern to them. They considered themselves a critical mass representing two-thirds of the world. For instance there was a working group on "How to Reach Refugees" but there were no working groups for those who were most responsible for the refugee situation around the world. These included politicians, the armed forces, freedom fighters and those who wielded significant global economic and financial power.

I convened a special meeting of those who shared this dissatisfaction. We drafted a statement, which was submitted to the officials of LCWE and which was signed by a third of the delegates. The executive committee did not take our criticism seriously. Hence the radical evangelicals, as we were referred to, decided to convene a conference of the two-thirds world. The first conference, which I had the privilege of chairing, met at Bangkok in Thailand in March 1982. The conference was attended by 25 theologians from Asia, Africa and Latin America as well as like-minded people from the USA and Britain. The theme of the conference was "Sharing Jesus in the Two Thirds World". Thirteen theological papers on Christology presented at the conference were edited by Vinay Samuel and Chris Sugden and published by Partnership in Mission – Asia, Bangalore, India, in 1983 and by Eerdmans, Grand Rapids, Michigan, USA, 1986.

The immediate consequence of the Bangkok meeting was the need for a theological institution to assist theologians from the two-thirds world to do research leading to a Doctor of Theology degree. This idea led to the foundation of the Oxford Centre for Mission Studies. Vinay Samuel and Chris Sugden left Bangalore, India, to establish the centre. I was the first chairman of the centre and Vinay was the first Director. The centre has been in existence for more than 29 years and has helped many two-thirds world students to undertake doctoral programmes.

The second conference was held in Tlayacapan, near Mexico City, in 1984. The theme of the conference was "Life in the Holy Spirit". The conference was organized by the Latin America Theological Fraternity. Unfortunately, no written report of the conference was published. But the conference was attended by theologians from the two-thirds world. The Africa Theological Fraternity was founded during the Mexico conference. I was elected the first chairman of Fraternity and Kwame Bediako of Ghana became the first General Secretary.

The Africa Theological Fraternity organized the conference, which was held at St Andrew's College, Kabare, Kenya, in July 1985. Having held conferences on the themes of Christology (the study of the Person of Jesus Christ) and Pneumatology (the study of the Person of the Holy Spirit), it was necessary to hold a conference on God the Father. Hence the theme of the conference was "The Living God".

Seventeen papers were presented at the conference and were edited by G. P. Benson and myself and published by Uzima Press, Nairobi, in 1986. I presented a paper on "The Churches' Witness to the Living God in Seeking Just Political, Social and Economic Structures in Contemporary Africa" (see *The Living God*, pp. 119-139). The conference was attended by 54 participants, most of them from Africa. The conference coincided with the United Nations meeting in Nairobi to evaluate the UN Decade of Women. During the conference two significant developments occurred on the African continent. There was a *coup d'état* in Uganda and the apartheid regime in South Africa declared a state of emergency.

The Diocese of Mt Kenya East was celebrating its 10th anniversary since its foundation in July 1975. The 1985 conference was intended to prepare members of the Africa Theological Fraternity who were to host the third INFEMIT conference in July 1987. The conference was held at St Andrew's College of Theology and Development, Kabare, Kenya, and was attended by delegates from Asia, Africa and Latin America as well as friends of INFEMIT from the USA, Britain and Yugoslavia.

The fourth INFEMIT conference was held at Osijek, Yugoslavia, in April 1991. It was attended by 85 theologians from 32 countries, who reflected on the theme "Freedom and Justice in the Church–State Relationship". The conference was hosted by the Revd Dr Peter Kuzmic, a citizen of Yugoslavia and a leading evangelical theologian in the former communist countries of Eastern Europe. We met at the Osijek Bible Institute, a brainchild of Dr Kuzmic. We also met after the death of Josip Broz Tito, the leader who had sustained a united Yugoslavia. Soon after Tito's death, the country started disintegrating. After our meeting, the town of Osijek was bombed, though the Bible Institute was spared. It was at Osijek that I presented a detailed paper on Church and Politics in Kenya. Some of the papers presented at Osijek appeared in *Transformation Magazine*, Vol. 8, No. 3, 1991. The conference prepared and adopted the declaration of Osijek on "Freedom and Justice in Church State Relationships".

Pastors' Conferences

In the late 1970s, the NCCK established a Pastors' Conference desk and I was requested to be its first chairman. The committee started planning for the first National Pastors' Conference in about 1977. The first National Conference was held at Kenyatta University from 8 to 12 September 1980. I chaired the meetings of the inaugural conference in my capacity as the chairman of the NCCK and also the chairman of the Pastors' Conference Committee. The Revd Dr John Stott led the Bible studies and Ugandan bishop Festo Kivengere was the main speaker. Kivengere had played a great role in the Christian revival in Uganda but had had to flee his country for speaking out against the oppressive leadership of dictator President Idi Amin. This conference brought together pastors from various denominations and faiths from all over Kenya.

The second National Pastors' Conference was held in August 1986 at the same venue at Kenyatta University. About 1,200 pastors and their wives attended the conference. Once again Dr Stott and Bishop Kivengere were among the main speakers. The conference is remembered more for its rejection of a resolution of the ruling party KANU that was adopted by a National Delegates Conference held at the Kenyatta Conference Centre about the same time. The resolution declared that all electoral positions in Kenya would be contested through a queuing system of voting under which one had to stand in line and the vote was one's physical presence. I will elaborate this dark phase of Kenya's history in the next chapter.

Early in 1979, I was invited by Jack Dain to join him as a speaker during the meetings of bishops from the Church of South India, North India and Bangladesh that were held in New Delhi. During this visit, I addressed the Pastors' Conferences of the Dioceses of Bangalore and Madras. This was the first time I had met Vinay Samuel and Chris Sugden, who have remained close friends and partners in the Gospel ever since. While in New Delhi, I had the privilege of meeting Indira Gandhi, the Prime Minister of India and daughter of the first Prime Minister of India, Jawaharlal Nehru.

World Vision International was particularly interested in organising and facilitating Pastors' Conferences all over the world. Samuel Kamaleson had been appointed by World Vision to co-ordinate the Pastors' Conferences. Kamaleson invited me to join him as one of the speakers at a conference of Aborigine Pastors held in the city of Adelaide in Australia. This was a very interesting conference which brought together Australian Aborigine church leaders to share the blessings and tribulations of their ministry to their own people.

Kamaleson also invited me to join him in another Pastors' Conference held in the city of Bangui in the Northern Philippines. There were protests from some fundamentalist pastors because the organizers invited the local Roman Catholic Archbishop to address the conference. One of the things that shocked me especially in Manila, the capital city of the Philippines, was to see so many young street girls holding little babies and begging for money at the traffic lights.

I attended another pastors' conference in the Transdanubian region of Hungary near Lake Belaton, the largest lake in central Europe. I was also there at the invitation of Kamaleson. The delegates appeared to be very unhappy for reasons I could not quite understand. They did not reflect Christian joy or say with St Paul, "Rejoice in the Lord always and again I say rejoice" (Philippians 4:4).

I am most grateful to Samuel Kamaleson for having given me opportunities of ministering to pastors in various parts of the world. Being in those gatherings was also a great blessing to me, because the pastors also ministered to me and I was able to share what I gained with the clergy of the dioceses I served in Kenya.

Visit to Burma (Myanmar): 18 November to 8 December 2003

A year after my retirement in 2002, I was requested by Roger Bowen, who was then the General Secretary of Crosslinks (formerly the Bible

Churchmen's Missionary Society), to pay a visit to Burma on behalf of the organisation. I could not get a visa to go to Burma from Nairobi and I had to travel to London to obtain one. I stayed for a week at the Oxford Centre for Mission Studies, where I was hosted by my good old friends Vinay Samuel and Chris Sugden. After seven days of waiting, I got a visa and travelled from Heathrow Airport to Bangkok in Thailand and then changed plane for the short flight to Rangoon, the capital city of Burma.

I attended some sessions of the Provincial Synod held at Myitkyina in the North and led Bible studies on the three ministries of Jesus, teaching, preaching and healing, as recorded in Matthew 9:35-38. We thoroughly enjoyed the cultural entertainment by the youth of Kachin. After the Council meetings we visited the mountain town where their British colonisers had once settled. We addressed theological students in preparation for the ministry of the Church. We traveled from Mandalay to Toungoo by train, a twelve-hour journey. This was a very taxing experience for me as the train was overcrowded. We had a wonderful time with the Bishop of Toungoo, who was also the Dean of the Province. We then went to the Yangon, where we were well received by Samuel San Si Htay, the Primate of the Province of Burma. We visited the school for blind and deaf children and addressed students at the Holy Cross Theological Seminary. On the last Sunday, I preached at the Anglican Cathedral on the theme "Render to Caesar what is Caesar's and to God what is God's".

Myanmar, which until 1989 was known as Burma, has an area of 671,000 square kilometres and is sandwiched between Thailand and Laos to the east and Bangladesh to the west with India and China bordering on the north. On 4 January 1948 Myanmar became independent from the British. Almost immediately the new government faced total disintegration and suffered a series of civil wars. Myanmar has been ruled by the armed forces and their political junta with an iron fist. In 1990 the military government allowed the first free elections in 30 years, which were won by the National League for Democracy (NLD) led by Aung San Suu Kyi, daughter of national hero Bogyoke Aung San, who was assassinated in 1947 but is considered the father of modern-day Burma. Her party won 59% of the national votes and 81% of the seats in Parliament.

The military government however refused to hand over power to her and put her under house arrest. She had already been under house arrest before the elections. During my visit to Rangoon, I tried to visit her home but I was not allowed to enter her compound. In October 1991 she was honoured with the Nobel Peace Prize as a tribute to her selfless leadership of Burma's pro-democracy movement. Elections were held again in November 2010 but her party boycotted the elections as a sham. She was released from house arrest and given a hero's welcome by her supporters. It now seems her release will herald the end of military rule and the dawn of new hope for the country.

The total number of Christians in Burma was estimated to be about 4 million of the total population of 55 million in 2000. The largest Christian denomination in Myanmar is the Burma Baptist Convention, which owes its origin to the pioneering activity of American Baptist missionaries. Other Protestant churches include Lutherans, Methodists, Salvation Army, Assemblies of God, Presbyterians and Anglicans.

In 1961, Buddhism, the largest single religion in Burma (85% of the population) was declared the state religion, though the rights of minority religions were guaranteed. Christian schools and hospitals were nationalised in 1965 and 1966, with the exception of seminaries and medical institutions. In 1966, the government refused to renew the residence permits of all foreign missionaries who had not worked in the country before independence. Nearly 375 missionaries, the majority of them Roman Catholics (234) were expelled; 29 Anglican missionaries were also expelled. Since 1976, however, the churches have not been interfered with.

The BCMS missionaries arrived in Burma in 1924 and directed their attention to upper and western Burma. The Anglican Church is relatively small and introverted and appears to suffer from an inferiority complex, having no dynamic vision for evangelism. It has not clarified its theology of church-state relationships and is scared to challenge the injustices of the military government.

What shocked me most during my visit was the large number of lorries transporting logs of precious wood. Indeed, deforestation poses the greatest threat to the inhabitants and the wildlife there. The state-owned Myanmar Timber Enterprises accounts for most of the logging undertaken throughout the country. The most valued woods are teak and cherry wood. Illegal logging in areas of the country controlled by the insurgent armies continues unabated. The timber is smuggled mainly to China.

Student (1955-59) at Kangaru Secondary School, Embu with Joseph Mwangi. (Chapter 2)

Student at Royal Technical College Nairobi 1960 (Chapter 2)

As chairman of the Christian Union in 1962 welcoming Rev John Stott, the leader of the first mission to Royal Technical College, Nairobi in the University of East Africa, later to become the University of Nairobi (Chapter 2)

Graduated from the University of East Africa B.A. of London University 1964 (Chapter 2)

With grandchildren
Kirk David Gitari
Mwendwa and
Splendour Grace
Wanjiru, 2005

My mother,
Jessie Njuku Mukuba

With clergy outside St Paul's Cathedral Embu, 1987

St Paul's Cathedral, Embu Consecrated in 1987

With the staff of St Andrew's Kabare after the attack on my house 21 April 1989 (Chapter 22)

On June 30 1990, the Diocese of Mount Kenya East was split into two, the Diocese of Kirinyaga and the Diocese of Embu. After the farewell service held at St Paul's Cathedral, Embu, I was escorted to the boundary of the two dioceses (Rupigazi River). The Embu people bade me farewell and the Kirinyaga people in a convoy of 120 vehicles received me and escorted me to St Thomas Cathedral Kerugoya 40 kilometres away where prayers were held for the new diocese which I served from 1990-1997. (Chapter 6)

Ordaining Pamela Wilding as one of the first three women priests of the Diocese of Kirinyaga at St Andrew's Kabare June 1991 (Chapter 12)

With Rt Rev Eliud Wabukala Bishop of Bungoma (now the fifth Archbishop of the ACK)

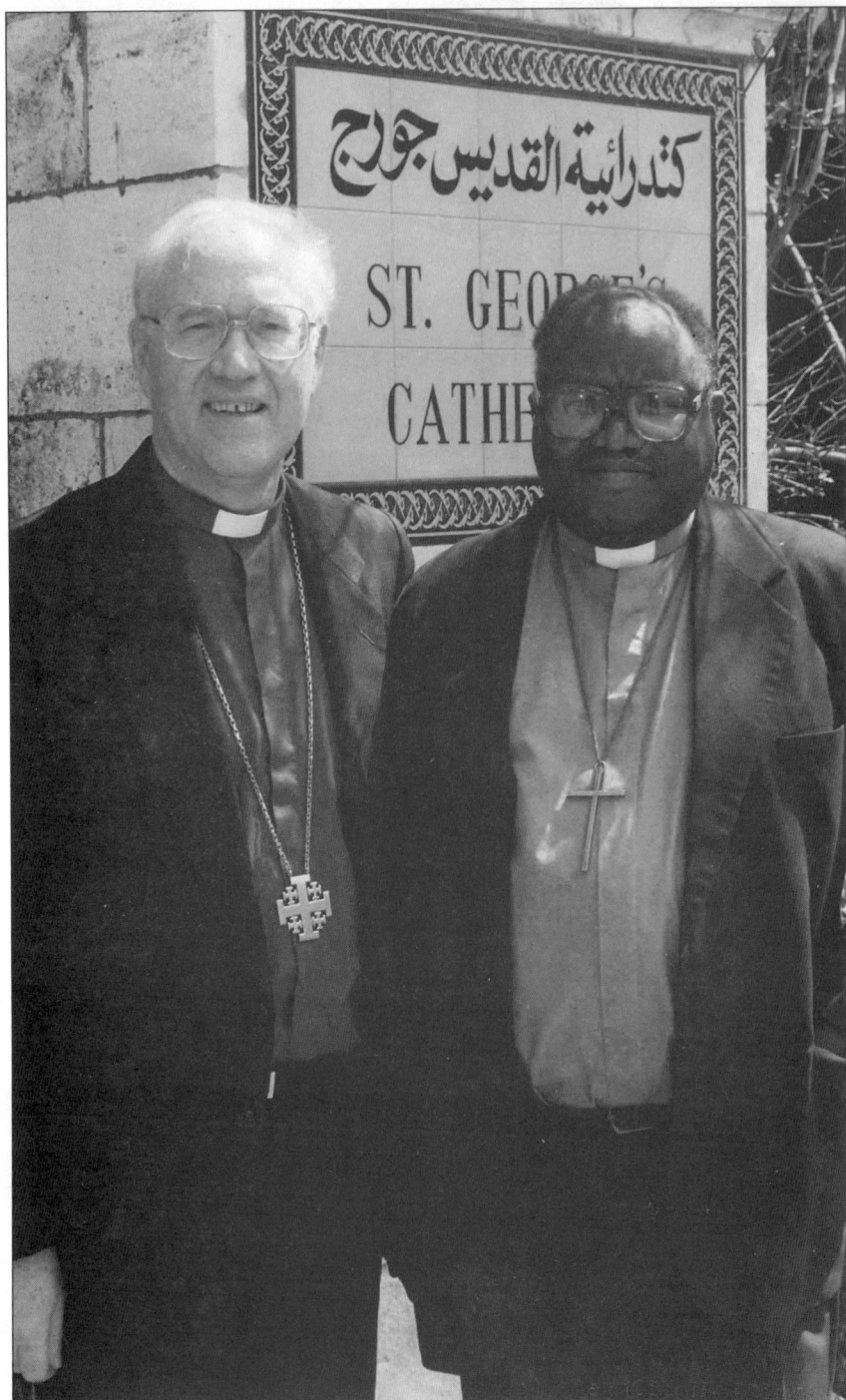

With Archbishop George Carey of Canterbury at St George's Cathedral Jerusalem, 14th March 1997 for Primates' Meeting (Chapter 15)

Presenting BD Degree to Peter Andrew as best student as Chairman of the College Council of St Paul's University, Limuru, 2000

With Bishop Samir Kaffity of Jerusalem and the Middle East (centre) and President Yasser Arafat outside the Yasser Arafat's offices in the Gaza Strip March 14 1997 (Chapter 15)

Chairman of the House of Bishops of the Anglican Church of Kenya 1997-2002 in the Chapter House 22 January 1998 (Chapter 11)

Chapter 14

Rwandan Genocide

As the World and Church Watched...

In 1994, the world watched in shock as the people of Rwanda turned against each other. In about 100 days, 800,000 people were dead. The official death toll announced by the government was even more morbid. They announced that 1,174,000 people had died in the period. This can be translated to mean that an average of seven people were killed every minute, 400 every hour and in all a whopping 10,000 people lost their lives daily, 20% of whom were Hutu and 80% Tutsi. Rwanda had a population of 7.3 million people; 84% of them were Hutu, 15% Tutsi and 1% were the marginalized pigmoid, the Twa. The first day of genocide was 7 April 1994, a day after the aeroplane carrying President Juvenal Habyarimana of Rwanda and President Cyprien Ntarymira of Burundi, who were both Hutu, crashed as it was about to land at Kigali Airport. The death of these two presidents served as the catalyst for the genocide.

The cause of this worst genocide in modern-day Africa can be traced back to the machinations of the Belgian colonial government, which supported the Tutsi monarchy. The Tutsi, though a small minority, were the ruling class and they subjected the majority Hutu to servitude.

During the 1950s, the Hutu majority became more resistant and in 1962 the Hutu overthrew the monarchy and established a republic headed by Gregoire Kayibanda. The regime persecuted the Tutsi in turn, especially those who constituted the aristocracy. Many of the most educated Tutsi fled the country to take refuge in Uganda, Kenya and other neighbouring countries.

Large numbers of Tutsi refugees in Uganda joined the National Resistance Movement, which eventually removed Idi Amin from power. They created a separate Tutsi movement with some 6,000 warriors, who invaded Northern Rwanda to try to regain power. This invasion caused great concern among the Hutu. The magazine *Kangura* was the Hutu response to the Tutsi journal *Kanguka*. Active from 1990 to 1993, the publication was instrumental in stoking Hutu disdain for the Tutsi on the basis of their ethnicity, rather than on that of the previously existing tensions based on economic advantage. The *Kangura* journal published the ten Hutu commandments, which summarized the Hutu ideology of hatred of the Tutsi. The commandments were taught in schools.

In August 1993, the Tutsi rebels and the Hutu administration held a peace conference in Arusha and signed the Arusha Accords, 5 protocols and treaties to end civil war. The accord proposed a government of national unity with representatives from all political parties, including the Rwandan Patriotic Front (the Tutsi rebel group). The extremist Hutu Coalition Group for the Defense of the Republic (CDR) was strongly opposed to sharing power with the RPF and refused to sign the Arusha Accords but later put pen to parchment. However the RPF opposed the accords in turn.

But the government of Rwanda had organized the genocide long before the death of the Presidents of Rwanda and Burundi in the aeroplane crash in early April. The Rwandese militia had already recruited about 30,000 members (or one militia member for every ten families) and they were organized nationwide. The genocide was openly discussed in Cabinet meetings. Caution, ethics and professionalism were thrown to the wind as the media, both electronic and print, freely broadcast and published statements of hate. It is to be highly regretted that the church leaders, both Catholics and Protestants, failed to intervene or condemn the hostility that fuelled the embers of genocide.

During the genocide the international community did very little to stop the ethnic cleansing at Rwanda's greatest point of need. The United Nations Security Council was reluctant to have the UN involve itself in the internal affairs of Rwanda. In addition, the UN peacekeepers were sent with specific instructions not to interfere unless a fellow peacekeeper was in danger. When President Bill Clinton visited Rwanda in March 1998, he stated that "the biggest regret" of his Presidency was not acting decisively to stop the Rwanda genocide.

Rwandese Patriotic Front (RPF) Renewed Invasion

The Rwandese Patriotic Front (RPF) battalion of Tutsi rebels stationed in Kigali under the Arusha Accords came under attack immediately after the shooting down of the plane carrying the president. The battalion fought its way out of Kigali and joined up with RPF units in the north. The resulting civil war raged concurrently with genocide for two months. The Tutsi rebels, though few, fought their way from the North, occupied the capital and won the war. Approximately two million Hutu participants in the genocide fled from Rwanda to Burundi, Tanzania and the Democratic Republic of Congo. Thousands of them died in epidemics such as cholera and dysentery. Later, many were repatriated to Rwanda. The victorious RPF organized a coalition government. It was called the Broad Based Government of National Unity. Its fundamental law is based on a combination of the Arusha Accords and political declarations by parties. The first post-war presidential and parliamentary elections were held in August and September of 2003 respectively. The current government prohibits discrimination on the basis of ethnicity, race or religion. In March 2000, Kagame became the President of Rwanda. On 25 August 2003 he won the first national elections since the RPF took power in 1994.

The biggest problems facing the Government of National Unity are the integration of the more than two million refugees, ending the insurgency among ex-soldiers and *interahamwe* militia who are mainly Hutus and the victorious Rwandan Patriotic Army in the north and south-west of the country. In addition to mass killings during the genocide, there were numerous sexual assaults against the Tutsi women. Military leaders encouraged and ordered Hutu men to rape Tutsi women as an instrument of war. In the 1996 report on Rwanda, the United Nations Rapporteur stated that "rape was the rule and its absence the exception". Estimates were that between 250,000 and 500,000 women and girls were raped. The proximate result was that 70% of all sexual assault victims from the Rwandan genocide are reportedly infected with HIV. The Broad Based Government of National Unity, under a democratically elected president, Paul Kagame, must be commended for the efforts it has made in bringing peace and economic recovery to Rwanda even though a lot more can still be done.[6]

6 Additional material in this article is extracted from Wikipedia (accessed 4 May 2011).

Pastoral Visit to Rwanda After the Genocide

As the fighting in Rwanda subsided, CAPA held a meeting in Botswana in November 1994 where it was resolved that a strong delegation of the organisation be sent to Rwanda on a pastoral visit. In preparation for the main CAPA delegation to Rwanda, the chairman of CAPA, the Most Revd French Chang-Him, requested the Ven. John Kago, the General Secretary of CAPA, Bishop Simon Chiwanga of Tanzania and myself to make the preliminary pastoral visit there. Bishop Chiwanga was not able to join the preliminary delegation. It was therefore left to the Ven. John Kago and me to make the initial pastoral visit and I prepared the report. We arrived at Kigali International Airport at about 11.00am and were met by Bishop Jonathan Ruhumuliza, the Coadjutor Bishop of Kigali Diocese and Bishop Alexis Bilindabago, the Assistant Bishop of Kigeme Diocese. We were rushed to Kigali Anglican Cathedral where 400 worshippers were anxiously waiting to welcome us.

Within the first few minutes in the cathedral we had learnt a lot. The vestiges of war were evident; the walls were still defaced and the broken window glass of the beautiful cathedral was yet to be replaced. I was requested to preach at rather short notice but I accepted the offer. I expounded on Philippians 4:1-9. After the sermon, the congregation sent word that they had two questions for the CAPA visitors. We accepted the request though we did not feel competent enough to answer questions about Rwanda before orientation.

The first question was asked by a lady: "Why have you come here and where have you left our bishops? Why didn't you come with them?" Five of the bishops had taken refuge in Kenya.

The congregation clapped her for asking that question. The questions that followed were direct attacks on the Coadjutor Bishop of the diocese, Ruhumuliza.

The questions went along these lines: "How valid is the election of Ruhumuliza and why did he assume the responsibility of the diocesan bishop by entering the Cathedral carrying the Episcopal staff while Bishop Adonia Sebumunguri is still alive and well though staying in Nairobi?"

They even read a copy of a letter that Bishop Ruhumuliza had written to the Revd Jose Chipenda on 12 May 1994. He had written:

> After the settling in of the new government, we see that things are changing in a good way. The ministers are doing their best to bring back peace in the country although they are facing many problems.

The bishop was asked "how on earth" he could say in May 1994 that things were changing in a good way when the government in power at that time was responsible for the killing of thousands of citizens of Rwanda. It appeared to us that the questions were meant to humiliate the bishop, who remained calm and composed. These were only our first moments in Rwanda, yet we had found ourselves deeply immersed in the realities of the Episcopal Church there. I must say here that Jonathan was the first Hutu Bishop to return to Rwanda after the genocide in August 1994.

On Monday 16 January, Bishop Ruhumuliza took us to Ruhanga, 28 kilometres from Kigali, the setting of incredible events during the genocide. One day in April 1994, the militia came to Ruhanga Episcopal parish and demanded that the Tutsi be separated from the Hutu so that the Tutsis could be killed. The Christians with one voice said, "Here in Ruhanga there are no Tutsis or Hutus, as all people are one in Christ." As the militia were rather few, they went back to Kigali for reinforcements. When they returned, people took refuge in the church assuming that the church was safe. The militia shot everyone in the church, both Hutu and Tutsi, and killed a total of 150 people. The vicar and his wife were killed and the vicarage burnt. The soldiers buried the 150 people in two common graves using tractors. The church was abandoned and worship did not resume until October 1994. On 17 December 1994, Bishop Ruhumuliza confirmed 159 candidates. Those who died at Ruhanga died because of their faith in Christ, in whom there is "neither Jew nor Greek, there is neither slave nor free, there is neither male nor female…" (Gal. 3:28).

During the afternoon of Monday 16 January, Bishop Alexis Bilindabago took us to Gahini, the oldest station that CMS missionaries had set up in Rwanda. The first missionaries had arrived in Gahini from Uganda in 1921. It was there that the East African Revival Movement began in 1934. Dr Joe Church (from the UK) and Blasio Kigozi and Yasio Kimuka, who were born of Mugandan parents, spent many hours praying for a revival. From Gahini the revival spread to Uganda, Kenya and Tanzania. The impact of the Revival Movement is still being felt throughout East Africa.

The Hutu militia invaded Gahini in April 1994 and started killing the Tutsi. Many of them had wanted to take refuge in the Episcopal church but the Revd Titus Ruvugabigisi would not allow them in. So many Tutsi went to take refuge in the Roman Catholic church four kilometres away. The militia threw grenades into the church over a period of three days. A total of 6,000 Tutsi were killed.

During our visit there we met Helen Nsinyumurinya, a lady who spent two weeks among the dead in the Roman Catholic church. It was a very traumatising period for her. The militia also destroyed the Gahini Mission Hospital in search of the Tutsi. The RPF liberators reached Gahini on 17 April 1994 and many Hutus had to run away. Revd Titus, the vicar of the parish, and his wife were killed by a mob for their refusal to protect the Tutsi.

Before we returned to Kigali that evening, we had a discussion with eight people who had just returned to Gahini after having been refugees in neighbouring countries for more than thirty years. They were:

- The Revd Misheck Nvuni Ngoma, who lived in Uganda for 33 years
- The Revd Canon Gideon Kabano, who lived in Tanzania for 37 years
- Enock Kayumba, a lay reader, who lived in Uganda for 33 years
- Nicodemus Nwabarida, who lived in Uganda for 33 years
- Dinah Shalita, who lived in Uganda for 33 years
- Augustine Ngwabarida
- Helen Nsinyumuriwa, the resident of Gahini who escaped death narrowly in April 1994 and stayed with the dead at Karuambu Roman Catholic Church for two weeks
- Majoro Muriel, who ran away from Gahini and Rwanda in 1961 and has now returned after 33 years

The Revd Patrick Butera, the new vicar of the parish, was unable to be with us. Our host was Majoro Muriel, who was by then occupying the bishop's house (because the bishop was away).

Majoro seemed to be the natural leader of the new community, which was mainly composed of returnees. Under her leadership, life in Gahini was returning to normal. There was an orphanage, a school and a hospital at the Gahini Mission Station and they were all functioning.

The greatest concern of this new community was that they had no bishop. They intimated that unless the bishops who ran away returned to their flock, they would lose their authority to govern the church. "How do they expect Christians to obey their directives issued from Nairobi?" Bishop Alexis Bilindabagabo did everything possible to set an appointment for us to meet government authorities but in vain. This was mainly because of the short notice of our visit to Rwanda.

However there were government representatives at the funeral of the Most Revd Augustine Ndandali, formerly the Archbishop of Burundi, Rwanda and Zaire, who had died at the Nairobi hospital and was buried at the altar of his cathedral in Butare on Wednesday 18 January 1994. I preached at the funeral, which was attended by about a thousand people. During the sermon I made it very clear that church leaders should not be too close to the powers that be. They should keep a critical distance so that when the governing authorities do what is right and just they are supported and praised and when they do what is wrong in the eyes of God they are criticised fearlessly. "Our relationship with authorities should be like our relationship with the fire," I said. "If you go too close to the fire you get burnt and if you go too far away from the fire, you freeze. Hence keep a safe distance," I concluded. The sermon was greatly appreciated by the government representatives who attended the funeral.

On Tuesday 17 January 1995, we held three meetings with three separate groups of church leaders. In the morning we met three priests of the Diocese of Kigali who were all returnees.

The Revd Anastasis Kajugiro

He was a refugee in Burundi for 34 years. When RPF won the war, he returned to Kigali only to find that the cathedral was closed and only dogs were roaming around the site. On 17 January 1995, he started mobilizing people and worship at the cathedral resumed. Though he was not licensed by the bishop, there was no doubt that he was effectively the provost of the cathedral.

The Revd Francis Karemera

He was a refugee in Uganda for 34 years. Francis has been assisting in leading English services at the cathedral.

The Revd Prudence Zachary Ngarambe

Prudence left Rwanda with his parents when he was a baby. They took refuge in Uganda, where Prudence undertook general education. During the reign of terror of Idi Amin, Prudence ran away to Kenya and studied theology at Pentecostal Assemblies of God College at Nyang'ori near Kisumu. He was appointed a pastor of the PAG church but decided to become an Anglican. After serving for a while as an evangelist in one of the parishes of the diocese of Mt Kenya East, he joined St Andrew's College, Kabare. I ordained him as deacon and priest and he served in a number of parishes. He then joined St Paul's United Theological College, Limuru, for three years and graduated with a Bachelor of Divinity. After teaching at St Andrew's, Kabare, for a while, he went to take a two-year Masters program in Seoul, South Korea. By the time of the writing of this book he had served as Education Secretary in the diocese of Embu for two years. He has recently returned to Rwanda and has joined the team of returnee clergy.

These three returnee clergy expressed great concern that the bishops who ran out of the country were staying away too long before returning to their flock. The longer they stayed, the more the vacuum they left became bigger. They also stated that their reluctance to return could be interpreted as an admission of guilt for having been compromised by those who were responsible for genocide in April and May 1994. They alleged that when the interim government relocated to Gitarame, some bishops moved with that government. The three clergy rejected the six resolutions adopted by the bishops of Rwanda who met in Nairobi on 15 December 1994. They urged CAPA to assist the church in Rwanda to reorganise parish councils, diocesan synods and provincial synods so that they could start operating once more.

The second meeting was attended by representatives of clergy from four dioceses:

Diocese of Kigali:
> The Revd Augustine Rurinda
> The Revd Josiah Sedegeiah

Diocese of Butare:
> The Ven. Ndoreraho Uzziah
> The Revd Murechesi Ernest

Diocese of Shongwe:
> The Revd Jerad Karimba
> The Revd Mutimura John

Diocese of Kigeme:
> The Ven. Joash Ruchikanshuro

Except for the Revd Josiah Sedegeiah, who had returned from exile in Burundi, all the clergy present had never fled into exile and had experienced first-hand the horrors of the genocide. They informed us that the war left many people dead and that many had fled to Zaire and other neighbouring countries. They admitted that the church in Rwanda had not reflected seriously on the whole question of church-state relationships. Joash said that sometimes the church tries to keep away from politics only to become a victim of politics.

Those who did not want to be involved in Tutsi-Hutu politics were seen as enemies of the respective groups. Jerad from Shongwe diocese informed us that the war left the country so devastated that poverty was the order of the day. He said that the Church in Rwanda had been forgotten even by its historic partners. The clergy emphasised the importance of the bishops returning to their flock, otherwise any resolutions they made from Nairobi or anywhere else (except Rwanda) would be of no effect to the Church of Christ in Rwanda.

They said that Christians were like sheep without a shepherd, no development projects were being undertaken and many candidates awaited confirmation by the bishops. The clergy informed us that there were many priests and Christians who risked their own lives to stand against the killings. But there were others (including bishops) who identified themselves so closely with those in authority that they could not prophesy. Had the church stood firm for justice, and had the bishops refrained from rubbing shoulders with the powers that be, then that tragedy might not have occurred, at least to the extent of becoming genocide. The clergy informed us that in the 1960s there was such great respect for church institutions and buildings that people who took refuge in churches were not harmed. But in 1994, the situation was different: many people were killed in church buildings.

Our last meeting was with the three bishops who had returned to Rwanda. They were:
- Bishop Jonathan Ruhumuliza
- Bishop Alexis Bilindabagabo
- Bishop Norman Kayumba

We informed the three bishops that their presence in the country provided the starting point of re-establishing the authority of the Church. We urged them to make themselves available to all the eight dioceses for Episcopal and pastoral duties. We recommended that in the first instance they should organise a fellowship meeting for the clergy who were inside the country, including the returnees. These meetings should be an opportunity to gather information from the clergy about the situation in each diocese. The meetings should make recommendations to all the bishops of EER concerning the future of the church. The meetings, we said, should recommend how the parish councils, diocesan synods and provincial synods should start their functions. The bishops agreed to call the meeting of all clergy on 1 and 2

February 1995. The clergy were expected to arrive at Kigali on Tuesday 31 January 1995.

After the three meetings, Bishop Norman Kayumba, the acting Dean of Province, took us to Kigeme in the south-western part of Rwanda. We drove through some of the most beautiful parts of the country. He informed us that he had had to move from Gikongoro to Kigeme to save the life of his colleague. Bishop Alexis Bilindabago had informed us that 7,000 people were killed at Gikongoro. Of these, 300 were civil servants who had requested protection from the government but were taken and killed together with other people. At Kandula, 11,000 people were killed, and 10,000 people lost their lives at Chibeho. Bishop Jonathan Ruhumuliza estimated the number of people killed within the two months range between one and two million, the majority of them Tutsi.

Bishop Kayumba pointed out to us that there was a very high number of ex-refugees who were still displaced from their homes, especially in his Kigeme diocese. On one of our trips we saw Rwandese who were returning from exile in the DRC disembark from United Nations vehicles. Apparently the government was assisting those who had opted to return to reclaim their homes and their land that had been taken over by some of their assailants.

After the funeral of Archbishop Augustine Ndandali, we were driven to Bujumbura by the Rt Revd Pie Ntrukamazina, the Bishop of Bujumbura, and the Revd Bernard Ntahoturi, the Provincial Secretary of the Church of the Province of Burundi. We arrived in Bujumbura just before the curfew, which commenced from 7.00pm and ended at 6.00am. We had a breakfast meeting with the Archbishop of Burundi, the Most Revd Samuel Sindamuka. The Archbishop agreed to participate during the Rwanda Clergy Retreat on 1 and 2 February as a facilitator. We returned to Nairobi on Thursday 19 January 1995 at 3.00pm.

Historical Facts about Genocides

Genocide or ethnic cleansing has been defined as a systematic elimination of unwanted racial, tribal or cultural groups from a society. Human history has numerous examples of genocide. When the Europeans occupied and colonized the New World they virtually hunted the Native Americans and the same happened to the aborigines of Australia. The occupation of Canaan by Israelites was made possible by elimination of the occupants of the Promised Land.

However it is the Jews who have suffered from genocide or holocaust probably more than any other people. The Babylonians forced the Jews from Palestine to exile in Persia and Media. The book of Esther is a revelation of plans to have more than 40,000 Jews eliminated from Persia, thwarted only by the intervention of Esther, a Jewess who had become the Queen. In 70 AD the Romans invaded Palestine and destroyed Jerusalem completely. The Jews were scattered all over the world and returned to Israel only in 1948 after Hitler had killed more than 6,000,000 Jews in the Holocaust of the Second World War.

Just before and after the First World War, the Armenian population of the Ottoman Empire was virtually eliminated through wholesale massacre and deportations. This was the first modern genocide, at the beginning of the 20th century. In addition to the Nazi Holocaust, as recently as 1992-1995 the Serbs committed genocide against the Muslims in Bosnia, leaving about 200,000 people dead. Black African farmers in Darfur in West Sudan have been systematically displaced and murdered at the hands of the Janjaweed, a government supported militia recruited from local Arab tribes. The genocide in Darfur has already claimed more than 400,000 lives and displaced over 2,500,000 people. The Darfur genocide has nothing to do with religion, as the majority of the people of Darfur and the Arabs killing them are Muslims.

The ethnic clashes that followed the general elections of 2007 in Kenya could be classified as ethnic cleansing, for the violence targeted people of particular ethnic, political and cultural extraction who were consequently believed to sympathise with either of the two rival parties, the Party of National Unity (PNU) or the Orange Democratic Movement (ODM). Over 1,300 people died and more than 300,000 were internally displaced. Although it is believed that the violence surrounding the 2007 election was elaborately planned and systematically executed, the Kenyan Government has so far not arrested, prosecuted or punished the planners, funders and those who murdered and destroyed property of fellow Kenyans. Six powerful individuals alleged by the prosecution of the International Criminal Court to bear the greatest responsibility for the violence have undergone confirmation of charges hearings at the Hague-based court. The court has confirmed that four of them have a case to answer. But ever since the violence, the government has demonstrated that it has not been keen to investigate and prosecute the perpetrators of the violence, even as it failed to show support for the effort of the ICC to bring the perpetrators of the crimes against humanity to justice. Every half-hearted effort in this cause is only clear evidence that impunity in Kenya has become a culture that will take a long time to eliminate.[7]

Lessons and Observations from the Rwanda Genocide

Before I visited Rwanda, I found it difficult to understand why the Hutus and Tutsi were killing one another. Unlike in Kenya, where each ethnic group lives in specific geographical areas, for instance Luos and Luhyas in Western Kenya, Kalenjins in the Rift Valley, Kambas in Machakos and Kitui and Maasai in the South Rift, the Hutu and Tutsi have lived in the same geographical area and speak the same language. The Tutsi emigrated to Rwanda many years earlier and were taller than the Hutu and had lighter skin, but they have intermarried over generations and it would be difficult to conclude accurately whether someone is Hutu or Tutsi just by looking at their physical features.

The blame in establishing the divide between the Hutu and the Tutsi peoples lies with Belgian colonial rule. The Belgians introduced separate identity cards (ID) for the two tribes. When the Belgian rule ended, they left most of the land and power in the hands of the Tutsi, while the Hutu were driven into forced labour or *Akazi*. The colonialists therefore created these ethnicities that came to hate each other over time through systematised inequality and struggle for power. The colonialists had in their usual divide-and-rule fashion created cultures to perpetuate their control over Rwanda.

Rwanda is one of the most evangelised countries in Africa. David Barrett in his *World Christian Encyclopedia*, published in 1982, predicted that by 2000 AD Christians in Rwanda would be 85% of the total population, of whom 64.7 would be Roman Catholics and 13.5% Anglicans (estimated total population 7,400,000). It is a surprise that in a country with such a high Christian population there should be genocide and ethnic cleansing. It appears as if the doctrine of the sanctity of human life was not given the priority it deserves by evangelists, preachers, priests and bishops. The book of Genesis begins by stating that on the sixth day of creation God said, "Let us make man in our image, after our likeness... So God created man in his own image, in his own image he created him; male and female he created them" (Genesis 1:26-27).

7 Additional notes by Professor Marion Mutugi, Jomo Kenyatta University.

It is this divine image in human beings which gives us intrinsic dignity or worth, a worth that belongs to all human beings by creation regardless of race, religion, colour, culture, class, sex or age. Because a human being is made in God's image there is sanctity in every person and for that reason every human being should be respected, served and loved, not exploited or eliminated. When Christians, and indeed humanity, grasp this fundamental Biblical doctrine, then they will begin to see the evils of racial or tribal discrimination, social prejudice and murder. These are an offence to human dignity and therefore to God in whose image we are made.

When Cain murdered his brother Abel, God asked him, "Where is your brother?" His answer was, "I do not know; am I my brother's keeper?" (Genesis 4:9). This answer demonstrated that Cain was arrogant, unrepentant and remorseless. Whenever there is ethnic cleansing, it is Cain striking again. And God is still asking those responsible, "Where is your brother?" They answer God arrogantly, "Am I my brothers keeper?

My other surprise is that the great East African Revival Movement originated at Gahini in Rwanda in about 1934. The message of revival was repentance, walking in the light and assurance of salvation. The movement spread to Uganda, Kenya and Tanzania. Those who were spiritually weak were strengthened and became committed members of their respective churches. It was those who belonged to the Revival Movement in Kikuyu land who kept the church alive and fearless during the time of the Mau Mau emergency. When I visited Gahini in January 1995, I was shocked to learn that 6,000 Tutsi who took refuge in a Catholic church there were mercilessly killed and that the Anglican priest who refused to allow the Tutsi to take refuge in his church was also killed. Why should these crimes against humanity take place at the birthplace of the East Africa Revival Movement? Had the message of revival became irrelevant?

When ethnic cleansing occurs where the majority of people claim to be Christians, irrespective of their denominational affiliation, it really means that they have not taken the Gospel of Jesus Christ seriously. Jesus Christ told his disciples, "You are the salt of the earth, but if the salt has lost its taste, how shall its saltiness be restored? It is good for nothing except to be thrown out and trampled under people's feet" (Mathew 5:13). In addition to giving taste to food, salt was applied to raw meat to arrest decay. We live in societies that are decaying owing to corruption, jealousy, hatred, immorality and numerous other social ills. It is the duty of Christians to arrest societal decay. Otherwise we become like salt that has lost its taste and is good for nothing.

The greatest mistake that church leaders can make is to identify their mission in this world with the powers that be in our respective countries. Our relationship with the powers that be should be like our relationship with fire. If you go too close to the fire you get burnt. If you go too far away you freeze. Hence church leaders should position themselves at a strategic point where they are free to praise and support those in authority when they do what is just and righteous before God and to criticise them fearlessly when they do what is not right.

The danger of being too close to the powers that is be is that if those in authority are removed, for instance during a *coup d'état*, the new government will consider the church leaders as having been collaborators with the previous government. As a result, those church leaders will suffer together with the previous rulers. This happened to the Coptic Church of Ethiopia when the communists removed the regime of Emperor Haile Selassie. The close relationship that the church had with the emperor was symbolised by the fact that the throne of the Head of the Coptic Church and that of Emperor Haile Selassie were placed together, side by side, at St George's Cathedral in Addis Ababa.

At one time the second Archbishop of Kenya, Manasses Kuria, published a calendar with portraits of then President Daniel arap Moi and the Archbishop on the front page. The Archbishop wanted us to sell the calendar to Christians in all the dioceses across Kenya. I informed him that my diocese would not sell the calendar as it was the most dangerous calendar that the church in Kenya had published. I asked him, "Suppose the government of Moi is overthrown? Won't that calendar be used to prove that the Anglican Church collaborated with the regime of Moi in all its mistakes?" Other bishops in Kenya followed suit in their rejection of the calendar.

Sadly, the church leaders in Rwanda were not spared during the genocide for having been too close to the powers of the day. In June 1994, the Roman Catholic Archbishop of Kigali was killed with two bishops and ten priests. If you go too close to the fire, you will be burnt! Keep a strategic distance. Finally Christians everywhere should proclaim clearly and loudly the words of St Paul: "There is neither Jew nor Greek, there is neither slave nor free, there is neither male nor female, for you are all one in Christ Jesus" (Galatians 3:28).

154

Chapter 15

Service to the Global Anglican Communion

Lambeth Conferences

The Lambeth Conferences are assemblies of bishops of the Anglican Communion that are held about once every ten years. The first conference was held in 1867 at Lambeth Palace, the official residence of the Archbishop of Canterbury in London, and was attended by 76 bishops. The conferences are chaired by the Archbishop of Canterbury. The functions of the conferences are consultative and advisory and their findings or resolutions are not binding upon any part of the Anglican Communion unless and until they have been adopted by the appropriate canonical authority. The resolutions are however significant expressions of the opinions of the Anglican Episcopate.

I had the privilege of attending three Lambeth conferences, all held at the University of Kent in Canterbury. I attended my first conference between July and August in 1978. It was chaired by the Most Revd and Rt Hon Donald Coggan, the then Archbishop of Canterbury. Those who attended the conference remember me for having seconded more than half of the resolutions. The main theme of the conference was "The Ministry of the Bishop". This was very helpful to me as I had been consecrated as a bishop only three years earlier and I had no experience in administering a parish, let alone a diocese. During this conference I met John Trillo, the Bishop of Chelmsford. The Diocese of Mt Kenya East started a partnership with the Diocese of Chelmsford that has continued to present day.

My second Lambeth Conference was again held at the University of Kent in Canterbury between July and August 1988, and was chaired by Archbishop Robert Runcie. I was requested to become a member of the Resolution Draft Committee, which was chaired by Michael Nazir-Ali, the then General Secretary of CMS. I was also requested to share the platform with Bishop David Jenkins of Durham and Bishop Bashir Jeevan of Pakistan in one of the evening sessions on the theme of Evangelism and Culture.

Bishop Bashir Jeevan spoke on the task of presenting the Gospel in the context of other faiths. He spoke with fervour for over twice his allotted time and attacked Bishop David Jenkins for not believing in the bodily resurrection of Jesus Christ. He argued that disbelief in the bodily resurrection of Jesus Christ and a claim that it was only a spiritual experience of resurrection in the minds of his disciples damaged missionary and evangelistic tasks in Asia. Bishop Jenkins was outraged by this affront and declared that he would not speak as the first speaker had already taken his time. I however persuaded him to speak as most bishops had attended the session to hear his views.

Bishop Jenkins then took the podium and spoke on "Evangelism in Secular Society". The bishop said that in the post-Christendom and post-Christian culture of Britain, with all its religious pluralism and secular approaches and practices, primary evangelism, in the sense of preaching the Gospel and receiving a positive response by which people are recruited to membership of the body of Christian believers, did not work. He said:

> To preach and practice a "churchly" gospel which endeavours to recruit people into cultic community which is aligned chiefly on their individual salvation and their pastoral care is simply to deny, or at any rate devastatingly to diminish, the actual and realistic claims of the gospel of the New Testament. (See Vinay Samuel and Chris Sugden, *Lambeth: a view from the two-thirds world.* London: SPCK, 1989, p. 64.)

I was the third and last speaker that evening. I took the microphone when the session should have ended. But I was pleasantly surprised that many bishops stayed on to hear me speak on "Evangelism and Culture: Primary Evangelism in Northern Kenya". Concerning culture and the Gospel I quoted Bishop Stephen Neill, who once said, "There are some customs which the gospel cannot tolerate, there are other customs which can be tolerated for the time being and there are customs which are fully acceptable to the gospel." I expounded a model of incarnational evangelism and gave the example of the Revd Andrew Adano, a Gabbra who was evangelizing the pastoralists in Marsabit District in Northern Kenya by living as a pastoralist. I also said that appropriate evangelism in Northern Kenya is not calling individuals to accept Jesus Christ but evangelising communities so that they can embrace the Christian faith. I concluded by stating:

> The incarnational model of evangelism is based on the perception that Jesus "emptied himself" and chose to "become flesh" and to "live among us" by entering on the stage of human history, he was able to identify himself with humanity and to reveal God and serve mankind. The incarnational model of evangelism demands our Christian presence in the world so that we may be able to share Jesus Christ with people and communities we encounter. The incarnational model also invites us to proclaim the Gospel not from a distance, but rather by penetrating communities and cultures. In the process of this penetration, the customs of the community and culture are either endorsed, challenged or transformed by the Gospel. In this way we believe we are obeying the Great Commission and as a result, the Lord is adding to our numbers those who are being saved and the church of Christ is growing. (See Vinay Samuel and Albrecht Hauser (eds.), *Proclaiming Christ in Christ's Way: Studies in Integral Evangelism.* Oxford: Regnum Books, 1989, pp. 118-119; reprinted Oregon, Wipf and Stock, 2007.)

In their assessment of the three lectures that night, Vinay Samuel and Chris Sugden noted that Bishop Jenkins saw in Bishop Gitari "someone who had taken the given gospel, applied it creatively and made it work. For it seemed that Bishop Jenkins recognized in Bishop Gitari's example a contemporary situation where the gospel was at work. Bishop Jenkins could not say the same about his hard situation in England with David Gitari's degree of confidence and certainty, but he was open to examining the situation from outside his context and learning from it." (Samuel and Sugden, *Lambeth*, p. 69.)

It was in my presentation that I raised the issue of church and polygamy. I appealed to the conference to revisit the decision of the 1888 Lambeth Conference, which had resolved that "persons living in polygamy be not admitted to baptism, but that they be kept under Christian instruction until such a time as they shall be in a position to accept the law of Christ." The conference agreed to review that resolution and resolved that people who were polygamists before becoming Christians could be baptised with their wives and children after further instruction. Putting away all wives except one should not be a condition for baptism. (See further David M Gitari, "The Church and Polygamy", *Transformation Magazine*, Vol. 1 No. 1 January-March 1984, Oxford Centre for Mission Studies, www.ocms.ac.uk.)

My comments on Church and polygamy were reported in the Kenyan media. I was rebuked by President Daniel arap Moi for going to England to ask for permission from former colonialists to allow Africans to be polygamists. He posed the question of whether I had consulted the Mothers Union of the diocese of Mt Kenya East before I went to request that the polygamists be allowed to be full members of the Church.

The Administrative Secretary of the diocese, the Revd Jepthah Gathaka, called a press conference to respond to the comments of the President. He informed him that the Anglican Church of Kenya had debated the issue and that the Provincial Synod had approved the recommendations made by the Provincial Board of Theological Education six years before the 1988 Lambeth Conference. Hence Revd Mr Gathaka said that the Bishop was reporting to Lambeth what the Anglican Church had already approved.

I attended my third Lambeth Conference in 1998 as the primate of the Anglican Church of Kenya. The Archbishop of Canterbury, the Most Revd and Rt Hon George Carey, had recommended to the University of Kent at Canterbury that it award me the degree of Doctor of Divinity *Honoris Causa*. The Bishop of Jerusalem and I were awarded this degree. The night before graduation I developed some pain in my feet and was taken to hospital and the administration there refused to release me to attend the graduation. But the Vice-Chancellor came and convinced them that it was important that I attend the graduation ceremony even though it meant taking me in a wheelchair. After the ceremony my friends Vinay Samuel and Chris Sugden took me to the Nuffield Orthopaedic Centre in Oxford, where I was thoroughly checked. They discovered the pains were caused by gout. I was also given good treatment and since that time the condition and the pains have not recurred. I was deeply moved that the Kenyan Liturgy for Holy Communion was selected for use during the opening ceremony of the 1998 Lambeth Conference. This was recognition of the work done by the Liturgical Committee of the Provincial Board of Theological Education under my chairmanship.

Lambeth Debates Homosexuality

Lambeth 1998 is probably more remembered for the debate on human sexuality. The majority of bishops from the Episcopal Church of America and the Anglican Church of Canada were in favour of Lambeth 1998 legit-imising blessings of same-sex unions and ordination of those involved in same-gender unions. But an overwhelming majority of bishops from the rest of the world were opposed to such a move. The African bishops were most vocal in opposing the blessing of same-sex unions and the ordaining of homosexuals and lesbians. I made contributions during this debate that were well received. When the vote was taken, only 70 bishops out of 770 were in favour of the blessing of same-sex unions and the ordination of homosexu-als. The Conference adopted Resolution 1.10 on human sexuality, which reads in part:

> This Conference...
> 2. In view of the fact that the teaching of scripture, upholds faith-fulness in marriage between a man and a woman in life long union, and believes abstinence is right for those who are not called to mar-riage.
> 4. While rejecting homosexual practice as incompatible with scripture, calls on all our people to minister pastorally and sensitively to all irrespective of sexual orientation and to condemn irrational fear of homosexuals, violence within marriage and trivialization and com-mercialization of sex.
> 5. Cannot advise the legitimizing or blessing of same-sex unions nor ordaining those involved in same gender unions.

The Episcopal Church (USA) General Convention of 2003 approved same-sex unions and encouraged exploration of liturgies celebrating and blessing same-sex unions. The following year, Gene Robinson, a confessed active homosexual, was consecrated the Bishop of the Diocese of New Hampshire. The Diocese of New Westminster, Canada authorised a public rite of blessing for those in committed same-sex relationships. Before Gene Robinson was consecrated, the Archbishop of Canterbury called a special meeting of the Primates, which met at Lambeth Palace on 16 October 2003. The Primates were categorical:

> If his consecration proceeds, we recognize that we have reached a crucial and critical point in the life of the Anglican Communion and we have had to conclude that the future of the communion itself will be put in jeopardy... This will tear the fabric of our communion at its

deepest level, and may lead to further division on this and further issues as provinces have to decide in consequence whether they can remain in communion with provinces that choose to break communion with Episcopal Church (USA).

This prediction has been vindicated as a number of provinces in Africa have broken communion with the Episcopal Church (USA) and rejected any form of support or partnership with those churches. (See *The Windsor Report*, Anglican Communion Office, 2004, p. 82; http://www.aco.org/commission /windsor_continuation/WCG_Report.cfm.)

The Year of Jubilee

The issue of special interest to the bishops from developing countries was international debt. I was among 80 bishops who met at Kuala Lumpur, Malaysia, in 1997 for the Second Anglican Encounter in the South in preparation for the 1998 Lambeth Conference. The church leaders from the southern Hemisphere decried "the crippling effect of International Debt" and called on "churches of the west to put pressure on their governments and on the World Bank and the IMF to respond to the many appeals coming from various quarters worldwide to make the year 2000 a year of Jubilee to cancel the two thirds world debt". Consequently debt relief became a major issue for discussion during the 1998 Lambeth Conference. The conference acted decisively to support debt cancellation. The conference resolved that:

> ...substantial debt relief including cancellation of unpayable debts of the poorest nations under an independent, fair and transparent process, is a necessary, while not sufficient pre condition for freeing these nations, and their people, from the hopeless downward spiral of poverty. (Ian T. Douglas and Kwok Pui-Lari (eds.), *Beyond Colonial Anglicanism*. New York: Church Publishing Incorporated, p. 182.)

The Anglican Consultative Council

The Anglican Consultative Council (ACC) was established by Resolution No. 69 of the Lambeth Conference of 1968. Its function was to continue the responsibilities hitherto entrusted to the Lambeth consultative body and the Anglican Council on Missionary Strategy. The Anglican Executive Officer was to be replaced by a General Secretary appointed by and responsible to the council. The first General Secretary was Bishop John Howe of Scotland, who was later succeeded by Canon Sam Van Culin. The first meeting of the ACC was held at Limuru, Kenya, in February 1972. The council was expected to meet at least three times between the Lambeth Conferences.

I attended my first ACC conference in Badagry, Nigeria, in 1984 in my capacity as a consultant in the section on Mission and Ministry. This section was chaired by the Bishop of Southwark, the Rt Revd Ronald Bowlby, while Edmond L. Browning (who later became the Presiding Bishop of the Episcopal Church of America) was the facilitator. I drafted the statement on Mission, which was discussed and refined by the group and which appears in the report of ACC – 6 (*Bonds of Affection*, London, Anglican Consultative Council, 1984, pp. 46-66). It was at this conference that I first met the Archbishop of Canterbury, Robert Runcie, though I had represented the ACK during his enthronement at Canterbury Cathedral in 1980. The Archbishop became a good friend of mine. I recall the many humorous stories he used to tell. In one of the ACC meetings he told us that when he went to Uganda an artist asked him to stand on the steps of the Namirembe Cathedral wearing his cope and mitre so that he could draw a portrait of the Archbishop. In a very short while the artist had completed his work and presented the Archbishop with the portrait. Archbishop Runcie asked him how he was able to finish it so fast. The artist replied that during the visit of Pope John Paul II, he had done a complete portrait of the Pope. This time he said that all he did was to remove the head of the pope and insert the head of the Archbishop of Canterbury. We all burst into laughter.

I attended the ACC-7 in Singapore in 1987 as a delegate from the ACK and I chose to be in Section 4, where we deliberated on Christianity and Social Order. We discussed issues such as power and politics, international debt, power through technology, media, militarism, racism, the Palestine/Israel situation, HIV/AIDS, women and men, the environment and community development. The ACC-7 requested the Lambeth Conference of 1988 to place the issue of militarism and fundamentalism on its agenda. The official report of ACC-7 was published in a book entitled *Many Gifts One Spirit* (London, Anglican Consultative Council, 1994). ACC-8 was held in Cardiff, Wales, from about 22 July to 4 August 1990. This was the last ACC that Robert Runcie attended as the Archbishop of Canterbury before his retirement. It was decided that future conferences would be held at the same time and venue as the primates' meetings.

The first joint meeting of Primates and the ACC was held in Cape Town, South Africa, in January 1992 at the University of Western Cape. The theme of the Conference was "A Transforming Mission". The conference was hosted by Desmond Tutu, the Archbishop of Cape Town. I had the privilege to ride along in the car of the Archbishop a number of times from the halls of residence to the venue of the conference. Before driving the car, he always said a prayer to commit the day to the Lord. I found him a man of great spirituality and courage.

The climax of the conference was the closing Eucharist at the Good Hope Centre with over 10,000 people present. Archbishop Tutu started by saying, "You are all very beautiful," clearly referring to the rich blend of nations and races present, for there were blacks, whites, Indians and many others. He then told the Biblical story of Joseph and Mary who could not find a room in the inn. This is what he said: "Joseph pleaded with the innkeeper, 'Can't you see how pregnant my wife is?' The innkeeper answered, 'But I am not responsible for her pregnancy!' Then Joseph said in consternation, 'But I am also not responsible for her pregnancy.'" This set the whole congregation roaring with laughter.

This was the best organised ACC conference that I had attended. As the retiring ACC General Secretary, the Revd Canon Samuel Van Culin, said:

> As we gathered at the University of Western Cape, January 1993, we saw the beauty of the land, the people and weather. We affirmed the courageous witness of the Church of Southern Africa, being hosted by the compelling person of Archbishop Desmond, and under confident leadership of Archbishop George Carey. These were experiences and encounters that made me sad – those that made me glad – all combining to allow me to end my term as General Secretary knowing fully well that out of political, ecclesial and personal struggle and suffering can come glory. (See *A Transforming Vision: Cape Town 1993*. London: Church House Publishing, 1993, p. 1.)

Archbishop Carey observed:

> The sights, sounds and experiences of South Africa overwhelmed us and constantly lifted our spirits... As the days progressed, however, we realized that our theme was particularly appropriate to South Africa, whose struggle has been aided by a strong faith in the power of resurrection. (*Ibid.*, p. 5.)

We met three years after global icon Nelson Mandela was released from prison after 27 years of incarceration on Robben Island. During the conference we had the privilege of being addressed by both Mandela and Chief Buthelezi of Zululand. At the close of the conference, we agreed on the content of a Pastoral Letter on the theme of "A Transforming Vision: Suffering and Glory in God's World" which was sent to all parts of the Anglican Communion.

It was a wonderful experience to be in South Africa just a year before independence which was granted in 1994. The joy of the black citizens was everywhere. To have daily contact with Desmond Tutu, who did so much to fight apartheid, was an experience that I cannot forget. I went back home energised and filled with joy and armed with the document "A Transforming Vision", prepared to share it with the Church in Kenya.

Primates' Meetings

Having completed three terms of membership representing the ACK in Singapore, Cardiff and Cape Town, I retired as a member of ACC and was succeeded by Bishop Joseph Wasonga of Maseno West. I however remained a *bona fide* member of Primates' Meetings during my tenure as Archbishop between January 1997 and September 2002. The first meeting of Primates that I attended was held in Jerusalem in March 1997, two months after my enthronement as 3rd Archbishop of the ACK. The meetings were held at St George's College from 11 to 16 March.

On Friday 14 March, we travelled to Gaza and were hosted by Chairman Yasser Arafat at the Presidential Palace. We then proceeded to the new medical library, which was officially opened by Chairman Arafat. We then proceeded to the refurbished church of St Philip the Evangelist and a service of dedication was conducted by Bishop Samir Kafity and Bishop Riah Abu El Assal. The service was also attended by Chairman Arafat and his wife. Lunch was hosted by Chairman Arafat and the Palestinian authority. I noted that Arafat spoke very few words to us. But this is not a surprise as Arafat was a soldier and not a politician. He presented each one of us with his trademark head scarf with black and white stripes. At 4pm we left Gaza for Erez and had vespers (a sunset evening prayer service) and supper with the Benedictines at Abu Ghosh. Tradition has it that it was in this village that the risen Lord revealed himself to Cleopas and his friends when he broke bread (Luke 24:13-35).

The second Primates' Meeting I attended was held in Porto, Portugal, in March 2000. The conference was chaired by the Most Rev. and Rt Hon. George Carey, the Archbishop of Canterbury. Plenty of time was spent discussing issues of human sexuality, especially because some bishops in the Episcopal Church of the USA had started ordaining active homosexuals and lesbians and were also blessing same-sex unions. We were visited by Baroness Linda Chalker, who gave an address on the strategy for eliminating poverty by the year 2015. Other issues discussed included international debt and the HIV/AIDS pandemic. On Friday 24 March 2000, I presented a paper on "The Role of Primates in Social Political Activities".

The third Primates' Meeting I attended took place in the USA at the Kanuga Conference Centre, North Carolina, from 2 to 8 March 2001. On my way to Kanuga, I stopped in Boston for a few days to meet the large number of Anglican clergy from Kenya who were settled there. They included Ivan Irungu, who hosted me, James Kibe (formerly a provost of St James and All Martyrs Cathedral, Murang'a), Frederick Thanji and the Revd Gatitu, both of Mt Kenya South, and Stanley Mwea of the Kirinyaga diocese. One of the significant developments in the USA was the emergence of various congregations who used local Kenyan languages for their services. One evening I addressed a congregation of about 60 Kikuyu resident in the Boston area. I was informed that there were three Kikuyu congregations in the area that were struggling with the issue of whether to be part of the Episcopal Church of America or not. I also visited the Episcopal Divinity School and met Dr Ian Douglas, who gave me a copy of a manuscript of a book he was writing, entitled *Beyond Colonial Anglicanism: The Anglican Communion in the Twenty-First Century*. I also went to New York, where I spent a night, and on the following day we travelled by air together with the Most Revd Frank Griswold, the Presiding Bishop of the Episcopal Church of the USA, his wife Phoebe and Patrick Manney. Security was so extremely tight at the Kanuga conference venue that even the Presiding Bishop himself was not spared thorough frisking. It was however very clear to the delegates that we were going to discuss sensitive issues and every measure was necessary to prevent uninvited guests from gate-crashing the venue.

Among the issues we discussed was the role of Archbishop of Canterbury in the Anglican Communion, human sexuality (especially in view of the ECUSA proposal to ordain practising homosexuals and the blessing of same sex unions), HIV and AIDS and its impact, especially in Africa, discipleship, forgiveness and mission, and canon law. At the end of the conference a pastoral letter was written and sent to various parts of the Communion.

I left Kanuga on 7 March 2001 together with Lord Hurd, who was British Foreign Secretary under Margaret Thatcher and John Major. Hurd had presented a report from the commission appointed to prepare a paper on the role of the Archbishop of Canterbury in the Anglican Communion. I returned home via Washington DC, where I visited offices of the World Bank and held a meeting with some of the members of staff. We had a candid discussion about the World Bank and its role in Kenya.

The last Primates' Meeting I attended was held in Canterbury, England, in April 2002. I went to Portsmouth en route to Canterbury to address the deans and provosts of the cathedrals of England, Wales and Scotland on the theme of "Culture and the Gospel". This is an important base of the Royal Navy and I was taken on a tour of HMS Victory, the ship used by Nelson when Napoleon's navy was defeated in 1805.

The Primates met at the Canterbury New International Study Centre from 11 to 17 April 2002. I was privileged to lead a Bible study group whose members included the Archbishop of Canterbury, the Presiding Bishop of the Episcopal Church of America and Peter Akinola, the Primate of All Nigeria. Professor David Ford gave Bible studies on reconciliation from St John's Gospel. On Sunday 14 April, I preached at Canterbury Cathedral on the theme "Blessed are they who believe without seeing" (John 20:29). This was the last Primates' Meeting that both the Archbishop of Canterbury, George Carey, and I attended before retirement in October and September respectively.

International Anglican Liturgical Consultation

The progress which the Anglican Church of Kenya had made in liturgical renewal, especially the publication of *A Modern Service of Holy Communion* in the Advent of 1989 and *Modern Services* at Pentecost in 1991, was recognised worldwide. I find this definition of liturgy by Paul Gibson very helpful.

The Church's Liturgy is the way by which it describes and celebrates its vision. Through mission we bear witness to Jesus Christ who has proclaimed the Kingdom or reign of God and taught his disciples to pray for its coming. When we assemble for worship, we recall and

recite what God has done in the lives of his people now and throughout history. In doing so we begin to learn the life-style of the
Kingdom.

I was invited to become a member of the International Anglican
Liturgical Consultation (IALC). The first consultation I attended was held in
Toronto, Canada, in 1991. The main issue we discussed in Toronto was children and the Eucharist. We dealt with questions such as: Should young children have communion alongside their parents in Anglican churches? What is
the precise meaning and place of confirmation in the Anglican understanding of Christian initiation? Must confirmation always be administered by a
bishop? These were some of the issues that the church was grappling with
then.

Bishop Colin Buchanan of the Church of England urged strongly that
baptism was a sufficient sacrament and that once someone is baptised, no
other ceremony is needed to admit them to the Holy Communion. It was
observed that in Orthodox churches, baptised infants receive Holy
Communion together with their parents. The consultation recommended
that this issue be discussed by the Provinces and appropriate action taken. It
was also recommended that adults should be admitted to Eucharist immediately after baptism. It was also noted that in the Roman Catholic Church, a
bishop can delegate confirmation services to a senior priest at the level of
vicar-general and others.

Another question we thought through was: What work would a bishop
do if the role at confirmation services was taken away? It was recommended
that when a bishop visits a parish, then his main work is the ministry of the
word and sacrament. When a bishop visits a parish then all those who have
been baptised and are already partakers of Holy Communion would be invited to come forward and the bishop would lead a special liturgy commission-
ing them to lay ministry, for we believe in the priesthood and witness of all
believers. So the bishop could commission all those who were baptised and
those who were already communicants to lay ministry and witness. The
Commission produced a report entitled *Walk in the Newness of Life* and recommended serious study of the report.

The Toronto Consultation inspired a need for participants from Africa
to have a CAPA consultation on liturgy. I was requested to convene and chair
the consultation. The consultation, on "African Culture and Anglican

Liturgy", was held at Kanamai, near Mombasa, Kenya, from 31 May to 4 June 1993. It was attended by 43 liturgists from South Africa, Central Africa, Kenya, Uganda, Tanzania, West Africa, Nigeria, Sudan, Zaire, Burundi and Rwanda. Also present was Paul Gibson, the ACC co-ordinator of Liturgy, and Bishop Colin Buchanan. I edited the report of the consultation which was published by Grove Books as Alcuin/Grove Liturgical Study No. 28.

The second IALC, held in Dublin, Ireland, in 1995 was designed to provide principles and guidelines for consideration in the Communion "as the development of Eucharistic prayers continues and members of the communion pursue a style of praying which is better inculturated, more inclusive, more aware of social dimensions of the gospel, and richer in both form and content" (see *Being Anglican in the Third Millennium*, Official Report of ACC-10, ed. James M Rosenthal, London, Anglican Consultative Council, 1997, p. 114).

The third IALC consultation was held at Kottayam, India, in August 1999. We had been scheduled to meet at the Seeri Conference Centre but police officers turned up and said that our meeting was illegal and could not be held at the centre. We were however invited by a Christian to meet at his Green Park Hotel. Some of the delegates were turned away by the authorities on arrival at the International Airport for stating that they were entering India to attend a Christian conference.

On Sunday I went to worship at the Syrian Orthodox Church. The worshippers stood most of the time during the liturgy. They sat on the floor during the brief homily. During the Communion, only the Bishop and his assistants took the elements (bread and wine). At the end of the service, which took one and half hours, the bishop blessed each participant by touching them on the face and as they went out each was given a little piece of bread.

The goal of the Kottayam consultation was "to continue reflection from the point of view of liturgy on Baptism, Eucharist, and Ministry, by development of statements on Ministry and order in the framework of a church which is defined by the Gospel and its effective expression in baptism and Eucharist, and which exists to minister in and to the world" (see *The Communion We Share*, Report of ACC XI, eds. James M.Rosenthal and Margaret Rodgers, London Anglican Consultative Council, 2000, p. 143).

I also served as a member of the steering committee of IALC for about eight years. The meetings of the steering committee were held at least once a year to prepare for the full meeting of the consultation. When I retired in

1999, the Revd Joyce Karuri Kirigia, the Provincial Liturgical Editor, was appointed to succeed me as the representative of Africa. My participation in IALC enhanced my interest in liturgy and gave me the inspiration and strength to continue with liturgical renewal for the Anglican Church of Kenya to the very end.

Chapter 16

Building Bridges

Restoring Anglican-Roman Catholic Relations

On 29 May 1982, Pope John Paul II visited Canterbury at the invitation of Archbishop Robert Runcie. The Pope and the Archbishop of Canterbury, along with representatives of the English churches and of the whole Anglican Communion, proclaimed and celebrated the one baptismal faith we all share. They also gave thanks to God for the work of the Anglican/Roman Catholic International Commission (ARCIC), whose final report had just been published. The Pope and the Archbishop of Canterbury agreed to the establishment of a new commission (ARCIC II) to continue the work of ARCIC I. Twelve Anglican and twelve Roman Catholic scholars were appointed to be members of ARCIC II. The Rt Revd Mark Santer, the Bishop of Kensington, London, UK, and the Rt Revd Cormac Murphy–O'Connor, Bishop of Arundel and Brighton, UK, were the co-chairmen of ARCIC II. Archbishop Robert Runcie appointed me to join the Anglican team of twelve in the commission.

Archbishop Michael Ramsey had made a historic visit to the Vatican in March 1966, where he met Pope Paul VI. They expressed in a common declaration the need for a programme of "growing together" with a view to restoration of full organic unity. The first ARCIC did its work from 1970 to 1982 and reached an agreed statement on Eucharistic doctrine, ministry and ordination, and authority in the church. I served on the commission from

1982 to 1989. During that time we held meetings in Venice, Rome, Dublin and New York. The primary task of ARCIC II was to examine and try to resolve those doctrinal differences that "still divide us". During the first three years we worked on the subject of justification and salvation. The agreed statement, entitled "Salvation and the Church", was published in 1987. The conclusion of the 27-page statement reads:

> The balance and coherence of the constitutive elements of the Christian doctrine of Salvation had become partially obscured in the course of history and controversy. In our work we have tried to discover that balance and coherence and to express it together. We are agreed that this is not an area where any remaining differences of theological interpretation or ecclesiological emphasis, either within or between our communions, can justify our continuing separation. We believe that our two communions are agreed on the essential aspects of the doctrine of salvation and on the church's role within it. We have also realized the central meaning and profound significance which the message of justification and sanctification, within the whole doctrine of salvation, continues to have for us today. We offer our agreement to our two communions as a contribution to reconciliation between us, so that together we may witness to God's salvation in the midst of the anxieties, struggles and hopes of our world. (See ARCIC, *Salvation and the Church*. London: Church House Publishing, 1987, pp. 26-27.)

ARCIC II produced a second agreed statement, published in September 1990, on "The Church as a Communion". On communion between Anglicans and Roman Catholics, the statement says:

> The conviction which this commission believes that Anglicans and Roman Catholics share concerning the nature of communion challenge both our churches to move forward together towards visible unity and ecclesial communion. Progress in mutual understanding has been achieved. There exists a significant degree of doctrinal agreement between our two communions even upon subjects which previously divided us. In spite of past estrangements, Anglicans and Roman Catholics now enjoy better understanding of their long-standing shared inheritance. This new understanding enables them to recognize

in each other's church a true affinity. (See ARCIC, *The Church as a Communion.* London: Church House Publishing, repr. 1998, p. 31.)

The co-chairmen of ARCIC II produced yet another statement entitled "The Gift of Authority", which was launched at Westminister Abbey on 12 May 1999. According to the co-chairmen, it was:

> ...building on the agreement about the bishop of Rome in ARCIC's previous work and offers agreement about his specific ministry within the college of Bishops concerning the discernment of truth which has been such a source of difficulty and misunderstanding. It seeks to make clear how in certain circumstances the bishop of Rome has a duty to discern and make explicit, in fidelity to scripture and tradition, the authentic faith of the whole church that is the faith of all the baptized in communion. The Commission believes that this gift to be received by all the churches and is entailed in recognition of the primacy of the Bishop of Rome. (See *The Communion We Share*, Report of ACC XI, *ibid.*, p. 246.)

My membership of ARCIC II for about seven years (1982 – 1989) was full of blessings and also frustration. It was a great privilege to meet some of the leading scholars and theologians from the two communions from various parts of the world. The Revd Professor Henry Chadwick of Peterhouse, Cambridge, was the most learned church historian on the commission. The Anglicans also had The Revd Professor Robert Wright, Professor of Church History at General Seminary, New York, the Revd Professor Oliver O'Donovan, Regius Professor of Moral and Pastoral Theology, University of Oxford, the Revd Dr Kortright Davis, Associate Professor of Theology, Howard University Divinity School, Washington, DC, and Professor John Pobee of Ghana. From the Roman Catholic Church we had Father Jean Tillard, Professor of Dogmatic Theology, Ottawa, Canada, the Revd Brendan Soane, Spiritual Director, Pontificio Collegio Beda, Rome, Italy, Sister Dr Mary Cecily Bowling, lecturer in Systematic Theology, Durham, UK, and the Revd Dr Edward Yarnold, theology tutor at Oxford, UK.

It was also a blessing to be visited by the Pope during one of our meetings in Rome. It was also exciting to be taken on a tour of the Vatican. My membership of the Commission helped me better to understand Roman Catholicism and even to eliminate some of the prejudices I had before becoming a member. The greatest frustration, I think, for all of us was that though we could worship together, we could not share the Eucharist. We attended worship daily, which was presided over by an Anglican or a Catholic alternately. An Anglican could read a lesson or even say a prayer during the Catholic mass, but we were left on our seats when Catholics went to receive the elements. We could invite Catholics to come and receive the elements when it was our turn to conduct Eucharist, but they could not come forward, for their church does not recognise Anglican orders.

There are historical reasons for this. In 1896 Pope Leo XIII in *Apostolicae Curae* rejected Anglican ordinations as invalid because of the break in Apostolic succession during the Reformation. ARCIC I had called for the re-appraisal of this verdict. As we continued with our meetings we reached a compromise that when a Catholic was celebrating the Eucharist, Anglicans could go to the communion rails, not to receive the elements, but to be blessed by the celebrant, and vice versa.

The other frustration was the limitation of our mandate. Even though the Commission provided unanimous conclusions, the agreed statement was not an authoritative declaration by the Roman Catholic Church or by the Anglican Communion, who had to evaluate the documents in order to take a position on them in due time. This of course is quite logical, but it was obvious that the Roman Catholic Church was not keen to take a position. As I was informed by Professor Tillard, the Vatican can take centuries to change its position. In view of this, it appeared to me that our work was a waste of time and I was happy to retire in 1989 after serving on the commission for about seven years. There are some Catholic doctrines, such as the Pope's infallibility when he speaks *ex cathedra*, that are no longer tenable. The Vatican will not be in a hurry to change them, but hopefully we planted a seed that will be a reference point for change when the time comes.

The other frustration was the tendency of some of the Anglican Commissioners of ARCIC II to want visible union with Rome at whatever cost. I am glad I was not party to the statement entitled "The Gift of Authority" launched in May 1999. The authors of the statement believed that the gift of authority to be received by all churches entails the recognition of the primacy of the Bishop of Rome, who in certain circumstances has a duty to discern and make explicit the authentic faith of the whole church. There are many Anglicans in our Commission who would not subscribe to this statement, as it seems to surrender our freedom of expression of our faith to one person, the Bishop of Rome, who might reject advances in theological understanding, as he did with the liberation theologians in Latin America, or impose Roman Catholic positions on such matters as family planning or ordination of women.

I must however add that the blessings I received as a member of ARCIC II far exceed the frustrations. During the Eucharistic Congress held in Nairobi in 1985, I shared the blessings I had enjoyed as a member of ARCIC II in a speech I gave to thousands of Catholics at Uhuru Park. My better understanding of Roman Catholics has given me the freedom to work closely and harmoniously with Kenyan Catholic bishops in promotion of our ecumenical activities and in the search for justice in our nation.

World Peace Conference

In April 1968, John Kamau, the General Secretary of NCCK, requested me, together with seven other Kenyans, to represent the council in the World Peace Conference, which was held in Prague, Czechoslovakia. Among the seven was Amos Kiriro, a leading Anglican layman, with whom I established close friendship during the trip; he has remained a good friend since. The invitation came from the Orthodox Church of Russia; hence we were required to travel to Prague via Moscow. There were no direct flights from Nairobi and we had to travel to Dar es Salaam, where we boarded an Aeroflot flight to Moscow. We stopped in North Yemen, where the plane offloaded arms. At that time North Yemen was fighting against South Yemen. We were then flown to Cairo and boarded a Hungarian flight that took us to Moscow. We were met by members of the Russian Orthodox Church and stayed in a Ukrainian hotel for a few days.

For the first time I found myself in a Communist country. At the hotel where we were staying different shifts of women were cleaning the same floor on hourly basis. This was to ensure full employment. There were also long queues in shopping centres, shoppers queuing to buy goods in short supply. Everywhere we went people wanted us to exchange roubles for American dollars. I asked one of our hosts, "How is Khrushchev?" the former president of the country. He told me that he had retired and had a house and a car. Because cars were in short supply one had to book and wait for at least ten years before getting the chance to buy one.

After a short stay in Moscow we were flown to Prague, where the Christian Peace Conference was being held. Most of the delegates were from the Soviet Union and other Eastern European communist countries. The most memorable speech was that of Dr Josef Hromadka, a great Czech theologian. We went to Prague when a revolt against the USSR had just taken place in Czechoslovakia. Dr Hromadka said that the people of Czechoslovakia wanted communism with a human face. Two weeks after we left Prague, the Russians entered Czechoslovakia with tanks and crushed the revolt.

I left Prague before the conference ended and flew to Moscow because I had very bad flu and did not get much help from our hosts. An official of the Kenyan Embassy came to see me. I then flew from Moscow to London to meet Dr Oliver Barclay, the General Secretary of the British Inter-Varsity Fellowship. I arrived in London on the same day that American civil rights leader Martin Luther King Junior was assassinated. We saw on television the looting of shops and the violence that followed the death of the man who had led a powerful non-violent movement against racial discrimination. King achieved more in his death than in life. The fruits of his work and his great speech "I have a dream" have no doubt influenced the thinking and policy of individuals, institutions and governments against racism and discrimination. Even though there is still much to be achieved in this area, like Moses, he had been to the mountain top and seen Canaan, as he said, even though he did not himself get into the promised land.

Back in Nairobi I attended the Martin Luther King memorial service at St Andrew's Presbyterian Church. One of the speakers was Tom Mboya, who had met King just before he was assassinated. Mboya gave a very moving speech. But he also died from an assassin's bullet in July 1969. In his death Kenya lost one the most brilliant and able politicians that the country had known.

Experiences in Apartheid South Africa

I first visited South Africa from 26 June to 5 July 1975. I had already been elected the first Bishop of Mt Kenya East in April but I had not as yet been consecrated and enthroned, which was done fifteen days after my return from South Africa. I was invited as one of the speakers for the National Student Christian Movement (SCM) of Southern Africa. The SCM was in actual fact a South African evangelical student organization. The SCM was the university students' movement for black students and there was another Evangelical University Student Fellowship for white students only. I was met at Jan Smuts International Airport by Ian Hill on Thursday 26. I spent the night at his home and the following day he and his wife took me to the University of the North, 200 miles away from Johannesburg.

At lunchtime we stopped at a petrol station to fuel the car and have lunch. Since we were in a whites-only area, Smith told me that he had to seek permission as to whether or not I could be allowed to join him and his wife in the restaurant. He told the restaurant attendant that he had an international visitor and asked whether I could be allowed to have lunch with him in the restaurant. He was asked the colour of his visitor and when he said that I was black, he was told that my food could be delivered outside but he and his wife could eat in the restaurant. "Then we will all have our lunch outside!" he responded. So we ate our lunch outside and used the bonnet of the car as the table for the plates.

The conference at the University of the North brought together students not only from the black universities of South Africa, but also from South West Africa (now Namibia), Mozambique, Botswana, Lesotho and Swaziland. I gave five Bible expositions that were well received by the students. Ebenezer Sikakane of Africa Enterprise was one of the speakers. The students sang vibrantly in their mother tongues and there was great jubilation. Andronica Poo, the Singing Sister of South Africa, also entertained us. During one of my addresses, I remarked that a visitor noting the joy in Christ in those present could not imagine they are the same people suffering from the injustices of apartheid.

In one of the afternoons, I was taken to the Holy City of Moria not far from the University of the North. The city of Moria is a centre of a very strict independent church in South Africa, the Zion Christian Church. Residents of the city and visitors must be very carefully searched so that they do not bring alcohol, cigarettes and any other "immoral items". The leader is highly venerated and it is difficult for visitors to see him. Though we had made a booking to see the leader, we could not see him as our names were not found in the "book of life". At certain times in the day, the bell is rung, and residents must assemble for worship. The members of the sect, who use the Star of David as their symbol, are trusted throughout South Africa for their honesty and hard work. They easily find employment where honest men and women are needed as watchmen, domestic workers, custodians of money, etc.

The following year, I was invited once again to visit South Africa. This time I was one of the speakers at the conference of the South Africa Christian Association (SCA), a whites-only university Christian student organisation. I arrived in Johannesburg a week after student rioting in Soweto. The Soweto students were protesting against being compelled to learn the Afrikaans language. They wanted this language to be dropped from the syllabus. The riots led to a large number of students being shot dead with impunity.

I arrived at the University of Natal in Pietermaritzburg, the venue of the conference, just before lunch on 2 July 1976. The white student delegates to the conference were given their rooms and settled down before the first session of the conference, which was to start at 8.00pm. About twenty coloured or mixed-blood students from the University of the Cape also arrived but they, like myself, were not allocated rooms.

When the first session ended at 10.00 pm, the coloured students and I were told that the law did not allow any non-white student to sleep in the university campus as it was for whites only. We were taken by bus to an ecumenical centre, seven miles away, where we were accommodated. Though I was given a room at the university where I could rest during the daytime, and though I was one of the main speakers, I was not allowed to spend a night in that room. I found it very strange that I could use the room during the daytime and not at night when I would be asleep and harmless.

During the evening of the second day of the conference, the coloured students protested. For coloured students and me to be refused rooms in the whites-only University of Natal meant that the white Christian students were not prepared to suffer for the sake of the Gospel. Yet the coloured students had themselves taken a great risk, as they had defied the student union of the University of the Cape, which punished any student group that co-operated with white students from whites-only universities by banning them from using the student union facilities. They had come to the University of Natal to protest against racial discrimination only to find the white Christian students were not prepared to suffer for the Gospel by defying unjust apartheid laws. If black and coloured students were allowed to sleep in the university, all participants would have been arrested and charged, including the hosts, for inviting coloured students to attend the conference. The following day, the twenty coloured students packed their luggage and left for the Cape before the conference had ended.

Compared with the joy I had witnessed at the conference of the black students the previous year, this conference was dull, disappointing and miserable. This made me conclude that the end of apartheid in South Africa would be liberation not only for the blacks but also for the white South Africans. For the time being the blacks were looking forward with great hope to a free South Africa, whereas the whites, though holding on to power, were filled with fear of the inevitable future.

Before I returned to Kenya I attended another conference of about 50 black and coloured university students at Cyara about 30 miles west of Johannesburg. I shared the platform with Beyers Naude, a Boer who had nearly reached the top position in the hierarchy of the Dutch Reformed Church but who became theologically convinced that the apartheid policy was contrary to the teaching of the Scriptures and was evil. He boldly fought against apartheid throughout his life despite much persecution by his own church and the government. It must have been a great joy for him to be alive when South Africa gained independence in 1994. Beyers Naude went to be with the Lord in 2004, ten years after independence.

It was a joy to meet him again in July 1996 at the Potchefstroom University for Christian Higher Education. I was invited to participate at an International Conference on Christianity and Democracy in South Africa. There I met Naude, twenty years after we first met at Cyara in July 1976. He appeared to be very pleased that his role in the struggle for the independence of South Africa was not in vain and that the Dutch Reformed Church had at last come to accept his theological position that apartheid could not be supported by the Scriptures.

Before I conclude this chapter on South Africa, I must make reference to an encounter with some white South Africans at a congress sponsored by Brother Andrew of *God's Smuggler* fame that was held in Blantyre, Malawi, in May 1978. "The Love Africa Congress" was mainly financed by white South Africans who were supporters of the ministry of Brother Andrew in smuggling Bibles to communist countries. Daniel Kyanda, a friend of mine from Uganda who was based in Nairobi after fleeing the atrocities of Idi Amin, was one of the organisers of the congress. He invited me on behalf of Brother Andrew to give daily Bible expositions on 1 Peter before about 300 delegates drawn from nearly every part of Africa. The main thrust of the congress was to inform the African delegates on the dangers of communism.

On the third morning, during my exposition of 1 Peter 2:13-25, I stated that apartheid in South Africa was making communism more attractive. I said South Africa claims to be a Christian country and yet promotes discrimination by colour by misinterpreting certain passages of the Bible and thus makes communism appear more humane. I said that the anti-communist policy of the government of South Africa could not help to end communism. Instead, as long as apartheid remains the political philosophy of that government, its policy promotes rather than curtails communism. When I finished speaking, Dr Malan, the chairman of the congress stood up and said, "We love Bishop Gitari so much that we paid his air ticket to enable him to attend this congress."

What I did not know was that my anti-apartheid stance would be the subject of tension and confrontation between blacks and whites right at the conference. At tea break, the twenty-five Kenyan delegates held an emergency meeting and called Dr Malan.

"What was the cost of the ticket of the bishop so that we can refund you and extend his stay to enable him to speak his mind?"

When I went outside where tea was being served, I was surrounded by five whites who took issue with me for challenging the apartheid policy of South Africa. All of a sudden the other black delegates came and formed another circle. I was right in the middle, a small circle of whites surrounding me and then an outer circle of about 300 black delegates.

"Stop attacking apartheid or go home," the whites said.

The black delegates responded, "If the bishop leaves the congress, we shall all pack and go home!"

Clearly the continuation of the congress now depended on whether I was to continue giving the Bible studies or leave the conference as demanded by those five whites. Later in the day, Brother Andrew called a meeting of congress organisers and me. I was asked to continue giving Bible studies but not to attack the South African government. I answered that no human being can stop me from speaking what the Holy Spirit urges me to say. Brother Andrew and the committee persuaded me to stay at the conference with no conditions as they considered my presence more critical for the success of the conference.

After independence in 1994, I visited South Africa a number of times and it was most refreshing to see the changes that were taking place. The advent of the end of apartheid in South Africa is a blessing not only to the people of South Africa but to the entire continent of Africa and indeed to the whole world.

Chapter 17

Breaking the Shackles
of Debt and Poverty

Participation in Jubilee 2000 Movement
for Debt Cancellation

> And you shall consecrate the fiftieth year and proclaim liberty
> through out the land to all the inhabitants; it shall be a jubilee for you,
> when each of you shall return to his clan (Leviticus 25:10).

During my enthronement charge as the third Archbishop of the Anglican Church of Kenya at All Saints Cathedral on 12 January 1997, I told the large congregation, "I feel greatly honoured and privileged that the Church has bestowed upon me the responsibility of ushering ACK into the 21st Century and the third millennium of the Christian era." The first three years of my term as the Archbishop of the ACK were in the 20th century (1997 to 1999) and the last three years were in the 21st century (2000 to 2002).

There was excitement throughout the world that we were about to move from the 20th century to the 21st century and many countries constructed new millennium monuments. The Christian Church throughout the world was determined to celebrate this beginning of the third millennium of the incarnation of our Lord Jesus Christ. The Church adopted the concept of the celebration of the Year of Jubilee that the Jews were commanded to observe in Leviticus 25.

The eighth assembly of the World Council of Churches, held in Harare in 1998, which I attended as a representative of ACK, was reminded, through the sabbath-jubilee tradition, that the Hebrew and the Christian scriptures offer a critical mandate:

The WCC is firmly committed to joining people of faith and communities of conscience in implementing the Sabbath jubilee mandate, sounding the trumpet and rejoicing in the hope of jubilee when debt is cancelled. We offer this policy statement for reflection by all members of the ecumenical community, call our churches to action and commit ourselves to achieving debt cancellation.

The issue of the cancellation of debt of impoverished countries was discussed at length. The G8 Countries and Bretton Woods Institutions (the World Bank and International Monetary Fund) were severely criticised for imposing conditions whose purpose is to generate revenues for debt service.

Structural Adjustment Programmes impose unacceptable conditions on debtor nations and drain them of precious resources. Unless present debt-management plans are transformed into debt-release opportunities, the devastating cycle of debt accumulation will repeat itself, condemning millions more people to suffering.

After attending the eighth Assembly and also the 1998 Lambeth conference, I felt the urge to participate in the Jubilee 2000 Campaign for Debt Cancellation. For this purpose I visited Australia and Japan.

Visit to Australia October 1999

I became deeply involved in the Jubilee 2000 Coalition Movement. In October 1999, I visited Australia at the invitation of the Most Revd Keith Rayner, the Primate of the Anglican Church. I addressed synods in Melbourne, Canberra and Perth on the issue of cancellation of international debt. I was the guest speaker at the launching of the Archbishop of Melbourne's International Relief and Development Fund (AngliCORD). In Canberra, I addressed a meeting of Australia's Council of Overseas Aid (AUSAID) on cancellation of international debt. I received a standing ovation when I addressed the Synod of the Diocese of Perth on the same issue.

Visit to Japan April 2000

The British Church Mission Society decided to send three Christian leaders from East Africa to the Japan Jubilee 2000 Campaign for Debt Cancellation. The three were the Revd David Zak Niringiye from Uganda, Joseph Ngereza from Tanzania and myself from Kenya. The Britons at CMS felt that we, coming from countries hit hard by the international debt, could make a greater impact on the Japanese government if we spoke for ourselves.

We were in Japan from 4 to 12 April 2000. I visited Okinawa and Kumamoto, where I addressed members of the Jubilee 2000 Coalition Movement. David and Joseph visited other cities. On Saturday 8 April, we addressed the Tokyo Symposium, attended by about 100 people and organised by Jubilee 2000 Japan. We addressed the symposium on the history of international debt and the effect of the structural adjustment programmes of the Breton Woods institutions on poor countries.

The climax of our visit was Tuesday 22 April 2000, which was the action day for the Japanese 2000 Coalition Movement. We went to the Ministry of Foreign Affairs led by a powerful Japanese lady to confront the officials of the ministry on the cancellation of international debt. We then visited the officials of the Ministry of Finance. Outside the building were 157 demonstrators supporting our campaign. In both ministries we were received very well. The officials were very diplomatic but repeated the same inflexible government policy of refusal to cancel debts. Despite their adamance, we believe that we were heard. It was during this visit to Japan that I bought my first mobile phone, for US $292, then an equivalent of Ksh 21,000. In those days mobile phones were very rare in Kenya.

Faith in Development Conference on Alleviating Poverty in Africa – Nairobi, March 2000

This chapter cannot be complete without reference to an important conference on alleviating poverty in Africa held in Nairobi in March 2000. This was the first ever conference that brought together the representatives of African churches and senior staff from the World Bank to discuss a topic of mutual and urgent concern: "Alleviating poverty in Africa". This first conference between African churches and the World Bank grew out of conversations between the then president of the World Bank, James Wolfensohn, and the then Archbishop of Canterbury, the Most Revd and Rt Hon Dr George Carey.

As a result of Wolfensohn's speech to the 1998 Lambeth Conference, a process began that led the council of Anglican Provinces of Africa (CAPA) to invite 137 African church leaders from 21 nations and 19 Christian denominations. The World Bank was represented by 20 senior staff, led by Callisto Madavo, the vice-president for Africa. The conference lasted five days (6 to 10 March 2000). As the Archbishop of Kenya and a member of CAPA, I was the main host of the conference and chaired a number of sessions.

The holding of this conference took many people by surprise, not least the participants. The 20 World Bank staff who attended (many of them country directors and sector managers) were eager to engage with the churches and the church leaders, and we found them to be very open to spiritual concerns and perspectives. At the end of the conference a joint communiqué was produced in an atmosphere of anticipation, enthusiasm and warm cooperation.

The full report of this conference was published in 2001 in a book entitled *Faith in Development: Partnership between the World Bank and the churches of Africa*, and was edited by Deryke Belshaw, Robert Calderisi and Chris Sugden. The foreword of the book was written by the president of World Bank and the Archbishop of Canterbury. It is a co-publication of the World Bank and Regnum Books International.

Chapter 18

The First President of Kenya, Mzee Jomo Kenyatta (1963–1978)

I was nine years old and was in Standard 3 at Ngiriambu primary school in Gichugu division, Kirinyaga District, when Jomo Kenyatta returned from England in 1946. In August 1948 Jomo Kenyatta addressed a large gathering at Kiamutugu market not far away from my home village. It was a sports day organized by three schools: Ngiriambu, Ngariama and Thumaita. My father, Samuel Mukuba, worked together with Jeremiah Kabui (Ngariama) and Richard Githae (Thumaita) to make the day a success. Kenyatta arrived at Kiamutugu in the late afternoon and was welcomed to the platform by my father. This was the first time that I saw Kenyatta and I was very impressed by what he said. During the closing prayers, when all eyes were closed, Kenyatta went quietly to his car before the Amen and continued with his journey to Embu and Meru. It was a great privilege to see the man whom everybody admired for his courage in his struggle against colonialism.

The Mau Mau emergency was declared when I was a Standard 7 pupil at Kabare intermediate school in 1952. I recall how much I was affected when I learnt that Jomo Kenyatta had been arrested. I did not see Kenyatta again until his return home in August 1961. I had followed the events surrounding his life and tribulations with much interest. I was a student at Royal College, Nairobi, when he was released but since it was August holiday, I had gone to my home village at Ngiriambu. I had bought myself a small radio and keenly followed the news of his release.

The following day, 15 August 1961, I decided to go to Gatundu to see Kenyatta. Our bus had to stop about three kilometres away from Kenyatta's home and we had to walk the rest of the journey. A multitude of humanity from all walks of life completely filled the entire three kilometres. I would agree with Joshua Nkomo, who also visited Kenyatta at this time and told correspondents in Nairobi, "…people flocked towards the house at Gatundu, in unbroken streams, on every day, anxious to see for themselves that Kenyatta was there… people crammed into comparatively small channels and vantage-points around the perimeter must have numbered about thirty thousand" (Jomo Kenyatta, *Suffering Without Bitterness*. Nairobi: East African Publishing House, 1968, p. 143.) Kenyatta came out of the house and spoke to us briefly amidst ululation.

The year leading to Madaraka day (1 June 1963) and Jamhuri day (12 December 1963) were very exciting years for the African students at the Royal College, Nairobi. We kept abreast with the activities of political parties and we often invited leading politicians of the day to come and address the students. The most popular politician with the students was Tom Mboya. I was present on the occasions when Kenya was granted internal self-government (1 June), which was celebrated on Harambee Avenue, and when Kenya attained full independence (12 December), which was commemorated at what is now known as Freedom Corner on Langata Road.

The Royal College, Nairobi, merged with Makerere University College and Dar es Salaam College to become the University of East Africa. The first chancellor was Mwalimu Nyerere, the first President of Tanzania. The first graduation ceremony was held in the great court of the University College of Nairobi in May 1964. Hence I was awarded the Bachelor of Arts Degree by Mwalimu Nyerere with President Kenyatta by his side. Since the graduands were not many, each candidate received the degree document from Nyerere and shook hands with both presidents. That was the first and last time that I shook hands with the first President of Kenya.

After teaching briefly as an untrained teacher at Thika High School (June 1964 to September 1965), I went to study theology in Britain. I returned in July 1966 to serve as General Secretary of Pan African Fellowship of Evangelical Students (July 1966 to September 1968). I then returned to Britain, completing my theological studies in June 1971.

On 5 July 1969, my wife, our little son Sammy and I were on holiday in Aberystwyth, Wales, when we heard on BBC News that Tom Mboya had been shot dead on a Nairobi street. This was a great shock to me. Mboya was a seasoned politician whom I deeply admired. He was definitely the most polished politician we had at that time, a great orator with great mastery of both the Swahili and English languages. He had probably done more than anyone else in the peaceful struggle for independence. For one week I was unable to sleep or eat properly as I thought about this great loss to Kenya and Africa. Had Mboya lived longer (he died when he was only 37 years old), I am certain that the history of Kenya could have taken a different course. As I continued following events back home, it became clear that some close associate of President Kenyatta had had a hand in this assassination.

Following the death of Tom Mboya, news started filtering through that many Kikuyus were going to the home of Kenyatta at Gatundu in Kiambu District in their thousands. They were going to have "tea", which really meant particpating in tribal oathing, to ensure that the government of Kenya remained within the house of *Mumbi*, the Kikuyu. According to Gideon Githiga, "Large numbers of Kikuyu people were to swallow an oath of a goat's meat and blood, a spittoon for the squeamish was provided at ceremonies which catered for the bureaucratic elite in Nairobi. Many ceremonies were held at the President's home in Kiambu, with oath-takers arriving in lorry-loads to have 'tea' with the President. The oathing that started as a voluntary event ended in compelling all the members of the House of Mumbi to pay allegiance to Kenyatta by taking the Oath." (Gideon Githiga, *The Church as the Bulwark against Authoritanianism*. Oxford: Regnum International, 2001, pp. 53-54.)

Many people went to Gatundu without knowing the real purpose of the visit and were deeply shocked to see what was going on. On my return from England in 1971, I talked to a number of top civil servants, who confessed to me that the oathing at Gatundu was the most humiliating experience they had had in their lifetime. They were made to squat and ordered around by unruly youth and given the most unpalatable concoction to drink. Those who resisted were beaten up and some were killed. This brought President Kenyatta into his first major conflict with the Church. Many members of the East African Revival Movement had refused to take the Mau Mau oath, because they could not mix the blood of Jesus that had washed their sins away with that of goats. Many revivalists had been killed for refusing to take the Mau Mau oath, and were willing to die rather than drink the "tea" at Gatundu with the President.

In early September 1969, church leaders went public in condemnation of the oathing at Gatundu. On 9 September 1969, 200 Christians signed a covenant against secret oaths. Protests also came from the Africa Inland Church, Presbyterian Church of East Africa and the Anglican Church of Kenya. A number of church leaders, who included Bishop Obadiah Kariuki (a brother-in-law of Kenyatta), John Cauri Kamau, the General Secretary of NCCK, the Revd John Mpayeei of Bible Society, the moderator of PCEA Church, the Rt Revd Charles Muhoro Kareri, and John Gatu went to see Kenyatta to plead with him to bring the oathing to an end. Bishop Obadiah Kariuki called an ecumenical gathering at St James and all Martyrs Cathedral, Murang'a, which was attended by thousands of people and during which a statement agreed by the synod of the Diocese of Mt Kenya was read. It stated:

> We declare our loyalty to Jesus Christ and then to the President of the Republic of Kenya Mzee Jomo Kenyatta, and his duly elected government... we deplore the beating, coercion, brutal treatment and torture resulting to death of which we have instances, being given by those in obedience to our Lord's teaching refuse to take part in such oathing... we earnestly desire an atmosphere in which peace and tranquility will be maintained in our beloved country. We therefore request the vigilance of the security forces to maintain order and guarantee the safety of the citizens. (*East African Standard*, quoted by Githiga, *ibid.*, p. 56.)

Soon after this gathering, the oathing at Gatundu came to an abrupt end. Though I was not in the country, I greatly admired the part that the Church had played in challenging the tribal oathing. As stated earlier, I was appointed the General Secretary of the Bible Society of Kenya in July 1971 soon after my return from three years study in Bristol, England. I did not have much confrontation with the Kenyatta administration until the assassination of J. M. Kariuki on 3 March 1975 (see chapter 4).

I heard the news of Kenyatta's death during the one o'clock news on 21 August 1978. Very much against the wish of my wife, I got into my car and drove from Embu to Nairobi to hold an emergency meeting with Kamau, the General Secretary of NCCK. As I drove towards Nairobi, I could see many cars driving in the opposite direction. People were running away from Nairobi to safety in their up-country homes. Many people expected trouble in the city once the news spread that Mzee was dead.

As chairman of NCCK I felt strongly that I should be in the city at a time like that. The city remained calm and quiet but had been deserted by many people. Moderator John Gatu of the PCEA co-coordinated an ecumenical church committee to prepare the liturgy for the burial of the father of the nation. His body lay at State House, Nairobi, for several days, and thousands of people went to pay their last respects. The mourners were entertained by ACK St Stephen's Choir led by Darius Mbela. *Nyakinyuas* (Kikuyu traditional dancers) who used to entertain the president when he was alive were nowhere to be seen! The non-believers have songs of joy for the living but not for the dead.

Chapter 19

The Second President,
Daniel Toroitich Arap Moi (1978–2002)

Soon after the death of Mzee Jomo Kenyatta, I went to Mombasa with my family on a brief holiday. On Sunday I preached at an ecumenical service at St Luke's Church, Makupa. The service was broadcast live on KBC. I called upon Kenyans to support Daniel arap Moi, who was acting President. When Moi was elected the second President of Kenya, I in my capacity as Chairman of NCCK was the only church leader requested to say a prayer during the swearing-in ceremony that was held at the Agricultural Show Grounds in Nairobi. Many groups of people started going to pledge loyalty to the new president at State House, Nairobi. The member churches of NCCK requested me to lead a delegation to State House so that they could pledge their loyalty. I found myself at a loss in choosing the words to use in pledging loyalty. I felt our loyalty to the President could not be unconditional since a time might come when our loyalty to God was in conflict with our loyalty to the President. The Holy Spirit led me to read one verse (Philippians 4:8):

> Finally, brothers, whatever is true
> Whatever is noble, whatever is right
> Whatever is pure, whatever is lovely
> Whatever is admirable – if anything is
> Excellent or praiseworthy – think about such things.

I then told the President that member churches of NCCK would fully support him on things that were true, noble, right, pure, lovely, admirable, excellent or praiseworthy. I then sat down, and left it to the President to think through those things on which we as churches could not support him. This virtually meant the opposite of the eight things in the above verse.

I was once again the Chairman of NCCK in 1982-1983. On 1 August 1982 Kenya experienced an attempted *coup d'état* led by the air force. Trouble started in the early hours of Sunday morning but by the end of the day the other armed forces led by the Kenya army and the police had quelled the revolt and the government was in full control. However, numerous shops were looted in the capital city, especially those belonging to the Asian community. The diocese of Mt Kenya East had hired three buses to take Christians to Meru for a fundraising event for the first Anglican church there, a function that had been scheduled to take place at Kinoru Stadium. We heard about the coup when we arrived at Kerugoya and I cancelled the trip as it meant traveling via Nanyuki, an important air base of the Kenyan Air Force. Instead we held prayers at the grounds of St Thomas' Church, Kerugoya, during which we fervently prayed for Kenya and the safety of the President. By late afternoon the rebellion was quelled, but at least 145 people were killed and several hundreds injured in the crackdown that followed.

Two weeks before the attempted coup, I had preached a sermon from the book of Esther during the consecration of St Andrew's Church Kiamaina, in Ndia constituency, Kirinyaga District. The occasion was attended by, among others, the cabinet minister Jeremiah Nyagah, G. K. Kareithi, a former Permanent Secretary in the Office of the President and Head of Civil Service, and David Musila, the then Provincial Commissioner of Central Province, and many other dignitaries from Kirinyaga and Embu were present.

The text of my sermon appears in Chapter 4 of my book *In Season and out of Season* (Oxford: Regnum International, 1996). Esther, a beautiful Jewess, had been selected by King Xerxes to become the Queen of Persia to replace Vashti, who had refused to obey the King during a banquet attended by princes, nobles and diplomats at Susa. Mordecai, a cousin of Esther, learned that there was a plot to exterminate all Jews in the empire. He sent a message to Queen Esther, in which he said, "Do not think, that because you are in the king's house you alone of all the Jews will escape. For if you remain silent at this time relief and deliverance for Jews will arise from another place, but you and your father's family will perish. *And who knows but that you have come to the royal position at a time like this*" (Esther 4:13-14, emphasis added).

During the sermon I challenged all those who are in positions of authority to meditate upon the words of Mordecai to Esther, "Who knows but you have come to your present position at a time like this… only do not remain silent." I also made reference to the prophet Jeremiah, who said "'Peace, peace,' they say, when there is no peace" (Jeremiah 8:11b). After the sermon, I invited the Provincial Commissioner to greet the congregation. The PC assured the congregation that there was peace in Kenya. However, shortly after that we had the attempted *coup d'etat*.

The political climate in Kenya at this time was getting increasingly volatile. Parliament had earlier passed a constitutional amendment bill to make Kenya a *de jure* one party state in a motion that was hastily passed in a record 45 minutes. The motive was to stop the doyens of opposition politics, Jaramogi Oginga Odinga and George Anyona, from effecting their plan to form a new political party. Soon after Anyona was arrested and detained without trial and Oginga was put under house arrest.

The haste with which the constitution was amended did not augur well for the peace of the country. The president consolidated his rule, became more autocratic and took steps to silence all opposition against his government. The most outspoken politicians were rigged out of parliament. Even the majority of church leaders preferred to remain silent. But there were a few of us who took the words of Mordecai seriously: "And who knows but that you have come to your royal position at such a time as this? Only do not remain silent."

A Critique of *Nyayo* Philosophy

When His Excellency President Daniel Arap Moi became the second President of Kenya in August 1978, he told the nation that he was going to follow in the footsteps (*Nyayo*) of his predecessor, Mzee Jomo Kenyatta. The standard Swahili dictionary printed by Oxford University Press in 1971 defines footsteps as "*hatua, kishindo cha mguu; wayo, unyayo, alama ya mguu, mguu.*" To follow his footsteps means "*nifuate, fanya Kama alivyofanya yeye, mwingine.*" By saying he was going to follow the footsteps of Mzee Jomo Kenyatta, President Moi was virtually declaring that he was going to lead this country as his predecessor had done. However, the President and his advisors must have seen that the term *Nyayo* needed an official definition if it was not going to be a mere empty slogan.

Consequently the President told the nation and the world that his leadership would be patterned on the Nyayo Philosophy, which was defined by the terms Peace, Love and Unity. Before the end of 1978, the word *Nyayo* was already being used in this elaborate sense and it was declared a protected word. After the attempted coup on 1 August 1982, there was intensified national focus on Peace, Love and Unity and the President declared that the Nyayo Philosophy must be taught in schools and universities.

One of my achievements as chairman of NCCK was the publication of the book *A Christian View of Politics in Kenya: Love, Peace and Unity* in September 1983. I felt that the council could make its contribution to the Nyayo Philosophy by publishing a book which gave a clear interpretation of what the Bible says about Peace, Love and Unity. My proposal was accepted and I was requested to be the chairman of the theological group that would reflect on what the Bible says about Peace, Love and Unity and then draft a book for publishing after approval by the council. At first I wanted to write the book myself but since it was going to be a critique of the President's leadership, I felt it would be safer to involve the council.

I prepared a first draft of the Biblical exposition of all three terms with help from the theological fraternity at St Andrew's College of Theology and Development, Kabare, which I had founded in 1977. Theologians were called to study the draft during a number of meetings at the Limuru Conference and Training Centre. My draft on Peace and Love were adopted with minor amendments. The draft of Bishop Henry Okullu on Unity was also adopted. The book was published by Uzima Press in September 1983, about thirteen months after the attempted *coup*. The book was given the title *A Christian View of Politics in Kenya: Love Peace and Unity.*

Biblical Meaning of Love

The Theologians at Limuru Conference Centre felt the title should be *Love, Peace and Unity* instead of *Peace, Love and Unity*, because true love is the quality that leads to peace and unity; after all, Jesus said that the greatest commandment is this: "Love the Lord your God, with all your heart and with all your soul and with all your mind and all your strength. The second is this: Love your neighbour as yourself" Mark 12:29-31. The first obligation on those whom God loves is to reciprocate God's love by loving him. This is not just an obligation. It is a commandment which must be total. Israel was commanded to love God with her whole being. Israel is to love God with her whole heart, her whole life, soul and her whole might. It is an obligation that demands total commitment. This means that to God we must give a total love, a love which dominates our emotions, a love which directs out thoughts, a love which is dynamite of our actions. Kenyans will be paying lip service to the term "love" unless love takes its root in our accepting and obeying the command to love God, with all our heart, with all our soul and with all our might. Our total love for God will radically direct the life of the society, including the politics of the nation in achieving a loving society. Without such a response to God's love, the word love will but remain an empty slogan appropriate for political rallies."[8]

The book notes that the second response to God's love is to be obedient to God and the third response is to live righteously. "When Kenya chooses LOVE as one of the terms which defines the *Nyayo* Philosophy, then the nation should seek to love God, obey his commandments and exercise justice in all walks of life and be especially concerning the plight of the poor. Failure to do this, the nation which embraces love as a guiding philosophy in nation building will be visited by a holy and righteous God full of wrath for the sins of the nation and will be punished accordingly."

> The Lord in his anger
> Covered Zion with darkness
> Its heavenly Splendour
> He has turned into ruins.
> (Lamentations 2:1)

I was convinced that we should emphasise the biblical teaching about love for a neighbour. The story of the Good Samaritan in Luke 10:25-37 clearly teaches that a neighbour to whom we should extend our love is not necessarily the person who lives next door to us or a fellow tribesman but rather any person we come across who is in need. Love must be love in action and a humble service to others. Compassion, to be real compassion, must issue in deeds. The book noted that "during the chaos in the city of Nairobi on 1 August 1982, there were few Good Samaritans. It was evident that the Asian shops and other business premises suffered more looting than those of Africans. Though for years Africans seem to have lived in peaceful co-existence with Asians, the events of that Sunday morning clearly show that there

---

8 See *A Christian View of Politics in Kenya: Love, Peace and Unity* (Uzima Press, 1983, pp. 5-6).

is a hidden bitterness against the Asians, which like a volcano can erupt with devastating consequences.

"The teaching of the Bible is that aliens living in our midst deserve our love and no harm should be done to them. The New Testament goes further to say that all people irrespective of their tribal, racial, religious or geographical background deserve our loving service. If Nyayo philosophy is to be true to scriptures, Kenyans should extend their love to their neighbours, that is the people they come into contact with day by day, whether they belong to our respective tribes or not, whether they are Kenyan citizens or not." The section on love was concluded with these words: "Just as fish is made to live in water and when it is there it can fully enjoy life, we are made to live in the atmosphere of love. Let us swim in the sea of love, in which we can strengthen the moral fiber of the nation in love and service. That is the true Nyayo."[9]

Biblical Meaning of Peace

I found my study of the Biblical meaning of peace very interesting. The English word "peace" translates two biblical words: the Hebrew *shalom* and Greek *eirene*. Broadly speaking, God is the author of *shalom*, which includes everything given by God in all areas of life to make life complete. This may include tranquility, contentment, material security, political stability and salvation. *Shalom* describes right relationships and uninterrupted goodwill between humans. Hence *shalom* does not only describe absence of war and strife but also describes happiness and well-being in life, and perfection of human relationships. The Greek word *eirene* occurs more than eighty times in the New Testament and it is found in all twenty-seven books of the New Testament. According to the New Testament *eirene* can mean tranquility, concord, unity, harmony and every kind of blessing and good. *Eirene* is also connected with reconciliation, for Christ by his death brought us the peace of God, and therefore we are able to live at peace with all human beings. The Nyayo Philosophy must be enriched by taking full account of the positive Biblical meaning of peace.

The Bible makes it very clear that God is the author of peace. In the book of Numbers, Moses was instructed to give Aaron and his sons the words they would be using in blessing the people.

9 *Ibid.*, p. 16.

The Lord bless you and keep you.
The Lord make His face to shine upon you,
and be gracious to you.
The Lord lift up His countenance upon you
znd give you peace [*shalom*].
(Numbers 6:25-26)

Here "peace" sums up all other blessings which come from God, such as kindness, graciousness and favour. When there is peace in the land it is because God has given it. God does not give His "peace" unconditionally. For a nation to enjoy peace, it must fulfill two conditions. These are obedience to God's commandments and establishment of justice and righteousness. If a nation obeys God's commandment, the consequences of such obedience is abundant peace and many blessings:

O that you harkened to my commandment
Then your peace would have been like a river,
And your righteousness like the waves of the sea.
(Isaiah 48:18)

God can also withdraw His peace, as a judgement on those who disobey him. In Jeremiah the Lord says that He has abandoned Israel, the chosen nation, and has given the people He loves into the power of their enemies. This is because God's chosen people have turned against Him; and because of their disobedience, the Lord says:

For the sword of the Lord devours from
one end of the land to the other, no flesh had peace.
(Jeremiah 12:12b)

The second condition of God granting His "shalom" to a nation is establishment of justice and righteousness:

Then justice will dwell in the wilderness
And the righteousness abide in the fruitful field
And the effect of righteousness will be peace [*shalom*]
And the result of the righteousness quietness and trust forever.
(Isaiah 32:16-17)

Justice and righteousness as conditions of peace are central themes of the preaching of the prophets. The false prophets promised peace when the conditions for peace were not fulfilled. But Micah, Jeremiah and Ezekiel made it clear that there could be no peace unless Israel turned away from evil. While the false prophets comforted people by saying "peace, peace", Jeremiah reminded them that there cannot be peace when injustices continued among the people.

- Everyone is greedy for unjust gain (Jeremiah 6:13).
- They are stubbornly rebellious (Jeremiah 6: 28).
- All of them act corruptly (Jeremiah 6:28).

The way of peace in Kenya is justice and righteousness in social, economic and political activities.

The prophet Isaiah was very emphatic in stating that injustices cut us off from God. In Isaiah 59, the prophet concentrates on injustices and states:

1. The lawsuits were not just; people went to law courts without a good case.
2. They did not go to law courts honestly; they were ready to use bribery or even threats to secure the verdict that they wanted.
3. They relied on empty pleas: they gave false evidence and swore untrue affidavits.
4. They conceived mischief: their whole purpose was to cause trouble for their neighbours. They did not consider that the true nature of courts is to be defenders of justice.

The task of the government is to protect courts from external interference, and ensure that the cases are always decided according to truth and justice, and not according to wealth or political influence. Unfortunately during the *Nyayo* era there was too much interference in the courts and some judges made decisions not based on the truth but on what they thought pleased the powers that be.

The seventh beatitude in Matthew's Gospel states, "Blessed are the peacemakers, for they will be called sons of God" (Matthew 5:9). The beatitude does not say that "peace lovers" are blessed but "peacemakers". A peace lover is a person who loves peace so much that he will let a dangerous situation develop in the family, the church or even in the society, because he does not want to be involved in potentially sensitive problems. Such a person may be called peaceable, but he is certainly not a peacemaker. The longer a potentially dangerous situation is allowed to continue, the more serious its consequences and the harder the cure. To keep quiet and say or do nothing because one is a peace lover results in the accumulation of trouble for the future.

A peacemaker is a person who is prepared to face difficulty, unpleasantness and trouble for the sake of peace. The peace which this beatitude describes is not the spurious peace that comes from evading problems and issues. It is the peace that comes from being prepared to give everything in toil and sacrifice that the situation demands. As the book of Proverbs says:

A man who holds back the truth causes trouble
But one who openly criticizes works for peace.
(Proverbs 10:10)

During the *Nyayo* era, those in authority were very much against those who criticized the government, even branding them anti-*Nyayo*. The President himself tended to think that those who criticised him were anti-government. It was out of sheer love for our country that we felt duty bound to speak against injustices. We were following in the footsteps of the prophets who loved Israel so much that they felt duty bound to prophesy courageously concerning the consequences of injustices. They were peacemakers, compelled by the desire for peace and their love for their country to speak what they believed God had sent them to say. And so prophet Micah could tell leaders and false prophets:

Listen, you leaders of Jacob
you rulers of the house of Israel
should you not know justice,
you who hate good and love evil,
you tear the skin from my people
and the flesh from their bones,
who eat my people's flesh.
strip of their skin
And brake their bones in pieces;
Who chop them up like meat for the pan
Like flesh for the pot
Then they will cry out to the Lord but He will not answer them.
At that time He will hide His face from them because of the evil they
have done.
(Micah 3:1-4)

Micah did not spare the land grabbers of his day:

> Woe to those who plan iniquity and those who plot evil on their beds. At morning's light they carry it out because it is in their power to do it. They covet fields and seize them, and houses, and take them. They defraud a man of his home, a fellow man of his inheritance. Therefore, the Lord says:
> I am planning disaster against the people,
> from which you cannot safe yourselves.
> You will no longer walk proudly,
> for it will be a time of calamity.
> (Micah 2:1-3)

In John 14:27 Jesus gave his disciples a peace that is different from the peace the world promises. "Peace I leave with you: my peace I give you. I do not give you as the world gives. Do not let your hearts be troubled and do not be afraid." This peace is both a legacy that Jesus leaves behind and also a treasure that Jesus gives his disciples. The peace that the world gives implies absence of a troubled and fearful feeling. The peace that Jesus gives is contrasted with the kind of peace the world promises.

The world can never give the kind of peace that Jesus bestows upon his followers. The world can give monetary peace or the peace of escapism from the realities of life. A man who has a lot of problems at home might decide to seek peace by going to a night club to drink to try and forget his problems at home. But once he becomes sober, he will find them right there where he left them. The world may give outward pleasure, physical rest and enjoyment, honour, wealth, but never the peace which passes all understanding, the inner tranquility that no one can take away.

Paul teaches that Christ, by his atoning death, has brought a comprehensive peace, one that includes complete wholeness spiritually, and a right relationship with God ensuing in a right relationship with fellow humankind. As a result of his atoning death, there is a vertical relationship with God and a horizontal reconciliation with humans. Consequently in Christ there is "neither Jew nor Greek, there is neither slave nor free, there is neither male nor female, all are one in Christ Jesus" (Galatians 3:28).

Biblical Meaning of Unity

My paper on unity written in 1983 was not included in the NCCK publication *Love, Peace and Unity*. However, it now forms one of the chapters in my book "Responsible Church Leadership", published in February 2005 by ACTON Publishers, Nairobi. The paper begins by exploring the Biblical doctrine of humanity and underlines the fact that humankind is a unity of body and soul. Unlike ancient Greek philosophers who saw the soul as the prison of the body, the Bible regards a human being as psychosomatic unit. As Alan Richardson puts it, "for Biblical writers, man is a living body (rather than a living soul in the modern sense of the word), and his body being God-created is not vile. It was an essential part of him, the means of self-expression, not his 'prison' or 'tomb': hence it was natural for St Paul to speak of resurrection of the body – that is, of man as a total personality; not a ghost or yet a purely 'spiritual' being, but having the essential means of self-expression, communication, recognizability and all other things that are included in what we would today call 'personality'" (Alan Richardson. *Genesis 1-11.* Norwich: SCM Press, 1962, p. 62).

This Biblical understanding of humanity is a challenge to those preachers who like only to win "souls" to Christ and do not care about the body. It is equally a challenge to materialists who assume that if a person got all the wealth he/she needed, he/she would find satisfaction in life. We need to raise the living standard of our people but we also need to uphold the dignity of men and women as well as to recognise that the deepest need of human beings cannot be satisfied by money or wealth alone.

The paper then emphasises the equality of the male and the female. The original intention of God at creation was not to create man as a superior being and woman as inferior. The division of humankind into two sexes is not the result of the fall. It is part of God's original plan, which he saw as "very good". The unity of male and female is clearly demonstrated by means of the figure of a woman being formed from the rib of man.

> So the Lord caused a deep sleep upon man, and while he slept took one of his ribs and closed up its place with flesh, and the rib which the Lord God had taken from the man he made into a woman and brought her to the man. (Genesis 2:21-22)

The first ever transplant operation is a wonderful allegory of how God made Adam's helper out of a part of his body, significantly his side. Woman stands by man's side, not behind him or before him. Man is not complete until a helper is made for him and a woman has no separate existence apart from man. When God presents Eve to Adam, the man recognises her as "bone of my bone and flesh of my flesh". The creation story emphasises that sexes are complementary:

> It is not good that man should be alone, I will make him a helper fit for him. (Genesis 2:18)

This complementality and equality is not merely biological, because she is described by her maker as a "helper fit for him", which means equal to and adequate to him. The Biblical symbolism of Adam and Eve implies what Martin Buber calls an "I – thou" relationship between equal persons. But in the Biblical view these two persons are one flesh. Though one flesh, each, person has his or her own personality. Though they are different individuals, they are nevertheless complementary in function. The Biblical teaching on the unity of the male and the female leads us to two conclusions. Firstly there is a need to emphasize that man and woman are equal before God. Secondly, the Biblical symbolism of Adam and Eve refers not to two specific individuals but to humankind as a whole. The original purpose of God at creation was not to make man superior to the woman, but rather to create equal partners who have to complement each other.

Throughout human history, however, women have been exploited by men politically, socially and economically. We cannot talk of national unity unless we go out of our way to eradicate discrimination against women at all levels. Since independence, much progress has been made in promoting the welfare of women, and many women have entered into what used to be "man's" dominion. We now have women administrators, magistrates and judges, engineers and architects; we have women in the police force and in the military, air force and navy. We also have women priests and bishops in some of our churches. Despite these advances, and despite the fact that women are slightly more numerous than men, there are very few women in the decision-making bodies either in church or in society. The World Council of Churches advised its member churches that in all decision-making bodies of the church at all levels women should be not less than 40%. Little has been done to increase the number of women in the National Assembly. It is however a step forward that the new constitution promulgated on 27 August 2011 took affirmative action seriously.

In the National Assembly, women are guaranteed a minimum of 47 seats out of 290 and in the senate 18 seats out of 67. This however is merely 16.21% and 26.9% respectively. The constitution should be amended to ensure that a minimum of 30% of seats are reserved for women in both houses. The increasing rate of defilement, rape and other forms of sexual abuse of girls and women is a great concern. All people of good will must join hands together to fight against these evils and promote the dignity of every individual.

Having explored the Biblical concept of a human being as a psychosomatic unit, and the equality of men and women before God, my paper discussed "the individual and community". Humans are not isolated individuals; they are both one and many. Humans in Hebrew thought are interrelated with each other. They have a common ancestry in one person, Adam, and a common destiny in death. Yet each individual, man or woman, in Old Testament thought is truly an individual person. Therefore "a man is like finger on a hand. Each finger is an individual finger. Yet all the five fingers have a common root in the hand which carries them" (G.A.F. Knight, *A Christian Theology of O.T,* 1964).

The concept of the individual and the community also implies that the sin of one individual affects other members of family or community. The penalty of idolatry in the second commandment involved the punishment by God upon the third and even the fourth generation (Exodus 20.5). This "corporate" view of people reminds us that the sin of one person has far-reaching consequences for other people. However, this insight does not mean that an individual is completely lost in the society or does not bear any responsibility even for his or her own faults.

The Old Testament recognizes the place of the individual and his or her responsibilities. In his message addressed to disillusioned exiles who were complaining that they were suffering because of a situation inherited from their father, Ezekiel told them, "When a wicked man turns away from his wickedness he has committed and does what is lawful, he shall save his life" (Ezekiel 18:26-27).

The Biblical concepts of the individual and the community are similar to the corresponding African concepts. In the African cultural heritage, there is a strong community solidarity. A human is not a human in isolation, but realises his or her full potential only as a member of a community. Problems of an individual are also the problems of the family, the clan and the community. An individual's blessings are blessings of the family, the clan and the community, who take an interest in his or her affairs. To decide to marry is such an important decision that the family, the clan and the community get involved in the various steps that lead to marriage. The African philosophy of being was summarized by John Mbiti in the words: "I am because we are, We are therefore I am." This differs drastically from the philosophy of the French philosopher René Descartes (1596-1650) who said, "I think, therefore I am," thus emphasising Western individualism.

To some extent, this African feeling of solidarity within a community is decreasing, primarily because of urbanisation. Young people who go to work in urban areas away from home seem to lose contact with their parents and relatives and might even make important life decisions without consulting their parents and relatives. The ideal would be to keep in touch with their parents and relatives in rural areas and at the same time to establish new relationships with their work-mates and neighbours in urban areas. It is here that the local church in the urban areas can form the alternative loving community for those who move to urban areas.

The story of the Good Samaritan demonstrates that a neighbour is not necessarily a person who lives next door to us. According to the norms of Jewish religion at the time of Jesus, the commandment of love for one's neighbours related only to persons who were pure Jews. In the parable of the Good Samaritan, Jesus teaches clearly that love for one's neighbour knows no bounds of nationality, tribe or ethnicity.

A neighbour is any person, whatever his or her background, who might become a victim of circumstances and to whom we should extend our loving care. As we belong to one nation, we are brothers and sisters and we should extend our love to all people in need, including visitors and strangers.

But unity does not necessarily mean uniformity. We should not assume that Kenyans can be united by obliterating all the peculiar characteristics of each tribe, clan or ethnic group. It is possible to have unity in diversity. Diversity is an important aspect of God's creativity. Created beings of the same species have their own individual peculiarities. So also do human beings, even within the same family (including identical twins); each of us has our own characteristics that distinguish us from all other people: our voice, the way we walk, our fingerprints, the iris in our eyes, and our genes, among numerous other unique aspects. Creation itself confirms that uniformity is not God's will, but rather unity in diversity.

Commenting on the story of the Tower of Babel, Alan Richardson observes: "...it contains in story-form the essential biblical verdict upon secular civilization, represented in the parable by the city and tower of Babel – that Babylon which throughout the Bible remains the symbol of man's megalomaniacal attempt to achieve the world peace and unity by world's dominion and exploitation" (Richardson, *Genesis 1-11*, 1953, p. 100).

Uniformity tends to force people to follow a certain line and does not help them to develop their own peculiar potential and talents. Similarly in a multi-tribal society like Kenya, we do not promote unity by seeking to ignore the existence of tribes and their cultural heritage. Our efforts should be directed towards encouraging individual people or tribes to be themselves and make the best use of their talents, and at the same time seek interactions with other people or tribes and learn from them. A person who has found self-identity can go forward with confidence to seek fellowship with other people. The national life will be enriched when each tribe makes its distinctive contribution from its cultural and social heritage.

One of the big mistakes Moi made during his presidency was to ban tribal associations. As long as the associations remained cultural and social, they had a positive contribution to make in nation-building. The second mistake the president made was to ban political parties and not only to make KANU the *de facto* political party but also to change the constitution in 1982 to make KANU the only *de jure* political party in Kenya. The Lancaster House Constitution was based on multi-party democracy. KANU led by Jomo Kenyatta won the elections. Within a very short time, KADU and APP dissolved themselves and joined KANU. Attempts by Oginga Odinga to form another political party (KPU) in 1966 were frustrated by the government.

Constitutionally Kenya remained a multi-party state but as a matter of fact there was only one party (KANU) in existence. From 1963 to 1982, anyone could legally have started a political party. But the political environment made it very difficult for any politician to dare start a new party. Passing a constitutional amendment to make Kenya a *de jure* political state did more to divide Kenyans than any other event since independence. The immediate consequence was the attempted coup on Sunday 1 August 1982.

The Death of *Nyayo* Philosophy

I have already indicated that I felt strongly convinced that no complete philosophy of *Nyayo* could be formulated without careful reflection on what the Bible says about love, peace and unity. I did not have any doubts that when the President chose these words to summarise the Nyayo Philosophy he did so in good faith and with a determination to make Kenya a land of peace, love and unity.

However, the events of Sunday 1 August 1982 must have shocked the president so much that he abandoned the ways of peace, love and unity to apprehend and punish all those people (real or imagined) who threatened his presidency. One of the first victims of Moi after he abandoned his own philosophy of peace, love and unity was Kenya's first African Attorney General, Charles Mugane Njonjo. Njonjo had become extremely close to Moi because of the instrumental role he played during the transition from President Kenyatta to his vice-president Moi. The assassinations of Tom Mboya and JM Kariuki had eliminated potential successors of Kenyatta but the president was in his 80s and frail. But the clique of powerful individuals who constituted the inner circles of the Kenyatta regime, particularly those in KANU from the Gikuyu, Embu and Meru Association (GEMA) felt threatened that their influence and the accruing benefits would be "lost" should an "outsider" ascend to the presidency. Vice-President Moi belonged to the Kalenjin community and the core concern of those who did not like him was a constitutional provision that empowered the vice-president automatically to take over the reins of power for 90 days in the event that the office of the president fell vacant for any reason. In September 1976, they formed the Change-the-Constitution Campaign and held anti-Moi rallies while the president was still alive. In a master stroke, Njonjo, a Kikuyu, warned that it was treasonable to premeditate, imagine or discuss the possible death of the President. Kenyatta supported Njonjo in a cabinet meeting that eventually endorsed the position. The anti-Moi rallies championed by Kihika Kimani, Paul Ngei, Njenga Karume, James Gichuru, Jackson Angaine and Dr Njoroge Mungai came to a sudden end. Moi owed Njonjo a favour.

When Moi ascended to power, Njonjo resigned, became a member of parliament in an intrigue-filled by-election and was appointed Minister for Justice and Constitutional Affairs by the President. In the early years of Moi's regime, Njonjo appeared to be very close to the President and must have helped him to formulate the Nyayo Philosophy. But after the attempted coup, Njongo became the first politician to become a victim of Moi after the President abandoned the Biblical values of peace, love and unity. He underwent ninety days of humiliation as he was publicly investigated for being *msaliti* or a traitor. Some argued that Njonjo was only swallowing some of his own medicine but here was the man who as Attorney General had done all that he could to help Moi to succeed Kenyatta.

From 1982 to 1992 the so called Nyayo Philosophy was dead and buried. President Moi had come up with a new philosophy of perpetuating his peace, love and unity, by crushing all opposition as ruthlessly as possible. Those suspected to be members or sympathisers of Mwakenya were hunted down like deer and many left the country into exile.

Moi devised a way of consolidating his hold on the National Assembly by ensuring that politicians who were most outspoken against the excesses of his rule did not get elected. Some of these so-called radical thinkers were described by Njonjo in derogatory tone as the "seven bearded sisters". They were Abuya Abuya, Chelagat Mutai (yes, a lady), Chibule wa Tsuma, Mwashengu wa Mwachofi, Koigi wa Wamwere, Lawrence Sifuna and James Orengo. The method of choice was the queuing (*mlolongo*) system of election, which Moi and KANU found to be the best way of rigging the elections. Voters were counted as they stood in line behind their preferred candidate, but very often, candidates with the shorter queues were declared winners.

Consequently, virtually all opposition against KANU and Moi was silenced, at least in Parliament, where speech was privileged. The only leaders KANU and Moi found difficult to silence were outspoken church leaders. The majority of church leaders preferred to play it safe by either supporting the government or by remaining silent or neutral on political issues. The few church leaders who became the voice of the voiceless were Bishop Henry Okullu, Bishop Alexander Muge and the present writer, all from the Anglican Church of Kenya. The then Archbishop of ACK, Manasses Kuria, was not critical of Moi's regime until the time when Kenneth Matiba and Charles Rubia were detained without trial in July 1990. Rubia's son had married the daughter of Manasses Kuria. Voices of protest from the Catholic Church included Bishop Raphael Ndingi Mwana a' Nzeki and Bishop John Njenga. From other churches, only the voice of Timothy Njoya of the Presbyterian Church was openly critical of the Government.

The death of the Nyayo Philosophy of peace, love and unity did not herald the end of the use of the term *Nyayo*. The term continued to be repeatedly used in KANU political rallies. In the decade between 1982 and 1992, the term had mutated and evolved to personify President Daniel Toroitich arap Moi. People started calling Moi *Nyayo*, just like it was his name, and he responded accordingly. The term no longer embodied peace, love and unity. In time, Daniel arap Moi had become *Nyayo* and *Nyayo* was Daniel arap Moi.

Moi then embarked on projects that were all baptized *Nyayo* projects. In 1986, he embarked on a project to manufacture a car that was called the

Nyayo Pioneer car. Hundreds of millions of shillings were sunk into the project. It collapsed. The Nyayo Bus Service came into existence in 1988 with a fleet of nearly 300 buses. The company was declared insolvent in mid-1995. Primary school children were given free milk twice a week. The milk was called Nyayo. The project was just not sustainable. Moi vigorously promoted the construction of wards in public hospitals; those wards were and are still called Nyayo Wards. Tea plantations were expanded by the destruction of a zone of protected forests, and those plantations were called Nyayo Tea Zones.

When Moi appointed Uhuru Kenyatta to succeed him, the media quickly referred to him as the Nyayo Project. All the so called *Nyayo* projects failed miserably for they no longer reflected "peace, love and unity" as we understand these from the Scriptures. Consequently Moi's *Nyayo* projects became white elephants and of no economic benefit to the country.

Prior to the 2002 general elections, before my retirement on 16 September, I visited Anglican dioceses in various parts of Kenya and told Christians that all the *Nyayo* projects had failed, and that even the Uhuru for President project would fail. The *Nyayo* projects failed because President Moi, acting like a jack-of-all-trades, refused to listen to experts in various fields and disciplines. For instance, at one time he went to a country in the Far East and found that rice was being grown in two seasons each year. He visited Mwea in Kirinyaga where rice was grown in only one season per year. Without consulting experts, he issued a presidential decree that in future rice will be grown in two seasons per year. The farmers obeyed the president and planted rice soon after the harvest of the first season. The rice grew in the second season but produced no rice.

Had he consulted them, the experts would have informed him that the Mwea black cotton soil must be given time to be baked by the sun so as to develop cracks that enable nitrogen, the most important plant nutrient, to penetrate the soil to enable the next crop to be fruitful. After the failure of the second crop ordered by the President, the Mwea farmers decided that they would not follow the presidential directive on rice farming. Then when the Ministry of Education included the teaching of new mathematics in schools, Moi issued a presidential decree banning the teaching of new mathematics in our schools. He never bothered to find out the value of new mathematics in the age of computers. The leading mathematicians in our universities dared not disobey a president who had now become a jack-of-all-trades and a self-declared professor of politics.

Chapter 20

Let the Bishop Speak

Let the Bishop Speak is the title of my book that was published by Uzima Press in 1988. The title was inspired by a direct quote from President Daniel arap Moi on 30 June 1987 during his address to the employees and directors of the Kenya Posts and Telecommunications Corporation when they visited him at State House. On 1 July 1987, the *Daily Nation* wrote a story with a banner headline "Let the Bishop Speak." The *Nation* report continued

> President Moi said yesterday that the outspoken Bishop David Gitari of the CPK should be allowed to speak his mind as Kenya was a democratic country. But the President said the Anglican prelate of Mt Kenya East had wronged Kenyans by making unwarranted criticism of his motherland in presence of foreigners.

The president's speech brought to an end weeks of public political outbursts by KANU politicians over me. For the first time in my ministry as the Bishop of the Church, the media had taken a very special interest in four sermons I preached in June 1987. They were:
- "Harassed and Helpless" (Matthew 9:35-38), preached at Immanuel Church, Mutira, on 7 June 1987.

- "Idols of our times" (Jeremiah 1:4-10 and 7:1-8), preached at St Andrew's, Kabare, on 14 June 1987.
- "The Truth is always Triumphant" (Daniel 6:1-28), preached at St Peter's, Nyeri, on 21 June 1987 during the occasion of the annual Civic Service Day.
- "All scripture is inspired by God" (2 Timothy 3:14-4:7), preached during the occasion of consecration of the church of Good Samaritan, Kathiga, on 28 June 1987.

The first sermon was preached at Immanuel Church, Mutira, in Ndia division of Kirinyaga district. It was during the occasion of creating the Archdeaconry of Mutira and installation of Ephantus Muriuki as the first archdeacon of that archdeaconry. I expounded Matthew 9:35-38, which says, "And Jesus went about all the cities and villages teaching in their synagogues, preaching the gospel of the Kingdom, and healing every kind of disease and infirmity."

I informed the congregation that Jesus did not stay at his home or office or what we would today call a vicarage waiting for people to come to him. Instead He is the one who went out, to every village and city to meet the people. His ministry was threefold: teaching, preaching and healing every kind of disease. And when He saw the crowds, they were harassed and helpless like sheep without a shepherd. As a consequence, Jesus was moved to the very deepest parts of His being. Consequently He had to respond to the needs of the people. In applying this message to contemporary Kenya I touched on two issues that must have troubled Moi and the entire KANU fraternity. The first issue was the registration of voters for the general election that was due to be held in early 1988. On 9 May 1987, *The Standard* newspaper had reported that the president had set a date for registration of voters. Here is part of the story as it appeared in *The Standard*:

> Registration of voters will start on 15th June 1987 throughout the country... President Moi, who was meeting with Provincial Commissioners and District Commissioners at State House Nakuru, told DC's to prepare for the exercise well in advance. Only people registered as KANU members, and have national identity cards will be eligible to register as voters, he added.

The issue was that Kenya at this point was a single-party state and this in effect meant that failure to have a KANU membership card deprived the citizen of the right to participate through the only outlet for democratic expression on a matter that was totally separate from intra-party processes and operations. In my sermon, I said:

It has been announced that registration of voters for the next general election will commence on 15th June 1987. As citizens of Kenya we must register ourselves in great numbers. Pastors and evangelists do not stay at home, but go and see for yourselves how this exercise will be carried out, and urge people to register. I would only wish to make a plea to those in authority. Membership of KANU should not be made a condition for registration. That would be unconstitutional, as section 43 page 27 of our constitution which spells our qualification and disqualification for registration as a voter, does not make membership of a party a qualification to vote. If that were to be made a condition then there are many poor people who cannot afford to pay party membership fee and who will be denied their democratic right to elect their parliamentary representatives. There is also a danger that some rich politicians will pay fees for party membership on behalf of the poor people on condition that they vote for them. To avoid such, the constitution should be upheld and all citizens who qualify constitutionally should be allowed to register as voters whether they have paid party membership fees or not. Otherwise many *wananchi* or ordinary citizens will look harassed and helpless like sheep without a shepherd, unable to participate in the General election (*Let the Bishop Speak*, p. 18).

Following my sermon, there must have been many consultations concerning what exactly I had said. The office of the then Vice President, Mwai Kibaki, telephoned me and asked me to send the newspaper cutting that stated that only paid-up KANU members could register as voters. Three days later the President had to issue a clarification. The *Daily Nation* of 10 June 1987 had a banner headline stating that ALL KENYANS FREE TO VOTE SAYS MOI. But a KANU card was a must in party polls. The newspaper read, "Any Kenyan registered as a voter and has an identity card will be free to vote in the presidential, parliamentary and civic elections President Moi said yesterday. But only registered KANU members may vote in party polls and preliminaries to the General Elections. The president clarified the ballot issue yesterday when he addressed a Nandi District delegation." I was glad that raising my concerns with regard to possible disenfranchisement of non-KANU members led the president to retract instructions he had given to provincial and district commissioners at State House, Nakuru, on 19 May 1987 that they would not allow anyone who is not a KANU member to register as voter.

However, what surprised me most was the attack I received from Moi and other politicians concerning a reference I had made in my sermon with regard to the giant Kenya Planters Cooperative Union (KPCU). I urged the pastors to mingle with coffee farmers and listen to their uncertainties as they ponder the implication of dissolution of KPCU and the creation of NCCU. I said that many appear harassed and helpless and added that it is our prayer that this matter may come to a good conclusion so that there can be stability in coffee industry (*Let the Bishop Speak*, p. 17). After the service at Mutira, a convoy of cars drove towards the home of the chairman of KANU in Kirinyaga District, James Njiru, to discuss my sermon. A statement was written and signed by Njiru, who said, "When President Moi addressed the nation from Kerugoya last week, coffee farmers were concerned at the way KPCU was handling, their affairs; the President gave mandate to take any action to streamline it (*The Standard*, 8 June 1987). The following day, *The Standard* had a banner headline: KPCU: MOI HITS OUT AT BISHOP.

The President was reported to have told a KANU recruitment rally at Bukhungu Stadium in Kakamega, "I expect the Church to pray for the weak. If the Church's aim is to sympathize with the oppressors then there must be something brewing." The KPCU, he pointed out, catered for and protected the interests of a few farmers who had more than 50 acres under coffee, leaving out the 65% of ordinary coffee farmers. "The Bishop now asks we pray for oppressors – '*Mungu turehemu*'" (God have mercy on us), he added. Despite the President's statement, the proposed National Coffee Co-operative Union (NCCU) never came into being and KPCU continued serving the farmers for many years until too much interference by the KANU government and corruption made it virtually bankrupt. However, the coffee industry, like many other industries in Kenya, has never recovered its past glory, not because of KPCU but because of the policies of the KANU government.

Idols of Our Times

The second sermon was preached at St Andrew's, Kabare, on Sunday 14 June 1987. On that day, I was inaugurating the Kabare Archdeaconry and insKereritalling the Venerable Linus Njuki as the first Archdeacon. On the previous Sunday at Immanuel Church, Mutira, I had invited two members of parliament from Kirinyaga who were present (John Matere Keriri and Nahashon Njuno) to greet the congregation. Njuno, the member for Gichugu Constituency, had been suspended from the party for a period of five months. Allowing Njuno to greet the people had aroused the wrath of some District KANU officials. They plotted to ensure that the suspended legislator would not address the gathering at Kabare.

Before the service began I received information that some KANU officials had recruited about 300 youth wingers who were given Ksh 40 each to come and heckle me if I allowed Njuno to address the gathering. Before I left home that morning I was telephoned by the priest in charge of Kabare parish and other friends who told me about the plans by KANU youth wingers to disrupt the service. He advised that I should not allow Njuno to speak. When I arrived at the Kabare shopping centre, I found a lorry full of police in anti-riot gear parked there to pre-empt any riots. I then went up the hill to the mission centre, where I found a huge congregation of about 5,000 people seated and waiting for the service to start.

After the induction of Njuki as Archdeacon, and after licensing lay readers, I invited the local political leaders to greet the congregation. Before doing so, however, I told the congregation that I was pleased to see so many KANU youth wingers present and I was going to pray for them so that they might be vigilant in promoting the Nyayo Philosophy of peace, love and unity. I also reminded the youth wingers that we were on holy ground for the purpose of worshiping God and that anyone who had come to interrupt the service had come to the wrong venue. After my prayers for the youth wingers, the congregation responded with a resounding "Amen!"

After that prayer, I invited the local leaders to speak, starting with G.K. Kariithi, the then chairman of KANU in Gichugu Division. He was followed by Njuno and Keriri. The youth wingers had been completely disarmed by my prayers for them. Some of them withdrew quietly. The rest of the service continued with no incident. The text of the sermon on that day was Jeremiah 1:4-10 and 7:18.

Jeremiah was born near Jerusalem in 650 BC. When God called him to be his prophet among the nations, Jeremiah felt most inadequate. He told God, "I do not know how to speak" and "I am only a child." But God told Jeremiah, "Do not say 'I am only a child.' You must go to everyone I send you to and say whatever I command you. Do not be afraid of them for I am with you and will rescue you." I told the congregation that "to be called by God to prophesy is not a request, it is a command. Once God commands, the prophet has no alternative but to deliver the message he receives from God, however unpopular the message might be" (*Let the Bishop Speak*, p. 26). God set Jeremiah over the nations and over the kingdoms and commissioned him "to pluck up and break down to destroy and over throw to build and to plant".

Negatively, the prophet Jeremiah was to pluck up and tear down, destroy and overthrow idolatry and other wickedness among humans. I told the congregation that the idols of our time are putting our trust in things made by humans, which is tantamount to worshipping idols. Idolatry has been defined as worshipping idols made by humans instead of worshipping God who created humans. This is what Paul Tillich called "Being ultimately concerned by that which is not ultimate". Among the idols of our time are money, military power, political groupings, personalities, buildings, etc. The men of Judah trusted in the temple so much that they believed that as long as they had the temple, they were secure. Jeremiah stood at the gate of the temple where false prophets and priests were passing on their way to the outer court of the temple and Jeremiah told them:

Do not trust in these deceptive words,
"This is the temple of the Lord, the temple of the Lord!"
(Jeremiah 7:4).

Jeremiah's message was very simple. The people of Judah had reached a point in their history where they thought that as long as they had the temple, all was well. The temple, they thought, was a bulwark of security. They thought that the northern kingdom had fallen to the Assyrians more than a century earlier, in 722 BC, because it did not have a temple. So the people of Judah at the time of King Jehoiakim considered the temple as their security. The temple had become like an idol to be worshipped. This is why Jeremiah felt duty bound to tell them not to trust in these words, "The temple of the Lord". Jeremiah went on to tell the leaders of Judah that the temple would not save them. The only way the southern kingdom would be saved from destruction was not by the temple but by justice.

If you really change your ways and your actions and deal with each other justly, if you do not oppress the alien, the fatherless or the widow and do not shed innocent blood in this place, if you do not follow other gods to your own harm, then I will let you live in this place, in the land I gave to your fathers for ever and ever. But look you are trusting in deceptive words that are worthless. Will you steal and murder, commit adultery and perjury, burn incense to Baal and follow other gods you have not known, and then come and stand in this house, which bears name, and say, 'We are safe' – safe to do these detestable things? Has this house which bears my name become a den of robbers to you? But I have been watching! declares the Lord (Jeremiah 7:5-8).

The people of Judah refused to listen to Jeremiah's advice. In 597 BC the Chaldean armies invaded Judah and attacked Jerusalem. The temple was looted and the treasures were taken to Babylon as booty. Egypt supported the rebellion against Babylon in 588 BC. This led to the siege of Jerusalem, which lasted 18 months. Nebuchadnezzar ordered the Babylonian army to destroy all that could be destroyed and to deport leading citizens.

I concluded the sermon by calling the people of Kirinyaga to pull down the deceptive idols of our times. "At the time of Jeremiah, people were saying 'peace, peace' when there was no peace. And today we continue to say 'peace, peace' and at the same time we plant our idols firmly. Unless these idols are removed there will be no peace. Let us pull down, our idols, whatever they might be, and instead of idols let God be asserted in the life of the church and society" (*Let the Bishop Speak*, p. 31). As I passed the shopping centre, I found the lorry carrying the riot policemen had left, as there was no need for police intervention. On Monday 15 June 1987, the *Kenya Times*, the mouthpiece of ruling party, wrote the following editorial entitled MISUSING THE PULPIT. It said:

Kenyan Church leaders of all the denominations will hopefully accept the sound advice handed by the ruling party's Secretary-General, Burudi Nabwera, who said on Saturday that all places of worship should be used relevantly and not for politicking. It is unfortunate that some of the CPK and PCEA clerics have of late been misusing the pulpit. It is a point of note, in this respect, that the Kanu Secretary-General rightly praised the Catholic Church in the country for not getting involved in political matters. He also made the point that the ruling party does not interfere with church affairs. Indeed, since the departure of foreign missionaries, some of the gentlemen who took over from them on the various Anglican and Presbyterian churches have all along been double acting, concentrating more on political agitation than on preaching the gospel. Look at the various mission stations in almost all parts of the country which, barely 30 years ago, were admirably maintained by foreign missionaries and the Kenyans they were grooming and coaching. All the school and hospital buildings were properly maintained and occasionally renovated; one used to admire every stretch of the carefully-tended flower and other gardens there were – and the mission stations were not free-for-all gazing zones. What's going on today, really? While some of the markedly well-educated Kenyan clerics in the "Protestant fold" have been globe-trotting, others have been politicking from the pulpit (or in open air), feigning constitutional immunity. Incidentally, they all live in the lap of luxury! (*Kenya Times* editorial, 15 June 1987)

The Truth is Always Triumphant

The third sermon was preached at St Peter's Church, Nyeri, on Sunday 21 June 1987. It has been a tradition that in June every year a civic service is held at St Peter's Church, Nyeri, and all Nyeri Members of Parliament and councillors are invited to attend. The Provincial Commissioner and District Commissioners are also invited to attend the service. The then Bishop of Mt Kenya Central diocese, the Rt Revd. John Mahiani, invited me to be the guest preacher on that day. When I arrived, the vicar of the Parish, the Revd. Ben Kanina Kirikiru, gave me a warm welcome.

It was also a tradition that the Provincial Commissioner of Central Province reads the lesson, and in his absence, the District Commissioner takes up that role. The text of my sermon on that day was Daniel 6. The Provincial Commissioner, John Etemesi, was unable to attend the service, but the District Commissioner, a Mr Mukhalule, was present. Also present was Isaiah Mathenge, the area MP, and the Nyeri KANU sub-branch chairman, the Nyeri mayor Mr Nderi and nearly all the councilors.

The dignitaries present were not aware that I was the preacher. I gave the DC the lesson for the day, but he decided that he would not read. Hence the lesson was read by the Principal of Kagumo College the Revd. Michael Kagume. The leaders present were then asked to greet the congregation. In his brief speech, the mayor reminded church leaders not to bring politics into the church. Another councillor said, "We go to Kamukunji Stadium for politics and we come to church to worship God. Hence we have come here not for politics but to hear the word of God." The DC and the chairman of the County Council repeated the same words. Because of the two sermons I had preached in Kirinyaga on the previous two Sundays, the Nyeri leaders assumed that I was going to preach "politics" and so they tried to preempt my sermon even before I preached.

I introduced the theme of my sermon by assuring the District Commissioner and the leaders that my task was to give a faithful exposition of Daniel 6. I had written the sermon in English, but the vicar had telephoned me a day before to tell me that the civic sermon is always in Kiswahili. So I had to re-write the sermon in Swahili. The media was well represented during the occasion.

Exposition of Daniel 6

Daniel was one of the leaders who were taken as hostages to Babylon with other Judean captives by Nebuchadnezzar. There he was trained along with certain other compatriots for the service of the royal court. I told the congregation that Daniel was a very capable, hard-working civil servant, stating, "It pleased Darius to appoint 120 satraps to rule throughout the kingdom, with three administrators over them, one whom was Daniel. The satraps were made accountable to them so that the king might not suffer loss. Now Daniel so distinguished himself among the administrators and satraps by his exceptional qualities that the king planned to set him over the whole kingdom" (Daniel 6:1-3). I told the congregation that "Daniel, a very hard working civil servant and very capable man was eventually removed from his position.

> Those who conspired to remove him were other ministers and civil servants who did not want Daniel promoted to the position of Prime Minister… In Daniel's case there were particular reasons why a conspiracy was made to remove him. One was racism. His fellow ministers and provincial administrators did not want to see a Jew made the top civil servant. Tribalism and racism in this case may be defined as denying a qualified and capable person a job or a responsibility simply on the grounds of his tribe or race. So a conspiracy was hatched on grounds of Daniel's race to stop him from becoming the Prime

Minister. Secondly, he was so faithful that he insisted on what was true, and refused to be bribed. There are many people who are not liked for the simple reason that they stand for truth, for honesty and faithfulness. Daniel was disliked because of his honesty and frankness (*Let the Bishop Speak*, p. 38).

The conspirators tried to look for faults that they could use against the Prime Minister-designate. They started looking for faults in his work, but could not find any. "They could find no corruption in him, because he was trustworthy and neither corrupt nor negligent" (Daniel 6:4b). I told the congregation, "If all those who are civil servants were to emulate Daniel, it would be a wonderful thing, then even if our enemies were to try to find fault in our work they would find none. Probably if we were to be investigated, faults would be found in our work. All faults or sins can be divided into two categories: sins of omission and sins of commission... Daniel could not be blamed for any faults, either of omission or commission. If Daniel was an administrator in Kenya today, he would sell KANU tickets to every citizen who qualifies and he would not register anybody as a voter who is not supposed to be registered" (*Let the Bishop Speak* page 39).

I went on to tell the congregation that as the Kikuyu saying goes, "Anyone who tries to look for fault in another will always find it." The conspirators having failed to find faults in Daniel's work, they had to look for fault elsewhere. After much consideration, they decided to remove Daniel by changing the constitution. The Persian constitution guaranteed freedom of worship. The administrators and satraps went to the King and advised him to issue an edict and enforce the decree that "anyone who prays to any god or man during the next thirty days, except you O King, shall be thrown into the lion's den" (Daniel 6:7b). Without much consideration of the implication of this decree, the king signed it.

The fellow administrators and civil servants went to see whether Daniel was going to disobey the new law. The Bible tells us that, "Now when Daniel learnt that the decree had been published, he went home to his upstairs room where the windows opened towards Jerusalem. Three times a day he got down on his knees and prayed, giving thanks to God just as he had done before" (Daniel 6:10). The conspirators then went to tell King Darius that his top civil servant was breaking the law which he had signed. The king was taken by surprise to realise that the law he had signed was aimed at removing his beloved and most capable and faithful top civil servant. The Bible says that, "When the King heard this, he was greatly distressed; he was determined to rescue Daniel and made every effort until sundown to rescue him" (Daniel 6:14). But the king was reminded, "Remember, O King, according to the law of the Medes and Persians, no decree or edict that king issues can be changed" (Daniel 6:15b).

Then I told the congregation, "The attempt to remove a leader by changing the constitution rings a bell in our ears when we recall the 'change the constitution' campaign of 1976. Though they did not say it, the campaigners wanted the constitution of Kenya to be amended so that the then Vice President of Kenya would not automatically become the president before the election in the case of death of the President. We did a better job in Kenya in 1976 than they did in Persia in the time of Daniel. The matter was discussed publicly and in the end a cabinet meeting at Nakuru discussed the proposal and rejected it. However in Persia the King approved the change of the constitution without any debate. *The greatest mistake we can make in our national life is to allow important decisions to be made without allowing sufficient time for all those concerned to debate the issues.* If King Darius had allowed this matter to be discussed publicly a number of problems would have emerged. Firstly, people would have asked, "Why make a law to worship the King for only thirty days? Secondly, Daniel and his fellow Jews would have made it very clear that they could not worship a human being because this would be contrary to the first commandment, "Thou shall have no other God but me".

Because the king did not allow public debate, he was caused to make a blunder which he greatly regretted. *The rulers of this world should be extremely careful of those advisers who claim to be loyal to the king while at the same time plotting to undermine efficient, capable and honest servants of the king.* On the one hand they say they are true and loyal followers of the king, and yet at the same time they plot to remove the faithful Daniels from positions of authority. King Darius made the mistake of allowing the constitution, which affected fundamental human rights, to be changed before it was thoroughly discussed by all concerned. He also erred by allowing himself to be worshipped, when worship is reserved for God the Almighty alone.

Daniel in the Lions' Den

When Daniel learned that the King had signed the decree, he went to his house and as usual opened the windows and there, facing Jerusalem, worshipped God three times a day. Daniel was not afraid. His enemies came to watch how the Prime Minister-designate was disobeying the new law. In this respect Daniel chose to obey God rather than humans even if this meant suffering the capital punishment of being thrown into the lions' den. Daniel was a courageous man: he knew, as Paul did years later, that:

> If God is for us, who can be against us?... Who shall separate us from the love of Christ? Shall tribulations, or distress, or persecution, or famine, or nakedness, or peril, or sword?... No, in all these things we are more than conquerors through Him who loved us. For I am sure that neither death, nor life, nor angels, nor principalities, nor things present, nor things to come, no powers, nor heights, nor depths, nor anything else in all creation will able to separate us from the love of God in Christ Jesus our Lord (Romans 8:31-39).

Without any fear, Daniel chose to give "Caesar what was Caesar's and God what was God's". Daniel is in effect saying that if the king wants that which does not belong to him, then he will reply, I can give to you only that which belongs to the king and I shall give God what belongs to him. The enemies of Daniel saw him worshipping God and they went to accuse him to the king. Those who caused the constitution to be changed told the king, "Your Prime Minister-designate is breaking the law". We read that when the King heard these things, he was greatly distressed. He even tried hard to save Daniel from morning until evening, but all was in vain. The King lacked one thing: wisdom. Wisdom has been described as "being wise before the event rather than after it." Now his most beloved civil servant had disobeyed the law that the King himself had approved. King Darius must have become much wiser on that day. He would readily have declared, "Never again shall I rush to make major decisions without careful research, investigation and consultation." When such leaders come with that kind of request in future, the King must have resolved that he would refer them to the appropriate government ministry. He must have said from now onwards, "I, King Darius, shall not allow anyone to influence me into making any major decision until the matter has been thoroughly discussed by all concerned."

Daniel was put into the lions' den, but God was with him. We read that the king spent a sleepless night and early in the morning he was the first person to visit the den. He called Daniel and asked him whether he was all right. Daniel's answer is found in verse 21-22: "O King, Live forever! My God sent His angel, and shut the lion's mouths, and they have not hurt me because I was found blameless before Him and also before you O King I have done no wrong." Daniel was in effect telling the king that when the constitution is illegally changed so as to interfere with a fundamental human right – such as freedom of worship – that new law can be disobeyed. It is a choice between obeying God and obeying humans, and a man of God has no alternative but to obey God. This can be called holy defiance.

The king was of course exceedingly glad and ordered Daniel to be removed from the den. The king commanded those who had accused Daniel to be cast into the den of lions, together with their wives and children. That was done, and before they reached the bottom of the den, the lions overpowered them and broke all their bones into pieces. The people who had claimed to be so close to the Persian seat of power and who had used the opportunity to mislead the king ended up rather badly. History keeps repeating itself; we have seen giants fall out of favour for misuse of the privilege of being close to the powers that be.

Conclusion

The faith and courage of Daniel remained unshaken, and this event became a witness to the living God throughout the empire. The King sent a decree to all people, nations and languages in all the earth. His message is contained in verse 25-27. "My dear friends," I said, "the Nyeri leaders, civil servants and all those here present, let us emulate Daniel who was such a loyal, capable and honest civil servant that no faults could be found in him. Because he was devout and blameless before God and was loyal and faithful to the King, God himself delivered him from the mouth of lions. My dear friends, when you hold a position of influence and you do your work well, then do not fear any opposition. Only trust in God. Even if you are accused unfairly, the truth will, in the final analysis, be triumphant."

When the service ended the District Commissioner, Mr Mukhalule, told me that was the best sermon he has ever heard. But on the following day, on the one o'clock KBC News, I was greatly surprised to hear the DC disassociate himself with my sermon, which he said was bordering on sedition. Soon after the one o'clock KBC news, I received a telephone call from the Provincial Commissioner, John Etemesi, who told me to go at once and see him. I therefore went to Nyeri and the PC told me that after the sermon someone telephoned the President, who was at Eldoret State House. The caller told the President that the PC had invited his friend Bishop Gitari to come to attack the President at St Peter's Church, Nyeri, and that the Bishop had spent most of the time talking about Daniel! Daniel! Daniel! The truth was that I had been talking about Daniel in the Bible and not Daniel arap Moi. He had informed the President that he was not even aware that I was the guest preacher during the civic service.

According to the PC the President sounded extremely annoyed on telephone. The PC called the DC to his house and the DC informed him that the sermon was very good. However, journalists were rounded up and requested to surrender copies of the sermon I had given them. The *Daily Nation* of 27 June 1987 reported:

> Nyeri District Commissioner Mr Mukhalule said the sermon by Bishop Gitari bordered on subversion and sedition. "The Bishop seemed to have been calling on his foreign masters to come to his assistance." The DC said the hand written text of the sermon circulated to the press by the Bishop after the service was clandestinely distributed and was at total variance with what the Bishop had preached in the church earlier. "I lead all the Nyeri people in condemning it." Mr Mukhalule said there was an unreported paragraph in the sermon which stated "Any leader who allows himself that which can only be given to God leaves a lot to be desired. Only God should be worshipped. To worship man is idolatrous."

He was unhappy with the paragraph too. The whole of that week from Monday to Saturday (22 to 27 June 1987), politicians, even those who were not present at St Peter's Church, were falling over each other in trying to condemn me. Ngumbu Njururi, the assistant minister in the office of the President, called upon me to withdraw remarks that I had made concerning KPCU and requested me to withdraw my call for a public debate before any changes are made in the constitution. He said the question of lining up during preliminary elections and the restructuring of KPCU had been sufficiently discussed. (See *The Standard,* 24 June 1987.) The National Chairman of KANU, David Okiki Amayo, called a press conference and gave me the official party reply to my sermon. The *Daily Nation* published KANU's reply to me on Saturday 27 June 1987; the reply is hereby reproduced verbatim.

KANU Replies to Gitari Sermon

The KANU National Chairman David Okiki Amayo yesterday accused Bishop David Gitari of the Church of the Province of Kenya of "seeking to create chaos, confusion and incite wananchi against their popularly elected leaders. He said: "The likes of Bishop Gitari, could only destabilize the country for reasons known to themselves." Addressing a press conference in his office yesterday, Mr. Amayo asked: "what is Bishop Gitari up to? Kanu's primary objective is to form the Government of this country. In this role, the party must be concerned with stability, harmony, rule and respect for the law and order in Kenya. Further-more, the party undertakes to promote unity and understanding among all the people of Kenya and to break down tribal, linguistic, racial and cultural barriers." He said the party was alarmed by Bishop Gitari's remarks, and is unable by any stretch of imagination, to understand the comparison of King Darius, a pagan King who ruled over a conquered kingdom and worshipped idols, with the leadership in this country." He told the Bishop that Kenya was led by democratically-elected leaders, and no one had been perse-cuted for his religious beliefs "in the history of independent Kenya." Bishop Gitari's Biblical reference to the book of Daniel Chapter 6, about Darius and Daniel has no parallel in Kenya. Such comparison can only be made with the aim of confusing the God fearing and peace-loving Kenyans. "The question of lining up in the election of party candidates for the national and local election was debated at var-ious levels in the republic. It was as a result of these extensive discus-sions that a consensus was reached. If the majority of Kenyans were not in favour of the system, he said, they would have rejected it as they did the move to change the constitution in 1976. Both the coun-try and the party have dynamic constitutions which have been sub-jected to the necessary amendments and changes previously. In 1965, there was a change in the country's constitution and that process took only one day. In 1970, there were further changes and indeed there have been some changes in both constitutions, all of them were done constitutionally." The chairman declined to comment on the support given to Bishop Gitari on the contents of the sermon by Nyeri Kanu Branch Chairman, Isaiah Mathenge. He said his statement should serve as a warning to the Bishop and "all those that support him. Churchmen, he said have a right to comment on all national issues.

But they must do so at the right time. In this case, Bishop Gitari is commenting on an issue that has already been resolved and finished by the state and country, he said. (*Daily Nation*, 27 June 1987)

The *Kenya Times* wrote an editorial which was published on Monday 29th June 1987 entitled CPK SHOULD DISOWN DR GITARI'S ANTICS.

Kenya churchmen and all other religious zealots and the laity are perfectly entitled to their respective beliefs and, in fact, freedom of worship and conscience is enshrined in the country's constitution. Nevertheless, the laws of the land do not allow any of them, or any foreigner resident on Kenyan soil, to indulge in any manner of subversion; and it is a penal offense to incite disaffection. Dissemination of subversive literature, too, constitutes a penal offense and all those clerics who are nowadays circulating written sermons among worshippers should be extremely careful lest they are caught red-handed breaking the laws of the land. One can preach about heavenly marvels, including signs of the zodiacs, but one cannot misuse the Holy scriptures as mere escape literature and, in the process, try to whip up disaffection and despondency. Preaching in Nyeri recently, the Rt Rev Dr David M. Gitari, Bishop of the CPK diocese of Mt. Kenya East, misinterpreted parts of the Old Testament in a vain effort aimed at justifying his own radical disposition. To which "advisors" for example, does the prelate specifically refer when he said they claimed "to be true Nyayo followers?" The Bishop glibly talked about King Darius of Persia, adducing a patently irrelevant argument which cannot justifiably be applied to present-day Kenya. When he attends his next CPK seminar or "refresher course" someone will hopefully remind him of the diversity of Persian mythology. Some of King Darius' subjects were Zoroastrians!

The only politician who supported me and was present when I preached the sermon at St Peter's, Nyeri, was Isaiah Mathenge, whose statement was published by the *Daily Nation* on 25 June 1987. He said the criticism was "totally unworthy and ill motivated". Mathenge said the sermon was "intellectually satisfying and spiritually uplifting". The criticism of my Nyeri sermon continued into the week that followed. Moses Mudavadi, the Secretary of KANU, had just returned to the country from overseas. On Monday 29 June 1987, he issued a statement reprimanding central province MPs for not condemning me over my sermon. He also told me to "keep politics out of church and guide church members on social-economic activities" rather than "cause trouble and misuse freedom of worship".

On Saturday 27 June 1987, I had pastoral duty to do in Meru. However when I read the criticism of the chairman of KANU, Okiki Omayo, I decided to stay at home and prepare a response to the criticism. On Sunday 28 June 1987, I was due to consecrate the Church of Good Samaritan, Kathiga. which is half way between Kutus and Kagio in Kirinyaga District. I decided to preach from 2 Timothy 3:14 to 4:7.

All Scripture is Inspired by God

The main purpose of my fourth sermon in June 1987 was to explain the value of all Scripture and in doing so to answer Amayo. In his statement, the National Chairman of KANU had said, "Bishop Gitari's Biblical reference to the book of Daniel has no parallel in Kenya. Such a comparison can only be made with the aim of confusing the God fearing and peace loving Kenyans" (*Daily Nation* 27 June 1987). The Chairman had also described the book of Daniel as irrelevant for Kenyans today. The *Kenya Times* wrote an editorial entitled CPK SHOULD DISOWN DR GITARI'S ANTICS in which I was accused of "misinterpreting parts of the Old Testament in a vain effort aimed at justifying his own radical disposition ..."

But in 2 Timothy 3:14-17, Paul tells the young Timothy, "But as for you, continue in what you have learnt and have become convinced of, because you know the Holy Scriptures, which are able to make you wise for salvation through faith in Christ Jesus. All scripture is God breathed and is useful for teaching, rebuking, correcting and training in righteousness, so that the man of God may be thoroughly equipped for every good work."

I told the congregation that at the time when Paul wrote this letter, the Old Testament was the only Bible. Paul is telling Timothy that the whole of the Old Testament is God-inspired. In other words, every book of the Old Testament is a book written by the inspiration of God. When the church added the New Testament to the canon of Scripture, it recognized that both the Old and the New Testaments were inspired by God. What this means is that every book of the Bible is the very word of God. I told the congregation that the second fundamental truth about the scriptures is that "all Scripture is profitable". There is no part of scripture that is useless even for the present generation... But now the chairman of KANU, speaking on behalf of our beloved party, had come forward to tell us what is not profitable in Scripture. If he was quoted correctly, he had said, "Bishop Gitari's Biblical reference to the book of Daniel Chapter 6 about Darius and Daniel has no parallel in Kenya." We were being told that Daniel 6 is not profitable for the modern Kenyan. There was therefore no profit in telling *wananchi* to emulate the example of Daniel, who served King Darius so faithfully that no fault could be found in his work. There was a great issue at stake here. Had KANU the right to tell church leaders which passages in the Bible were profitable to Kenyans or which were not profitable? As far as we preachers were concerned, all Scripture, including Daniel 6, is profitable for every generation and is profitable for Kenya Today "(*Let the Bishop Speak*, p. 50). I told the congregation that we now had two authorities concerning scriptures. On one hand we had the chairman of KANU who told us some parts of the Bible are not profitable for Kenyans; on the other hand we had the apostle Paul, who tells us that all Scripture is profitable for teaching, rebuking, correcting and training in righteousness. I challenged the congregation to choose between the Chairman of KANU and the apostle Paul. With a resounding response the entire congregation chose the apostle. That was the last time Akiki Amayo was heard criticising me publicly.

The Secretary of KANU, Moses Mudavadi, on his part had also issued a statement in which he said, "The government welcomes constructive criticism and suggestions from any quarters, including the church, provided that the time is appropriate." In response, I told the congregation that in 2 Timothy 4:2, Paul instructed Timothy, "Preach the message, insist upon telling it whether the time is right or not." Here we have another fundamental issue at stake, I told the congregation. Has any politician a right to tell the preacher when it is convenient to preach on certain issues and when it is not convenient? If I have to choose what a politician tells me and what St Paul commands I will take the side of the apostle. The preacher is captive to the Holy Spirit and he has to preach on any issues the Holy Spirit leads him to touch. Preacher, press the message home on all occasions! We have to be on duty at all the times, convenient or inconvenient.

Mudavadi had allegedly said that I was not loyal to Kenya because I was not a Kenyan. In response I told him that I was born not far from the equator on the southern slopes of Mt Kenya and provided my identity card number. After that I did not get any further criticism from Mudavadi. The

President had also said that he wanted civil servants to be consistent. I therefore criticized the Nyeri District Commissioner, Mr Mukhalule, for his inconsistency. On Sunday, after the Nyeri sermon, he had said that was the best sermon he has ever heard. On Monday he was quoted as saying, "The sermon by Bishop Gitari bordered on subversion and sedition." Such inconsistency is not worthy of a District Commissioner.

KANU had asked me to withdraw my statement that "any leader who allows himself that which can only be given to God leaves a lot to be desired. Only God should be worshipped. To worship man is idolatrous." I told the congregation that I could not understand the logic of those who were calling on me to withdraw that statement. I said I would be like Martin Luther, who stood before the Imperial Court at Worms in 1521, and, asked to recant, said, "Unless I am convinced by the Scriptures and plain reason, my conscience is captive to the word of God. I cannot and I will not recant anything, for to go against my conscience is neither right nor safe. Here I stand: God help me." With those words, I ended the sermon.

On Monday 29 June 1987, I became the target of three Cabinet Ministers, Dr Robert Ouko, Andrew Omanga and Nicholas Biwott. After touring the abandoned giant molasses plant at Otongolo area, Kisumu, they called upon me and other clergy to "keep their churches clean by not preaching on controversial issues". They referred to my sermons as provocative. Dr Ouko was reported by *Kenya Times* to have said, "We in Kenya, right from our beloved President Daniel arap Moi, are God-fearing people and are not worshipping an individual as claimed by Bishop Gitari... Rejecting Bishop Gitari's sermon, Dr Ouko asked the prelate as to whether he was referring to this country in his sermon or another country, 'because it's only in Kenya where freedom of worship is greatly observed'. He called clergymen to stop interfering with the affairs of elected leaders and instead make the churches 'pure' to attract more worshippers." The scathing attack on me, the *Kenya Times* reported, "was began by minister for Energy and Regional Development Biwott, who questioned why some church leaders abused freedom of worship instead of using it to preach love for one another." (*Kenya Times*, 30 June 1987)

The Assistant Minister for Co-operative Development, Peter Ejore, called upon KANU to discipline me for "serving his foreign masters and not God". He wondered why the congregation did not shout me down for the "nonsense" I was preaching.

A group of ex-freedom fighters led by General Chui Muhoro told the *Kenya Times* that "we feel time has come for our children to be told in plain terms that some of the most dangerous traitors are masquerading in our midst wearing robes of piety and purporting to talk in the name of Christ. These must be watched carefully and told to shut up and leave the work of national development to those who genuinely care for the future of this nation" (*Kenya Times*). The newspaper went ahead to publish this editorial.

Enough of All That, Dr David Gitari…!

KENYANS everywhere in the republic, who are all aware of their constitutional rights will persist in their refusal to be taken for an occasional ride by any of those clerics who have of late been audacious enough to make the precious Holy Bible one of the best misused books of the year. In nowhere does the Holy Book question the legitimacy of any properly-established authority of State. A countrywide hue and cry, spearheaded by patriotic elected members of Parliament, among them Ministers and Assistant Ministers, local councilors and officials of the ruling party Kanu, has been aroused by the remorseless attitude adopted by the Rt Rev Dr. David Gitari, Bishop of Mt Kenya East Diocese of the Church Province of Kenya, who has refused to retract any of the offensive utterances he made in a recent sermon. The prelate, ostensibly responding to the current hue and cry against his own ill-conceived onslaught on the ruling party and the echelons of the country's leadership, was at the weekend reported as having bragged at yet another church service; "We do not preach the gospel to please leaders of political parties, As long as we are faithful to the scriptures and to Jesus, it does not worry us what the rest of the world (may) say about us …" Unlike their colonial era's predecessors, who persistently confined their activities to spiritual matters a number of Kenyan clerics who succeeded them are now at war with elected leaders and burning their fingers in confrontation with the ruling party and the government. Dr David Gitari belongs to this category of the undoubtedly well-educated Kenyan clerics who are vainly trying to create an unacceptable lobby within the Republic's Christendom – which must be nipped in the bud. Kenya's popularly-elected political leadership is constitutionally obliged to uphold the Constitution.

Section 78 of the constitution makes it crystal clear that no person shall be hindered in the enjoyment of his freedom of conscience, which freedom either alone or in private, to manifest and propagate his religion or belief in worship, teaching, practice and observance... What's all the fuss about, Dr Gitari? Are we Kenyans not freer, markedly civilized and affluent than those cavemen, herdsmen and other folk of yore days upon whom his favorite King Darius sat and spat? (*Kenya Times*, 1 July 1987)

After three weeks of this, the President himself decided to bring the debate to an end by saying, "Let the Bishop Speak". Owing to the interest my four sermons generated and vigorous condemnation by politicians, most of whom had neither been present nor read the actual texts of my sermons, I decided to have the sermons published and to include in the book photocopies of newspaper cuttings about reactions by politicians. Hence Uzima Press agreed to publish the sermons under the title *Let the Bishop Speak*. The book was published in 1988 and sold like hot cakes. Within a short time it was out of print. The inclusion of press statements condemning my sermons was aimed at exposing the ignorance of politicians who react to sensational newspaper reporting rather than responding to the actual text of my sermons. Some of the statements of condemnation had no bearing whatsoever on what I had actually said. Included in the book was an additional chapter on church and politics in Kenya. Since the book is long out of print, I hereby reproduce the chapter summarising the lessons I learnt from June 1987 events.

Church and Politics

The first lesson from the debate is that there seems to be some confusion within the country on the proper place of the church in national affairs. It was most refreshing to hear the President, as quoted above say publicly that the Church has the duty to speak out against corruption and other evils. Yet it is precisely at this point that there is confusion. Every time a church leader speaks openly against corruption and injustice, he is told to leave politics to politicians.

However, the current confusion demands urgent and open debate between political and church leaders on the proper relationship between the Church and Politics. The key issues in this debate are an understanding of the role of the Church in society, and an understanding of what constitutes politics. The debate is not purely an academic exercise; there are urgent practical questions to be answered. For example, does the statement that "church leaders should not involve themselves in politics" mean that they should not become members of the ruling party? Does it mean that they should not use their vote in the election of councilors and members of parliament? Does it mean that they themselves should not stand as candidates for a council or for a parliament position? I suspect that if we were to ask a group of politicians for their answers to these questions we would find that the majority see no problem in church leaders becoming KANU members, or exercising their right to vote. Some would also say that there is nothing wrong with a church leader seeking election as a councilor or parliamentarian. The logical conclusion to which we would be forced is that our politicians do not consider that becoming a KANU member, or voting in an election, or even standing as a candidate, as involving oneself in politics. Some politicians allow church leaders wide freedom to discuss "political" matters. In a recent sermon a bishop of an indigenous church touched on many political issues, including voter registration and loyalty to the government and to KANU. He even threatened to use his Church's disciplinary machinery to expel any member who opposed the Government or KANU. The bishop, as far as I am aware, has not been criticized as interfering in KANU affairs, or mixing religion with politics. The Standard Newspaper reported on 2nd June 1989 that; "A bishop of the African independent Pentecostal church of Africa (AP-CA) The Rt Revd Samuel Gichuki has said that the church will expel any member who opposes the government or KANU".

The Proper Relationship between the Church and the State

The question of the right relationship between the Church and political powers is not a new one, and it is not confined to Kenya. In August 1976, a conference organized jointly by the World Council of Churches and the Ecumenical Institute of Bossey, Switzerland, provided a useful outline of four possible attitudes of churches to Political powers;

1. The churches adapt themselves actively when they identify themselves with the goals and intentions of the power or the state.
2. The churches adapt themselves passively when they withdraw into the sphere of the purely religious and refrain from making any statements on decisions and activities of the power of the state.

3. The churches can engage in critical and constructive collaboration with the power of the state by evaluation on the basis of their understanding of the gospel, political decisions and proposed programmes.
4. The churches may be led to resist or oppose the power of the state. The obligation to resist which may arise under certain circumstances has no destructive intention; the attitude of resistance will be adopted to serve society and even the state, because the state as well is called to be the servant of God and of the people (Romans 13).

The fourth position – direct resistance by the Church to the state – is a comparatively rare phenomenon. It was seen in the resistance of the confessing Church to Hitler's government in Nazi Germany. In our own day, many Christians in South Africa also take a position of total rejection of the Apartheid State. However, the first three of these positions are well represented in Kenya today. An example of the first position where a church actively identifies itself with the goals or intentions of the Government may be found in the indigenous Kenyan Church.

It is interesting to note that one of the indigenous Churches, whose present political position is to give the government one hundred per cent support, was in the forefront of the struggle against colonialism. During the *Mau Mau* emergency, the Church was banned by the colonial government. At that time, the Church was acutely aware and critical of mistakes which the colonial government was making; but now that independence has been granted, the church no longer sees the need to criticize the government. I find it difficult to commend a church for giving the government or a political party unconditional support whether it is right or wrong. In the final analysis this position does no good to either the Church or the State.

The second position is also well represented in Kenya. This is where the Church withdraws into the sphere of purely religious activity and abstains from making statements on government activities or decisions. It is probably the position that most politicians would like the Church to adopt.

This position was well demonstrated by the statement issued by the moderator of the Baptist Church of Kenya and published by the *Daily Nation* on 28th June 1987.

Meanwhile, the Moderator of the 800 Church Baptist Convention of Kenya, the Reverend Arthur Kinyanjui, has criticized Archbishop Kuria's views on the queuing system adds KNA. Speaking in Nakuru yesterday, Revd Kinyanjui said it was a member of the CPK who had brought up opposition to the system at the recent National Council of Churches of Kenya pastors conference. He asked what verse of the Bible the CPK leader had based his criticism of the system, adding: "Caesar's should be left to Caesar and God's to God. He told critics of the new voting system to concentrate on saving souls. The Moderator said the NCCK pastors had gone "astray" and called upon the clergy men to leave political matters in the hands of Kanu. The Revd Kinyanjui said his church fully backed the President, the Government and KANU and that the NCCK pastors should have consulted the State on the issue before passing their resolution. The moderator added that his church stood by the freedom of expression and worship upheld in the country's Constitution.

The words of Jesus about what is Caesar's and what is God's are commonly quoted by those who wish to silence the Church on matters of public policy. It is less common to hear a proper exegesis of the passage. Jesus was responding to a question on the specific issue of paying taxes. His answer authorizes Christians to pay taxes, and also gives general approval to the function of government which taxes are needed to support. Jesus' words do not mean that God and his Church have no interest in what the Government does. Questions of justice and righteousness belong to God, not to Caesar; it is Caesars' work to uphold God's standards. If Caesar makes a mistake, God will correct him.

The third position is constructive but critical collaboration. It is the position which the National Council of Churches of Kenya (NCCK) took in its resolution on queuing in August 1986. Those who adopted this position were aware of the breadth of what the Bible says about political authority in this world. The same Bible that contains Romans 13 also contains Revelation 13. In Romans 13, Christians are advised that the state at its best is a servant of God, upholding His standards in the world and deserving all honour and obedience. The ruler is a God's servant for your good. However, Revelation 13 shows how the state may become a demonic force, opposing the will of God and doing evil, and deserving only destruction.

The Church's task is to steer the state away from evil doing, and to remind it of its high calling as the servant of God. It cannot fulfill the task by 'concentrating on saving souls' while ignoring other duties. The church must be ready to encourage and praise the good which the state does, while challenging and advising the government whenever it is in danger of doing ill. This indeed was the purpose of my June 1987 sermons. The Church's commitment to this prophetic ministry is not just confined to Kenya. For instance, in Europe, the Church has been deeply involved in political issues. The abolition of the slave trade and the introduction of labour laws, the confessing churches resistance to Hitler in Germany and Archbishop Temple's preaching on the need for social justice in Britain, were all thoroughly political. The then Archbishop of Canterbury, the Most Revd Robert Runcie has been very critical of some aspects of the ruling Conservative Party. The church has also vigorously debated issues such as unemployment, inner city renewal, the miners' strike, nuclear weapons and apartheid in South Africa. The Church worldwide regards it as part of her responsibility to guide and comment on national affairs.

The Role of the Press

In June 1987, the readers heavily relied on press reports to know what I had said in my four sermons. When I check what the press has reported about my sermons, I am generally satisfied that the press has done a good job of presenting the message fairly. However many times the media in covering our sermons gives prominence to issues even those present during the sermon would not consider as the main thrust of the preacher. I am aware that editors have to sell newspapers and that many times they have to write sensational headlines and stories to catch the attention of readers. I also understand that they have news values that they use to judge what aspects to give prominence. But sometimes spiced up stories fail to present an accurate account of events, and sometimes reports are taken out of context and the reporting on some of my sermons has ended up causing some degree of misunderstanding. Therefore I have learnt that when I read in the newspapers that someone 'attacks' me or 'blasts' me I do not necessarily take it personally. I would rather find out what the individual who was quoted actually said and try to answer them sensibly. Journalists tell us 'when a dog bites a man that is no news. But when a man bites a dog that is news!'

The Decision-Making Process in Kenya

According to the constitution, sovereign authority in Kenya belongs to the people. The people entrust their sovereign power to the elected representatives in the National Assembly and to the President who is both the Head of State and the source of executive authority. The responsibility for making and implementing policy rests with those to whom the people have entrusted it. It is their inescapable task to seek just and practical policies in public life. If those in authority are wise, they will consult widely with the people in their search for good policies.

It was interesting to read a statement published in the Media by the Catholic Bishops, "We have all seen the enthusiastic support that President Moi has received at mass meetings in which he raised this matter. We believe that this represents the overwhelming personal support and loyalty enjoyed by the president rather than a reflective response to the issue itself. It is on this basis that we appeal to your fatherly concern for the nation to allow further discussion of the issue... When the President asks people who support what he says to raise their hands, they have no alternative than to raise their hands even if they do not believe in what he says. When the president is looking at you it is very difficult not to raise your hands."

The Purpose of Public Rallies

The president has explained clearly what the purpose of a public meeting is:

> A harambee rally is not only a fund-raiser exercise, it is much more. Normally, it is also a forum for public education, for political education to explain policies, for whipping up national favour for a cause, and for giving the people a sense of dignity and communal belonging – in short, for welding us into one people for one cause. At the occasion, everyone present is made to feel for everyone else, and to absorb the galvanizing spirit thereby created. The rally promotes fraternity; and gives satisfaction to all, poor and rich.

In other words, the purpose of a rally is not to discuss or make policy; it is to explain policies which have already been made, and to build national solidarity. The making of policy is still the responsibility of the committees, councils and parliament. If there is a call for policies to be discussed, they cannot shelter behind the idea that "the policies were fully debated at a public rally". That is not purpose of rallies.

True Loyalty

The question of loyalty and being pro-Nyayo emerged as the main issue in the debate that followed my sermons in June. The best comment on these attitudes is to quote again from the Catholic Bishops' memorandum of 13 November, 1986:

> The commitment of your Excellency to love, peace and unity is the inspiration behind the strengthening of KANU as a symbol and instrument of unity in the country. However, we are disturbed by the claims of politicians that the power of the party is the paramount, exceeding even the power of parliament. The suggestion is made that anyone who says otherwise is disloyal to Your Excellency and is anti-Nyayo.

This view seems to have been the result of excessive zeal for party unity which had not been fully thought out by its exponents. We believed that there was a danger of totalitarianism if the trend was not checked. It represents a fundamental change in our political system. If our people genuinely want it, they should have it. However, it must not be allowed to happen without very serious and considered discussion.

At present, discussing is precluded by the allegations of powerful party officials that any questions of the system are tantamount to disloyalty. Already, the party is assuming a totalizing role. It claims to speak for the people and yet does not allow the people to give views.

Let the last word go to the wisest of human rulers, King Solomon. As a King, he was no doubt surrounded by his share of flatterers. He must have heard the praises of those who in the last resort were treacherous, as well as hearing the challenges of those who in the last report were loyal. His conclusion recorded in Proverbs 10:10-11, was as follows: "A man who holds back the truth causes trouble. But the one who openly criticizes works for peace."

Chapter 21

The Queuing Debate:
August 1986 to November 1991

In August 1986, I chaired the second National Pastors' Conference organized by NCCK, which was attended by 1,200 pastors and their spouses and held at Kenyatta University near Nairobi. While the pastors were meeting at Kenyatta University, the National Delegates' Conference of KANU was holding its annual conference at the Kenyatta Conference Centre in the city. The conference passed a resolution that in future all national elections were to be held by queuing behind candidates. The party argued that since the queuing was to be done during broad daylight, everyone would see which candidate had the longest queue. When this decision was published in the daily newspapers, the pastors at Kenyatta University were very concerned. Bishop Henry Okullu came to see me as the Chairman and told me that it was imperative that the pastors' conference issue a statement rejecting the queuing system of election. I drafted the statement with the help of Bishop Okullu, which was signed by the General Secretary of NCCK, John Cauri Kamau, after it was discussed and approved by the 1,200 pastors.

The pastors' conference statement said the pastors would not participate in the exercise of nominating party candidates for the obvious reasons that the pastors preferred the "secret ballot" method to that of queuing behind a candidate. The pastors' statement of 21 August 1986 went on to say

We therefore urge KANU and parliament to find an alternative method in which church leaders can participate in primary election so that they can exercise their democratic rights as citizens of this nation. If the procedure of lining up behind candidates is followed and if many church leaders or other Christians refrain from taking part in the elections, (Nominations) they will have been denied their human and political rights. (See *Weekly Review*, April 1986).

Soon after the pastors issued their statement, President Moi expressed his displeasure with the NCCK statement and later announced that "irrespective of the pastors' objection, a bill will be taken to parliament to make queuing part of the country's election law". The president went on to say that he was "surprised at the stand taken by the NCCK pastors that queuing behind a candidate meant that they were taking sides". The president went on to say, "People who truly believe in God cannot be afraid of any repercussions simply because they have openly elected a candidate of their choice through parliamentary and civic elections."

According to the *Weekly Review* of 29 August 1986, the pastors' conference statement was also criticized by, among others, then cabinet ministers Nicholas Biwott (Energy and Development) and Dr Robert Ouko (Planning & National Development). Dr Ouko said, "Truth and honesty are virtues cherished by Christianity and there is nowhere where lining up behind a candidate can be considered to be inconsistent with Christian values." Mulu Mutisya, a man described as the strongman of Ukambani politics, asked the pastors to make a written apology to the President for undermining the party.

Following this controversy some churches withdrew their membership of NCCK. These included the African Inland Church (AIC), the African Independent Pentecostal Church of Africa, the Church of God, the Full Gospel Churches of Kenya, the Pentecostal Assemblies of God and the Salvation Army. Some of these churches returned to the fold of NCCK later, but some never returned. The president, who is a member of AIC, played a major part in persuading the church to pull out of the NCCK.

A number of church leaders continued to criticize the queuing system of voting. Archbishop Manases Kuria of ACK had called the system "un-christian, undemocratic and embarrassing". Bishop Alexander Muge of the Diocese of Eldoret urged the pastors who had participated in the conference not to worry even if they were attacked for their stand, as they had a pastoral duty over their flock. He said that it was the role of the church to stand up against the pressures of totalitarianism in the name of one-party systems and against the detention of political opponents without trial. The Chairman of the Roman Catholic Church Episcopal Conference said that the church could not support queuing because such a procedure would create schism in church ranks (see *Weekly Review*, 29 August 1986).

The queuing system was used for the first time during the nomination of KANU candidates for the general election held in February 1988. Owing to the refusal by church leaders to participate in the party nomination, the president had issued a statement excluding people in the armed forces, senior civil servants, senior administrative officers and church leaders from voting by lining up behind candidates. A booklet was published by KANU on 2 February 1988 giving guidance concerning the forthcoming nomination. I immediately issued a statement, which read;

> We have cadres of civil servants, members of the armed forces and the religious leaders who have been exempted from queuing, but the booklet released recently on rules to be followed during the nomination did not indicate what system these people would follow to exercise their constitutional rights... I am concerned that the rules do not give guidance on how those members of KANU who were exempted from queuing will exercise their rights to vote.

The General Secretary of KANU, Burudi Nabwera, responded to my enquiry. He said, "There is no special way of voting without queuing. You either stay away or join the queue" (*Standard*, 11 February 1988). During the KANU nomination exercise, most of the Anglican bishops were attending the Partners in Mission consultation conference held at St Andrews College of Theology and Development, Kabare, in Kirinyaga district. We decided to take a day off so as to witness with our own eyes how the nominations were being done in some parts of the district. Bishop Henry Okullu went to the southern part of Ndia constituency. Bishop Alexander Muge went to Mutira Polling Station and I went to Kamuiru. All the chiefs and assistant chiefs who were not supporters of James Njiru were sacked some months before the elections and new ones appointed. They were under instruction not to allow anyone who was not a supporter of Njiru into the queue. This was obeyed to the letter.

I went to Kamuiru Polling Station accompanied by Canon Burgess Carr, formerly the General Secretary of the All Africa Conference of Churches, and the Ven. John Kago, the ACK Provincial Secretary. I was abused by a young youth winger, a supporter of James Njiru. The police were standing by and were doing nothing to stop the young man from insulting me. When supporters of John Matere Keriri came out of the polling station, they chased the youth winger out of the school compound. The youth wingers went on to the other side of the fence and started throwing stones. It was not until a stone hit a policeman that the officers retaliated by shooting bullets in the air. We were escorted to Kagumo Market by supporters of John Matere Keriri. Burgess Carr was understandably very frightened by this incident, though such was somewhat usual to many Kenyans.

When we arrived at Mutira Polling Station, we found that the assistant chief had stopped the returning officers from counting the people in the queues. There were only a handful of supporters of James Njiru and the assistant chief was ordering election officials to wait for Njiru's people to come. Bishop Alexander Muge kept vigil for many hours observing how the queuing system was being abused. He asked me to contact State House concerning this matter. We drove to Karatina, about ten miles away, where I telephoned the comptroller of State House, Abraham Kiptanui. Kiptanui then telephoned the DC Kirinyaga and ordered him to send the DO to supervise the nomination. When the DO, who was a Kalenjin like Muge, arrived, Muge told him to his face that the Kalenjin administrators were spoiling the name of KANU and the president in the district.

At the end of the day, Kenya Broadcasting Corporation (KBC) announced that James Njiru had won the election by 88% of the vote. Nahashon Njuno had also been defeated by rigging in Gichugu constituency. I wrote a letter of protest to the president, which I took to State House personally. I told the president that the people of Kirinyaga will never again support KANU and the queuing system of elections because of violence and the injustices of the system. The president never replied to my letter.

I issued a press statement condemning the queuing system of voting and in response KANU said I was a communist serving my foreign masters. I answered that I did not need a foreigner to tell me which were the shorter and the longer queues and to know that declaring candidates supported by the shorter queues winners was a travesty of justice and a blow to democracy. I had after all witnessed this first-hand in a number of polling stations in Kirinyaga and Nyeri.

The rigging of elections continued even in the national elections held in April 1988. Bishop Henry Okullu was very right when he said 75% of members of the 6th Parliament were selected not elected. *Beyond* magazine, sponsored by NCCK, gave a detailed analysis of how the elections were rigged. As a result of this exposure, *Beyond* magazine was proscribed and the editor

Bedan Mbugua arrested, prosecuted, found guilty and imprisoned at the G.K. Manyani Prison for one year. His employer, the NCCK, did not protest or defend him, but abandoned him at his greatest hour of need. The editor of *Society* magazine, which was also seen as critical of the government, Pius Nyamora, was also arrested.

Beyond magazine had quoted me as having said that G.K. Kariithi was "rigged in". This attracted the wrath of supporters of Kariithi. After the elections Kariithi walked into my office in Embu and informed me that he was now my *bona fide* member of parliament. I told him, "Mr Kariithi, you have been rigged in and very soon you will be rigged out". Five months later he lost his post as Chairman of KANU in Gichugu constituency when the election was rigged. I am the only person who called a press conference to state that Kariithi had won the KANU chairmanship elections but that Nahashon Njuno had won by rigging them. Kariithi telephoned me and we arranged to meet at St Andrew's, Kabare, where he told me that he had at last come to realize that I stood for the truth.

I was present during the historic KANU annual delegates conference at Kasarani Sports Complex in November 1991. To my great joy, KANU abandoned the queuing system of voting during the preliminary nominations. I thanked God that the seven-year struggle against the system was not in vain.

Parliament Debates a Bishop

On Thursday 29 September 1988 Parliament suspended its normal business to debate a matter of national importance. The matter of national importance was my criticism of the method used by KANU to pass twelve resolutions in ten minutes during the annual delegates' conference. The conference that year was held at Nyayo Stadium on Saturday 24 September 1988. More than 3,000 delegates representing KANU branches throughout the nation attended the conference. According to the newspapers of Sunday 25 September 1988, twelve resolutions were passed in ten minutes.

On Sunday 25 September, I was taking a confirmation service at ACK Church, Kinoru, in Meru Town. About 400 people attended the service. I confirmed 92 candidates on that day. During the sermon I told the congregation that the 3,000 KANU delegates who had attended the annual delegates' meeting the previous day were treated like a rubber stamp. They passed twelve resolutions in ten minutes. The motions were proposed, seconded and passed by acclamation. I complained that the delegates were not given an opportunity to debate each motion before it was passed. I was particularly concerned by two resolutions that had been passed. One motion called on the government to reconsider its stand on NCCK and if necessary ban the organisation for its involvement in politics. Another motion called on the delegates and the party to appreciate the services of civil servants who had officiated at the nationwide preliminary elections.

I told the congregation that I was sure that there were some KANU delegates present who, if given the opportunity, would have cautioned the delegates from threatening to ban the NCCK. I also said that it was a big joke that civil servants were being appreciated for their role in the preliminary nominations in February and the elections in April. I said there was sufficient evidence that the elections had been rigged by the civil servants, who should have been condemned, not praised, at the annual delegates conference. I said the 3,000 delegates were made to endorse regulations they had no part in formulating, and that they did not even understand, as they were not even given time to discuss them.

I went to Nairobi on Tuesday 27 September 1988 and called a press conference at the provincial office. My statement was published on Wednesday 28 September 1988. MP Johnstone Makau moved a motion for parliament to adjourn business that Wednesday afternoon but the speaker told him to move the motion the following day. And so parliament suspended its normal business that Thursday afternoon. More than 20 members of parliament spoke against me and the debate lasted for two and a half hours; thus I became the first church leader to be debated for so long by parliament. Bishop Muge had been debated before, but it was for one and a half hours.

The *Weekly Review* of 7 October 1988, covering the debate, said:

> Politicians quickly read into Gitari's statement a deliberate plot by churchmen to continue discrediting the political establishment, so, rather than respond to Gitari alone, MPs lumped together with Gitari three other outspoken clerics in the country, Dr Henry Okullu, the Bishop of the CPK's Maseno South Diocese, Bishop Alexander Muge of the CPK's Diocese of Eldoret and the Rev Dr Timothy Njoya of the PCEA and lambasted the lot at a go for their several criticism of the government. For two and half hours, the lawmakers took turns in making increasingly scathing attacks on the four church leaders.

I was in several instances referred to as a tribalist, a political activist, a champion of political groupings, a member of *Mwakenya* (the underground political movement) and a messenger of foreign masters. All four of us were accused of being sympathetic to the apartheid regime of South Africa (*Weekly Review*, 7 October 1988, p. 8).

The *Weekly Review* went on to say, "Perhaps the most censorious attack came from the Vice-President Dr Joseph Karanja who is also the leader of Government Business in the House. He descended on the four clergymen as frustrated politicians who should leave the pulpit if they are interested in politics rather than using it as a platform from which to criticize the government and party..."

As the *Weekly Review* observed, the contributions by parliamentarians during the debate did not respond to the issue I had raised. Twelve resolutions were passed by the 3,000 delegates in ten minutes. None of the issues was debated and the delegates were used as rubber stamps. Fourteen years later, some of those who attacked me were removed from the leadership of the party by acclamation.

The statement by the General Secretary of KANU, Moses Mudavadi, that if church leaders did not refrain from criticising the government they "should not be surprised if their freedom to do so was removed through parliament", was a great surprise. Bishop Alexander Muge responded by telling Mudavadi that if freedom of worship was curtailed, the government should prepare sufficient prison cells and graveyards because "many will continue to worship, whether Mudavadi likes it or not".

Some politicians tend to assume that freedom of worship is given by the state. Freedom of worship comes from God and no one can take it away. When they tried to stop Daniel from worshipping God, Daniel continued worshipping the true God even in the lions' den. The duty of the state is not to give freedom of worship but to guarantee it.

Chapter 22

Kirinyaga's Era of Misguided Politics

The Misfortunes of Political Rivalry

When I was consecrated and enthroned as the Bishop of Mt Kenya East Diocese, I found myself immersed into the volatile politics of Kirinyaga district. The member of parliament for Ndia, James Njiru, had styled himself as the most important person in the district. He had endeared himself so much to both President Jomo Kenyatta and his successor Daniel arap Moi that he was feared by even the most senior of civil servants from Kirinyaga. Despite the fact that he was not well educated, he was appointed assistant minister, before President Moi made him the first ever Cabinet minister from the district. He became the minister for National Guidance and Political Affairs and he seemed to have assumed that his responsibility was to supervise ever government ministry. During elections, he would carry out a reign of terror by making assistant chiefs expel from polling stations voters who were known to favour other candidates. Top civil servants from Kirinyaga held their positions at his pleasure as he claimed to be very close to the president. He was responsible for recruiting KANU youth wingers to shout down preachers and grab microphones from them if they mentioned KANU adversely. When KANU youth wingers attempted to grab microphones from me as I was preaching at St Thomas's Cathedral, Kerugoya, in April 1989, I posed the question as to whether this was what was meant by "National Guidance and Political Affairs". By this time the ministry had virtually become the Ministry of "National Misguidance and Political Thuggery." It did not take long before the ministry was dissolved by the president, who realized that it was not serving any purpose, and Njiru was sacked as minister.

In the early 1970s, the long time MP for Gichugu, Nahashon Njunu, was having drinks with his friends at a bar in Kutus when Njiru turned up and shot at him with a pistol. The bullet narrowly missed him as he and his colleagues went scampering in all directions for dear life. The matter was investigated by police but to the best of my knowledge no action was taken against Njiru.

The bitter rivalry between the two politicians also played out during KANU grassroots elections. Njiru had obtained a permit to hold public meetings in various parts of the district, starting from Kiini location in the west of the district. Njunu and Gachii, the Chairman of the County Council, were denied entry to the venue where Njiru was recruiting new KANU members. A scuffle ensued in which the two grabbed and tore a permit before the two politicians were hunted down, arrested and charged for behaviour likely to cause a breach of the peace. They were remanded at the King'ong'o Prison in Nyeri. The MP for Mwea constituency, Stephen Kiragu, came to see me and requested that I speak to the powers that be and plead for the release of the two.

We went to see Njenga Karume, the then powerful leader of the Gikuyu, Embu and Meru Association (GEMA), in his Kiambu office. This was the first time that I had met Njenga and he surprised me when he asked why I had invited the vice-president Daniel arap Moi to be the guest of honour for a fundraising event in my home church, St Matthew's, Ngiriambu, in Gichugu division. He told me it would have been a lot better had I invited GEMA. This was the era of the intriguing Change-the-Constitution campaign intended to move an amendment to ensure that Moi did not automatically become acting president in case of the demise of the president. Moi came to Ngiriambu and conducted the fundraiser. Njuno and Gachii were still remanded at King'ong'o. In my sermon, I said that it was unfair for one person in Kirinyaga or elsewhere unilaterally to have discretion to hold party meetings. When I finished the sermon, Njiru, who was present, shouted, telling me not to interfere with KANU affairs. I told him that we were in church worshipping God and that he should hold his peace. Soon after this, the KANU administration changed the method of issuing permits to hold political meetings.

The second person that we visited was James Karugu, who had succeeded Charles Njonjo as Attorney General. Kiragu had accompanied me and we pleaded with Karugu to have Njuno and Gachii set free. In his response he expressed surprise that "a whole Bishop of the Church can come to my office to seek interference with the cause of justice." I then reminded him that Njiru had attempted to shoot Njuno with a pistol and that nothing had been done to have Njiru apprehended. I posed the question, "Is attempting to shoot to kill a person a lesser crime than tearing documents? The process of justice in Kenya today seems to favour some people who are in good books with the government over others." The attorney general was so touched by my comments that he admitted that the file of the investigation into the shooting incident had been brought to his office. He however added that he had received instructions from higher authority to close the file. I then told him that this was the reason why I felt duty bound to go and see him concerning the plight of Njuno and Gachii. He then told me that I was justified in visiting his office. He then assured me that if there was no interference from other quarters, then he would ensure that justice was done or at least would be seen to have been done. I was very impressed with James Karugu and probably it was because of his stand that he served as attorney general for a very short time.

My final attempt to have Njuno and Gachii released was a telephone call that I made to the powerful Mbiyu Koinange, who was at Mombasa State House together with President Mzee Jomo Kenyatta. Though he did not give me a clear response, my pleas seemed to have been heard. The magistrate at Nyeri courts was ordered to convene a hearing on Sunday and the two gentlemen were released.

The two politicians also shocked the country when they fought within the precincts of the National Assembly, a matter that was widely reported. After the incident, leaders from Kirinyaga, including myself, were called to a meeting in Kerugoya, which was chaired by cabinet minister G.G. Kariuki. Kariuki wanted the two politicians to tell the people of Kirinyaga why they had fought in parliament. When we were all seated, Njiru entered the hall with a plaster on his left hand and spoke as though he was in great pain. This made some people sympathize with him. But to his rivals, Njiru was known to pretend to have suffered injury so as to win public sympathy.

Njiru masterminded the rigging of the 1988 preliminary elections. Njuno was defeated by rigging in favour of G.K. Kariithi, who succeeded Njuno as MP for Gichugu. Njuno realized that he could not survive politically if he did not reconcile with Njiru. The new friendship culminated with Kariithi being defeated by rigging as KANU Chairman for Gichugu. Though Njuno was a popular politician in Kirinyaga, he coined the tag 42 and 21, which he used to demonstrate the inequality between the rich and the poor in the district. The 42 were the poor people and 21 were the rich. He used the tag to demonstrate that the poor were more than the rich and therefore it would always be inevitable that he would win the elections – but that was until he was defeated by rigging in 1988.

Raid on Our Philadelphia Home

At about midnight during the night of 21 and 22 April 1989, our home was raided by political thugs. All the five members of the family, Grace, Sammy, Jonathan, Mwendwa and I, were present. The Revd Andrew Adano Tuye (who later became the assistant Bishop of the Diocese of Mt Kenya East) was also present as well as a friend of the children, Anthony Kirea.

The thugs, who were carrying very powerful torches, started by going around the house and breaking windows and the glass on the doors. It was a rainy night, there was no power and we could not call the police as (we later learnt) the thugs had first cut the telephone lines that night near the house before the attack. Mobile phones were at that time unheard of in our part of the world.

We went to the western balcony of the house, where we found Adano already talking to them.

"What do you want?" Adano asked.

"*Tuko hapa kumaliza askofu! Ako wapi?*" ("We are here to finish the Bishop! Where is he?")

I sent Jonathan to our bedroom to go and bring me a spear and his younger brother Mwendwa followed him. But a number of the thugs had gone straight to the window of the main bedroom and started cutting the grills, which fell on the bed just as the children were entering the room. I heard Jonathan say, "They are coming in!" as they scampered up the stairs.

My wife Grace, Andrew, and I climbed to the roof of the house via the balcony. Our firstborn, Sammy, had jumped from the balcony to the ground and jumped over the gate.

"*Huyo!*" ("There he is!") we heard them shouting as they tried to run after him but he was too fast for them and disappeared into the darkness through the farm in terrain he was very familiar with. He ran for about a kilometre to look for a telephone. At the same time the other boys returned to the guest room on the eastern side of the first floor and closed the door to the balcony. The thugs hesitated before climbing up the stairs but then mustered enough courage and found Jonathan, Mwendwa and Anthony in the guest room. They were armed with axes, machetes and other crude weapons which they kept threatening to use on the boys if they did not show them where I was.

"Where is the Bishop?" they menacingly and repeatedly asked with the weapons directed at the heads of the boys.

"We do not know," they replied over and over again.

From the top of the roof I raised distress calls and about fifty neighbours responded and came with all kinds of weapons. The children had locked the door and the thugs tried in vain to open the door to the balcony that would lead them to the side of the roof where we were. They went searching through each and every room then suddenly disappeared, but not before causing a lot of damage to the house and stealing radios, video players and other electronics. We could see their torch lights retreat into the darkness some distance away. When the boys opened the door to the balcony, the key that the gangsters had tried over and over to open easily turned. It was a miracle that the children were not harmed and that the door to the balcony had jammed when the thugs tried to open it.

I drove to the Embu Police Station ten kilometres away with a few neighbours and was informed that my son had already telephoned to report the raid. I then drove to Kerugoya (twenty kilometres away). At reception I was informed that the Officer in Charge of Police Division (OCPD) was having a telephone discussion with the District Commissioner, Joseph Mengitich. Apparently they were discussing whether the mission to eliminate me had succeeded.

Police from the four stations (Embu, Kerugoya, Wang'uru and Kianyaga) came to our home that night. The police from Embu, who had sniffer dogs, were able to arrest three of the thugs in a nearby church where there was a *Kesha. Kesha* is a Swahili word which refers to spending the whole night worshipping God. The thugs had gone and mingled with worshippers but the police dogs traced their footsteps to the church. Since the church was in Mwea, the Embu police handed over the thugs to the police from Wangu'ru Police Station. Being part of the plan to eliminate me, the Wangu'ru police released the thugs immediately even without interrogation, investigations or parading them for identification before my sons and their friend who had clearly seen some of them in the house.

On the following day, which was Sunday 22 April, I went to preach at St Paul's Cathedral, Embu. My voice was hoarse owing to the distress calls I had made from the roof of the house. I however delivered a sermon from 1 Thessalonians. The news of the raid into our home was well covered by the local and international media. All the daily newspapers gave detailed coverage of the story on Monday 23 April. There was protest from various churches and church organisations. The Primates of the Anglican Communion, meeting in Larnaca, Cyprus, sent a protest note to President Daniel arap Moi. Other protest messages were issued by NCCK, ACC, and WCC.

On Wednesday 25 April 1989, the President announced from Jomo Kenyatta International Airport that he had appointed a special commission to investigate the matter. He said that as soon as the commission completed its work, he would make its report public. President Moi retired in December 2002 without ever making the report public. Within three hours of his announcement five policemen from Nairobi led by Nathan Ombati of Interpol visited our home and started investigating the matter. They were in the area for about a month and we know they completed their assignment and gave their report to the President. The President however found it difficult to make the report public as it may have implicated some of his own ardent political supporters.

Four days before the raid on our home four politicians from Gichugu constituency issued a press statement saying that they had evidence that there were plans to damage my property. The five young men were arrested and charged but were later released without being prosecuted. On Sunday 29 April 1989, I preached to one of the greatest gatherings ever assembled at St Thomas's, Kerugoya. During the service, two KANU youth wingers tried to disrupt the service but did not succeed. In the Eid ul-Fitr holiday, politicians from all over Central province gathered at Kerugoya Stadium and spent the whole day condemning me. I found it preposterous that MPs from Central province should spend a day condemning a church minister instead of condemning the political thugs who had raided my house barely two weeks earlier.

In May 1990, the President invited me to meet him at State House, Nairobi, on a Tuesday morning. The meeting lasted for about 50 minutes. I had been warned by people who worked with him that such a meeting can be a monologue and I should chip in from time to time if it was going to be a useful dialogue. Before the meeting ended I asked him what became of the report on raid into my house. He answered me that some state matters are very delicate. After the meeting I was telephoned by the Provincial Commissioner of Central Province, who invited me to go and meet him at his Nyeri office, for further discussion on how we could co-operate with the government. I went to Nyeri and met the PC, Victor Musoga and the DC of Kirinyaga.

They informed me that the President had instructed them to meet me and discuss details of how I could help Kirinyaga people to renew their support for KANU. I told them that I was greatly surprised that they were now asking me, a church leader, to be involved in politics when I had been warned many times to confine myself to spiritual matters and leave politics to politicians. I am sure they must have reported to the President that I had not changed one iota despite our meeting with him.

Confrontation with Grabbers of Public Land

When I became the Bishop of Mt Kenya East in 1975, I was informed that the Kirinyaga County Council had in 1969 allocated 40 acres to the Diocese of Mt Kenya for development of an old people's home. The application was made by Revd Mr Kamau, who was then priest in charge of Kerugoya parish. The 40 acres were allocated adjacent to Gathigiriri GK Prison in Mwea division, Kirinyaga district.

When I wrote to the clerk of the county council requesting him to confirm the allocation, I never received a reply. However, the then District Commissioner, David Musila, informed me that the councillors had allocated the land to themselves and had been summoned by the then Provincial Commissioner, Simeon Nyachae, to explain why they had grabbed church land. By that time the Ministry of Lands office in Nairobi had already issued title deeds to individual councillors. The PC ordered the councilors to issue the Diocese of Mt Kenya East alternative land. The councilors gave only sixteen acres within Wang'uru Town. The Christian Community Services of Mt Kenya East made this one of the six centres for integrated development. It also developed a demonstration farm, which was even used by the Ministry of Agriculture to train farmers.

The Embu County Council also grabbed 12 acres out of 40 acres allocated to the diocese at Macumo. The twelve acres were given to the community to build a primary school. I started a youth polytechnic at the site in

1989 but was ordered to close it by 31 December 1989. I however wrote to the council, to inform it in no uncertain terms that the youth polytechnic would not be closed. The land is now used by the Christian Community Services of Mt Kenya East region as another centre of integrated development.

On Friday 26 October 1994, the *Standard* newspaper reported that 200 acres of KARI land in Mwea division of Kirinyaga district had been grabbed by senior civil servants, politicians and tycoons. When I condemned the grabbing, Victor Musoga, the then Central Province Provincial Commissioner, was reported to have told a meeting at Ngekenyi Chief's Camp that "the much talked about land belonging to KARI was non-existent contrary to allegations by a certain clergyman". The PC was clearly referring to me though he did not mention my name. He however challenged the unnamed church leader to indicate where the land he was talking about was.

I issued a press statement to inform the PC that I would on All Saints Day, 1 November 1994, show the PC the 200 acres of KARI land that had been grabbed. Thousands of people from Mwea and other parts of Kirinyaga came by bicycles, matatus and on foot to see the drama of the Bishop showing the PC the grabbed land. The PC did not turn up. After a brief church service at ACK Mathanguta Church near Kimbimbi, I took the congregation on a tour of the grabbed land and the story was well covered by the *Standard* and *Nation* newspapers. The *Standard* of Wednesday 2 November had a banner headline: PC FAILS TO TOUR LAND. I later learnt that he had instructed the police at Nyeri to come and arrest me but they refused his orders in view of the fact that he was the one who had challenged me to show him the grabbed KARI land I was talking about.

The grabbing of public land in Kirinyaga continued unabated. This phenomenon was the subject of a well attended church service held at Wang'uru CCS Centre on 16 January 1994. The sermon was published in my book *In Season and out of Season*, pages 145 to 153. The sermon, entitled "Let the farmer have the first share of his labour", was based on 2 Timothy 2:4-6. I exposed the grabbing of 60 acres of red soil near Kimbimbi, and the grabbing of public land in urban centres of Kerugoya, Kutus, and Wang'uru, among others.

The climax of my confrontation with land grabbers was a special service I held at Trinity Church, Mutuma, near Kamuruana Hill on Sunday 19 May 1991. I had learnt that on 19 February 1991 the Kirinyaga County Council Ordinary Works, Town Planning, Marketing and Housing Committee had passed a resolution giving ten acres of Kamuruana Hill to M/s Kariko Jaken Tress Nurseries. The committee also approved an application by Jimka Developers and Lodges Company to build a motel at the top of Kamuruana Hill.

My sermon, entitled, "Was there no Naboth to say NO!" was based on 1 Kings 21:1-29. In the story King Ahab had gone to request Naboth, a poor man, to let him have his vineyard to extend his vegetable garden but Naboth refused the king's request. I challenged the councilors for surrendering the public land to a powerful politician without a single protest. As a result of this gathering Kamuruana Hill was spared from public land grabbers. We know that this request had come from the minister for National Guidance and Political Affairs. I observed that the minister for National Guidance and Political Affairs had now become the minister for National Misguidance and Political Thuggery. Before very long, this ministry did not seem to serve any useful purpose and the President wisely scrapped it from the list of ministries.

My sermon was published in my book *In Season and out of Season*, pages 102 to 110. When I made so much noise about land grabbing in Kirinyaga, the councilors met and offered me part of Kerugoya forest on condition that I would not preach against public land grabbing. I told the chief who was sent to deliver the message to me that "you have now given me the subject of my sermon next Sunday which will be on the attempt of the county council of Kirinyaga to silence me by bribing me with public land".

Throughout my life I refused to be compromised by accepting such bribes. Though I had every right to apply to the council for land or a plot I deliberately refused to make such applications. The land I have was either given to me by the clan of the Agaciku or bought with money from my own savings.

Chapter 23

Struggle for Multi-Partyism

At the time of independence in 1963, it was assumed that Kenya would continue to be a multiparty state. Indeed the general elections just before Kenya gained self-independence on 1 June 1963 were contested by KANU, KADU and APP In November 1964. However, KADU and APP dissolved themselves and joined KANU; hence Kenya became a *de facto* one-party state. President Kenyatta did not want to change the constitution so as to make Kenya a *de jure* one party state. It was therefore quite legal for other political parties to be formed.

A good number of politicians were becoming dissatisfied by some key KANU policies, especially the KANU development blueprint entitled "Sessional Paper No. 10" of 1965 on "African Socialism and its Application to Planning in Kenya". Led by the then Vice-President, Oginga Odinga, vehement critics of the government decided to form a new party, which was called the Kenya Peoples' Union (KPU).

The party was formed in April 1966 with Oginga Odinga as the president and Bildad Kagia as the vice-president. Twenty-nine members of the lower house and ten senators defected from KANU and joined the new party. This led the government to introduce a bill in parliament for a constitutional amendment to the effect that a member who defects from the party under which he was elected must seek fresh mandate from the constituency that elected him. The bill was debated, put to the vote and became law. The little election was held in 1966. KPU won seven lower house seats and two senate seats. The rest were won by KANU. Because it won only a few seats, KPU was not recognized as the official opposition. It was then however given the status of a parliamentary party and became the unofficial opposition without privileges.

The government administrative machinery massively harassed the Kenya Peoples' Union. The assassination of Tom Mboya on 5 July 1969 sparked angry protest by KPU leaders and their supporters. Mzee Jomo Kenyatta went to Kisumu for official duties and during a public rally he was booed and the meeting became unruly. The security forces opened fire and many people were killed. Consequently, in October 1966, KPU was banned and some of its leaders detained.

Kenya remained a *de facto* one-party state until June 1982. Following a rumour that Oginga Odinga and George Anyona were about to announce a new political party, a bill to amend the constitution so as to add clause 2A making Kenya a *de jure* one-party state was debated by Parliament on Wednesday 9 June 1982. The bill sailed through Parliament in 45 minutes. In my contribution to the 1983 NCCK publication *A Christian View of Politics in Kenya: "Love, Peace and Unity"*, I wrote, "Kenya has now legally become a one party state. History will tell whether the hasty decision made by parliament to change the constitution, thus making it illegal for anyone to start another political party, was right or not" (see page 63).

As Nick Wanjohi has observed, "The hardest hit institution by the introduction of section 2A was the national assembly itself. In 1983, KANU became assertive, insisting that henceforth the supremacy of parliament could have meaning only as an expression of the supremacy of the ruling party. What the party did not state was that KANU itself was an expression of the supremacy of the President. By 1988, a new political reality had come to be and the supremacy of the President over all other institutions in the land was complete."[10]

For some time, I was not very keen to join the multi-party democracy campaign. I was more or less convinced that a one-party government could also be democratic so long as everyone was free to exercise his or her human rights under the umbrella of one party. Important decisions would be made in the African traditional way. In the days gone by, elders met, discussed

---

10 Nick Gatheru Wanjohi, *Challenges of Democratic Governance*. NCCK, 1993, pp. 29-30.

issues and reached agreement by consensus rather than by casting votes. A number of independent African countries had also become *de jure* one-party states. The argument was that in a young nation, opposition parties are a luxury, as they will unnecessarily delay important decisions from being reached. When Kenya became a *de jure* one-party state, I started to realise how impossible it was to have a true democracy in a one-party system of government.

KANU became very much like a monolithic Biblical tower of Babel. Indeed this was symbolized by the attempt by KANU to build at Uhuru Park the Kenya Times Complex, which was to be the tallest building in Africa and the headquarters of KANU. The construction of the KANU "tower of Babel" was abandoned primarily because of the campaign against the project by Professor Wangari Mathai of the Green Belt movement. I was deeply concerned that instead of promoting democracy within the one-party system, KANU devised elaborate ways of disciplining and expelling members from the party. Many politicians, including those who were outspoken, were silenced and could not speak their minds in case they were expelled from the only political party there was. Every party branch was encouraged to hunt down people who were not faithful to the president and the party, and recommend them to the KANU National Governing Council for expulsion.

The big purge came in June 1989 when the National Governing Council expelled 14 people from the party. Among those expelled were Dr Josphat Karanja, one time party stalwart and former Vice President, Charles Rubia, who was the former MP for Starehe, Professor Joseph Ouma, the former MP for Rangwe, and John Koech, the former minister for Public Works. Other politicians were suspended following recommendations by their respective branches. These included Eliud Mwamunga, the former minister for Works, Housing and Physical Planning, and G.K. Kariithi, the former MP for Gichugu. The first victims of expulsion after the addition of clause 2A to the constitution in 1982 were Oginga Odinga and George Anyona.

Between 1982 and April 1990, a total of 30 politicians were expelled from KANU. After the expulsion of Oginga Odinga and George Anyona, there was another major purge in 1984 when the former Attorney General, Charles Njonjo, and 13 others were expelled. Recommendations for expulsion were made by branches on flimsy grounds and for no good reasons other than that some branch leaders wanted to remove their arch-rivals from leadership. My member of parliament G.K. Kariithi was suspended on allegations that he had made a secret trip to Uganda that was financed by the Uganda government. I was with him at St Paul's Cathedral, Embu on the day he was alleged to have made the clandestine trip, attending the wedding of the daughter of Jeremiah Nyaga, a long serving minister in the government. Kariithi was not only suspended from KANU but was also dismissed as an assistant minister. It later emerged that this was a case of mistaken identity as it was another G. Kariithi, a pharmacist, who had gone to Uganda, on a normal business trip. But even after the truth came out, the government did not apologize to Kariithi or reinstate him in his portfolio as an assistant minister.

Strangely I was even summoned by the Gichugu KANU branch, chaired by Nahashon Njuno, to answer some questions regarding my public attacks on the ruling party, even though I was not a member. I told a large congregation at St Thomas Cathedral, Kerugoya, that I had accepted the summons but would go to meet KANU wearing my full bishop's attire and together with all the Kirinyaga priests, who would also be wearing their robes. Njuno visited me that same evening at my Philadelphia home and confided to me with a touch of humour that when I entered through the door, the disciplinary committee would disappear through the window.

The campaign for multi-party democracy was triggered by Pastor Timothy Njoya when he preached at St Andrew's Presbyterian Church, Nairobi, on 1 January 1990. He told the congregation that Kenya must revert to multi-party democracy. Bishop Henry Okullu supported Njoya in a sermon preached at St Stephen's Cathedral, Kisumu. Following these two sermons, Kenneth Matiba convened three secret night meetings at the home of Phillip Gachoka at Karen to plan the campaign strategy for multi-party democracy. The meetings, chaired by Matiba, were attended by Bishop Henry Okullu, Joe Owino, Paul Muite, Phillip Gachoka and myself.

Matiba, who had earlier resigned from his position as a government minister, and Rubia started a public campaign for Kenya to revert to multi-party democracy as at the time of independence. They demanded a licence from the government to hold a rally at Kamukunji grounds on 7 July 1990. They were denied the licence but declared that the rally to demand an end to KANU's dictatorship would go on "with or without a license". They were detained one week before the ordained day and the grounds were sealed off by police in anti-riot gear. But the drive for multipartyism had obtained its own momentum and riots broke out in various parts of the capital. Activists were arrested and members of the public were brutally beaten. Police also broke into houses in various estates in Eastlands and beat whoever they found there. From that time 7 July was celebrated each year as Saba Saba (Seven Seven) day. Despite the arrests, the multi-party campaign continued unabated for the rest of the year and most of 1991. Politicians including Jaramogi Oginga Odinga, Martin Shikuku, Masinde Muliro, Ahmed Bamariz, George Nthenge, Philp Gachoka, Paul Muite, James Orengo and Rashid Mzee called for another meeting on 16 November 1990. Holding hands, they advanced towards Kamukunji but security agents rounded them up and transported them to various towns in the country and charged them with incitement to violence.

On Friday 29 November 1991, the ACK Standing Committee of the Synod met at All Saints Cathedral parish hall and requested that a pastoral letter be prepared by the Justice and Peace Commission for distribution to the entire Church. I was given the task of drafting the letter, which addressed itself to the prevailing social, economic and political climate in Kenya to give guidance to the Christians as they sought to participate positively in the welfare of the nation. As we met in the All Saints parish hall, Nairobi, the following events were very fresh in our minds:

- On Saturday 16 November 1991, the Forum for the Restoration of Democracy (FORD) had threatened to go ahead and hold a political rally at Kamukunji, despite having been denied a licence. The police stopped the rally and arrested and charged nearly all the leaders of FORD.
- The commission chaired by justice Evans Gicheru, which was probing the mysterious death of the former Minister of Foreign Affairs and International Co-operation, the late Robert Ouko, had suddenly been ordered to stop its proceedings at Kisumu just when it appeared to be making real progress towards finding the truth about the murder.

Little did we know that within five days of our meeting, both external and internal pressures would cause far reaching changes to the political landscape of the nation. During the KANU Delegates Conference, the ruling party threw in the towel and voted for the removal of section 2A of the constitution. Parliament met just before Jamhuri Day to legalize multi-party democracy. By the turn of the year, FORD was registered as a political party under the chairmanship of Oginga Odinga, and at the beginning of the year the Democratic Party was also registered under the chairmanship of Mwai Kibaki. These events virtually marked the nexus of the second liberation. Many more parties were registered in preparation for the December 1992 elections. Kenneth Matiba returned from London, where he was recuperating after detention, and formed the Ford Asili party, which was also registered.

As the date of the December 1992 general election approached, the three strongest parties were FORD, Ford Asili and KANU and the strongest candidates for the presidency were Oginga Odinga, Kenneth Matiba, Mwai Kibaki and Daniel arap Moi. The religious leaders met and strongly felt only one candidate should face the incumbent. Three church leaders were sent to see each of the three opposition candidates separately and invite them to a meeting to discuss the possibility of two of the candidates withdrawing their candidature so as to leave one to face the chairman of KANU. I was sent to see Kenneth Matiba, whom I met at his Alliance office opposite the University of Nairobi. He received me very warmly but when I told him the subject of my visit, he gave me a one-hour lecture and would not let me speak. He rejected any meeting with the other two candidates. I was later informed that Oginga Odinga had agreed to attend the meeting but he flew to London on the date set. Only Mwai Kibaki accepted the invitation. The meeting was therefore cancelled. When the elections came, the opposition divided their votes and Daniel arap Moi was sworn in for a fourth term as the President of Kenya. The votes of Mwai Kibaki and Kenneth Matiba combined were more than those of Moi.

The opposition was very keen to have the constitution amended before the next elections in December 1997. The President however was very adamant that the constitution would not be amended until after the elections. The opposition showed their anger by grabbing the mace in parliament on the day the June 1997 budget was read. They made so much noise on the floor of the National Assembly that no one could hear what the Minister for Finance was reading. Only the media was able to inform the public what the budget was all about.

In August 2011, the Prime Minister, the Rt Hon. Raila Odinga, invited many of those who participated in the second liberation to a dinner to celebrate the promulgation of the new constitution. More than 100 people attended from various parties and civil society organisations. I was invited, alongside Dr Timothy Njoya, to represent church leaders who actively participated in the second liberation. During the occasion, the Prime Minister refused to sit on the ceremonial chair reserved for him. Instead he looked for me and ushered me into his chair, to the surprise of everyone. Later he told the particpants that he was there not as the Prime Minister, but as one of those who struggled to expand Kenya's democratic space. He said because the Prime Minister's chair could not remain empty, he looked for the retired Archbishop so that he could sit on it. For a few minutes, I indeed felt like I was the Prime Minister.

Chapter 24

Security Forces Invade
All Saints Cathedral, Nairobi

Saba Saba Day, 7 July 1997

On Saba Saba day, 7 July 1997, opposition leaders decided to hold a rally at Uhuru Park (which is adjacent to All Saints Cathedral, Nairobi) with or without a licence. A large number of pro-reform supporters and leaders of opposition parties were ready by 9.00am to address the gathering. The main purpose of the gathering was to push for the amendment of the constitution before the election in December 1997. The police descended on the gathering with tear gas canisters and batons and people were scattered in all directions. A number of leaders, including Mwai Kibaki, the leader of the official opposition, went into All Saints Cathedral in the hope that they would find refuge. The police followed them into the Cathedral, threw and fired tear gas canisters at them, beat up the leaders and injured some of them. The Revd Timothy Njoya was present, wearing a chasuble, and was beaten thoroughly until his robe was soaked in blood. Mwai Kibaki was also clobbered.

I was not present myself but the provost of the cathedral, the Very Revd Peter Njoka, kept me fully informed by phone on what was happening in our Cathedral. The event got plenty of coverage in the local and international media. I decided to hold a special service of cleansing for the cathedral on the following Sunday, 13 July 1997. The special service was well advertised by the media and thousands of people attended. I blessed the water, and, assisted by the bishops of ACK, we went round the Cathedral sprinkling the holy water and then entered the Cathedral in a colourful procession of bishops, clergy, lay readers, and others. The cathedral was packed and many people stayed outside but followed the proceedings by television monitors that had been placed at various strategic places.

I preached from the Book of Daniel, chapter 5. The chapter tells the story of King Belshazzar, the son of Nebuchadnezzar who ruled Babylon from 562 BC to about 560 BC. Though his city was surrounded by the forces of King Cyrus of Persia, he assumed that he was secure and he decided to have a banquet, which was attended by thousands of his lords. Belshazzar made three main mistakes. Instead of proclaiming a fast, he proclaimed a carousing feast. Secondly, he used gold and silver goblets taken by his father Nebuchadnezzar from the Jerusalem temple and used them to serve wine to his nobles, government ministers, wives and concubines. About 1,000 people were present. Thirdly as they drank wine they praised idols. They used the holy vessels from the Jerusalem temple to worship and praise a human being instead of worshipping God who created them.

It was while they were feasting that "the fingers of a human hand appeared and wrote on a plaster of wall of the king's palace, *MENE, MENE, TEKEL, PARSIN*". As the enchanters and wise men of Babylon were unable to read and translate the words written on the wall, the queen recommended to the king that Daniel be invited to translate the words. Daniel came to the palace and told the king, "this is the inscription that was written:

MENE, MENE, TEKEL, PARSIN
MENE: God has numbered the days of your reign and brought it to an end.
TEKEL: You have been weighed on the scales and found wanting.
PARSIN: Your kingdom is divided and given to Medes and Persians (Daniel 5: 25-28).

I told the president that the hand of God had not as yet written "Mene, Mene, Tekel, Parsin" on the wall of State House. However, if he did not fulfill the following conditions the hand of God would write the words there. I said:

- The Constitution should be reformed to ensure that the holder of the office of president is expressly elected by a majority of voters, and rigging of elections should come to the end.

- A truly independent Electoral Commission (ECK) with adequate power to organise, control and manage elections should be put in place.
- The establishment of an independent inter-parties Transitional Consultative Forum (TCF) is necessary, with an equal representation from the government, the opposition and the organised sectors of civil society, whose decisions will be binding on government and whose mandate will be discussed and act on all transitional issues.
- The Constitution shall provide the formation of a coalition government and provide for formation of a government of national unity after the next elections with express responsibility of undertaking comprehensive democratic reforms.
- The constitution shall declare that Kenya will always remain a multi-party state, with the provision of the state co-funding for all registered political parties.
- The laws should be changed to allow for fair political competition by removing the provincial administration and police from the electoral process, ending the practice of seeking licences to hold rallies and assemblies, allowing for more equitable access to the public funded media and facilitating the use of transparent and lockable ballot boxes.

The hand of God has not yet written "Mene Mene Tekel Parsin" on the wall of State House because there is still hope. However, if those in authority refuse dialogue and to hear the cries of people of Kenya and continue to harden their hearts, then the hand of God will write on the wall of State House "Mene Mene Tekel Parsin" and Daniel will have to invite Daniel to interpret the writings on the wall.

The politicians have often told church leaders to leave politics to politicians and not to use the pulpit for politics. This we cannot accept as politics is too important to be left to politicians alone. Left on their own they have caused the Hiroshimas of the world with their devastating effects. God has called upon us not only to deal with the spiritual matters but also the social, physical, environmental needs of humankind. After all a human being is a psychosomatic unit – he is the spirit and body which cannot be separated. Martin Niemoller, a Lutheran Pastor during the Nazi reign of terror uttered these words to demonstrate the danger of the church ignoring involvement in politics:

"In Germany the Nazis came for communists and I did not speak as I was not a communist. They came for Jews and I did not speak as I was not a Jew. Then they came for Labour Unionists and I did not speak up because I was not a Labour Unionist. Then they came for Catholics; as I was a Protestant I did not speak. Then they came for me. By that time there was no one left to speak for anyone." We refuse to be silenced by any one. If God tells us to read the writings on the wall, we shall read them, however unpalatable they are to those in authority.

The sermon received much publicity locally and internationally. Letters of protest addressed to me for onward transmission to the president were read during the service. The protest letters came from George Carey, then the Archbishop of Canterbury, Archbishop Robin Eames of Ireland, Crosslinks, the Church of England, the Diocese of Egypt, the Primate of the Episcopal Church of America, the Most Revd Edmond Browning, the Primate of Brazil, the Primates of the Provinces of Africa (who were meeting in Johannesburg), the Primate of the Anglican Church of Korea, John Peterson, the General Secretary of the Anglican Communion, the representative of the World Anglican Church at the United Nations, the Rt Revd James Ottley, and Michael Peers, Archbishop and Primate of Canada, who had preached during my enthronement seven months before.

The Archbishop of Canada wrote his letter to the president himself and told him, "I am distressed by action that harasses worshippers who gather to pray for the well being of your country. I join my voice with others around the world to protest acts of violence carried out against people who had gathered peacefully. I hope you will disassociate yourself from such action by making an apology on behalf of the government to the leaders of All Saints Cathedral... I urge you to seriously consider entering into dialogue with the opposition leaders. Surely dialogue is far better than violence."

We bound all the letters of protest we had received and handed them over to the Office of the President. Two days later, on 15 July, a number of church leaders were invited to State House to meet the president. To my surprise I was also invited. The president told us that he had accepted that the constitution should be amended before the December polls. The president also requested the church leaders to chair a meeting between the leaders of the opposition and government ministers to work out the logistics of reviewing the constitution.

Chapter 25

Relationship with President Moi in 2002

In 2002 I was due to retire as Bishop of Nairobi and Archbishop of the ACK. I visited various dioceses and often said, "I have one thing in common with President Moi; we are both supposed to retire this year. My retirement date is 16 September 2002, when I will reach the age of 65. President Moi should also announce the actual date he will retire." I repeatedly made this statement because there were some KANU activists who were already urging Moi to continue ruling Kenya for a sixth term of five years.

A few months before the December 2002 general election, President Moi said he had nominated Uhuru Kenyatta to succeed him. The media quickly coined the term "the Moi Project" for Uhuru's candidacy. In my farewell visits to various dioceses I told congregations that none of the *Nyayo* projects had succeeded. I gave examples of Nyayo School Milk Project, Nyayo wards (which had no medicines), Nyayo Tea Zones, Uhuru car, among others. I said that even the Uhuru Nyayo project will not succeed. I also recall that some months before I retired, four cabinet ministers who were all Anglicans demanded to meet me. We met at the board room of the Church Commissioners for Kenya and I was accompanied by Bishop Eliud Wabukala of Bungoma Diocese. The Ministers were led by Marsden Madoka. The other three were Gideon Ndambuki, Joe Nyaga and the assistant minister Albert Ekirapa.

Madoka took the chair and Bishop Wabukala said the opening prayers. I had no doubt that the ministers had been sent to see me by powerful state operatives. They said they had come to see me as their Archbishop. They all gave a summary of their membership and long association with the ACK. But they told me that they now feel rather embarrassed to be associated with the church. The reason for their embarrassment was that every time I opened my mouth to preach they knew exactly what I was going to say: attack the government of Moi of which they are ministers.

In response I told them that they do not know the style of my preaching but what they know is what they read in the newspapers. Newspapers write what is sensational and what can make their newspapers sell. I then told them that my preaching is what is known as "expository preaching". I read the Scriptural text and I give the background of the passage, then I expound every verse faithfully. Then in application of the text, the Holy Spirit urges me to make my preaching relevant to the contemporary situation in our nation and to the world at large.

I informed the ministers that bishops and priests are like the prophets of old who were appointed by God over nations and kingdoms "to uproot and tear down, to destroy and overthrow, to build and plant" (Jeremiah 1:10). And when God appoints and sends us, we have no alternative but to accept God's call and command to deliver his message courageously whether the hearers accept God's message or not. Ndambuki was the first to respond. He said many people do not know the expository aspect of my preaching. Then he posed the question on how this aspect of my preaching can be made widely known. I answered him that the Minister for Information, Joe Nyaga, would not let me speak live on the national broadcaster KBC, whether on radio or television. In response Nyaga said he would be taking a great risk if he allowed me to appear live on TV or radio as what I might say might be an attack on the government.

I told them that the greatest mistake they can make is to dispense with their bishop by concluding that his services are no longer necessary. I told them how I once went to see the vice-president, who was also the minister for finance, concerning importation of church vehicles duty-free, but the minister completely ignored me. Some years later, parliament wanted to discuss a motion of no confidence in him. Before the date of the debate, he requested the moderator John Gatu to see me and persuade me to make a public statement that that motion was unnecessary. I went public on the issue even before John Gatu had communicated the request to me. That a vice-president was seeking the assistance of a bishop he earlier had no time for was quite an irony. "You are ministers," I told them. "Do not even meditate dispensing with your Archbishop. You might need his services one day." After closing prayers the meeting dispersed and I went to Ufungamano House, where church leaders were anxious to know what the cabinet ministers were up to. They seemed to have already known that various church leaders were holding similar meetings with their respective ministers. This was yet another attempt to silence church leaders during an election year.

On 15 September 2002, I preached three sermons as my farewell messages to Anglicans and Kenyans in general. My three sermons were printed and distributed to each of the 2,000 people who attended the service. A day after my retirement, I was visited by four policemen at my Philadelphia residence. They said that they had been sent by higher authorities to come and find out how I would eliminate Uhuru Kenyatta so that he could not become the President of Kenya. Apparently the *Daily Nation*, in reporting one sentence of my sermon, wrote that I told the congregation at All Saints Cathedral, Nairobi, that "Uhuru will not live to see the presidency". As I had not read the *Daily Nation* on that day, the officers gave me their copy to read. I told the police that that was a grave misquotation and I gave them a copy of my three sermons, which I had distributed to all those who had attended the farewell service. I had said, "If we succeed in amending the constitution, Uhuru might not be elected the third President of Kenya." The police were taken by surprise, as they came assuming that they would arrest and charge me. However, there is a world of difference between saying, "He will not live to see the presidency" and "He might not be elected".

I wondered whether the president had consulted the head of Special Branch, who was obviously well represented by his team when I delivered the sermons. Intelligence officers at this time frequented church services. I told the police that the three sermons were also recorded on video and that they could review the footage at the Communications Department in our Nairobi office. At this juncture, I received a telephone call from television journalists from a media house who informed me that they were on their way to record the presence of the police in my residence. When the police heard that, they quickly retreated to their car and hurriedly drove towards Nairobi.

The following day, Wednesday 18 September 2002, the *Daily Nation* published an apology to me for having misquoted me. After viewing the video, the police arrested the *Nation* reporter who wrote the story. He was arraigned at the magistrate's court in the Nairobi Law Courts and I was summoned to be the government witness during the hearing. I attended the court and the young reporter was charged. I was then invited to give my statement.

I responded by saying that the *Daily Nation* had published an apology to me and I had forgiven the *Nation* and the reporter. The magistrate, after consulting the prosecutor, adjourned the proceedings for half an hour.

When the court reconvened, the magistrate told me I had no powers to forgive the reporter. I told the magistrate that, as a government witness and bishop of the church, I would suggest that the case be withdrawn and the reporter set free. To the best of my knowledge, the young reporter was summoned to court several times until KANU lost the elections and the file was closed by the new government. I found it interesting that President Moi was still pursuing this case even after my retirement but still without success. The following Sunday I said that President Moi had not ceased to spread unfounded rumours against me even after my retirement.

Corruption by Traffic Police

When I became the Archbishop of ACK in 1997, I occasionally commuted from my Philadelphia place in Kirinyaga near Embu town to my office in Nairobi, a distance of about 120km. I witnessed numerous instances of traffic police receiving bribes from motorists. I was so concerned about this that I decided to see the Commissioner of Police, the late Edwin Nyasenda, at his Vigilance House office. The Commissioner told me that if I saw any policeman taking bribes I should take his or her number and telephone him immediately. He gave me his direct telephone numbers.

One day I saw a policewoman receive a bribe from a lorry driver in Thika and I requested her to let me have her number so that I could inform the Commissioner. When she declined to give me the number I asked her boss for her number and he gave it to me. The policewoman called Anne started crying and pleaded with me not to report her to the commissioner. Her boss advised me that as a bishop I should give her counselling instead of reporting her to the commissioner. I asked her what church she belonged to and said she was an Anglican from the Diocese of Machakos. Then I told her I would request the Bishop of Machakos, the Rt Revd Joseph Kanuku, to call her for counselling. She told me that I would rather refer her to the Bishop of Thika, the Rt Revd Dr Gideon Githiga, instead of the head of her home church. I immediately telephoned Bishop Githiga, who arrived within a few minutes and made an appointment with the lady for counselling and fellowship. Later I met the bishop, who informed me that the woman was very repentant and assured him that she would not do it again.

On another occasion I was driving home from Nairobi and I stopped at a police road block after passing the Blue Posts hotel. I witnessed the police on both sides of the dual carriageway receiving bribes from *matatu* drivers. As soon as I got to the road block, I telephoned the Thika OCPD and told him what I was witnessing. He came after a short time and asked me to point out the policemen who had been taking bribes. I showed him all of them. He ordered the officers to dismantle the road block and return to the station. Bishop Githiga was with me and he followed the police vehicle up to their station in town. We knew that our efforts to fight corruption among traffic police would yield little fruit, as junior officers confess that they are ordered by their superiors to take bribes, which they share with them at the end of the day.

The police at Thika must have been very annoyed with me, as they staged an accident with my car. One day I left my home very early in the morning for official duties in Nairobi. On reaching the road block, a police car followed my car and passed it and without signaling that he was turning right. He then took a sharp turn to cross the road near Del Monte kiosk, which sells fresh pineapples. My car hit the police car. The two cars were towed to the police station and the police driver was charged for careless driving. My driver and I attended the court session as witnesses. To our surprise and the surprise of the prosecution, the lady magistrate ruled that nobody could be blamed for the accident. This was despite a telephone call that I received from the provincial police officer to the effect that everything would be done to establish the cause of the accident. The ruling by the Thika magistrate convinced me that I could not find justice under the Moi regime. After all, the report of the commission of enquiry into the raid on my house in April 1989 had never been made public despite the president's promises when he appointed the commission.

I have often told congregations that corruption is two-way traffic. The giver and the receiver are both corrupt. Some years back I was driving along the capital city's Moi Avenue at about 7pm in the evening and I made a U turn at Khoja Mosque. I was seen by five policemen and they stopped my car, entered it and ordered me to drive to the Central Police station to write a statement. When we reached Jevanjee Gardens, I was ordered to stop the car and park it on the side of the road. Then they asked me to give them "tea". I told them if it was tea they wanted I would take them to the nearest café and buy each one of them a cup of tea. One of them asked me, "Don't you know what tea is?" I answered him, "The tea I know is when you heat water in a sufuria; when it has boiled you add tea leaves, milk and sugar." All five policemen were quiet for a while, then one asked me, "But who are you?" I answered that I was the Rt Revd Dr David M. Gitari. "Bishop!" the officers retorted. "Yes," I answered. Then they all opened the doors and got out of my car and told me, *"Bishop, kwa heri ya kuonana"* meaning "Bishop, goodbye and hope to see you again."

Chapter 26

Attack by Muslim Youths at the Beginning of Ramadan

During the last week of November 2000, I was on official duties in Bangalore, India. I returned on Thursday 1 December and the following day went to Ufungamano House to attend a meeting of religious leaders from various faiths who were pushing for critical reform agendas under the banner of the Ufungamano Initiative. I had not even read the newspapers that day. There was a banner story that a mosque had been set on fire in Nairobi's South B the previous day.

After the meeting, which ended at about 1pm, we agreed that all the religious leaders present would go to South B and show our solidarity with Muslims in their protest against the burning of their mosque and wish them blessings during the month of Ramadan. I gave a lift to Abdulilahi Abdi, a good friend of mine and a keen member of Ufungamano Initiative. My vehicle led the procession to South B and as we neared the estate we saw hundreds of youth on their way to the burnt mosque, full of anger and shouting "Allahu Akbar" or "Allah is great." My vehicle was the first to enter the compound and it was stoned by the youth, who also stole Ksh 21,000/- from my pocket. My driver, Michael, removed my cross and went to the police, who were about 100 metres from the point where my car was being stoned. He told the police that the Archbishop was being killed and showed them my cross. The officers just stood by, watched and told the driver that the Bishop had no business there. The Muslim leaders who were with me at

269

Ufungamano tried their best to stop the stoning of my car. One stone passed through the rear screen and hit me on the back of the head and I started bleeding.

One brave young Muslim man entered the car and reversed it and took me to the Mater Meriscodie Hospital. As we drove to the hospital we could see huge flames at Our Lady Queen of Peace Catholic Church, South B, which had been set on fire by the youth. Within a short time Reuters News Agency issued a statement to the world media stating that after attacks by Muslims, I was taken to hospital unconscious, which was not true. My son John Mwendwa, who was working with Kenya Television Network (KTN), was among the first people to see me in the hospital. I was treated and discharged but as I walked out I found a large number of pressmen waiting to interview me about the incident. I told them that I would issue a press statement in my office at Bishops Garden House within a short time.

My driver had to navigate the badly damaged vehicle to the compound of the provincial office. In my statement I said I would have been killed if it were not for the Muslim leaders who had come to know me well in the meetings about the Ufungamano Initiative. Some Christian youths were prepared to retaliate by burning Muslim mosques. But in my statement and that of the priest of Our Lady Queen of Peace Church, we reminded the Christians the words of St Paul, "Do not pay anyone evil for evil... Do not revenge, my friends, but leave room for God's wrath, for it is written, 'It is mine to avenge; I will repay,' says the Lord" (Romans 13:17-19). A few other Christian churches were burnt but Christians did not take revenge.

I later learnt that the temporary mosque at South B was actually burnt by hawkers who had put up temporary kiosks on the plot. The temporary structures of these hawkers were burnt by Muslims when they wanted to start building a permanent mosque. It appeared that those who carried out the attacks on churches were convinced that anyone who is not a Muslim is a Christian; therefore they assumed that their temporary structure was burnt by Christians. I am not even certain how many of those hawkers were professing Christians or how many of them even attended church.

Within a short time a much better and more spacious Our Lady Queen of Peace Church emerged out of the ashes. Catholics and non-Catholics contributed funds for the construction of the new church. I was present during the first fundraising ceremony and was accompanied by a good number of Anglican clergy from the Diocese of Nairobi. We gave a generous donation for the reconstruction of a new church.

Chapter 27

Relationship with Mwai Kibaki, the Third President of Kenya

I retired as the third Archbishop of the Anglican Church of Kenya on 16 September 2002. Mwai Kibaki was sworn in as the third president of the republic of Kenya on 29 December 2002, about three and a half months after my retirement. Hence I did not have the opportunity to work with him when he became the president. I had however learnt about Mwai Kibaki ever since his student days at the Makerere University College of Uganda in the 1950s. At Makerere University College he obtained a first class Bachelor of Arts Degree in Economics, History and Political Science. The degree was granted by the University of London. At that time Makerere and Nairobi were constituent campuses of University of London. He was awarded a scholarship and completed his studies at the London School of Economics, where he was awarded a first class degree in public finance.

After completing his studies in London he returned to Makerere to lecture in the Department of Economics. After a short spell as a lecturer he was invited by Mzee Jomo Kenyatta, the then chairman of Kenya African National Union (KANU) to come and assist in the management of the party. It was actually Oginga Odinga who was sent to visit Kibaki at Makerere and persuade him to return home and take up the responsibility of the management of KANU. He left a prestigious and well paid job to take the job of KANU Executive Officer, with no salary, as at that time KANU had no money. Accompanied by John Keen, he travelled the whole length and breadth of Kenya on public transport, publicising KANU and recruiting new members.

Kibaki was first elected to parliament as the member for Bahati constituency, now Makadara, in 1963. In the first Kenyatta government Mwai Kibaki became Parliamentary Secretary (assistant minister) in the Ministry of Finance. He was appointed the chairman of the Commission on Economic Planning and served in that capacity from 1963 to 1965. During that time he wrote Sessional Paper No. I on African Socialism and its Application to Kenya. The paper was however published by Tom Mboya in his capacity as Minister for Economic Planning and bears his signature, but the mind behind it was that of Mwai Kibaki.

In 1965, Mwai Kibaki was appointed the Minister for Commerce and Industry, and he served in that capacity until 1969. He was then appointed the Minister for Finance from 1969 to 1982. As Minister for Commerce and Industry, he is credited with having initiated industrial development institutions such as the Industrial and Commercial Development Corporation (ICDC), the Development Finance Company of Kenya (DFCK), the Tourist Development Co-operation (KTDC), the Agricultural Finance Corporation of Kenya (AFCK) and the Kenya National Trading Company (KNTC).

It should be noted that he was MP for Bahati for two terms, after which he re-located to his home constituency of Othaya, Nyeri district, in 1974. Since he joined Parliament he has never lost any election and at the time of writing he is the longest serving Member of Parliament. When Mzee Kenyatta died in 1978 and Daniel Toroitich arap Moi succeeded him, he appointed Mwai Kibaki as his vice-president as well as Minister for Finance until 1982. While remaining vice-president he was then transferred to the Ministry of Home Affairs. In 1988 he was unceremoniously removed from the No. 2 position and was appointed Minister for Health.

During his days as Minister of Finance (1978-1982), and being a highly qualified economist, Kibaki is credited with having enabled Kenya's economy to attain 7% growth. From that time and until the time the KANU government was removed from power in 2002, the growth of the country's economy declined to 0.2%. During this period many of our once flourishing parastatals and institutions became white elephants. These included the Kenya Meat Commission factory at Athi River and the Kenya Co-operative Creameries Society Ltd. The Kenya Farmers Association (KFA) lost its former glory, and so did KPCU. Government sponsored centres for training farmers were closed and *Nyayo* projects collapsed.

While some international factors are often blamed for the downturn in Kenya's fortunes, it was clear that the government had for many years lost the vision, intentions and focus upon which the fragile foundations of the nation were built. The deliberate weakening of institutions and the politics of expediency and patronage all contributed to the mess that Kenya found itself in. Poor planning, poor social-economic policies that exacerbated poverty, unemployment amid a rising cost of living, inefficiency in government, disparities in distribution of resources and wealth, inequality in access to opportunities, corruption and impunity that thrived at all levels of government, poor infrastructure, dilapidated and potholed roads dotted the country. Many years and lives were wasted during Kenya's dark years. Still, Kibaki had been in cabinet until 1991, when he resigned his membership in KANU to form the Democratic Party of Kenya

When Kibaki became the third president of Kenya in December 2002 and during his first five-year term, the economy started recovering. During the first two years of his leadership, economic growth rose from 0.2% to 6%. Before the post-election ethnic clashes, the growth had reached 7%. The economic growth then dropped to 2% owing to 2008 post-poll clashes but at the time of writing (May 2012), the economy has picked up again to 5% growth.

I have been a great admirer of Mwai Kibaki ever since I came to know him when I was a student at the Royal Technical College (now the University of Nairobi) from 1959 to 1964. I have continued admiring Kibaki to date. But some of my expectations of him have been frustrated. Kibaki has remained an enigma, a person who is difficult to understand. No allegation of corruption has been directly proved to be linked to him, even though his close allies have had to step down over accountability issues. Yet in his position as Vice-President he did not oppose the adoption of the queuing system of election by KANU in August 1986, which became the most corrupt method of organizing national elections. During his inauguration as the third president he publicly said there would be zero tolerance of corruption in his government and yet he appears not to be as zealous in the fight against corruption as we expected.

I do however understand that the position of a vice president (a No. 2) anywhere in the world is very difficult. When No. 2 is opposed to some of the things his boss is doing, he has three possible actions he can take:

1. He can oppose his boss and risk being sacked.
2. He can resign his position and become an enemy of the top person.

3. He can patiently tolerate what he does not like and suffer in silence in the hope that one day he will take the reins of power and transform the nation.

Oginga Odinga opted for the second position and died before he had tasted the presidency. Both Moi and Kibaki opted for the third position. Moi was a faithful vice-president to Kenyatta and his first manifesto stated that he will follow the *Nyayos* (footsteps) of the father of the nation. This impressed many and Kenyans were happy to have him elected unopposed in the 1978 election. But we know the so-called Nyayo philosophy of "Peace, Love and Unity" was dead in the water after less than four years, especially after the attempted coup d'état in 1982. Similarly Kibaki chose to tolerate his boss even when he knew things were not going in the right direction. However, Moi took the initiative to remove him after ten years as the Vice-President for unknown reasons even though he retained him as a cabinet minister.

Mwai Kibaki as the Third President Of Kenya

As I have stated above, Kibaki became the president of Kenya after I had retired as the third Archbishop of ACK. I therefore did not have much interaction with him, as I chose to move away from the capital city and retreat to my Philadelphia country home in Kirinyaga district. I did not want to get too involved in the politics of Kenya and I deliberately refrained from making political statements. I wanted my successor, the Most Revd Benjamin Nzimbi, to take up the task of speaking on behalf of the Anglican Church of Kenya on matters of national importance.

I was therefore more of an observer of the politics of Kenya during the first term of Mwai Kibaki. I was very pleased when leaders of the opposition, including those who had resigned from KANU following Moi's anointing of Uhuru Kenyatta as his successor, worked together to remove KANU from power. A large number of KANU leaders, including Raila Odinga, George Saitoti, Stephen Kalonzo Musyoka, Joseph Kamotho, Moody Awori and Charity Ngilu, formed the National Rainbow Coalition so as to remove KANU from power. It was during this time that Raila Odinga uttered the memorable words "Kibaki Tosha", or "Kibaki is sufficient".

The opposition entered into a memorandum of understanding, as they had more members in the National Assembly in the 9th Parliament. Hence they formed the government, with Mwai Kibaki as the president. The marriage did not last long, especially when a number of the ministers voted against the referendum on the new draft constitution in 2005. Kibaki sacked all those ministers in the coalition who had campaigned against the new proposed constitution.

President Kibaki's failure to respect the memorandum of understanding and his sacking of Raila Odinga, Kalonzo Musyoka and others surprised me. I had assumed Kibaki would do everything possible to keep the National Rainbow Coalition together. This was one of the many reasons which made the 2007 election end up in post-election violence that left at least 1,300 people dead and more than 3,000 others as refugees in their own country.

Though President Kibaki achieved much in terms of the economic growth of the country during his first five years, his performance politically was not what I expected. He remained silent at a time when we expected him to speak on various national issues. So the country was left in darkness and was longing to hear his voice but he preferred to remain silent. He was quite the opposite of Moi, who spoke on every subject even when he knew so little. Moi's banning of the teaching of the new mathematics in schools without even understanding the value of new mathematics in the digital age was a good example of interference in areas where he should have let experts give guidance. But that was the style of the "professor of politics" who interfered with the work of the ministers instead of giving them liberty to do what they thought was good for their respective ministries.

President Kibaki, on the other hand, gave liberty to his ministers to take full responsibility for their ministries. The book of Ecclesiasties says, "There is a time to speak and a time to keep quiet" (Ecclesiasties 3:7). Sometimes President Kibaki behaves as if all time is the time to keep quiet even when the nation is anxiously waiting to hear his guiding voice. The observation that he is more of an economist or technocrat than a politician seems to summarise the personality of the third president.

There is no doubt that President Kibaki did great things economically in this country during his first term. The rate of growth started rising. The construction of a network of good roads all over the country has been a great achievement. The introduction of free primary education has been a great blessing to Kenya and to millions of children who have an entry point to a greater future. His ability to delegate responsibilities to other people leads to good administration. Moi was the chancellor of all the public universities, but as soon as Mwai became the president, he chose other people to be chancellors of all the public universities. There has also been some effort to improve service delivery in some government ministries and departments.

One thing I very much appreciate about Mwai Kibaki is his view of the relationship between the church and the state. While other politicians kept telling church leaders to leave politics to politicians and to confine their preaching to spiritual matters, Kibaki had a different view. He strongly believed that the church could not keep away from the issues of the day. He was once invited to address NCCK church leaders and I was greatly impressed when he told us, "Church leaders should not waste time praising politicians – we have enough people to praise us. But the church leaders should pray for us, support us when we do what is right and criticise us fearlessly when we do wrong."

Since Kibaki became president, the new generation of church leaders does not seem to have been so courageously aggressive in criticising the government as some of the church leaders of the 1980s and 1990s. Having helped in removing Moi from power they seem to have been satisfied to keep quiet even when things went seriously wrong. During the December 2007 elections, there was no doubt the church leaders in Kikuyu land supported Mwai Kibaki and those in Nyanza and Rift Valley supported Raila Odinga. The church leaders were so divided during the 2008 post-election violence that their prophetic voice could not be heard. The salt had lost its flavour and was good for nothing. (Matthew 5:13). It was only after the post-election violence that the NCCK member churches repented for having been silent during the destruction of property and senseless killings. But it was too late.

I attended the DP campaign at Kinoru stadium just before the 1997 general elections. When I was given the opportunity to speak, I told Kibaki, the presidential candidate, that if you are elected the president, I will praise and support you if you do what is right before God. But if you do what God does not expect of a president, then I will criticise you fearlessly just as I have been criticizing Moi. There are other people who feel Kibaki has not fulfilled their expectations in fighting against corruption and impunity. But we have to give credit where credit is due.

First and foremost Kibaki declared that he was keen to fight against corruption. He took the initiative soon after being sworn into office to legalise the Kenya Anti-Corruption Commission, giving it powers to investigate corruption. He has also strengthened the office of the Attorney General so that it can perform its constitutional duties without interference. He has also taken steps to improve and motivate the police force. Though it may appear as if he has not done much in dealing with scandals such as Goldenberg, Anglo-leasing and the sale of the Grand Regency hotel, it should be noted that he suspended some of his closest friends mentioned in these scandals: David Mwiraria, George Saitoti, Kiraitu Murungi, Amos Kimunya and Chris Murungaru. It was a brave decision to suspend such close political allies and to subject them to investigations. On the issue of impunity, some of us hoped that Kibaki would revisit the issue of the assassinations of J.M. Kariuki and Robert Ouko. It may be the president is waiting for the Truth, Justice and Reconciliation Commission to complete its work before he provides direction.

The other area that makes the third president of Kenya an enigma is his silence on issues on which the country expects him publicly to express his opinion and give guidance. The best example is the silence of the president with regard to the grabbing of Migingo Island by Uganda. Those who know Mwai Kibaki well and his closest associates say that he does not like rushing into addressing every issue but would rather study each issue very carefully before acting. He is good at resolving issues quietly and after careful consideration. He is also very secretive and prefers to keep confidentiality. Unlike former presidents, he seems to desist from protecting his friends who have been implicated particularly in corrupt deals, when it appears they are complicit. But he will also never attempt to destroy his enemies and will give a chance to both friends and enemies to redeem themselves. Though he will listen to some close friends and associates, his confidants argue that Kibaki does not like a permanent kitchen cabinet.

Those of us who are not politicians by profession should be very careful on how we pronounce judgment on the performance of our political leaders. The task of leading a nation is a difficult task. A president is entrusted not only with the task of economic growth, but also that of protecting all the people of Kenya against criminals and of punishing evildoers so that we can live in peace. Sometimes we get a president we might not understand. Our judgment might be based on naïvety or ignorance of the inside story. During the time of Kenyatta, Idi Amin threatened to extend the boundaries of Uganda to Naivasha. Some of us wanted Kenyatta to declare war against Uganda but the matter was resolved quietly. It should be observed that since independence, Kenya had never been at war with its neighbours, though we have been provoked many a time. We probably would have liked President Mwai Kibaki to give a stern warning to Museveni when he tried to grab Migingo Island. His silence might be seen as cowardice. But we would be naïve to pronounce such a judgment for we do not really know the inside story. When President Jimmy Carter was defeated by Ronald Reagan, he said in his concession speech, "I have realised in politics the truth is not enough." It is a strange statement uttered by a president whose aim was to apply Christian values to his presidency. Kibaki to many did the unexpected when he sanctioned the operation against al-Shabaab, who had been making incursions into Kenya and who had several active terror cells in East African countries.

But it is true that there are some truths that if exposed can cause more problems to a nation. That is probably the reason why every member of cabinet must take a vow not to reveal confidential matters discussed by the cabinet. The same is true of a family. It would be most irresponsible for any member of the family to go out to the world to reveal family matters that are supposed to be confidential.

Conclusion

President Daniel arap Moi used to invite me for mutual discussions with him at State House, Nairobi. Though Mwai Kibaki has never invited me to State House, I am nevertheless grateful for him having awarded me the order of the Moran of the Burning Spear (MBS) in recognition of the services I have rendered to this great nation. I am also grateful that during the Heroes Days observed (for the first time) on 20 October 2010, I was publicly recognised as one of the *Washujaa* (heroes) who struggled courageously for the second liberation. I was the only person in Kirinyaga County who received that honor.

Chapter 28

Cog in the Wheels of
Constitution Making (2002–2010)

During my retirement service held on Sunday 15 September 2002 at All Saints Cathedral, Nairobi, the General Secretary of the NCCK, the Revd Mutava Musyimi, announced to the congregation that the NCCK had appointed me to be one of the representatives of the council in the Bomas of Kenya Constitutional Assembly. The constitution of Kenya (National Constitutional Conference) was established by a legal notice entitled "The constitution of Kenya Review Act Chapter 3A" (revised edition 2001). The review conference was chaired by Professor Yash Pal Ghai and was held at Bomas of Kenya, Nairobi, from October 2002.

While the delegates were meeting at Bomas of Kenya, the president dissolved parliament on 25 October 2002. When the delegates received the news during morning tea break, they streamed back to the hall and started dancing on the floor and singing. There was a Christian song that originally went "*yote yawezekana na imani*" or "all is possible by faith", but the lyrics had been corrupted to "*Yote yawezekana bila Moi*" meaning "all is possible without Moi". As I watched the singing and dancing to this song in its distorted version, I concluded that this was the worst song that I had ever heard. I felt that after Moi is gone they will sing "all is possible without the successor of Moi" or any leader of any organisation.

The next meeting of the constitutional assembly was due to be held on Monday 28 October 2002. The delegates who arrived early were chased away by the police at the orders of the president. The president must have been very annoyed by the dancing and singing of "all is possible without Moi". In other words the delegates were singing "Whether the president likes it or not Kenya will have a new constitution."

Around this time KANU was undergoing a major crisis. A KANU delegates' conference was held at Kasarani sports grounds on 14 October 2002 to endorse Uhuru Kenyatta as the KANU presidential candidate by acclamation. Following this, several government ministers resigned including Raila Odinga, William Ntimama, Moody Awori, Dr Ardhi Awiti and Kalonzo Musyoka. On the same day the Rainbow Alliance Party held a mammoth rally at Uhuru Park to demonstrate against President Moi. It was during this KANU delegates' conference that George Saitoti, who had already been sacked as vice-president in August, and who now lost his position as the vice chairman of KANU said, "There come [sic] a time when the interests of a nation are more important than personal interests."

The Constitutional Review Conference did not resume its deliberations until after the elections of December 2002, when KANU was removed from power. The conference resumed on 28 April 2003 and was chaired by the chairman of the Constitution of Kenya Review Commission, Professor Yash Pal Ghai; the secretary was Dr P.L.O. Lumumba. There were 625 official delegates, among them the other commissioners from the review commission. All districts were represented, each with 3 delegates. There were also representatives from trade unions, non-governmental organisations (NGOs), professional groups, women organisations, religious organisations, political parties and special interest groups. All Members of Parliament were also delegates.

The conference was held in three phases and lasted for more than two years. Every delegate was given a copy of the draft constitution prepared by the commission and other relevant documents. During the first phase, delegates preferred to discuss the new constitution in plenary format. In one session, veterans of the Lancaster House Conference who were still alive came to enlighten us on their participation in the conference that gave independent Kenya its first constitution. One thing that shocked me was that some members of parliament, particularly from central Kenya, boycotted the Bomas review talks. They used only to go to the venue in the morning and register themselves then disappear. They would then turn up on pay day to claim their sitting and travel allowances. The very political leaders who are paid hefty salaries still wanted to drain the taxpayer of even more money through false claims.

During the second phase of the conference we were divided into various working technical groups to discuss, improve and amend the chapters and clauses of the draft. During the third and final phase, we met in plenary to discuss every chapter and clause as amended by the groups. Further amendments or additions were suggested by the plenary session before the final document was prepared.

During the second phase I was assigned to the technical working committee on culture, which I very much enjoyed and where I learnt a lot about the subject. I was however concerned that the draft of the commissioners stated, "The state shall respect, preserve, protect and promote the cultural heritage of Kenya." I argued in plenary that because a human being was created by God in his image, some of his culture is rich in beauty and goodness. But because of the fall, all our culture is tainted with sin and some of it is demonic. I told the conference we cannot preserve and respect such cultural heritage as female genital mutilation (FGM) and cattle rustling. I further said that Maasai *morans* were taught to believe that all the cattle in the world belong to them. They understood that taking cattle from Wakamba is not stealing but returning them to their proper custody. To my surprise no Maasai delegate or any other delegate stood to disagree with my statement. I was grateful to note that in the new constitution promulgated in August 2010, my concerns were taken into account. In the clause on Rights and Fundamental Freedom it is stated that children and youth will be protected from "harmful cultural practices". (See part 3, clause 53[d] and clause 55 [d].)

Numerous contentious issues were hotly contested during the constitutional conference. One of the most burning issues was the chapters on the Executive and Devolution. There were those, particularly in government, who advocated for a powerful president who would act both as head of state and government. There were also those who proposed a parliamentary system where leader of the party with most seats in parliament automatically became the Prime Minister, answerable to parliament. A Consensus Building Committee had been formed under Bishop Philip Sulumeti, which brought various players to the negotiating table, and a consensus report was drafted. The consensus position was to have a hybrid system with a President elected by universal suffrage and a Prime Minister from the leader of the parties with the largest number of seats in parliament. On 14 March 2004, a final plenary session of the Kenya Constitutional Review Conference was held to adopt the draft as amended by the delegates. The Sulumeti report was defeated, sparking a mass walkout from the conference by delegates led by the then vice-president, Moody Awori, who also boycotted the voting. Most of these were members of parliament and delegates from Central Kenya. I did not walk out. The draft constitution was passed by a large majority though a few abstained from voting.

There were several initiatives to break the deadlock without success until the Parliamentary Select Committee and the CKRC meeting at Naivasha brokered the Naivasha Accord. This accord supported a powerful president and a non-executive prime minister. More amendments were made to the draft during a meeting in Kilifi. The Attorney General Amos Wako published the final draft on 22 August 2005.

The referendum for the new constitution was held on Monday 21 November 2005. Voters could either vote YES or NO to the proposed new constitution. The symbol for "YES" was a banana and that for "NO" was an orange. The proposed new constitution was rejected by a huge majority. Members of parliament were sharply divided between those who voted YES and NO. President Mwai Kibaki expected his ministers to vote in favor of the new constitution. But a number of key ministers campaigned for rejection of the new constitution. Consequently the president dissolved parliament on 23 November 2005 and appointed a new cabinet on Thursday 8 December 2005. In his appointment of ministers, he took the opportunity to drop all those who campaigned against the proposed new constitution. These were Raila Odinga, Stephen Kalonzo Musyoka, Najib Balala, Anyang' Nyong'o, Ochillo Ayanko, Lina Kilimo and William Ntimama. He also dropped Chris Murungaru though he had campaigned in favour of the new constitution.

The victory of "Orange" inspired the formation of the Orange Democratic Party (ODM). The next general elections were held in December 2007. The ODM party led by Raila Odinga campaigned vigorously against the Party of National Unity, which was a coalition of several other parties. Before the elections were held, Kalonzo Musyoka broke away from ODM and formed ODM-KENYA which later joined PNU and thus weakened ODM. However ODM managed to gain slightly more Members of Parliament than PNU. But according to the Electoral Commission of Kenya, Mwai Kibaki defeated Raila Odinga in the presidential election and was sworn in as president for a second term. Election violence had already started in some of the western parts of the country but as soon as the KEC announced that Mwai Kibaki had won the elections, a huge fire was seen in Nairobi's Kibera slum, and killing and destruction of property began spreading through various parts of the Rift Valley, Western, Nyanza, Nairobi, Coast and Kiambu in Central province. This continued for two months, by which time 1,300 people had lost their lives and 300,000 persons had become internally displaced. These tragic disturbances ended when the former General Secretary of the United Nations, Kofi Annan, intervened and held reconciliation meetings with representatives of ODM and PNU. This led to the formation of the Grand Coalition with Mwai Kibaki as the president and Raila Odinga as the prime minister of the new government.

A commission of experts was appointed to draft a new constitution, taking into account the deliberations of Bomas of Kenya and other important documents that had been produced by other forums. The Attorney General published the second proposed constitution of Kenya on 6 May 2010.

Debate on Proposed Constitution, May to August 2010

The new draft constitution was debated by Members of Parliament for two consecutive days. They proposed 150 amendments but none of the amendments could garner the 145 votes required out of the 222. Hence the document as published by the Attorney General was presented to the voters to study and for each to decide whether he/she would vote YES or NO during the referendum to be held on 4 August 2010.

The debate on whether to accept or reject the new proposed constitution started even before it was officially published on 6 May. Daily newspapers had published the entire document and circulated it to all their readers throughout the country in April. William Ruto, MP for Eldoret North and member of ODM, became *de facto* leader of the movement to oppose the proposed new constitution. He travelled throughout the country accompanied by MPs and religious leaders who were opposed to the constitution. The majority of church leaders, the Roman Catholic Episcopal Conference, member churches of the National Council of Churches of Kenya (NCCK) led by the General Secretary Canon Peter Karanja, the Kenya Evangelical Fellowship, independent churches and many others opposed the constitution, mainly on two grounds. First and foremost the new draft constitution favoured Islam over against other religions, and secondly it allowed abortion in certain circumstances.

The Protestants, evangelicals and Pentecostal churches took the lead in opposing the entire constitution on the grounds that it favoured Islam. Indeed clause 8 of the draft constitution on state and religion reads, "There shall not be state religion" and yet in chapter 10 on the judiciary, part 3 clause 170 states, "There shall be a chief Kadhi and such number, being not fewer than three, of other Kadhis as may be prescribed under an act of parliament." The Kadhis, who must profess the Muslim religion, are civil servants paid by the taxpayers.

The inclusion of Kadhi courts in the constitution raised a hue and cry from the majority of churches. Reference was made to the Abuja declaration of 28 November 1989, which summarises a strategy for the spread of Islam in Africa so that within three decades Africa will become an Islamic continent. Among other things, the Abuja communiqué called upon Muslims to "support the establishment and application of Sharia law to all Muslims" and "to ensure only Muslims are elected to all political posts of member nations". I urged that instead of Christian leaders being concerned about the Abuja communiqué, they should hold a continental assembly to plan a strategy to win the entire African continent for Christ.

The inclusion of the Kadhi courts in the draft constitution appeared to some Christians as one step forward towards introducing sharia law in Kenya. In opposition to this view it was argued that the Kadhi courts were included in the Lancaster House constitution following negotiations between the Sultan of Zanzibar, the colonial government and Mzee Jomo Kenyatta. The Kadhi courts have been part of the judiciary since independence and the jurisdiction of Kadhi courts is "limited to the determination of questions of Muslim law relating to personal status, marriage, divorce or inheritance in proceedings in which all the parties profess Muslim religion and submit to the jurisdiction of Kadhi courts".

The Kenya Episcopal Conference was particularly opposed to clause 26 on Right of life, clause (4) which states that, "Abortion is not permitted unless, in the opinion of a trained health professional, there is need for emergency treatment or the life of the mother is in danger or if permitted by any other written law."

On Friday 30 July 2010 a joint statement was published by the Christian leaders during the ecumenical meeting held at the Holy Family Basilica. One paragraph stated, "The 4th August 2010 will be a day that will be a hall mark in the history of the republic of Kenya. We call upon each and every Kenyan to turn up in large numbers, to exercise their democratic right to vote, and to display their patriotism for our country and convincingly vote **NO** to this flawed proposed constitution that takes away your sovereignty now and forever, through subjection of international law. We are all aware that this project began as a beautiful dream for the whole country, a dream to make this nation a great nation in the eyes of God and of men. We can still realize that dream and should not give up or choose to accept a clearly flawed document with the excuse of fatigue or fear."

On the following day, Saturday 31 July 2010, the Kenya Episcopal conference issued a six-clause statement entitled, "Listen to the voice of the Lord" and signed by all the 25 Roman Catholic bishops in Kenya. Clause 2 stated:

> Brothers and sisters, we have raised our concerns about Article 26(4) which by other written laws, opens the gate to abortion on demand. The life of a person begins at conception, and unborn babies are therefore human beings and have a right to a life and this document declares that in essence, legislators and "health professionals" should have a free hand in ending the lives of these human beings. The contradiction is so clearly framed that it lends to words once written by Pope John Paul II: "The height of arbitrariness and injustice is reached when certain people such as physicians or legislators, arrogate to themselves the power to decide who ought to live and who ought to die." (Encyclical "The Gospel of Life" 2001).
>
> To legalize abortion is to legalize murder of the innocent. As a result the society will become more violent. If I can kill an unborn child because they are "inconvenient" or "unwanted" why refrain from killing others who get in the way of my greed, lust or ambition? Abortion causes harm to the unborn child, it causes harm to the father of the child, and the mother of the child, and to the whole society in general. Abortion is not good for our country, and the majority of Kenyans do not want abortion in this country. It has been introduced in this process contrary to the majority's will, making the proposed draft an undemocratic document. On this ground alone and to reject the imposition of a fundamentally anti life law, we urge all Christians to vote **NO** to this draft.

While appreciating the fact that the Kenya Episcopal Conference was making an important contribution to the debate on the clause on abortion, we felt duty bound to inform the voters that the proposed new constitution clearly stated, "Abortion is not permitted". The proposed draft constitution recognised the fact that in certain circumstances, it might be necessary to terminate pregnancy if "in the opinion of a trained health professional there is need for emergency treatment or the life or health of the mother is in danger". In case of ectopic pregnancy where the woman's seed is fertilised in the fallopian tube and does not move to the uterus, then the life of the mother would be in great danger and in such circumstances, neither the mother nor the baby would survive. Termination of the pregnancy would save the life of the mother. The opinion of a trained health professional is also necessary in cases of abortion when the life of the mother could be in danger.

We are all concerned, whether we are Catholics or not, when we read in the media of newly born babies being destroyed by their mothers or young pregnant girls going to seek abortion from unqualified medical practitioners and ending up going to hospital when complications arise. In such cases the blame should be shared equally by the parents and the church, which may have failed to teach young people, both boys and girls, the Christian morals they are supposed to uphold. Whether we like it or not, abortion will continue unless the church intensifies its ministry to the young people and teaches them the essence of being a committed Christian and parents play their role in counseling their children.

In preparation for the debate on the proposed new constitution, I had read the document (published in the newspaper) in April 2010. On Sunday 18 April 2010 I was invited by the provost of All Saints Cathedral, Nairobi to preach at both the 9 am and 11 am services. In both services the cathedral was packed. I preached on the theme of "Blessed are those who have not seen and yet have believed" (John 20:29b).

I was preaching about faith in view of the unbelief of Thomas when told by other disciples that they had seen the risen Lord. He said, "unless I see the nail marks in his hands and put my finger where the nails were, and put my hand into his sides, I will not believe it." But when the risen Lord revealed Himself to the disciples the second time, and Thomas was present, Jesus invited him to come and do his experiments. Thomas was so overwhelmed that all he could say was, "My Lord and my God!" Then Jesus told him, "Because you have seen me you have believed? Blessed are those who have not seen and yet believe." The writer of Hebrews defines faith as, "being sure of what we hope for and certain of what we do not see" (Hebrews 11:1).

It is always my policy to make my sermons relevant to the contemporary situation. As the great debate on the proposed new constitution had just begun, I felt urged by the Holy Spirit to make my contribution as I preached from the National Pulpit of the Anglican Church in Kenya. I reminded the congregation that a Christian lives in hope even when the situation appears to be hopeless. We have faith that God in his own appointed time can turn hopelessness to triumphant hope and a cause for joy for individuals, communities and the nation. The search for a new and more democratic constitution has been long and virtually hopeless. The Lancaster House constitution was amended many times and each time the powers of the president were enhanced until he became an imperial president who ruled the country with iron fist and his words seemed to have the final authority. Now we have to choose in the referendum either the Lancaster House constitution as amended over the years or the draft constitution published by the Attorney General.

I told the congregation, in Christian ethics, if one has to choose between two evils, you choose the lesser evil. The Lancaster House constitution is bad because first and foremost it has increased the powers of the president so that he has become an imperial president. The proposed constitution is bad because even the Members of Parliament wanted to amend 150 clauses but virtually all the proposers withdrew their notices of amendments once they realised they would not be supported by the required 65% (145 members). Hence we have to choose between these two evils. The proposed new constitution is better by far than the Lancaster House constitution. I asked the congregation whether they wanted me to tell them how I would vote. They said, "Yes," and I answered, "Yes." The congregation gave me a mighty clap and laughed with joy. The congregation of All Saints Cathedral, Nairobi, is known for not clapping at any preacher and sometimes not laughing even when he/she makes jokes. On that day I was given a mighty clap as if that "Yes" were what they were waiting to hear.

The following day I had a surprise telephone call from Charles Njonjo, the former Attorney General and a worshipper at All Saints Cathedral, Nairobi. When I was Archbishop, Njonjo used to attack my leadership by issuing press statements and he even took me to court for proposing to divide the Diocese of Nairobi into two. He was clearly my adversary. On that day however, he told me on the telephone, "We have been enemies for a long time. But as from today we have become friends for supporting the new proposed constitution." How wonderful it was to gain a friend as a result of my prophetic proclamation of the gospel.

The Anglican bishops met five days after my sermon and after a whole day's deliberation they passed a resolution not to support the new proposed constitution. This decision was not unanimous, as some Bishops in Nyanza disassociated themselves from the statement. However, just before the referendum the Archbishop of the Anglican church of Kenya, the Most Revd Eliud Wabukala, was reported to have said that Anglicans were free to vote either "Yes" or "No".

On 7 July 2010 (Saba Saba day), I was invited to preach at St Stephen's Cathedral, Nairobi. The service was attended by politicians and clergymen who participated in the struggle for multiparty democracy. Among those present were Pastor Timothy Njoya of PCEA, Professor Anyang' Nyong'o, Gitobu Imanyara and other veteran political activists. We were hosted by the Bishop of Nairobi, the Rt Revd Peter Njoka, who said that even if all Anglican Bishops vote "No" during the referendum, he would vote "Yes."

That afternoon the Prime Minister, Raila Odinga, invited pro-reform heroes to his Karen home to celebrate Saba Saba day with them. Those present included Paul Muite, who was the master of ceremonies, Gitobu Imanyara, Gibson Kamau, John Khaminwa, the Revd Timothy Njoya and myself. Raila wanted to celebrate Saba Saba day with us at home where he was convalescing after a minor operation.

From January to August 2010 the National Civil Society Congress organised press conferences held on Sundays at Serena Hotel to update the media on the progress that the "Yes" campaign was making. The theme of the press conference was "*Katiba Sasa* Campaign" or "Constitution Now Campaign". I was invited to attend two of the press conferences but the Revd Timothy Njoya attended most of them. In one of the press conferences one journalist informed us that one key church leader in the "No" campaign had issued a statement that we should keep out of debate on the proposed constitution as we were retired generals and our views on current matters were irrelevant and out of date.

In my response I said I was retired but not tired. We challenged the leading clerics in the "No" campaign to a live debate on television. This debate would enable the Kenyan viewers to decide for themselves whether we are no longer relevant in our comments on important current issues or not. One of the television channels organized the debate and invited the key "No" church leaders to come and face us. We were later informed all those "No" church leaders who were invited declined to come to participate in such a debate. We considered their refusal to come and face us as cowardice.

By early July 2010, the Central Kenya leaders were beginning to feel they were getting behind in educating voters in the area about the new proposed constitution. The "No" campaigners, led by William Ruto and some key church leaders, were touring Central Kenya and other parts of Kenya holding huge rallies to convince people to reject the proposed constitution. They seemed to be gaining many followers in the region. Leaders from central Kenya called an urgent meeting to discuss a strategy for urging central region voters to support the proposed new constitution.

They felt that I was the right person to convene such a meeting. I convened the meeting, which we co-chaired with the chairman of GEMA, Bishop Lawi Imathiu. The meeting, which was held at Limuru, was highly successful. It was agreed that leaders would return to their respective districts and hold meetings to drum up support for the new constitution.

In Kirinyaga I organised eight seminars attended by an average of 250 people per day from all parts of Kirinyaga. Several lawyers came to facilitate the meetings, which were attended by a total of 2,000 people, at Philadelphia Retreat and Conference Centre. I convened and chaired all the meetings. The purpose of the meetings was not to tell people to vote Yes or No. The purpose was to educate voters about the new constitution so that they could make informed decision on the day of the referendum. But the delegates who in the morning were in the "No" camp had by the end of the day converted to the "Yes" camp.

A few days before the referendum, on 30 July to be precise, Christian leaders issued a statement from the Holy Family Basilica calling upon the Christians to "convincingly vote 'NO' to this flawed proposed constitution…" The following day, the 25 Roman Catholic bishops issued a statement in which they urged all Christians to vote "No" and thus reject the "imposition of a fundamental anti-life law".

The referendum was held a few days later on 4 August 2010 and was approved by 5,954,767 voters or more than 67%; 2,687,183 voted "No". The results of this referendum should teach church leaders a number of lessons;

- Some church leaders, from the very beginning of the debate, convened prayer meeting to call upon Almighty God to intervene and have the proposed constitution rejected. My position was that if such prayer meetings were held it would be wiser to pray that "God's will be done" during the referendum. If, after prayers had been made for rejection of the constitution, a majority of Kenyans then voted in favour of the constitution, it would mean that God was hearing the prayers of the politicians and other "Yes" activists rather than those of church leaders.

- The second important lesson church leaders should learn is that the days have gone when Christians believed and obeyed the advice of church leaders to the letter. The voice of church leaders is no longer taken by Christians as the final authoritative mind of God. During the 2009 census, it was found that 82% of Kenyans profess the Christian faith. Had they all voted according to the wish of their church leaders the proposed constitution would have been rejected by 82% of the voters. Instead the proposed constitution was endorsed by 67% of voters, the majority of them Christians. I heard one Bishop say publicly that the government would be shocked by the results of the referendum, as the majority of voters are Christians who would be mobilised to vote "No". In the final analysis it was the church leaders who were shocked by the results as their followers rejected their advice.

I was asked by journalists whether I thought that the Church lost its credibility after the referendum. My answer was that the Church of Christ can never lose credibility, but church leaders' credibility can be questionable if they rely on their human convictions instead of seeking for "God's will to be done on earth as it is done in heaven" (Matthew 6:10).

The history of the church is full of examples of the church making wrong decisions or punishing individuals unfairly. One of the best examples is that of Galileo (1564-1642), an Italian astronomer and mathematician and a supporter of Copernicus's theory of the solar system. Copernicus found the centre of the solar system was not the earth but the sun. Galileo was condemned to imprisonment for "vehemently suspected heresy". Today the Copernican theory of the solar system is accepted universally as scientifically correct. It is not the earth that is the centre of universe but the sun.

Some of the Kenyan church leaders have lost credibility for keeping quiet when they should have vigorously united and courageously intervened during post-2007 general election violence. The church leaders should also bear in mind that Kenya is a secular republic and the church cannot impose its moral ethics on non-Christians. However, the church should be at the forefront of teaching and practising the message of the Holy Scriptures and reminding the nation that "justice is our shield and defender".

The new constitution was promulgated by President Mwai Kibaki at a colourful ceremony held at Uhuru Park, Nairobi, on 27 August 2011. Philadelphia Retreat and Conference Centre felt duty bound to be involved in civic education with regard to the constitution, especially the implementation of devolved government. Realising that the youth (that is, those who are 35 years and under) form 67% of the population of Kirinyaga, we planned to have fifteen seminars, each attended by 100 young people from every location in Kirinyaga. The last seminar was held on Thursday 25 November 2010. The 15 seminars were attended by a total 1,500 of young people. The main post-referendum issue discussed was the devolved government.

Each seminar targeted a particular group of youth professionals who are leaders in their own right. The groups included young pastors, youth involved in transport, particularly *boda boda* (motorbike taxis), young political activists, church youth leaders, university students, small-scale traders and businessmen/women, young village elders, single mothers and young widows, and accountants. There were also office secretaries and computer experts, young artisans, young farmers, self-help group leaders and young school teachers. The seminars started at about 10am and ended at 4.30pm each day.

The Philadelphia Seminar Planning Team met with representatives of Kirinyaga Professionals at Parklands Sports Club, Nairobi, on 19 October 2010. The meeting agreed on names of professionals who would facilitate the seminar. The professionals who facilitated these seminars included Paul Muite (Constitutional Lawyer), Prof. Joseph Wangomb'e (Health Economist), Prof. Marion Mutugi (Genetics), Prof. Octavian Gakuru (Sociology of Development & Education), Prof. Daniel Mukunya (Agriculturist), Ann Tei Mukunya (Agriculturist), Mercy Kangara (Lawyer & Company Secretary), the Revd David Nyoroku, the Revd Gerald Mwai and the Revd J.B. Mwangi (Theologians). Others who attended were John Kithaka (Architect now involved in mobilising the youth for meaningful investment), J.S. Mathenge (Retired Civil Servant and Businessman), Marcella Wanjiru (Superintendent of Police), Fredrick Konya (Police Base Commander), Wambugu Ngunjiri, Samson Ngengi Njuguna, Peter Kimaru Wamwea, Patrick Itumbi and Ernest Kiunguyu (Diplomat). I convened and chaired all the meetings.

After much discussion and dialogue between facilitators and the youth, the participants were divided into ten small discussion groups, each with ten people. The groups were requested to discuss five main questions;

1. What qualities should we look for in the person who will be elected as Governor of Kirinyaga County?
2. What part should we as young people play in ensuring that we get the right person to be our Governor?
3. What would you as a young person wish the Kirinyaga County Government to do to ensure that the youth are fully involved in the planning and management of economic growth and human development in Kirinyaga County?
4. Which town should be elevated to be the capital of Kirinyaga County and for what reasons?

After this process, the youth made the recommendations for further consideration by the professionals and other citizens of Kirinyaga. This was the "Message from the youth of Kirinyaga to the people of Kirinyaga" (see Appendix X). RevdThis message was presented to 100 Kirinyaga professionals from various parts of Kenya in December 2010, including senior civil servants, university professors and lecturers, businessmen and women, bankers, farmers, teachers, administrators and politicians.

The meeting, which I chaired, was held at Philadelphia Retreat and Conference Centre. The participants welcomed the message from the youth. They also decided to set up a committee composed of three people from each of the five districts to prepare a strategic development plan for Kirinyaga County.

Once agreed upon by the professionals, the strategic plan will be presented to a forum of Kirinyaga County for further discussion and approval. The aim is to have the strategic development plan ready in good time, before the next general elections.

I was elected unanimously to be the chairman of these proceedings. It is our prayer and hope that the strategic plan will be a great help as we begin to develop Kirinyaga County and as we implement the new constitution.

Chapter 29

The Challenges of the Twenty-First Century

It was a great privilege to serve the Anglican Church of Kenya as a bishop for a total of twenty-seven years. I was consecrated as a bishop at the age of 37 years and spent most of my active life as a servant of the Lord Jesus Christ until my retirement in 2002. I have no regrets for having spent my entire life in the service of the Lord Jesus Christ and his Church.

I was awarded my first university degree (BA London) only six months after Kenya became independent in December 1963. At that time university graduates were in great demand, especially in the civil service and corporates. My university contemporaries and friends could not understand how I preferred to work for the Church when there were so many opportunities for a better-paid job in the civil service and the blossoming private sector. However the call to serve the Lord was so irresistible that material gains could not persuade me to change my calling. The Kirinyaga leaders wanted me to be the clerk to the county council but I turned down the offer.

When today I meet those who were very much opposed to a university graduate going to serve the church, they tell me that I made the right choice. They admire the part I have played as a bishop in courageously challenging the injustices in Kenya and in the struggle for a more democratic country. Being called to be a bishop is indeed a great privilege and I enjoyed serving the church and the nation my entire life. There were many challenges and risks but God was faithful enough to see me through difficult trials and circumstances. I was misunderstood many a time, physically attacked by my enemies, deserted by friends, had false allegations made against me, received many abusive anonymous letters, and to crown it all, was attacked by the highest authority in the land. But I thank God that in all these tribulations I never spent a sleepless night and my faith in God became immovable. No threat succeeded in making me a coward. Even at the heights of all these tribulations, I continued with my ministry fearlessly and courageously.

It was a great privilege to be enthroned the third Archbishop of Kenya three years before the end of the 20th century and to have served the church in that capacity during the first three years of the 21st century. During my ten years of retirement I have been more of a spectator and observer of the life of the Church that I once led. I joined many other leaders who have retired and others have gone to be with the Lord. We who have retired and others who have gone before us form what the letter to the Hebrews call "the cloud of witness". We are like spectators in the athletics stadium and our work is to cheer on those who have taken up leadership. We cheer them on so that they may also finish the race. As the writer of Hebrews says:

> Therefore since we are surrounded by so great a cloud of witness, let us also lay aside every weight and sin which cling so closely, and let us run with endurance the race that is set before us, looking to Jesus, the founder and perfector of our faith who for the joy that was set before him endured the cross, despising the shame and is seated at the right hand of the throne of God (Hebrews 12:1-2).

For those competing in the athletic stadium it is imperative that they lay aside every "weight and sin". Weights are not sins but are hindrances to running the race successfully. Kenya has distinguished itself as a nation of champion long-distance runners. But if our marathon runners wear boots, overcoats and hats, then they cannot run successfully. But wearing boots and other weighty gear is not a sin but an unnecessary accompaniment in the race. The leaders who have succeeded us must consider what kind of weights they are carrying that might be hindering them in facing the challenges of leadership in these early days of the twenty-first century. The sins that cling so closely to us are called "besetting sins", those sins that keep recurring in our lives. These must also be laid aside for us to complete the race successfully. I can only summarise the challenges that I feel the Church and particularly the Anglican Church is facing and that must be courageously tackled.

Spiritual Challenges

Bishops, priests and lay leaders of our church must cultivate deep spiritual lives so that they can set an example to the believers. In geography we learn that the higher you climb a mountain, the colder it gets. Being elevated to a high position is like reaching the top of the mountain of leadership. There at the top of the mountain the leader can become spiritually cold. In the first instance, there are few people willing to visit the bishop for his spiritual encouragement. The other bishops who could provide such fellowship are far apart. It is important that the bishop gathers around himself a group of people, including leaders from other churches, who can have regular fellowship of prayer and Bible studies. The bishops are expected to give so much to the Lord's flock in preaching and teaching. They themselves should seek to have regular retreats and fellowships with brother bishops and clergy for spiritual nourishment. Jesus had twelve disciples but he selected three of them, Peter, James and John, who were like an inner cabinet for special consultations in his ministry. The bishop cannot run a diocese single-handedly; he needs fellowship and consultation with a smaller group, which should meet regularly for mutual encouragement.

Challenge of Evangelism

The clause on the nature of evangelism in the Lausanne Covenant states,

> To evangelize is to spread the good news that Jesus Christ died for our sins and was raised from the dead according to the scriptures, and that as the reigning Lord he now offers the forgiveness of sins and liberating gift of the spirit to all those who repent and believe. But evangelism itself is the proclamation of the historical, biblical Christ as saviour and Lord, with a view to persuading people to come to him personally and so be reconciled to God... The results of evangelism include obedience to Christ, incorporation into his church and responsible service in the world.

In modern history, CMS was the first Society to send missionaries to evangelise Kenya. In 1994 the Anglican Church of Kenya celebrated the 150 years since Johannes Krapf, the first CMS missionary, arrived in Mombasa. It is now 168 years since the coming of the first missionary. The Anglican Church of Kenya remains the largest single Protestant denomination in

Kenya and its impact is felt throughout the nation. The Comity Agreement made by various Protestant missions at Kikuyu in 1913 divided Kenya in to various areas of influence to avoid unnecessary competition in evangelism and planting of churches. Hence there were some parts of Kenya that CMS missionaries left to other Protestant missions. The main areas reserved for Anglicans were the coast (except Pokomo), Kiambu, Murang'a, Kirinyaga, Embu, Nyanza, Western Kenya and some parts of Rift Valley and Nairobi. CMS missionaries could not plant churches in (for example) Ukambani (reserved for AIM), Meru (reserved for Methodists and Scottish missionaries), Southern Nyanza and Kisii (reserved for SDA, etc.). At the time of independence in 1963, there were many Anglicans working in various parts of Kenya who initiated the planting of Anglican churches in areas that were not under our spheres of influence in accordance with the 1913 comity agreement. Other denominations also penetrated into areas reserved for Anglicans. So after independence, the Comity Agreement was a dead letter. Hence Anglican churches can now be found in nearly every part of Kenya.

The starting of Diocesan Missionary Associations in most of Anglican dioceses helped in the evangelism of the unreached areas, especially among the pastoralists of Northern Kenya and Maasai land. BCMS (now Crosslinks) pioneered missionary work in Samburu, Marsabit, West Pokot and other areas.

Though the Anglican Church is still the largest Protestant church in Kenya, it faces major challenges in evangelism. It should also be noted that we are losing many of our members to other churches. I therefore wish to call upon the Anglican Church of Kenya to consider the following challenges of evangelism.

Reviving the Revival Movement

The East African Revival Movement that began in Rwanda in the early 1930s and spread to Uganda, Kenya and Tanzania made a great impact during the first four decades (1930-1970). But it seems to have lost its influence in evangelism. There are many people in positions of church leadership who owe their strong Christian foundation to the revival movement. I consider its loss of momentum to be due to its introverted nature and legalism. The weekly fellowship meetings were meant for each individual to openly confess the sins they had committed since the last meeting. The brethren present welcomed the confession by singing "*Tukutendereza*". In the early decades, the members of the revival met for fellowship and spiritual encouragement and then went out to evangelise and to challenge members of the church who appeared to be lukewarm Christians. This is no longer the practice. The brethren have also suffered from leadership squabbles and have been split into groups, each with its godfather or mother. The movement has occasionally been affected by heretical teachings such as *Kufufuka* and *Kupaa*, which split the movement further. The *Kufufuka* (*kuzuzuka* in Kiganda) preached that many saved Christians were spiritually dead and needed to rise from death. But this rising from the dead meant to refrain from taking bank loans, which to the *Kufufuka* was a sin, and not to keep dogs. To keep dogs meant you put your security in dogs instead of Jesus Christ. The revival movement, being primarily a lay movement, was led by people who had not studied theology. Though it is a commendable thing for the movement to be led by laity, it is important that the bishops and pastors show their presence in revival fellowships so that they can also help the movement to steer away from heretical teachings.

The second key reason that the East African Revival Movement has lost its impact is its legalism. This is the one main reason that has made the movement unattractive to the young people. There are times when the movement was more concerned about the outward appearance of a person than his/her spirituality. A girl wearing earrings, necklaces, high-heeled shoes, trousers or miniskirts was condemned as unsaved. Boys were also condemned as unsaved because of the way they dressed or certain personality traits. Yet St Paul says, "Therefore let no one pass judgment on you in questions on food or drink or with regard to a festival or a new moon or a Sabbath..." (Colossians 2:16) and again, "Let no one disqualify you insisting on asceticism and worship of angels..." (Colossians 2:17). And in Romans 14:17 Paul says, "For the Kingdom of God is not a matter of eating and drinking but of righteousness and peace and joy in the Holy Spirit."

The Challenges of the Pentecostal Movement

The growth of Pentecostal or charismatic movement in Kenya, especially among young people, began towards the end of the 1960s. Joe Kayo, a young charismatic preacher from Kisii, began to gather around himself many young followers. He started a congregation in a hired hall at Kariokor in Nairobi and within a short time hundreds of young people were coming to hear him on Sundays. He was the founder of the Kenya Redeemed Church.

Kayo was a gifted preacher and an orator in his own right. He was invited to many secondary schools and started organising "explosion" conferences for students during school holidays. The main emphasis of his preaching was to call upon people to be filled with the Holy Spirit. The evidence that one was spirit-filled was talking in tongues. Healing, especially exorcism, were major activities carried out in those conferences. Though Kayo lost leadership of the Kenya Redeemed Church within a few years, the church has grown and spread to many parts of Kenya. Many other Pentecostal churches and ministries were started and attracted many young people.

The Kenya Students Christian Fellowship (KSCF) embraced the message of charismatic movement. I attended the annual KSCF conference in Machakos Teachers College in December 1971 as one of the speakers. I had just returned from Bristol, England, after three years undertaking my Bachelor of Theology Studies. I was concerned that all the other preachers, including Bishop James Mundia, were emphasising that the evidence of being spirit-filled was speaking in tongues. One evening I decided to read to the conference 1 Corinthians 13, 14 and 15 and emphasised that speaking in tongues was just one of the gifts of the Holy Spirit and not the most important.

I reminded the conference that Paul says:

Pursue love and earnestly desire the spiritual gifts, especially that you may prophesy. For the one who speaks in a tongue speaks not to men but to God; for no one understands him but he utters mysteries in the spirit. On the other hand, the one who prophesies speaks to people for their up building, encouragement and consolation. The one who speaks in a tongue builds up himself, but he who prophesies builds up the church. Now I want you all to speak in tongues, but even more to prophesy. The one who prophesies is greater than the one who speaks in tongues, unless someone interprets, so that the whole church may be built up (1 Corinthians 14: 1-5).

It should be noted that prophecy in the New Testament does not mean foretelling or predicting the future but rather forth-telling or the powerful proclamation of the gospel in such a way that the hearers are built up, encouraged and consoled.

My preaching that evening divided the conference into two. At the end of my preaching Watson Omulokoli stood and said the Holy Spirit has been quenched by my exposition and called upon delegates who so wanted to remain behind for prayers throughout the night that the Holy Spirit may return to the conference. I told those who wanted clarification to follow me to another classroom. Many remained with Watson for the whole-night prayer meeting. My exposition was however a relief to many young people who were being told they were not truly saved unless they spoke in tongues. Some were trying to force themselves to utter unintelligible words so as to appear to be speaking in tongues. The following Sunday morning during the prayer session one person prayed, "God deliver us from this demon of theology." At the end of the meeting I stood to say, "Theology means knowledge of God and therefore cannot be demonic."

That afternoon the Annual General meeting of KSCF was held and to my surprise I was elected by majority votes as the chairman of the fellowship. I remained in that position for four years: 1972 to 1975. It was my joy to see many who were opposed to my theological position accept the fact that speaking in tongues is not necessarily the evidence of being filled in the Spirit but is one of the gifts of the Holy Spirit and is not a must for every believer.

Many young, born-again Anglicans who joined secondary schools were bombarded by Pentecostal and charismatic preachers and started questioning the teachings of the Anglican Church on infant baptism and its lack of emphasis on the fullness of the Holy Spirit. Some of the young Anglicans were re-baptised by full immersion even in schools sponsored by the Anglican Church. The Anglican Church is not opposed to baptising candidates by full immersion if that is their choice. But there is also a strong biblical case for infant baptism. The greatest shortcoming of the Anglican Church is that our presence is not felt in secondary schools, even those we sponsor. My strong recommendation to all the dioceses is to ensure that well-trained clergy who are also qualified teachers are posted or are attached to every secondary school we sponsor. When I was the Bishop of Kirinyaga, I organised special courses for qualified secondary school teachers, whom we ordained and appointed as chaplains of the schools that they were teaching in.

In recent years the Pentecostal movement has made a great impact by using the media, especially television. Some of the Pentecostal leaders have money to buy air time to have their sermons transmitted on television. Many viewers are impressed, especially by healing and exorcism shown on television. Whereas I have no doubt that God uses the media to change many hearts, I am concerned about some of the Pentecostal preachers in the media. The following are some of my concerns.

Publicity of Healing Sessions

In the Synoptic Gospels (Matthew, Mark and Luke), there is a continuous theme of Messianic secrecy. Jesus did not heal for publicity purposes but because He was touched by the suffering of people who were harassed and helpless, like sheep without a shepherd. In many instances he healed people and ordered them not to tell anyone (see Mark 7:36; 8:26 and others). The Fourth Gospel, however, records only a few healing miracles and John concludes by saying that Jesus did many other signs, but "these are written that you may believe that Jesus is the Christ, the Son of God and that by believing you may have life in His name" (John 20:31).

Before He began His ministry, the Synoptic Gospels record that Jesus was led up by the Spirit into the wilderness to be tempted by the devil (Matthew 4:1-11, Mark 1:12-13 and Luke 4:1-12). After he had fasted for 40 days and 40 nights, the devil came to tempt him. During these 40 days and nights, Jesus was considering how He was going to carry out His mission. All three temptations by the devil were to persuade Him to adopt methods that would make Him popular immediately. If He commanded stones to become loaves of bread, He would be instantly popular. People would flock to Him in their thousands for free food. If He agreed to throw himself down from the pinnacle of temple, to be received by angels, He would instantly get a big following that would be attracted by His spectacular and sensational activities. In the third temptation, the devil takes Jesus to a very high mountain and shows Him the whole civilised world. The tempter tells him, "All this I will give you, if you fall down and worship me" (Matthew 4:9). This is the temptation to compromise. It is as if the devil was telling Jesus, "I have got people in my grip, don't set your standards so high. Strike a bargain with me. Just compromise a little with evil and people will follow you."

Jesus rejected all these three methods of winning people to Himself. In the first temptation, Jesus tells the devil, "It is written that man does not live by bread alone, but by every word that comes from the mouth of God." The tempter was suggesting that Jesus should bribe people with material gifts into following Him. Jesus' answer was that humans will never find life in material things.

The second temptation was to attract people to spectacular and sensational activities. But Jesus refused to use this method because what is sensational today will be ordinary within a short time. To keep the momentum one has to keep on producing new sensations. The third temptation was the temptation of compromise and to make the gospel cheap. There can be no compromise with evil, for good is good and right is right and wrong is wrong. Jesus refused to compromise with the devil in His ministry.

Instead of engaging populist activities or huge crusades, Jesus chose the difficult method of calling twelve disciples who were not themselves angels or saints. Some of them were rough fishermen; one was a hated tax collector; another was a guerilla fighter (Simon the Zealot); and Thomas was a man who could not believe unless he saw and touched. He chose ordinary people so as to transform them to become extra-ordinary people who after His resurrection and ascension would go to "make disciples of all nations, baptizing them in the name of the Father and the Son and the Holy Spirit, teaching them to observe all that I have commanded you" (Matthew 28:19-20). Jesus chose the way of the cross and by so doing conquered not only death but the devil himself.

My concern about some of the Pentecostal preachers is that they have chosen the populist way of winning men and women to Christ. They want to show on television the healing miracles they claimed to have performed. Though I have no doubt that God can heal the sick as a result of the prayers of faithful people, I am concerned about the publicity of these healing activities. I am concerned that there are many who go to those healing crusades and are not healed but are assured that they have been healed. Others are told they have not been healed because they have no faith. There were some people whom Jesus healed without their even first confessing faith in Him. The best example was the man who was sick for thirty-eight years at the pool of Bethesda. When Jesus asked this man whether he wanted to be healed, instead of saying "yes", he started complaining that he had no one to put him into the pool when the water was stirred up. Jesus said to him "Get up, take up your bed and walk". Asked by the Jews who had healed him and commanded him to break the Sabbath by carrying his bed, he said he did not know the man. This man was healed even before he was evangelised. It was after he was healed that later Jesus found him in the temple and evangelised him. "See you are well, sin no more, that nothing worse may happen to you" (John 5: 1-17). Some of our Pentecostal preachers leave a big pastoral problem by telling people that they are not healed because they have no faith.

The Anglican Church should embrace the healing ministry by visiting the sick and praying for them. But our prayers should be that God may do His will. We must never discourage the sick from going to hospital for treatment or from taking medicines. It is God who has led scientists to find cures for many diseases. To forbid believers to go to hospital for treatment is in itself a crime.

The Prosperity Gospel

The starting of new churches and ministries has become a major preoccupation of many Kenyan preachers. In the last three decades, close to 10,000 churches have been registered by the Registrar of the Societies, while thousands more applicants await registration for new churches and ministries. It is not difficult for the new churches and ministries to attract membership. In the city of Nairobi, all that a preacher requires for a crowd to hear him is some space and a public address system. At one stage, the lunch hour would see every empty space around public parks, bus termini and busy pathways such as the Aga Khan Walk occupied by a preacher calling people to turn to God, repent of their sins and be saved. New laws enforced by the National Environmental Management Agency have made this a little more difficult. But usually the sick are invited to come forward to be healed of all their diseases. The whole enterprise has become a money-making business exploiting those with spiritual and physical needs. It has therefore appeared as if the motive behind starting new churches and ministries is to make money and be rich rather than the extension of God's Kingdom.

The increase in the number of preachers who buy space on broadcasting stations to air their services on television has brought this prosperity gospel to our homes. Virtually all the preaching ends with a special appeal for viewers to send money to the preacher. The money is usually sent by mobile phone money transfer services through a telephone number shown on the television during the service. Some of the preachers have even gone to the extent of telling those who are sick to send a certain amount of money to the preacher and assuring them that as soon as the preacher receives the money, he/she will offer a prayer for healing and the patient will be healed instantly. Other preachers have told sick viewers to buy special healing oil that when applied can heal instantly. The oil ordinarily can be bought from supermarkets for a few shillings but it is sold at exorbitant prices by these preachers. Another preacher came on TV advertising small mats that he was selling at 5000/- to be used for kneeling when praying. So the buyer keeps in touch with the preacher by buying mats blessed by the preacher!

Some of these preachers have become millionaires, thus making the preaching of the Gospel a highly profitable business. Most of the victims of these preachers are young women who are displayed on the shows claiming to have been healed. Because they are discouraged from going to see a doctor, there is no medical evidence that they have been healed. For instance some people with the HIV infection are assured that they become HIV-negative immediately after a healing prayer or after giving some money or consuming an agent that should have healed them. They stop taking their antiretrovirals only for the infection to recur. This leads to further physical and spiritual suffering and even death. Meanwhile the preacher has taken away the little money they have, leaving them poorer economically and spiritually. The prosperity gospel preachers pick some verses in the Bible that refer to material prosperity as a consequence of generous contribution to the Lord's work.

Challenges of Politics in Present-Day Kenya

The Bishops and other clergy should always remember that their calling includes prophetic proclamation of the gospel. Our proclamation is not only to win souls to the Lord Jesus Christ but also to participate in their social, economic and political transformation. This will require constant challenge to the unjust structures of society. To succeed in this ministry, one has to study and understand the unjust structures and courageously challenge those in authority to uphold justice as required by God.

Some politicians are fond of telling church leaders to confine their preaching to spiritual matters and to leave politics to politicians. We cannot confine our preaching only to spiritual matters, as a human person is a psychosomatic being, both the spirit (*psyche*) and the body (*soma*) and the two cannot be separated. Politics is so important that it cannot be left to politicians alone. Our preaching must therefore be relevant to the contemporary situation. By challenging the unjust structures of society we shall be following the footsteps of the prophets of old who courageously challenged the rulers of Israel. We shall also be following the footsteps of our Lord Jesus Christ, who went throughout all the cities and villages, teaching in their synagogues and proclaiming the gospel of the kingdom and healing every disease and every affliction. When he saw the crowds, he had compassion for them, because they were harassed and helpless, like sheep without a shepherd (Matthew 9:35-36).

The Greek word used for "compassion" means being touched to the very depth of one's being. Having seen the harassment and helplessness of the crowd, Jesus was so touched to the very depth of his being that he could not allow the status quo to continue. Then he said to the twelve, "The harvest is plentiful but the labourers are few; therefore pray earnestly to the Lord of the harvest to send out labourers into his harvest" (Matthew 9:37-38). We should also be following in the footsteps of the apostles, who were prepared to say "no" to those in authority (the Sanhedrin) when commanded not to preach in the name of Jesus (Acts 4, 19-20). The saying of "no" to those in authority when they command us not to exercise our prophetic ministry is "holy defiance", which may be necessary at certain times.

At the time of independence, the politicians who struggled for our freedom said that they were going to fight against ignorance, poverty and disease. The fight was lost on all three fronts. By the time the second president retired after 24 years, Kenyans were poorer than they were in 1963. Our public hospitals and health centres had no medicine and essential equipment had broken down. Preventable diseases were still a major cause of death, particularly among children under five years of age, while maternal health care was for millions a distant mirage. New diseases such as HIV/AIDS were ravaging Kenyans. Though there was an increase in the numbers of public and private universities, there were many children who could not go to school for basic education as their parents could not afford school fees.

The struggle for the second liberation was waged by civil societies and some church leaders. It was not until the removal of KANU from power at the end of 2002 that we started having a taste of the gains of the second liberation. The climax of the second liberation was when the new constitution was promulgated in August 2010. However, we have to struggle against three other enemies: tribalism, corruption and impunity.

Negative Ethnicity

There are positive as well as negative aspects of our ethnic cultures. We should be proud of belonging to a particular ethnic group and should be proud of our varied cultural heritage. There are many good aspects of culture that should be protected and promoted; we cannot however embrace all aspects of our culture. The new constitution recognises that there are harmful cultural practices and children and youth should be protected from them (see clause 53 and 55). Such practices include female genital mutilation, cattle rustling and other life-threatening cultural practices. Kenya has forty-two ethnic groups and, being one nation, we should be prepared to learn and embrace the good things in all these cultures.

Ethnicity becomes a curse when people are so proud of their culture that they do not think anything good can come from other tribes. People tend to favour people who belong to their own tribes in employment, promotions, and distribution of other benefits. Ethnicity however raises its ugly head especially during the time of general elections. Tribalists are not comfortable if their own person is not elected to leadership positions. In the run-up to presidential elections, tribalists gang up and campaign for a person who comes from their ethnic group or region. Tribalism even finds its way into some of our churches when believers want a person from their own tribe to be elected to the position of bishop, moderator, or any other leadership position. Using local language in a cosmopolitan community sometimes puts off congregants who may be minorities in a particular church. It is these kinds of tribalism that we must fight against.

During presidential campaigns, the church should be at the forefront in discouraging that kind of tribalism. As Jethro, the father in-law of Moses, advised him, "You should always look for able men among all people, men who fear God, are trustworthy and hate dishonest gain; and set such men over [the people] as officers over thousands, hundreds, fifties and tens" (Exodus 18:21-22). Though there were twelve tribes in Israel, Moses was not advised to select people from a particular tribe. Every tribe was capable of producing a leader with those four qualities: capable, God-fearing, trustworthy and incorruptible.

We should learn from Jethro that each of the 42 tribes in Kenya, however large or small, is able to produce a leader with those four qualities. The first president of Tanzania came from one of the smallest tribes in that country and yet was elected by voters from every ethnic group. The large ethnic groups in Kenya have made those with smaller numbers feel insecure, as it appears that the tribalists who have the majority vote will trample over the rest and always elect their own person to the top position of leadership even if he is incapable, not God-fearing, untrustworthy and corrupt.

The Kikuyu, being the largest tribe in Kenya and supported by their neighbours in Central Kenya (Merus, Embus and Mbeeres), will go for their own son or daughter as the leader of this nation. The Luos, half of the Luhya and the Kalenjin felt they had enough votes during the 2007 general elections that their candidate could defeat the Kikuyu candidate. The Wakambas, who are the fifth largest tribe in Kenya, united behind a Kamba candidate. Unfortunately many church leaders at that time joined their fellow tribalists in supporting the candidate from their respective tribe. As a result, the church leaders of the day were not united and could only remain as silent observers of ethnic cleansing.

I urge the church leaders in every generation to cast away tribalism at all times. If I am asked what tribe I belong to, I would rather say that I am a Kenyan. Any tribal or regional ganging-up in search of a president is wrong. Remember, any tribe can produce a leader who is capable, God-fearing, trustworthy and incorruptible. Let the church be the church by abandoning negative ethnicity. Remember the words of St Paul: "There is neither Jew nor Greek, slave nor free, male nor female for you are all one in Christ Jesus" (Galatians 3:28).

Corruption

The second enemy that we must fight against is corruption. Even though corruption took new dimensions as the instruments of power were transferred from colonialists to the first government, the vice was perfected during the last three decades and corruption has become part of the culture of many Kenyans. We experience corruption every day. A good number of civil servants will not attend you unless they are bribed. For your child to join a government college, some of the principals will ask for a bribe, and once it has been given, you can be assured that a place will be found for him/her whether qualified or not. The pattern replicates itself during the recruitment of those who want to join the army or the police force. Many candidates for elective office bribe voters with money or in kind and the voters cast their votes in favour of the candidate who gave them the highest amount. You, Kenyan voter, you vote for an incapable person to become a parliamentarian because he/she gave you Ksh 500. Consequently you suffer for the next five years, as your member has nothing to deliver for the well-being of the constituency and the nation.

To crown it all, the people who are supposed to establish justice in this country have become very corrupt. That includes the police, magistrates and judges. A policeman will let a motorist driving an unroadworthy vehicle through after receiving a Ksh 50 bribe, yet the vehicle poses a threat to the lives of the driver and other road users. Public service vehicles (*matatus*) endanger the lives of passengers, adding to the number of fatal accidents on our roads. Though in our national anthem we sing, "Justice be our shield and defender", some of our judges and magistrates will condemn the righteous and set criminals free because they were bribed.

In our national anthem we pray among other things that the God of all creation may bless this nation with peace and unity. God does not give his peace unconditionally. God grants his peace to a nation that obeys his commandments and establishes justice and righteousness. The prophet Isaiah says that if these conditions are met:

> Then justice will dwell in the wilderness and righteousness abide in the fruitful field and the effect of righteousness will be peace, and the results of righteousness, quietness and trust for ever (Isaiah 32: 16-17).

In order for God to bless the nation with the gift of peace, Isaiah challenges Judah to fulfil the following conditions:
- Judges must do their work in a spirit of justice.
- The meek and poor (the oppressed) must be given cause for joy.
- Anyone who interferes with court procedures by perjury must be severely punished.
- Corruption must be removed from religious life.
- Foolish or wicked men in government must be exposed and dismissed.
- Wealthy people must stop being complacent.

Corruption is however a two way traffic. The giver and the receiver are both corrupt. Christians, who are now 82% of the population of Kenya, could transform this country if they pledged never to give or receive a bribe. It could be true that the culture of corruption has become the way of life in Kenya. If Christians were to say no to corruption, then this nation would be transformed.

Impunity

The last but not the least of the three evils that must be fought against in this era of the second liberation is impunity. The Oxford Advanced Learners' Dictionary states, "If a person does something bad with impunity, they do not get punished for what they have done." Impunity is therefore the freedom deliberately to commit a crime because one knows that even if one is caught, one will not be punished.

It is usually the "big fish" who have the courage to commit serious crimes because they know they are the untouchable, sacred cows. Numerous crimes have been committed in Kenya with impunity. J.M. Kariuki was assassinated in March 1975. Parliament selected a special commission chaired by Elijah Mwangale to investigate the murder of J.M. Kariuki. I went to the gallery of the chamber the day Mwangale was submitting the report of the commission. The commission gave names of the suspects and recommended that they should be investigated further by the police. The Attorney General stood and told Mwangale that his report was null and void. Consequently the government of the day did nothing to search for the assassins of J.M. Kariuki. All indications pointed to a cover-up. It appeared that powerful individuals in government knew who the killers of J.M. were, but the assassins did their job with impunity because they knew they could not be punished. Kenyans cannot be blamed for concluding that those in authority at that time sanctioned or even employed the assassins to commit the crime.

The same can be said of the assassins of Robert Ouko, the minister for Foreign Affairs, in 1990. They committed the crime with impunity because they knew they could not be punished. To cover up the crime and to ease growing tensions, a commission of enquiry chaired by Justice Evan Gicheru was appointed and began its work in Kisumu (near where the crime was allegedly committed). When the commission was on the verge of unearthing the truth, the commissioners were ordered to pack up and return to Nairobi. Then Detective Superintendent John Troon of Scotland Yard was appointed by the president to investigate the crime. His report was published and submitted to the president. All this time those in authority knew who the assassins of Ouko were, yet they spent millions of shillings in taxpayers' money on appointment commissions whose reports they knew would never be implemented to ensure that the murderers would not be punished.

I am writing this chapter a few weeks after the Chief Prosecutor of the International Criminal Court, Louis Moreno Ocampo, revealed the names of the six people whom the ICC believes bear the greatest responsibility, directly or indirectly, for causing the ethnic clashes following the 2007 general elections, after charges had been confirmed against four suspects. The way the leaders and some members of parliament have reacted is shocking. Soon after the grand coalition was set up in early 2008, attempts were made to set up a local tribunal to try those behind ethnic cleansing but Parliament voted against that move in favour of their being tried by ICC at The Hague. But as soon as the names of the six alleged masterminds behind the ethnic cleansing were published, frantic efforts were made by a section of the grand coalition to set up a local tribunal to try them. The people of Kenya are therefore justified in the general feeling that some of those in authority are not serious about the fight against impunity.

This is a great challenge to the church leaders of the present generation, just as Esther was told by her cousin Mordecai, "And who knows but that you have come to your royal position at a time like this?" (Esther 4:14). King Ahasuerus or Xerxes of Persia and Media (486 to 465BC) had married Esther, a Jewess, after divorcing his first wife, Vashti, in most unfair circumstances. Mordecai discovered there was a plan of genocide against 40,000 Jews living in the kingdom. Hence he urged Esther to inform the king about this plan and save her fellow Jews. Hence the question "And who knows, but that you have come to the royal position at a time like this?"

It may be that those who are leaders of our churches have come to their present position at a time like this. These are the days of tribalism, corruption and impunity. They can save the situation if only they do not keep quiet. Study the situation carefully and preach the gospel in season and out of season, "correct, rebuke and encourage - with great patience and careful instructions" (2 Timothy 4:2).

Chapter 30

Message to Church Leaders from the Retired Archbishop and Conclusion

I wish to conclude this autobiography by sending a special message to all persons holding positions of power and authority in our churches.

The first major responsibility bestowed upon you is to "care for the flock of God." Remember the flock under your care is not your flock. It is God's flock. A church overseer is a shepherd appointed to care for the Lord's flock. The overseer must be a good shepherd who calls his own sheep by name; they hear his voice and follow him and he leads them to the green pastures and besides still waters. A good shepherd does not flee when he sees the wolf, but he protects the sheep from the attacks of their enemies. A caring bishop or pastor will be among the first people to visit any of his flock who might be having problems, whether sickness or other kinds of suffering.

In the Anglican Church the bishop is made an overseer of a large area with many congregations. It is not therefore possible for him to know by name all the Lord's flock under his care. He therefore makes arrangements for suitably qualified persons to be trained for the ministry. After they have qualified, he ordains and appoints them to take charge of parishes on his behalf. The parish priest therefore does all the pastoral duties on behalf of the diocesan bishop. In view of this the bishop should be a loving and a caring bishop to all the clergy in his diocese. His first priority therefore is to pastor or shepherd the clergy so that on his behalf they can ably minister to the rest of the Lord's flock in the diocese.

There are complaints in some of quarters that some bishops tend to be harsh, inconsiderate and unloving to some of their clergy and other church workers. They will listen to accusations and take disciplinary action without even double-checking on whether the accusations are true or false. It is always important to give a chance to any accused person to defend himself or herself before any action against him/her is taken. Some bishops will be quick to terminate the services of their clergy even without following laid down disciplinary procedures spelt out in great detail in the Anglican Constitution. It is important that our bishops be caring bishops. During the consecration of a bishop, the candidate is exhorted, "You are to be merciful but with firmness; to minister discipline, but with mercy" (*Our Modern Services*, p. 124).

Our Lord Jesus Christ had twelve disciples for three years and he did not sack any except Judas Iscariot, who sacked himself. These disciples were not angels. Each had a weakness and the style of Jesus was to help each one of them to overcome his weakness and to shape or mould each to become what he should be. He chose ordinary disciples and made them extra-ordinary apostles. Only Judas Iscariot could not be moulded in the pattern Jesus wanted to shape him; consequently he destroyed himself.

The Preaching of the Gospel

One of the greatest privileges the bishop and pastors have is the opportunity to preach the gospel during the Sunday services. I do not know of any other institution that gives its leaders the privilege of speaking to a captive audience once a week throughout the year. People come to church on Sundays from all walks of life: children, boys and girls, men and women, the rich and the poor, farmers and businessmen, the downhearted and the motivated, the sick and the healthy. These people come to church voluntarily. This is unlike a chief's meeting in the past where a chief's order was used to compel people to attend the meeting, and if they failed with no good reason, they were punished accordingly. The Sunday church service is attended by people who come voluntarily to worship God.

The congregation is a captive audience when the bishop or the pastor is preaching; no one is supposed to interrupt the sermon. No one will dare raise his or her hands to ask for clarification of any statement made from the pulpit. This is contrary to the political meetings, where there is shouting and booing. That is why the politicians would love to be invited to "greet" the church congregation.

In view of this, it is very important that the preacher is very well prepared and understands the salient issues facing a community. A preacher should spend a good time preparing his sermon thoroughly and praying that the Holy Spirit will give him power to deliver his message to the point where each person present is either up built, encouraged or consoled (1 Corinthians 14:3). Every sermon must be relevant to the contemporary situation.

Theological Education

The surgeons who operate on the bodies of the sick are highly qualified people. Medical schools take the best high-school graduates in the country. They are trained for not less than seven years before they are commissioned to be surgeons. No sick person would like to be operated on by a quack or half-trained surgeon. Similarly a preacher is a healer of souls. To entrust the healing of souls to people who have not studied theology and all that it entails is futile. Unfortunately Kenya is filled with preachers who have not been to theological colleges and do not even aspire to spend time training as they consider that as a waste of time.

The disciples of Jesus underwent three years training; theirs was mobile theological training, day after day, from the Master Himself. They travelled with Jesus, their teacher, from place to place and learnt from the Lord himself not only how to preach but also how to deal with the numerous problems they encountered every day.

Spending time preparing for future ministry is not a waste of time. Moses was tempted to start liberating oppressed Hebrews in Egypt by using his own strength. "He saw an Egyptian beating a Hebrew, one of his people... he struck down the Egyptian and hid him in the sand. When Moses realized that his own people did not appreciate what he had done, he was afraid and he fled to Midian and stayed there for forty years" (Exodus 2: 11-15).

Moses had to go to the "University of the Desert" to learn how to depend on God in liberating the Hebrews from the yoke of Pharaoh. After forty years, he came to the mountain of God and the angel of the Lord appeared to him in the flame of the fire out of the midst of a bush. The bush was burning and it was not consumed. At last Moses received his calling from God Himself, to liberate the Hebrews. "Come I will send you to Pharaoh, that you may bring my people, the children of Israel out of Egypt" (Exodus 3:10). The forty years in the desert of Midian were not a waste of time; it was time to learn how to depend on God in fulfilling his great desire to liberate his own people from Egypt. This time round he was going to carry out this great mission guided by God Himself.

When Saul heard the voice of the Lord on his way to Damascus and was healed by Ananias, he did not start preaching immediately. He tells us that after his conversion he did not immediately consult with anyone, nor did he go up to Jerusalem to those who were apostles before him, but he went into Arabia and returned again to Damascus. After three years he went to Jerusalem to visit Cephas and stayed with him for fifteen days. He then went to Tarsus and stayed there for fourteen years (see Galatians 1:18-24, 2:1). It is Barnabas who went to look for Paul and brought him to Antioch after he had visited Jerusalem for a while. It was the cosmopolitan church in Antioch that chose Barnabas and Paul for their first missionary journey to proclaim the Gospel to the Gentiles.

Paul did not start to preach the gospel immediately after he was convert-ed. He spent some time in Arabia and three years in Damascus and then vis-ited Jerusalem to get acquainted for 15 days with Peter and James the broth-er of our Lord. He then went to Tarsus, the place he was born, and stayed there for 14 years. All this time Paul was learning more about Jesus Christ. When he emerged from his hibernation, he had mastered the message of the kingdom of God preached by Jesus Christ. He was already qualified as a doc-tor of law but he was then qualified enough to be a doctor of Christian the-ology and doctrine. Though he was not one of the twelve disciples of our Lord, he emerges as among the most learned of the apostles. He was able to articulate the message of Jesus to his disciples and his letters are a good source of Christian doctrine, systematic theology and moral theology.

I have given these two examples to urge those who feel called to be bish-ops and pastors not to neglect theological studies. In the Anglican Church it has been our policy not to ordain anyone who has not done three years of theological education (after "O"-levels) in our own theological colleges or other reputable or accredited colleges. It is also important that our bishops encourage students who have done well in our Bible schools to proceed to universities such as St Paul's, Limuru, for further studies leading to a Bachelor of Theology degree. Those who wish to go to overseas universities for masters and doctoral programmes should be encouraged by their respec-tive bishops to do so. A bishop must not be a stumbling-block to his clergy who wish to pursue further education.

I prepared myself for the ministry for not less than ten years and had obtained Bachelor of Arts (London) and Bachelor of Divinity (London) degrees before I was ordained. I was later to be awarded two doctorates *causa honaris*. This learning has given me the confidence to proclaim the good news of the Lord Jesus Christ powerfully, intellectually and fearlessly.

Kenya is now littered with the so many preachers who have probably attracted followers because of their eloquence. Some of these leaders buy themselves red shirts won by Anglican bishops assuming that the red colour is the colour for bishops, yet they are intellectually bankrupt. Others bestow upon themselves the title of "doctor" but cannot prove where they studied for their Ph.D. or even produce a genuine certificate to prove they were awarded their doctorates in any recognized university on earth. Though these preachers may be doing some good, some of them are a great liability to the Church in Kenya.

The Treatment of Retired Bishops and Clergy

As a retired Bishop and Archbishop, I have the *locus standi* to write on this issue on behalf of many who served the church faithfully and retired on reaching the mandatory retirement age. I am deeply impressed by the way the Presbyterian Church of East Africa (PCEA) treats their retired moderators of the National Assembly. After retirement they are given other assignments and continue serving the church. During the Annual General Assembly, the retired moderators are given a place of honour. If they raise their hands to speak they are given priority.

Unfortunately this is not the case with the Anglican Church of Kenya. Some bishops do all that they can to ensure that their predecessors are forgotten at the earliest possible moment. Though they are still strong and available, their successors deliberately refuse to invite them to assist them with episcopal duties such as confirmation, ordination or consecration of new church buildings. Though the ACK constitution states that a retired bishop should be invited to the diocesan and provincial synod, they are rarely invited. I cannot really understand why our successors are so reluctant to involve us in the ministry of the dioceses. Some of us laid the foundations of those dioceses, yet in our retirement our advice and services are no longer needed by our successors, though the Christians in the diocese would love to see us assist the bishops in visiting their parishes.

Some of the bishops will do everything possible to ensure that their predecessors are forgotten. One good example was the diocesan celebration of 100 years since the CMS missionaries first preached the Good News in the area. The book published to celebrate the 100 years does not mention anywhere the role played by the current Bishop's predecessor who served the area as a bishop for twenty-two years or 22% of the 100 years. It is an attempt at falsifying history. True records accurately reflect historical facts and give credit where credit is due. The bishops who behave in this way (ignoring their predecessors) seem to forget that one day they will also retire and I am sure they will not like to be treated by their successors the way they have treated their predecessors.

When we reach retirement age it does not mean we are a threat or no longer useful. The church should count it a blessing to have retired bishops and clergy. They have a wealth of experience that can still be beneficial to the growth of the church. Those who describe retired archbishops and bishops as "no longer of any use, out of date and irrelevant and … order them to keep off from comments on National Affairs" have no respect and are arrogant. I took a "yes" stand on the 2010 referendum and I am glad that I was on the right side of history. Those church leaders who campaigned for a "no" vote told us to keep out of the debate as we were out of date and had nothing valuable to offer. We were able to read the signs of the times in our retirement and took a stand that gave Kenya a new and more democratic constitution.

Lawsuits against Believers

In 1976, the Most Rev Festo Olang', the first Archbishop of the Anglican Church of Kenya, was taken to court by one of his own senior priests because the priest had been transferred from the parish he had served for many years. This was the first time in Kenya that an Anglican priest had taken his bishop to civil court. I was so concerned about this development that I telephoned the priest and tried to persuade him to withdraw the case but he would not listen. With connivance from the powers that be, the priest won the case and the Archbishop was greatly embarrassed. This event opened the way for those who were aggrieved to sue their respective church leaders in civil courts. This has been one of the most unfortunate trends in the history of the church. Taking church leaders to civil courts is not the best way of sorting out disputes within the church.

The gospel of St Matthew 18:15-17 records the teaching of Jesus concerning the procedures to be followed:

> If your brother sins against you, go and tell him his fault, between
> you and him alone. If he listens to you, you have gained your broth-

er. But if he does not listen, take one or two others along with you, that every charge may be established by the evidence of two or three witnesses. If he refuses to listen to them, tell it to the church. And if he refuses to listen even to the church, let him be to you as a Gentile and a tax collector.

There are two ways of handling disciplinary cases in the church. The cases can be handled either pastorally or legally. The pastoral way is to sit down with the alleged offender, give him/her counselling and persuading him/her to see his/her faults and repent. As a good shepherd, one gives him/her time to change.

The legal way is to follow strictly the constitution of the church to the letter. The Anglican constitution has a detailed canon dealing with the tribunals of the church (see Canon XV, pp. 59-69). The constitution forbids any offended person, whether bishop, clergy or laity, from instituting any legal proceedings in secular courts against the church before exhausting machinery set out in the constitution of the church. A person who feels s/he cannot find justice in the church and goes to the secular courts should know that the civil magistrate will follow the constitution of the church in his/her judgment. Bishops and other church leaders should be careful not to act unconstitutionally in disciplining those under them. This is why in the Anglican Church every diocese has a chancellor or legal advisor who should be consulted for his/her advice in all legal matters.

It is my strong recommendation that the church should use the pastoral method before instituting legal proceedings. St Paul was completely against believers taking their disputes to be heard by unbelievers. He says, "When one of you has a grievance against another does he dare go before the unrighteous instead of the saints? ... I say this to your shame. Can it be that there is no one among you is wise enough to settle a dispute between the brothers, but brother goes to law against brother and this before unbelievers? To have lawsuits at all with one another is already a defeat for you." (See 1 Corinthians 6: 1-11.)

The Struggle to Raise Money to Pay Diocesan Quotas

I have visited a number of congregations since my retirement and have witnessed the struggle that parish priests and parish councils undergo to raise funds to pay diocesan quotas allocated to the parish. A parish priest will be posted to a new parish, where he finds huge arrears from the previous years and also has to raise money to pay the quota for the new year. Trying to raise this money becomes a nightmare. Various methods are devised and much time is used during the Sunday service to persuade people to contribute generously.

There is the monthly tithe, which is supposed to be 10% of monthly income. There is the normal offertory. Then there is a special contribution for the Mothers' Union, the Kenyan Anglican Men's Association and the Youth, among others. The congregation may also use one of the congregants to give a special offering and to be assisted by other members of the congregation. Then those who wish to give thanks are invited to bring their thanksgiving offertory. This process might go on for about one hour. Some Christians will refuse to go to church because of these money-centred processes.

The church must revisit these issues and see whether there are better ways of raising money for quota payments and also payment of parish staff and for other local church needs. If one goes to church with an offertory of Ksh 500 in his or her pocket, and knows that the collection bag will come round five times, then he/she can divide the Ksh 500 into five notes each of Ksh 100. He will give 100 every time the collection bag comes round and will contribute a total of 500. Much time can be saved if the five different contribution categories can be reduced to one.

First and foremost we must teach our Christians good stewardship. We must impress upon them that the Sunday offering is not a church tax but rather an opportunity to give thanks to God for all his goodness. The money offered joyfully is for the ministry of the church and extension of the Kingdom. St Paul was opposed to what we call *harambee* or fundraising ceremonies. In 1 Corinthians 16:1-2 he says, "Now concerning the collection for the saints: As I directed the churches of Galatia, so you also are to do. On the first day of every week, each of you is to put something aside and store it up, as he may prosper, so that there will be no collecting [*harambee*] when I come."

It is probably in order for churches to organise fundraisers and invite wealthy people from outside to assist in fundraising for the construction of churches, church halls, dispensaries, etc. But to organize fundraisers and call outsiders to pay for the diocesan quota or the pastor's salary is not right. It is the people who benefit directly from the services of bishop, pastor or evangelist who should contribute for their financial support. They in turn must do their duty of looking after the Lord's flock as caring and loving shepherds. Pastors, and bishops for that matter, must give high priority to visiting the people in their homes and places of work and to praying and giving them encouragement in times of sickness and bereavement or any other tribulations. This will be following the footsteps of Jesus who "went throughout all the cities and villages, teaching in their synagogues, and proclaiming the gospel of the kingdom and healing every disease and every affliction" (Matthew 9:35).

For Christians to continue contributing to the work of the church there must be transparency and accountability in the way the money they give is being used. As far as possible every church should have an honorary treasurer with knowledge of financial matters and a qualified accountant who keeps a record of all money received and spent. There should be a financial committee that meets regularly to receive and discuss financial reports from the honorary treasurer.

Diocesan synods in the Anglican Church meet at least once every two years. One of the top items on the agenda of the synod is to receive audited accounts for the previous two years and to adopt the budget for the following year. If Christians start feeling that there is no proper accountability for the funds they contribute or there is no transparency, then this discourages them from generous giving. The church overseers must be prepared to defend their integrity in handling finances. I would strongly advise bishops, pastors and other overseers to leave financial matters to lay people. When there were complaints in the early church that the widows of Hebrews were being favoured and the Hellenists' widows were being neglected in the daily distribution of food by the apostles, the apostles did not sweep these complaints under the carpet. They met, discussed the complaint and decided to hand over the "serving of tables" to the seven deacons so that they could devote themselves to prayer and to the ministry of the word (see Acts 6:1-7).

The Importance of the Church Constitution

A constitution is an important document that gives guidance on how the church should be administered. The constitution should however not be a stumbling-block to the smooth running of the church. The constitution should not be static but dynamic. Should any clause of the constitution be an obstacle to the well-being of the church, then the clause should be revised or amended.

When the second Archbishop of the Anglican Church of Kenya, the Most Revd Manasses Kuria, retired in 1994, we could not elect his successor for two years. This was because the constitution stated that the election of an Archbishop could not take place until all vacant sees were first filled. The sees of Kajiado and Maseno North were vacant and it was extremely difficult for the bishops of those two Dioceses to be elected owing to court injunctions and other reasons. After two years, it became imperative that the constitution be amended so that sees with no bishops could be represented by a senior clergyman from that diocese approved by the House of Bishops. After that clause was amended we started the procedure of electing the third Archbishop, but we had two years with no Archbishop.

Should the church note that there are some clauses in their constitutions that are more of a problem than a blessing, then steps should be taken to amend them in accordance with the articles on the amendment of the constitution. The National Independent Church of Africa (NICA), founded by Bishop Willie Nyaga, went through a difficult time because the constitution did not specify at what age the leaders of the church should retire. He wanted to continue leading the church indefinitely. As the church was a member of NCCK, the council decided to intervene and a commission composed of John Gatu, Lawi Imathiu, Moses Njue and myself was appointed to visit the church and try to resolve the problem. I had the privilege of chairing the commission. We met several times with the founding father of the church and his supreme committee. After studying the constitution, we felt that the church needed to review its entire constitution. The commission, with full participation of the key church leaders, drafted a new constitution, suggested the creation of three dioceses instead of one and outlined the procedure for the election of bishops and archbishops and their age of retirement. We urged the church to give the founder a good retirement including building him a house and other retirement benefits. The new constitution was accepted, the founding bishop retired happily and peace prevailed in the church.

The Anglican Church has been accused of being tribalistic in the election of bishops. Kikuyus will elect a bishop who is a Kikuyu; Luos will elect a Luo bishop; and the Luhyas, Kalenjin, Embus and Mbeeres, Taita-Tavetas and all the other communities will elect their own sons to be their bishop. There is also no mechanism for transferring bishops from their home dioceses to serve anywhere in Kenya. The Roman Catholic Church on the other hand has a mechanism for appointing and posting bishops to any diocese in Kenya whatever their racial or tribal background. It must however be understood that the decision to appoint a bishop for any Catholic diocese is made by the Pope at the Vatican and the decision of the Pope is final. The Anglican Church tries to be democratic; members of the diocesan synod and the province nominate candidates, who are interviewed by a panel composed of representatives of the diocese and the province, and the electoral college that makes the final decision has more members from the diocese than from the province. In such situations, it is virtually impossible for a candidate from outside the diocese to be elected a bishop. The bishops and the chancellors of our church should seek ways and means by which any candidate from anywhere can be elected to be the bishop of any vacant see irrespective of his or her tribal background.

In Uganda for instance, diocesan bishops are elected by the House of Bishops under the chairmanship of the Archbishop. They can elect a qualified candidate and post him in any vacant see anywhere in the country. According to the present ACK constitution, a priest in good standing from anywhere in the Anglican Communion can be nominated to be elected a bishop of any diocese if he is at least 35 years old and not more than 60. If a priest who is 35 years old is elected, consecrated and enthroned, he/she can remain the bishop of that diocese for 30 years. If the diocese gets the wrong person as its bishop, it will have to wait for 30 years to have another bishop.

I would strongly suggest that the ACK constitution be amended so that a diocesan bishop serves initially for a term of five years. Then if elected for a second term he can serve for another five years, after which he must retire as a diocesan bishop whether he has reached retirement age or not. A bishop who knows he will have to face the electoral college after five years will be a more responsible shepherd in handling the flock of Christ under his care. Under the present system, a bishop knows that once he is elected and consecrated he will be in service until he retires, and he can do whatever he wants irrespective of any complaints from any quarters. It is the diocese and the whole church that will suffer in consequence.

The big question to be dealt with is what a young bishop who fails to win a second term will do after losing an election. The province can assign other duties to such a person, such as lecturing in our theological colleges if he is academically qualified. The moderators of the General Assembly of the PCEA serve for maximum of two terms of three years each, after which they are assigned other duties in the church as long as they are strong enough to serve.

Worship and Liturgy

It was and still is the practice of the Jewish people to rest on the seventh day because on that day, "God finished his work that he had done, and he rested on the seventh day from all his work that he had done. So God blessed the seventh day and made it holy, because on it God rested from all his work that he had done in creation" (Genesis 2:1-3). The Christian church adopted this practice but chose the first day of the week i.e. Sunday, as a day of rest and worship. Only the Seventh-Day Adventists rest and worship on Saturdays. Apart from the Seventh-Day Adventists, other Christians all over the world rest and worship on Sundays to celebrate the resurrection of our Lord Jesus Christ, the ascension and the coming of the Holy Spirit on the day of Pentecost.

It should be remembered that Sunday is a day of worship and rest. After working for six days our bodies require a day of rest so that we can begin a new week refreshed. There are some Christian groups who tend to regard Sunday as a day of worship only. They will gather in their places of worship early in the morning and spend the whole day there singing, praising the Lord and listening to lengthy sermons until the evening. I believe this is wrong, as they do not give worshippers time to go and rest. It is equally wrong to keep worshippers in church for too long. There are churches that begin worship about 10.30 am and continue long past 5 o'clock.

I believe it is possible to have a powerful Sunday service, full of blessings in two hours and then worshippers can go home and rest or visit their friends. To be able to do that, it is important that those leading services arrive on time and bring the service to an end on time. If a priest tells the congregation to gather at 10.30am and he himself does not arrive until an hour later, then members of the congregation will also start the habit of coming late. Pastors must be good stewards of their own time as well as the time of other people.

Part of the great heritage of the Anglican Church is its prayer book. Morning and evening worship includes;
- Call to worship, repentance and absolution
- A period of praise and singing psalms and hymns
- The affirmation of our faith by saying the Apostles' Creed (or the Nicene Creed during Holy Communion)
- Intercessory prayers
- The ministry of the word, which includes the reading of the scriptures and preaching

- Offertory
- Closing prayers and benediction

For many years Anglicans throughout the world used the prayer book published in England in 1662. The prayer book was translated into the vernacular whenever an Anglican Church was planted. The Lambeth Conference of 1958 acknowledged that the time for more dynamic prayer book revision had arrived and set forth guidelines that were more fully developed by the Anglican congress held in Toronto, Canada, in 1963. The Anglican provinces were encouraged to prepare their own prayer books using those guidelines.

In Kenya the Provincial Board of Theological Education (PBTE), of which I was the chairman for many years, set up a Liturgical Committee to draft an alternative prayer book. The first product of the committee was the Kenyan *Service of the Holy Communion* in 1989, which was hailed as one of the best in the Anglican Communion. The Kenya *Service of the Holy Communion* was used during the opening ceremony of the Lambeth Conference in 1998. A second booklet containing *Alternate Liturgy for Morning and Evening Prayer, Baptism and Confirmation* was published in 1991.

When I became the Archbishop in 1997, the Revd Joyce Gaturi Kirigia was appointed a full time Provincial Liturgical Coordinator with a mandate to complete the work of producing a new prayer book. The prayer book committee under the leadership of the Ven. Samuel Mawiyoo and Bishop Gideon Githiga completed the work and *Our Modern Services* was published by Uzima Press just before my retirement in September 2002. During the service for my retirement held at All Saints Cathedral, Nairobi, I offered the prayer book as my retirement gift to the Anglican church of Kenya in the 21st century.

I left it to my successors to have the book translated into the vernacular and made available to all our churches. As soon as I retired, the work stalled and the position of full time co-coordinator ceased to exist. The fifth Archbishop has however revived the liturgical committee and the Revd Joyce Kirigia has been recalled to continue with her work nine years behind schedule. It is my joy to know that the new prayer book has been published and is available to all Kikuyu-speaking congregations. It is my hope and prayer that translation to other vernacular languages will continue. When only the English-language version was available, it was said that the Kenya *Our*

Modern Services was used more in other English-speaking countries than in Kenya.

The Anglican prayer book has been described as dull and some Anglicans have defected to other churches where worship is considered full of joy and is participatory. The Anglican prayer book is not dull; it is some of those who lead the service who make the worship dull. Anglican worship does not restrain worshippers from raising their hands, jumping or even having liturgical dances. Those who lead worship must leave space for joyful singing. However time should also be given to the ministry of silence. We do not get blessing only in times of praising with our mouths; blessing can also be found in silence. When Elijah was hiding in a cave in Horeb, the mountain of God, "a great and strong wind hit the mountain, but the Lord was not in the wind. After the wind there was an earthquake, but the Lord was not in the earthquake, after the earthquake there was fire, but the Lord was not in the fire. And after the fire the sound of a low whisper - the Voice of God" (1 Kings 19:9-18).

After Elijah had demonstrated the power of the living God by calling fire from heaven to consume the burnt offering at Mt Carmel, he might have thought that God demonstrated his powers by such mighty natural phenomenon as wind, earthquakes or fire. But at Mt Horeb God was not in the wind, nor in the earthquake, nor in the fire. Elijah heard his voice when all was quiet. Hence let us not only make noise in worship but also give room for God to speak and bless us in silence.

Finally, remember that your calling to the ministry of the church is a great privilege. This privilege carries with it great responsibility. In his farewell message to the elders in Ephesians, St Paul told them, "Pay careful attention to yourselves and to all the flock in which the Holy Spirit has made you overseers, to care for the church of God which he obtained with his own blood" (Acts 20:28). And St Peter exhorted the elders as:

> ...a fellow elder and a witness of the suffering of Christ, as well as a partaker in the glory that is going to be revealed: shepherd the flock of God that is among you, exercising oversight, not under compulsion, but willingly as God would have you; not for shameful gain, but eagerly, not domineering over those in your charge, but being an example to the flock (1 Peter 5:1-3).

This privilege is inseparable from suffering. If I were to summarise my life-history in four words, I would choose the words, "Troubled but not Destroyed". A careful reading of this autobiography is a record of the joys, challenges and troubles I have experienced and the many humiliating circumstances I have found myself in. Yet in all these troubles I have experienced the divine power that redeems them and makes them occasions for further manifestations of God's glory.

This was St Paul's experience and should be of great encouragement when we find ourselves troubled. Paul says in 2 Corinthians 4:7-9, "But we have this treasure in jars of clay to show the surpassing power belongs to God and not to us. We are afflicted in every way, but not crushed, perplexed but not driven to despair, persecuted but not forsaken, struck down but not destroyed." Here we are given a contrast between the message and the messenger. As Professor R.V.G. Tasker says in his commentary on verse 7, "To know the glory of God in the face of Jesus Christ and to be called to spread this knowledge is the most treasured of all possessions. But the wonder of the divine dispensation is that while an earthly treasure is usually preserved in a container of fitting dignity and beauty, the treasure of the gospel has been entrusted to men [and women] subject to the infirmities and limitations, the instability and insecurity of their conditions. It is as though a most costly jewel was encased in an earthenware jar! Paul sees in this a supreme manifestation of the divine law that God's strength is made perfect in human weakness" (*Tyndale Bible Commentary 2 Corinthians*, RVG Tasker, Tyndale Press, 1958).

In verse 8 and 9, Paul contrasts the humiliating circumstances in which he often finds himself as a minister of the Gospel with the divine power that redeems them and makes occasions for further manifestation of God's glory. Paul is a hunted man but he is not forsaken or abandoned to the enemy, nor left solely to his own resources. In his missionary journeys, Paul was persecuted in one city, but often escaped to another city, only to find fresh opportunities for Christian witness.

Paul's greatest dream was to preach the gospel to the utmost part of the earth to fulfill the great commission that "...you will be my witnesses in Jerusalem and in all Judea and Samaria and to the ends of the earth" (Acts 1:8b). His dream was to preach the Gospel in Spain, which in those days was the end of the known world. We know that he ended up in a Roman prison cell waiting to appear for his appeal against accusations by the Jews to be heard by Emperor Nero. Paul did not consider being in prison as the end of his ministry. He saw it as an opportunity for the spread of the Gospel. He witnessed to the entire imperial guard of about 10,000 men who had fought many battles and were brought to Rome to guard the emperor. Each of these was allocated time to guard Paul so that he does not escape from prison. And Paul had a chance to tell each that he was in prison because of Jesus Christ. Had he gone to Spain he would not have had the opportunity to preach the gospel in the corridors of Roman power.

Paul also gave encouragement to all the Christians who came to visit him in the prison cells. He says, "And most of the brothers, having become confident in the Lord by my imprisonment, are much more bold to speak the word without fear" (Philippians 1:12-14). It is there in prison that he wrote the captivity Epistles – Ephesians, Philippians, Colossians and Philemon. Had he gone to Spain he would not have the time to write those spiritually stimulating letters, which have come down to us. Paul was able to turn what appeared to be a liability (prison) to a great asset for the gospel.

The troubles that Paul had during his pioneering work in the Gentile world are listed in 2 Corinthians 11:24-28. "Five times I received at the hands of the Jews the forty lashes less one. Three times I was beaten with rods. Once I was stoned. Three times I was shipwrecked; a night and a day I was adrift at sea; on frequent journeys; in danger from rivers, danger from robbers, danger from my own people, danger from Gentiles, danger in the city, danger in the wilderness, danger in the sea, danger from fake brothers; in toil and hardship, through many a sleepless night, in hunger and in thirst, often without food, in cold and in exposure. And apart from other things, there is daily pressure on me of my anxiety for all the churches." Paul believed the problems he had undergone were to humble him so that he did not become too elated by the surpassing greatness of the revelations.

To crown it all, Paul goes on to say, "…a thorn was given me in the flesh, a messenger of Satan to harass me, to keep me from being elated. Three times I pleaded with the Lord about this, that it should leave me. But He said to me, my grace is sufficient for you, for my power is made perfect in weakness. Therefore I will boast all the more gladly of my weakness, so that the power of Christ may rest on me. For the cause of Christ, then I am content with weakness, insults, hardships, persecutions and calamities. For when I am weak, then I am strong" (2 Corinthians 12:7-10).

There are few servants of the Lord whose list of tribulations can compare with that of Paul. Paul has listed more than twenty tribulations he encountered and yet he never gave up the proclamation of the Gospel. My list of tribulations is much shorter: born physically weak, failed key primary school examinations, expelled from teachers' training college after only three days because I was too short to reach the blackboard, discouraged from studying for a theological degree, rejected as a candidate for ordination, told never to preach again in the Diocese of Nairobi for telling the St Mark's Church, Westlands, congregation that "you are neither hot nor cold", spent a night in a police cell during an emergency, confrontation with atheists at the University, false accusations by leaders of one constituency in the Diocese of Mt Kenya East, abusive anonymous letters, road accidents, attacks by politicians, deceived by conmen/women, raid on my residence by political thugs, sued in court of law for planning to divide the Diocese of Nairobi, stoned by Muslim youths. Two days after my retirement, President Moi would not let me retire in peace. He sent four policemen to arrest me for allegedly saying in my farewell sermon that his anointed successor would not live to see the presidency. In retirement I was attacked by church leaders for urging Kenyans to vote "yes" during the referendum on the new constitution. Then last but not least and the most painful, being ignored during my retirement by a section of the Church that I spent all my energy in serving, even at the expense of my family and my economic advancement.

Like the Apostle Paul, who suffered much more than me, I would conclude, "Therefore I will boast all the more gladly of my weakness, so that the power of Christ may rest on me. For because of Christ, then I am content with weakness, insults, hardships, persecutions and calamities. For when I am weak, then I am strong". The title of this book is *Troubled but Not Destroyed*. The title summarises my life history. I have refused to give up the life of Christian faith because of any troubles I have had in the past; neither shall I allow any tribulation to make me give up my faith in God. With Paul, I conclude this autobiography by saying;

> For I am sure that neither death nor life, nor angel nor rulers, nor things present nor things to come, nor powers nor height nor depth nor anything else in all creation will be able to separate us from the love of God in Christ Jesus (Romans 8:38-39).

AMEN

Bibliography

Books and Articles by David Gitari

Books

God with Us – Fifth Anniversary: Diocese of Mt Kenya East Marches On (Embu: Diocese of Mt Kenya East, 1980)

In Season and out of Season: Sermons to a Nation (Oxford, Regnum Books, 1996)

Let the Bishop Speak, (Nairobi, Uzima Press, 1988)

Responsible Church Leadership (Nairobi, ACTON Publishers, 2005)

The Country we want – edited by David M Gitari and Joyce Karuri Kirigia FEP Publication

Witnessing to the Living God in Africa: Findings and Papers of Inaugural Meeting of Africa Theological Fraternity (Nairobi, Uzima Press, 1987)

Articles

"A Christian Perspective on Nation Building" in EFAC (Evangelical Fellowship in the Anglican Communion) Bulletin Issue 47, Trinity 1996 pp 210-22

"Church and Nationhood in a Changing World" in Lionel Holmes (ed) *Church and Nationhood* (papers from WEF Theological Commission consultation in Basel, Sept 1976), (New Delhi: WEF n.d.)

"Church and Politics in Kenya", Transformation Vol 8 no 3 July-September 1991 pp 7-17

"Church and Polygamy" Transformation magazine Vol I No I January-March 1984 (Oxford Centre for Mission Studies, www.ocms.ac.uk)

"Evangelisation and Culture" in Proclaiming Christ in Christ's Way edited by Samuel and Hauser (Oxford, Regnum Books, 1989; Oregon, Wipf and Stock, 2007)

"Mission of the Church in East Africa" in P. Turner and F. Sugeno (eds), *Crossroads are for Meeting* (Sewanee, SPCK/USA, 1986)

(with Ben Knighton) "On Being a Christian Leader in Africa" in *Transformation* Vol 18 No 4, October 2001

"The Unity and Diversity of the Worldwide Church" in P. Sookhdeo (ed.), *New Frontiers in Mission* (Exeter, Paternoster Press, 1987)

"We will serve the Lord- An exposition of the ten aims and objectives of Kenya Anglican Men's Association"- 2004, 2005

Books and Articles about David Gitari

G.P. Benson "Church Confrontation with the State during Kenya's Nyayo Era: Causes and Effects" Unpublished M.Phil thesis Open University 1993

Gideon Githiga The Church as the Bulwark against Authoritarianism – Development of Church-State relations in Kenya, with particular reference to the years after Politial Independence 1963-1992 (Oxford, Regnum Books, 2001)

John Karanja in Anglican and Episcopal History Volume LXXV December 2006

John Karanja "Evangelical Attitudes to Democracy in Kenya", Chapter 2 in Evangelical Christianity and Democracy in Africa edited by Terence O. Ranger (New York, Oxford University Press, 2005)

J.K. Karigia Eight Great Years 1994-2002 (Nairobi, Anglican Church of Kenya, 2002)

Ben Knighton: Editor "Religion and Politics in Kenya – Essays in Honour of a Meddlesome Priest" (USA, Palgrave/Macmillan, 2009)

John Moses Editor Chap.11 "Critical Encounter" A Broad and Living Way: Church and State – a Continuing Establishment (Norwich, Canterbury Press, 1995)

Index